THE JEWS AND THE ENGLISH LAW

BY

H. S. Q. HENRIQUES, M.A., B.C.L.

OF THE NORTHERN CIRCUIT, BARRISTER-AT-LAW
FORMERLY SCHOLAR OF WORCESTER COLLEGE
AND VINERIAN SCHOLAR IN THE UNIVERSITY OF OXFORD

THE LAWBOOK EXCHANGE, LTD.
Clark, New Jersey
2006

ISBN-13: 978-1-58477-645-1
ISBN-10: 1-58477-645-5

Printed in the United States of America on acid-free paper

THE LAWBOOK EXCHANGE, LTD.
33 Terminal Avenue
Clark, New Jersey 07066-1321

Please see our website for a selection of our other publications and fine facsimile reprints of classic works of legal history:
www.lawbookexchange.com

Library of Congress Cataloging-in-Publication Data

Henriques, H. S. Q. (Henry Straus Quixano), 1866-1925.
The Jews and the English law / Henriques, H.S.Q.
p. cm.
Includes bibliographical references and index.
ISBN 1-58477-645-5 (alk. paper)
1. Jews--Legal status, laws, etc.--England--History. I. Title.
KD4102.J4H45 2005
342.4208'73--dc22

2005026523

THE JEWS AND THE ENGLISH LAW

BY

H. S. Q. HENRIQUES, M.A., B.C.L.

OF THE NORTHERN CIRCUIT, BARRISTER-AT-LAW
FORMERLY SCHOLAR OF WORCESTER COLLEGE
AND VINERIAN SCHOLAR IN THE UNIVERSITY OF OXFORD

OXFORD
PRINTED BY HORACE HART, AT THE UNIVERSITY PRESS

Issued to Members of the Jewish Historical Society of England, in Commemoration of the fiftieth anniversary of the passing of Acts enabling Jews to sit in Parliament, July 23, 1858

July 23, 1908

OXFORD: HORACE HART
PRINTER TO THE UNIVERSITY

PREFACE

This book consists of a series of ten articles contributed to the *Jewish Quarterly Review.* I have to express my profound thanks to my friends Mr. Israel Abrahams and Mr. Claude G. Montefiore, the editors of that periodical, for their assistance in their republication. Dealing, as they do, with legal problems of considerable difficulty, and intended to be read by the general reader as well as by the lawyer, they of necessity run the risk of being found too difficult by the former, and not sufficiently deep or learned by the latter, even as Critias of old was said to be

ἰδιώτης μὲν ἐν φιλοσόφοις, φιλόσοφος δὲ ἐν ἰδιώταις.

Still, the subject is of such absorbing interest to so many that I hope that the distastefulness caused by the crabbed intricacies of style, which seem to be natural to the legal writer, may be overcome by the general reader, and the lawyer, if he desires to penetrate more deeply into the subjects dealt with, will find sufficient material for his researches in the authorities quoted in the footnotes.

The articles were written at different times and in the midst of other occupations, consequently it may be found that the order and arrangement of the topics discussed is neither as precise or logical as it should be. It would on this account have been better to rearrange and in part rewrite the articles, but, as it is desired that they should be republished before the fiftieth anniversary of the admission of Jews to seats in Parliament, I have been unable to find time for this purpose, and can only hope that the Table of Contents and Index, which have been added, will enable the reader to find the subjects in which he is interested.

One subject of great practical importance has been altogether omitted, namely the law as to Jewish marriages; this I have dealt with in two separate articles, which will shortly appear in the *Jewish Quarterly Review*, and may possibly be afterwards republished as a distinct treatise. The question of Sunday labour is also not dealt with, for the law in this respect is the same for Jews and Christians, with the single exception of the privileges conferred upon the Jews by the Factory Acts. The time may come when special provision as to Sunday work will be made for the Jews in other cases also; my views upon this subject will be found in the evidence I gave before the House of Lords Committee on the Sunday Closing (Shops)

Bill, 1905, and before the conjoint committee on Sunday Trading appointed by both Houses of Parliament, in 1906, which will be found in the reports of these bodies published as blue-books. As the law is now the same both for Jew and Gentile, I do not think the subject would rightly find a place in the present volume.

More than a generation has passed since complete equality before the law has been established between Jew and Christian, and every profession and public office has been thrown open to the Jews. The doleful prophecies, which were so freely indulged in by the opponents of Jewish emancipation, that it would result in the dechristianizing and demoralization of the country, have been proved by experience to be wholly unfounded. A new charge is now made against the Jews that they do not sufficiently avail themselves of the right to take part in public affairs, which has been conceded to them. On examination this complaint also seems to be equally unfounded; when the comparatively small number of the Jews in the United Kingdom is taken into consideration—they do not amount to more than ·05 of the population—and it is remembered that of this small number a very large proportion are foreigners, or the children of foreigners, and that the remainder have not started life with advantageous professional or political antecedents, the number of those who have made their mark in public life is by no means small.

The impression that Jews do not evince sufficient interest in public life can only be accounted for by the fact that they still retain that supremacy in the world of commerce and finance, which they acquired when no other field for their energies was open to them. They fortunately also afford many examples of that world-wide and farseeing philanthropy which does much to reconcile mankind to the great acquisition of wealth by successful financiers.

H. S. Q. HENRIQUES.

4 King's Bench Walk,
Temple, E.C.
March, 1908.

CONTENTS

	PAGE
TABLE OF CASES	xvii
TABLE OF STATUTES	xxi

I

The English Law has imposed no disabilities upon Jews as such	1
Attempts to suppress the Jewish religion by legal proceedings	2
The Act to oblige the Jews to maintain their Protestant children	3
Stringent administration of the Act in its early days	4
Its later administration	6
The Jewish religion protected though outside the benefit of the Toleration Act (1688)	9
Libel on the Jewish community (*R.* v. *Osborne*)	9
It is no crime to attack the doctrines of any religion if the decencies of controversy are observed	11

II

The Act against Blasphemy and Profaneness	13
History of the Act	15
Anti-Jewish amendment	16
Desire for the conversion of the Jews to Christianity	17
Practical freedom of the Jewish religion	18
Jewish religious endowments	18
The case of *Da Costa* v. *De Paz*	19
Other legal decisions	22
Benefit of the Toleration Act extended to the Jewish religion	23
Effect of this legislation	24
How Jewish endowments may still be defeated	25
In re Michel's Trusts	26
Superstitious uses	29
Prayers for the souls of the dead	30
Gifts for such a purpose are not charitable	30
Action to recover seat rentals in a synagogue	32

III

The right of Jews to participate in general endowments and charities	34
In re the Bedford Charity	35
Claim of a Jewess to participate in the Bedford Charity	37

	PAGE
Petition presented	37
Evidence in support of the petition	37
Evidence on behalf of the trustees of the charity	39
Hearing of the petition and decision of Lord Eldon	41
New petition presented. Formal judgment on the whole case	42
Order made on the petition	46
Comments on Lord Eldon's judgment	46
IV	
Date of the return of the Jews to England	49
Popular historical and legal theories	51
Early history of the Jews in England. Saxon times	51
Legal status of the Jews after the Norman Conquest	53
Exchequer of the Jews	54
Statutes restricting the Jews' civil rights	54
Banishment of the Jews	55
Effect of the banishment on the revenue of the King	56
Theories concerning the banishment:	
(1) Lord Coke's	58
(2) Prynne's	59
(3) That the expulsion was by a synod held in London	62
Period between the banishment and the return of the Jews	62
The disappearance of villenage	63
Consequences of the Reformation	65
The law of heresy	65
Alterations in the law of heresy	68
Heresy and the Court of High Commission	71
Abolition of the Court of High Commission	72
The law of Uniformity	73
Recusants	75
Legal position of the Jews at the beginning of Charles I's reign	77
Treaty with Spain, 1630. Spanish crypto-Jews	79
The Great Rebellion. Ascendancy of the Independents	82
Petition of the Jews of Amsterdam, 1648–9	84
Modification of the laws against recusancy	86
Freedom of worship not extended to all Christian sects	88
Continuation of the negotiations with the Jews of Amsterdam	88
Menasseh ben Israel	88
The Whitehall Conference, 1655	89
Result of the Conference	91
Menasseh's second petition, March, 1655–6	92
Departure and death of Menasseh	92

V

PAGE
Failure of Menasseh's mission 94
Cromwell's toleration 95
Theory that a "tolerance" was granted to the Jews by Cromwell in February, 1658 97
Theory that the Committee of the Council of State reported in favour of admitting the Jews 99
Theory as to the return of the Jews founded on the proceedings against Antonio Robles (March–May, 1656) . . . 102
The true bearing of the Robles case 105
Theory that Cromwell gave a special authorization to John Sadler to build a synagogue 107
Theory founded on the antiquity of the Spanish and Portuguese cemetery at Mile End 109

VI

Cromwell's attitude to the Jews 115
The legal position of the Jews under Cromwell the same as under Charles I 116
Cromwell did not grant and had no power to grant special privileges to the Jews in respect of their religion . . 117
Position at the time of Cromwell's death. Previous intrigues of the Jews in Holland with the Royalists 118
Menasseh's failure made the Jews of Holland incline to Charles II 119
Commission to Lt.-Gen. Middleton to treat with them . . 120
Their hopes destroyed by the battle of the Dunes 121
Interval between the death of Cromwell and the Restoration. Increase in the number of the Jews here 121
First mention of a Jewish synagogue in England . . . 122
No change in the legal status of the Jews till the Restoration . 124
The Restoration of the king and Resettlement of the Jews . 125
Charles II an advocate of toleration in an intolerant age . . 126
The Convention Parliament and toleration 127
The new Parliament, 1661 128
Members ordered to take the Sacrament 128
The Corporation Act 129
The Quakers' Act 129
The Act of Uniformity, 1662 130
First Declaration of Indulgence, 1662 130
The Conventicle Act, 1664 133
Bill for granting Liberty of Conscience rejected 134
The Five Mile Act, 1665 134
Second Conventicle Act, 1670 135

PAGE
Declaration of Indulgence, 1672 136
The power to issue the Declaration questioned in the Commons. The Declaration cancelled 138
The Test Act, 1673 139
The Parliamentary Test Act, 1678 140

VII

Petitions against the Jews at the time of the Restoration . . 142
Position of the Jews after the Restoration 144
The first synagogue 145
The secrecy surrounding the synagogue discarded at the end of 1662 or beginning of 1663 146
An organized community formed. 146
1664. Threatened attack on the Jews. Petition to the king. His gracious answer 147
Inquiry concerning the Jews ordered by the House of Commons 148
1673. Prosecution of the Jews for meeting for the exercise of their religion 149
The Jews petition the king and obtain an Order in Council to stay the proceedings against them 149
Entering a *nolle prosequi* on an indictment a new way of exercising the Dispensing Power 150
Progress made in the Establishment of a Jewish community in the reign of Charles II 151
Accession of James II. His religious policy 152
Jews arrested and charged with recusancy 153
On the petition of Joseph Henriques and others a formal Order in Council made staying the proceedings. 154
Dispute between James II and Parliament concerning the Dispensing Power 154
The struggle transferred to the Law Courts. James issues his Declaration of Indulgence. 156
The illegality of James's proceedings 157
Did not affect the Jews 157
Views on toleration at the time of the Revolution . . . 158
The Toleration Act 159
Extension of the benefits of the Toleration Acts 161
Relief from the Test and Corporation Acts 162
Legislative relief from the penal laws at length given to the Jews 162
Parliament and the Jews. Attempt to lay special taxation upon them 164
Mention of Jews in the Act imposing taxation on marriages . 166
The Act against Blasphemy 167

PAGE
The Act to oblige Jews to maintain their Protestant children. The de Breta case 167
Relaxation in favour of the Jews of the Act compelling land-owners to take the oath of abjuration 170
Similar privileges given the Jews by other Acts of Parliament. The Colonial Naturalization Act, 1740 170
Lord Hardwicke's Marriage Act, 1753 170
The Jewish Naturalization Act, 1753 171
The Jews admitted to the benefit of the Toleration Act, 1845 and 1846. Till then they were protected only by the Dispensing Power of the king 171
Resulting anomaly in the law as to the Registration of synagogues 173
Advantages of certifying a synagogue 174
Summary of the foregoing account of the legal recognition of the Jewish religion 175

VIII

Distinction between civil and political rights 177
The law of the land applied to the Jews on their return; but the abolition of villenage exempted them from the operation of the ancient statutes concerning the Judaei . . . 178
Right of a Jew to be a witness in a Court of law . . . 178
Witnesses not sworn on the New Testament may be guilty of perjury 180
A Jew may be sworn on the New Testament if he does not object 182
The Oaths Act, 1838 182
Arrangement of cause lists so that Jewish cases should not be taken on the Jewish Sabbath or holidays 183
Jewish religious scruples recognized by the law merchant. A Jew excused from giving notice of dishonour of a bill of exchange on a Jewish holiday 184
Capacity of Jews to bring actions 185
Coke's theory that infidels are perpetual enemies . . . 186
The capacity of a Jew to sue admitted in 1684 188
Coke's theory overruled by the Courts 189
Coke's theory not altogether groundless 190
Capacity of Jews to hold real property 191
Ordinance of 1271 forbidding Jews to hold land discovered by Dr. Tovey in 1738 192
Capacity of Jews to hold advowsons 194
Jews and the benefit of clergy 195
The practice of administering the necessary oath upon the New Testament the cause of the civil disabilities of the Jews . 198

PAGE
Jews excluded from the freedom of the city of London . . 199
Quakers in a better position than Jews in this respect . . 200
Jews and trade in the city of London. Not more than twelve allowed to be brokers 200
The disability removed, Dec. 10, 1830 201
Exclusion from the legal and other professions 202
The annual Indemnity Acts 203
Jews admitted to the bar, 1833 203
Admission of Jews as solicitors, 1770 . , ... 205
The profession of schoolmasters and tutors 206
Dissenters disabled from teaching in the public schools and colleges 207
The Religious Disabilities Act, 1846 208
The Universities and Dissenters 208
The Universities Tests Act, 1871 210
Jews and the lower branches of education 211
Private schools 212
Public schools 212
Endowed schools 213
The Endowed Schools Act, 1869 214
Public elementary schools 215
The Cowper-Temple clause 217
Religious instruction in non-provided schools 217
Higher grade and technical schools 218
Poor law schools 219
Reformatory schools 219
Industrial schools 220

IX

The obligation to take certain oaths the cause of Jewish disabilities 221
The oath of allegiance and supremacy 221
Persons on whom it was imposed 222
A new oath of obedience or allegiance, 1606 222
The oath directed against Popish Recusants 224
The oaths of allegiance and supremacy recast at the time of the Revolution 225
Introduction of the oath of abjuration in 1701 226
Jews unable to take the new oath 228
Later history of these promissory oaths 228
Mode of administering the oaths 229
Effect of promissory oaths 229
The acquisition of British nationality 229

PAGE
Former status and disabilities of aliens 230
The special taxation of aliens 230
Who are aliens by English law 233
The Roumanian Law as to aliens 233
How aliens can acquire British nationality 234
The colonial trade closed to aliens by the Navigation Act of 1660 235
Jews made denizens by Charles II 236
Naturalization by Act of Parliament 237
Naturalization confined to Protestants by a statute of 1609 . 238
General Naturalization Acts 238
The Plantation Act, 1740 240
The Jews Naturalization Act, 1753 241
The Jews Naturalization Repeal Act, 1754 243
Unsuccessful attempt to take away the right of Jews to be naturalized in the colonies 245
Recent changes in the law of naturalization 245
The Parliamentary franchise 246
Provision in the Ballot Act for voting on Saturday . . . 247
Offices in corporations and under the Crown 247
Motives of the Corporation and Test Acts 248
Repeal of the Corporation and Test Acts 249
Declaration not to injure the Established Church substituted for the Sacramental Test. 249
The Lords add the words "On the true faith of a Christian" to the new Declaration 251
Effect of the new Declaration on the political status of the Jews 251
Relief given to Roman Catholics and Quakers in 1829 and 1837 respectively 253
Declaration to be taken by Sheriffs Act, 1835 253
Mr. Salomons refused admission to the office of Alderman . . 254
The Jewish Disabilities Removal Act of 1845 255
The Oaths Act and the Jewish Relief Act of 1858 256
Subsequent legislation 256
Taking the insignia of office to a place of religious worship . 257
Device of fining Dissenters for refusing to serve the office of sheriff. 258
Jews not liable to these fines 261
S. 3 of the Jewish Relief Act of 1858, disabling Jews from holding certain high offices, repealed in 1871 261
A Jew may now be Lord Lieutenant of Ireland or Lord Chancellor 262
Ecclesiastical patronage attached to an office held by a Jew . 263

PAGE

X

Mr. Robert Grant's Jews' Civil Disabilities Bill, 1830–36 . . 265
1836–47. Minor measures of relief from political disabilities . 267
1847. Baron de Rothschild elected to represent the city of London in Parliament 267
1847–8. Lord John Russell's Jewish Disabilities Bill . . . 268
1849. Lord John Russell's Parliamentary Oaths Bill . . . 269
1850. Baron de Rothschild having resigned and been re-elected attempts to take his seat 269
1851. Lord John Russell's Oath of Abjuration (Jew) Bill . . 270
Mr. Salomons purports to take the Oath of Abjuration without pronouncing its final words 270
Mr. Salomons takes his seat in the House and refuses to withdraw 271
Subsequent proceedings in the House of Commons . . . 273
The case of Miller *v.* Salomons 274
The judgment affirmed on appeal 276
Lord John Russell's Jewish Disabilities Bill of 1853 . . . 277
1854. Lord John Russell's Parliamentary Oaths Bill refused a second reading by the House of Commons . . . 279
1856. Mr. Milner Gibson's Oath of Abjuration Abolition Bill . 280
1857. Lord Palmerston's Oaths Bill 281
The opposition to Jewish Emancipation grows weaker . . 283
The Bill is rejected by the House of Lords 284
1857. Lord John Russell's Oaths Validity Amendment Bill . 284
Not receiving facilities from the Government the Bill is abandoned 285
Baron de Rothschild again resigns and is re-elected . . . 285
Select Committee appointed to consider whether a Statutory Declaration might under the Act of 1835 be substituted for Parliamentary Oath 286
The autumn session of 1857: Lord John Russell's Oaths Bill . 286
Fall of Lord Palmerston's Government, and the formation of a Conservative Ministry under Lord Derby . . . 287
The Oaths Bill read a third time in the Commons . . . 287
The Bill in the Lords. The fifth clause, enabling Jews to omit the final words of the oath, rejected in committee . . 288
Baron de Rothschild appointed a member of the Commons' Committee for drawing up reasons for disagreeing with the Lords' amendments 288
The legality of the appointment 289
The Commons' reasons 290
Conference between the two Houses 291

PAGE
Lord Lucan's suggestion for compromise 291
The suggestion favourably received 292
The Lords insist on their amendments. 292
Carrying out the compromise 293
Lord Lucan's Jewish Relief Bill 293
The Lords' reasons for insisting on their amendments . . 294
The House of Commons and the compromise 296
Baron de Rothschild takes his seat in the House . . . 297
The real character of the "compromise" 297
The settlement hastened by the fall of the Liberal Government 298
The exclusion of the subject from the arena of party conflict a benefit to the Jews 299
The praiseworthy conduct of Baron de Rothschild and Mr. Salomons 300
An inconvenience arising from the form of the settlement remedied by Act of Parliament 300
The "compromise" upset by the Parliamentary Oaths Act of 1866 301
The power of the House of Lords to exclude Jews voluntarily abandoned by the former opponents of Jewish emancipation 302
Lord Rothschild created a peer in 1885 304
The Office and Oaths Act, 1867 304
The Promissory Oaths Act, 1868 304
The Promissory Oaths Act, 1871, throws open to Jews the high offices from which they were excluded by the Jewish Relief Act of 1858 305

CHRONOLOGICAL TABLE 306

ADDENDA AND CORRIGENDA 315

INDEX 318

TABLE OF CASES

PAGE

Anon. (1683), 1 Vernon, 263 . . . . 152 *n.*, 179
Anon. (1684), Lilly's *Practical Register*, vol. I, p. 4 . 188, 152 *n.*
Attorney-General *v.* Baxter (1684), 1 Vernon, 248, and (1689) 2 Vernon, 105 . . . . 19 *n.*
Attorney-General *v.* Drummond (1842), 1 Drury and Warren, 380 . . . . 25 *n.*
Attorney-General *v.* Lucas [1905], 1 Ch. 68 . . . 24 *n.*, Addenda
Attorney-General *v.* Mayor of Bristol (1820), 2 Jacob and Walker, 294 . . . . 21 *n.*
Attorney-General *v.* Pearson (1817), 3 Merivale, 353 . 14 *n.*, 19 *n.*, 24
Alderman Backwell's case (1683), 1 Vernon, 152 . 107 *n.*, Addenda

Barker *v.* Warren (1677), 2 Modern Reports, 271 . 152 *n.*, 183
Bedford Charity, *in re* the Masters, Governors, and Trustees of the (1818), 2 Swanston, 470 . . . . . . 35 seq.
Blundell's Trusts, *in re* (1861), 30 Beavan, 360 30
Bradlaugh *v.* Gossett (1884), L. R. 12 Q. B. D. 271 . . 300 *n.*
Bradshaw *v.* Tasker (1834), 2 Mylne and Keene, 221 . . . 25 *n.*
Breeks *v.* Woolfrey (1838), 1 Curteis' *Eccl. Rep.*, 880 . . . 29 *n.*
Britton *v.* Standish (1704), cases temp. Holt, 141, and 3 Salkeld, 88 74 *n.*

Calvin's case (1608), 7 Coke's Reports, 1 . . . . . 186, 190
Chamberlain of London *v.* Evans. *See* Harrison.

Da Costa *v.* De Paz (1743), Ambler, 224, 1 Dickens, 258, and 2 Swanston, 481 . . . . 19, 33, 42
De Wilton, *in re*, De Wilton *v.* Montefiore, L. R. [1900] 2 Ch. 489 . . . . 49, 51

East India Co. *v.* Sandys (1683–5), X Howell's *State Trials*, 371 seq., 2 Shower, 366, and Skinner, 132 . . 117 *n.*, 187
Edenborough *v.* Archbishop of Canterbury (1826), 2 Russell, 111 . . . . 247 *n.*
Edwards *v.* Bishop of Exeter (1839), 7 Scott, 676, and 5 Bingham, New Cases, 652 . . . . 194 *n.*
Egerton *v.* All of Odd Rode, L. R. [1894] P. 15 . . 29 *n.*, Addenda
Elliott, *in re* (1891), Weekly Notes, 9 . . . . 30 *n.*
Endowed Schools Act, 1869, *in re*, and *in re* Christ's Hospital (1890), L. R. 15 A. C. 172 . . . . 215 *n.*

PAGE

Fineberg *v.* Adler and the Liverpool Schechita Board (1904). *See* the *Standard*, Feb. 26 and 27 and Liverpool local papers of these dates 184
Fish *v.* Klein (1817), 2 Merivale, 431 . . . . . . 111 *n.*
Fleetwood, *in re*, Sidgreaves *v.* Brewer (1880), L. R. 15 Ch. D. 594 30 *n.*

Ganer *v.* Lady Lanesborough (1790), 1 Peake, 25 . . 182 *n.*
Gilbert *v.* Buzzard and Boyer (1821), 2 Haggard's *Consistory Cases*, 333 . . . . 111 *n.*
Goddard *v.* Smith (1764), 8 Modern Reports, 264 . . 150 *n.*
Godden *v.* Hales (1686), XI Howell's *State Trials*, 1166, and 2 Shower, 475 . . . . 156 *n.*, 173 *n.*
Gomez Serra *v.* Munez (1728), 2 Strange, 821 180

Habershon *v.* Vardon (1851), 4 De Gex and Smale, 467 . . 25
Harrison, Sir Thomas (Chamberlain of London) *v.* Evans (1767), 3 Brown's *Parliamentary Cases*, 465, and Cobbett's *Parliamentary History*, vol. XVI, pp. 313–27 . 160, 259, 260 *n.*
Heath *v.* Chapman (1857), 2 Drewry, 417 20
Hingeston *v.* Sydney [1908], L. R. 1 Ch. 126 . . 26 *n.*, Addenda

Inhabitants of St. Andrew's Undershaft *v.* De Breta (1701), 1 Lord Raymond, 699 168
Isaacs *v.* Gompertz (1783), Ambler, 228 *n.*, 1 Dickens, 169 *n.*, and 7 Vesey Junior, 61 . . . . 22, 33
Israel v. Simmons (1818), 2 Starkie, 356 32

Le Louis, the case of (1817), 2 Dodson, 210. . . . . 191 *n.*
Lindo *v.* Belisario (1795), 1 Haggard, *Consistory Cases*, 216. . 49
Lindo *v.* Unsworth (1811), 2 Campbell, 602. 185
Lyons, *ex parte* (1750), Ambler, 89 201

Marshall *v.* Graham, L. R. [1907] 2 K. B. 112 . 216 *n.*, Addenda
Mayor of Guildford *v.* Clarke (1690), 2 Ventris 247 . . 260 *n.*
Mellish *v.* Da Costa (1737), 2 Atkyns, 14 . . . . . . 8 *n.*
Michel's Trusts, *in re* (1860), 28 Beavan, 39. . . 25 *n.*, 26–30
Miller *v.* Salomons (1852), 8 State Trials, New Series, 163, 7 Exchequer, 475; 8 Exchequer, 778; 21 *Law Journal*, New Series, 161, 16 Jurist, 375 . . . . 225 *n.*, 274 seq.
Mirehouse *v.* Rennell (1833), 7 Bligh, New Series, 322 . 195 *n.*
Moggridge *v.* Thackwell (1802), 7 Vesey Junior, 36 . . 19, 22
Moses Marcus, *ex parte* (1722–3) and (1726–7), Sanders' *Orders in Chancery*, I, 457, 524 6–8
Musgrove *v.* Chun Teeong Toy, L. R. [1891] A. C. 272 . 117 *n.*

Nayler's Case (1656), V Howell's *State Trials*, 801 . . . . 82 *n.*

PAGE

Omychund *v.* Barker (1744), Willes, 538, 1 Atkyns, 21, and 1 Wilson, 84 . . . . 180–82, 189
Orme *v.* Nutt (1699), 1 Lord Raymond, 486 10

Pearson *v.* Stead, L. R. [1904] P. 66 . . . . . 29 *n.*, Addenda
Pigg *v.* Caley (1617), Noy, 27 63
Poulter's case (1610), 11 Coke's *Reports*, 29 197
Powell *v.* The Kempton Park Racecourse Co., L. R. [1897] 2 Q. B. 242 and ib. [1899], A. C. 143 64

R. *v.* Bosworth (1739), 2 Strange, 1112 . . . . 199, 200, 229
R. *v.* Richard Carlile (1819), 3 Barnewall and Alderson, 161 . 14
R. *v.* Francia (1717), XV Howell's *State Trials*, 897 179
R. *v.* Gilham (1795), 1 Espinasse, 286, and 6 Term Reports, 265 . 182
R. *v.* Bartholomew Legatt (1612), II Howell's *State Trials*, 729 . 70
R. *v.* Osborne (1732), 2 Barnardiston, 138 and 166; Wm. Kelynge, 231; 2 Swanston, 503 *n.*; and Sessions Cases, 260 . . 9, 10
R. *v.* Parry (1811), 14 East, 549 . . . . 249 *n.*
R. *v.* the Turkey Company (1760), 2 Burrows, 943, and id. 1000 200 *n.*
R. *v.* Edward Lord Vaux (1612), 1 Bulstrode, 199 229
R. and Morrice *v.* the Mayor of Lincoln (1698), 12 Modern Rep. 190, and 5 Modern Rep., 399-403 . . . . . 200 *n.*
R. and Reg. *v.* Larwood (1694), 1 Lord Raymond, 29, and 4 Modern Rep., 269 . . . . 261 *n.*
Reg. *v.* Humphery (1838), 3 Neville and Perry, 681, (1839) 10 Adolphus and Ellis, 335 255
Reg. *v.* Price (1884), L. R. 12 Q. B. D. 247 . . . . . 111 *n.*
Reg. *v.* Ramsey and Foote (1883), 15 Cox, *Criminal Cases*, 231 . . . . 12, 263 *n.*
Robeley *v.* Langston (1667), 2 Keble, 314 . . . . 152 *n.*, 179

Sidney, *in re*, Hingeston *v.* Sidney, L. R. [1908] 1 Ch. 126 26 *n.*, Addenda
Sommersett's Case (1771), XX Howell's *State Trials*, 1 . . . 63
Steavenson, *in re* (1823), 2 Barnwell and Cresswell, 34 . 249 *n.*
Straus *v.* Goldsmid (1837), 8 Simon, 614 23

Tassel *v.* Lewis (1695), 1 Lord Raymond, 743 . . . . 185 *n.*
Thomas *v.* Sorrel (1674), Vaughan, 330 . . . . . . 173 *n.*
Tirlot *v.* Morris (1611), 1 Bulstrode, 134, and Yelverton, 198 231 *n.*

Villareal *v.* Mellish (1737), 2 Swanston, 533 8
Vincent *v.* Fernandez (1718), 1 Peere Williams, 524 4

Wells *v.* Williams (1697), 1 Lord Raymond, 282, and 1 Salkeld, 46 189
West *v.* Shuttleworth (1835), 2 Mylne and Keen, 684 . . 28, 31

Zap Chea Neo *v.* Ong Cheng Neo (1875), L. R. 6 P. C. 396 . . 31

TABLE OF STATUTES

PAGE

Ancient Saxon Statutes 52, 53
Law of Edward the Confessor 53
Magna Charta . . . . 61, 117 *n.*, 229–30
54 & 55 Henry III (Ordinance prohibiting the Jews from holding land) 192, 54, 64
3 Edw. I (Statute *de la Jeuerie* or *de Iudaismo*) 54, 58, 59, 62, 64, 192
15 Edw. II (Act banishing the Despensers) 78
5 Rich. II, stat. 2, cap. 5 (for the arrest of preachers of heresy) . 66
2 Hen. IV, c. 15 (*De Haeretico*) 67
2 Hen. V, stat. 1, c. 7 (against Lollardry) 68
1 Ric. III, c. 9 (Restraints upon aliens) . . . . . 231 *n.*
1 Hen. VII, c. 2 (Customs to be paid by aliens made denizens) 231 *n.*
11 Hen. VII, c. 14 (Customs to be paid by aliens made denizens) 231 *n.*
14 & 15 Hen. VIII, c. 2 (Apprentices of strangers artificers) . 231 *n.*
22 Hen. VIII, c. 8 (Denizens strangers to pay strangers customs) 231 *n.*
23 Hen. VIII, c. 10 (Assurances of lands to churches, &c.) . . 29 *n.*
25 Hen. VIII, c. 14 (against heretics) . . . . 69 *n.*
25 Hen. VIII, c. 22 (concerning the King's succession) . . 221
26 Hen. VIII, c. 2 (Oath of obedience to the King and the heirs of his body by Queen Anne) 221
28 Hen. VIII, c. 7 (concerning the succession of the crown) . 221
31 Hen. VIII, c. 14 (Act of the six Articles) . . . . 69 *n.*
32 Hen. VIII, c. 2 (Statute of Limitations, 1540). 63
32 Hen. VIII, c. 16 (Aliens, alien artificers, and denizens) . 231 *n.*
35 Hen. VIII, c. 1 (for the establishment of the King's succession) 221
1 Edw. VI, c. 1 (the Sacrament) . . . . 69 *n.*
1 Edw. VI, c. 12 (for the repeal of certain statutes concerning treasons and felonies) . . . . 69 *n.*
1 Edw. VI, c. 14 (the Act for chantries collegiate) . . . 29 *n.*
2 & 3 Edw. VI, c. 1 (Act of Uniformity, 1548) . . . . 69 *n.*
1 & 2 Phil. & Mar., c. 6 (reviving the statutes against heretics) . 69
1 Eliz., c. 1 (Act of Supremacy) . . . 69, 76, 200, 208, 221–2
1 Eliz., c. 2 (Act of Uniformity) 73, 76

PAGE

5 Eliz., c. 1 (for the assurance of the Queen's Royal Power) 202 *n.*, 222

18 Eliz., c. 7 (to take away the benefit of clergy in certain cases) 196

23 Eliz., c. 1 (to retain the Queen's subjects in their due obedience) . . . . 2, 74, 87, 153, 207 *n.*

29 Eliz., c. 6 (for the due execution of the Act to retain the Queen's subjects in their due obedience) 74

35 Eliz., c. 1 (to retain the Queen's subjects in their due obedience) 75, 87, 133

35 Eliz., c. 2 (for restraining Popish recusants to certain places of abode) 75

1 (2 Ruff.) Jac. I, c. 4 (for the execution of the statutes against Jesuits, recusants, &c.) . . . . 207 *n.*

3 Jac. I, c. 4 (for discovering and repressing Popish recusants) 75, 76, 77, 222–4

3 Jac. I, c. 5 (to prevent dangers which grow by Popish recusants) . . . . 76, 77, 113, 194 *n.*

7 Jac. I, c. 2 (Naturalization and restoration of blood) . . 238, 241

7 Jac. I, c. 6 (for administering the oath of allegiance) 76 *n.*, 202 *n.*, 208, 223

21 Jac. I, c. 6 (female convicts and benefit of clergy) . . 197 *n.*

16 Car. I, c. 11 (for the abolition of the Court of High Commission) 72

Ordinance of March, 164$\frac{4}{5}$, cap. 51, substituting the Directory for Public Worship for the Book of Common Prayer . . 83

Ordinance of 23 Aug., 1645, cap. 57 ("The Directorie to be put in execution with Penalties for using the Book of Common Prayer") 83

Ordinance of May 2, 1648, cap. 114 (for punishing blasphemies and heresies) 82

Ordinance of September 27, 1650, cap. 27 (Repeal of several clauses in statutes imposing Penalties for not coming to Church) . . . . 87, 107 *n.*

Navigation Act, October 9, 1651, cap. 22 88

The Instrument of Government, December 16, 1653 . . 87, 117

The Humble Petition and Advice, May 25, 1657, cap. 6 Addenda, 97 *n.*, 117

The Ordinance for the better Observance of the Lord's Day, 1656, cap. 15 . . . . Addenda, 97 *n.*

12 Car. II, c. 4 (for granting a subsidy of tonnage and poundage) . . . . 231 *n.*

12 Car. II, c. 18 (Navigation Act, 1660) 144, 231, 235

13 Car. II, stat. 1, c. 12 (for explaining 16 Car. I, c. 11) . . 72

PAGE
13 Car. II, stat. 1, c. 14 (for confirming Acts of the Convention Parliament including the Navigation Act, 1660) . 144 *n.*
13 Car. II, stat. 2, c. 1 (Corporation Act, 1661) . . 129, 247, 258
14 (13 & 14 Ruff.) Car. II, c. 1 (against Quakers) . 129, 161 *n.*
14 (13 & 14 Ruff.) Car. II, c. 4 (Act of Uniformity, 1662) 9, 130, 206, 213, 249
15 Car. II, c. 15 (for encouraging the manufactures of linen cloth and tapestry) 239
16 Car. II, c. 4 (Conventicle Act, 1664) 133
17 Car. II, c. 2 (Five Mile Act, 1665) . . . . . 134, 161 *n.*
22 Car. II, c. 1 (Second Conventicle Act, 1670) . . 9, 135, 161 *n.*
25 Car. II, c. 2 (Test Act, 1672) . . . . . 139, 156 *n.*, 248
25 Car. II, c. 6 (Aliens Duty) . . . . 231 *n.*
29 Car. II, c. 9 (for taking away the writ *de heretico comburendo*) 73
30 Car. II, stat. 2 (Parliamentary Test Act, 1678) . . . 140
1 Will. & Mar., c. 1 (Declaring the Convention a Parliament) . 225
1 Will. & Mar., c. 8 (appointing new oaths of allegiance and supremacy). . . . . 225, 202 *n.*, 208
1 Will. & Mar., c. 18 (The Toleration Act, 1688) 159-62, 9, 19, 20, 173, 260
1 Will. & Mar., c. 26 (to vest in the Universities the presentations of benefices belonging to Papists) . . . . 194 *n.*
1 Will. & Mar., sess. 2, c. 2 (The Bill of Rights) . . . 76, 172
3 Will. & Mar., c. 9 (Benefit of Clergy) . . . . . 197 *n.*
6 & 7 Will. III, c. 6 (An Act for granting duties upon Marriages, &c.) 166
7 & 8 Will. III, c. 22 (The Act for preventing frauds and regulating abuses in the Plantation Trade) 235
7 & 8 Will. III, c. 27 (For the better security of His Majesty's Person and Government) 246
7 & 8 Will. III, c. 34 (Making the solemn affirmation of Quakers equivalent to an oath) . . . . 200 *n.*
9 (9 & 10 Ruff.) Will. III, c. 35 (c. 32 Ruff.) (For the more effectual suppressing of Blasphemy and Profaneness) 13, 167, 212
11 (11 & 12 Ruff.) Will. III, c. 4 (To prevent the further growth of Popery) . . . . 4, 161 *n.*
12 & 13 Will. III, c. 2 (The Act of Settlement) . . 234, 238, 240
13 & 14 (13 Ruff.) Will. III, c. 6 (For the further security of succession to the Crown in the Protestant line) 226, 228 *n.*
1 Anne, c. 16 (stat. 1, c. 22 Ruff.) (for alterations in the oath appointed by 13 & 14 Will. III, c. 6) . . . . 228 *n.*
1 Anne, c. 24 (stat. 1, c. 30, Ruff.) (The Act to oblige the Jews to maintain and provide for their Protestant children) . 3, 167

PAGE
6 (5 Ruff.) Anne, c. 9 (c. 6 Ruff.) (Benefit of Clergy) 197
6 (5 Ruff.) Anne, c. 11 (c. 8 Ruff.) (The Act of Union with Scotland) . . . . 228 *n.*
6 Anne, c. 41 (c. 7 Ruff.) (The Succession to the Crown Act, 1707) . . . . 228 *n.*
6 Anne, c. 64 (c. 37 Ruff.) (The Act for the encouragement of Trade to America) 239
6 Anne, c. 78 (c. 23 Ruff.) (The Scotch Representative Peers Act, 1707) 246
7 Anne, c. 5 (Foreign Protestants Naturalization Act, 1708) 233 *n.*
10 Anne, c. 6 (c. 2 Ruff.) (The Occasional Conformity Act, 1711) 257, 258 *n.*
13 Anne, c. 7 (12 Anne, stat. 2, c. 7 Ruff.) (The Schism Act, 1713) 257
13 Anne, c. 13 (12 Anne, stat. 2, c. 14 Ruff.) (The Presentation of Benefices Act, 1713) . . . . 194 *n.*
1 Geo. I, stat. 2, c. 4 (Disabling clause to be inserted in Naturalization Bills) . . . . 238 *n.*
1 Geo. I, stat. 2, c. 13 (For the further Security of His Majesty's Person and Government, &c.) 202, 208, 228 *n.*, 268, 277 *n.*, 289
5 Geo. I, c. 4 (For strengthening the Protestant interest in these Kingdoms) . . . . 257, 258 *n.*
5 Geo. I, c. 6 (The Act for quieting and establishing corporations) 248
8 Geo. I, c. 6 (Forms of Affirmation or Declaration for Quakers) 200 *n.*
9 Geo. I, c. 24 (To oblige persons refusing to take the Oaths to register their names and real estates) 170
10 Geo. I, c. 4 (To explain and amend 9 Geo. I, c. 24) 170, 191, 200, 206, 275
1 Geo. II, stat. 2, c. 23 (First annual indemnity Act) . . . 203
2 Geo. II, c. 31 (Indemnity Act, 1729) 202
4 Geo. II, c. 21 (The British Nationality Act, 1730) . . 233 *n.*
9 Geo. II, c. 26 (Indemnity Act, 1737) 202
13 Geo. II, c. 3 (For the better supply of mariners) . . . 239
13 Geo. II, c. 7 (The Plantation Act, 1740) . . . 170, 240, 241
20 Geo. II, c. 44 (Naturalization in the American colonies) . 241 *n.*
22 Geo. II, c. 45 (For the encouragement of the Whale Fishery) 240
22 Geo. II, c. 46 (Continuancy of laws; affirmations of Quakers) 200 *n.*, 268 *n.*
26 Geo. II, c. 26 (Jewish Naturalization Act, 1753) 241–5, 163 *n.*, 171, 192, 194
26 Geo. II, c. 33 (Lord Hardwicke's Marriage Act, 1753) . . 170
27 Geo. II, c. 1 (Jewish Naturalization Act Repeal Act, 1754) 243–5, 194
2 Geo. III, c. 25 (Naturalization of Protestants serving in America) 239

PAGE

6 Geo. III, c. 53 (The Act for altering the oath of abjuration, &c., now known as the Treason Act, 1766) . . . 226–8
13 Geo. III, c. 21 (The British Nationality Act, 1772) . . 233 *n.*
13 Geo. III, c. 25 (To explain 13 Geo. II, c. 27 and 2 Geo. III, c. 25) . . . . 241 *n.*
18 Geo. III, c. 60 (Sir George Savile's Act) . . . . 161 *n.*
19 Geo. III, c. 44 (The Nonconformist Relief Act, 1779) . . 207
20 Geo. III, c. 20 (For the better supply of mariners and seamen) 239
24 Geo. III, sess. 2, c. 16 (For discontinuing the petty custom on aliens' goods, &c.) . . . . 231 *n.*
26 Geo. III, c. 50 (For the encouragement of the southern whale fishery) . . . . 240 *n.*
28 Geo. III, c. 20 (Encouragement of the southern whale fishery Amendment Act) . . . . 240 *n.*
31 Geo. III, c. 32 (Roman Catholic Relief Act, 1791) . 161 *n.*, 173, 207
33 Geo. III, c. 4 (Lord Grenville's Aliens Act, 1793) . . . 232
34 Geo. III, c. 42 (For allowing aliens in foreign colonies surrendered to His Majesty to trade, &c.) . . . . 236 *n.*
35 Geo. III, c. 92 (For further encouraging the southern whale fisheries) . . . . 240 *n.*
37 Geo. III, c. 63 (For allowing aliens in foreign colonies surrendered to His Majesty to be merchants or factors, &c.) . . . . 236 *n.*
43 Geo. III, c. 30 (Roman Catholic Relief Act Amendment Act, 1803) . . . . 161 *n.*
45 Geo. III, c. 32 (For allowing aliens in foreign colonies surrendered to His Majesty to be merchants or factors, &c.) 236 *n.*
52 Geo. III, c. 155 (The Places of Religious Worship Act, 1812) 130 *n.*, 135, 161 *n.*, 173
53 Geo. III, c. 127 (The Ecclesiastical Courts Act, 1813) . . 187 *n.*
53 Geo. III, c. 160 (Unitarians Relief Act, 1813) . . . 15, 161 *n.*
6 Geo. IV, c. 67 (To alter and amend 7 Jac. I, c. 2) . . . 245
6 Geo. IV, c. 105 (To repeal the several laws relating to the customs) . . . . 236 *n.*
7 Geo. IV, c. 54 (Registration of Aliens Act, 1826) . . 232 *n.*
7 & 8 Geo. IV, c. 28 (For improving the administration of justice in criminal cases) 197
9 Geo. IV, c. 17 (Sacramental Tests Repeal Act, 1828) . 249, 129, 162 *n.*
10 Geo. IV, c. 7 (Roman Catholic Relief Act, 1829) 161 *n.*, 246, 253, 258, 261, 263, 279
2 & 3 Will. IV, c. 115 (The Roman Catholic Charities Act, 1832) 23, 161 *n.*, 208 *n.*
3 & 4 Will. IV, c. 30 (The Poor Rate Exemption Act, 1833) 174 *n.*

PAGE

5 & 6 Will. IV, c. 28 (Sheriffs' Declaration Act, 1835) . . 253
5 & 6 Will. IV, c. 36 (The Parliamentary Elections Act, 1835) Addenda, 247 *n.*
5 & 6 Will. IV, c. 50 (The Highway Act, 1835) . . . 174 *n.*
5 & 6 Will. IV, c. 62 (The Statutory Declarations Act, 1835) . 285
6 & 7 Will. IV, c. 11 (The Registration of Aliens Act, 1836) . 232
1 & 2 Vict., c. 5 (Quakers' Relief Act, 1837) 253
1 & 2 Vict., c. 15 (Quakers' further Relief Act, 1838) . . . 253
1 & 2 Vict., c. 105 (The Oaths Act, 1838) . . . 182, 271, 275
3 & 4 Vict., c. 77 (The Grammar Schools Act, 1840) . . . 213
7 & 8 Vict., c. 66, s. 5 (Mr. Hutt's Naturalization Act, 1844) 111 *n.*, 245
7 & 8 Vict., c. 102 (To repeal certain penal enactments made against Roman Catholics) . . . . . . 3, 77 *n.*, 162
8 & 9 Vict., c. 52 (Jewish Disabilities Removal Act, 1845) . 255, 286
9 & 10 Vict., c. 59 (The Religious Disabilities Act, 1846) 9, 23, 27, 65, 77 *n.*, 163, 174, 208
11 & 12 Vict., c. 20 (Removal of Aliens Act, 1848) . . 232 *n.*
15 & 16 Vict., c. 43 (Disabilities Repeal Act, 1852) . . 277 *n.*
16 & 17 Vict., c. 137 (Charitable Trusts Act, 1853) . . 174 *n.*
17 & 18 Vict., c. 81 (Oxford University Act, 1854) . . . 209
18 & 19 Vict., c. 81 (Places of Worship Registration Act, 1855) 174
18 & 19 Vict., c. 86 (Liberty of Religious Worship Act, 1855) 23, 174
19 & 20 Vict., c. 88 (Cambridge University Act, 1856) . . 209
21 & 22 Vict., c. 48 (The Oaths Act, 1858) . . . 236, 228 *n.*, 256
21 & 22 Vict., c. 49 (The Jewish Relief Act, 1858) 195, 228 *n.*, 261, 263, 293 seq., 305
23 & 24 Vict., c. 11 (The Endowed Schools Act, 1860) . . 213
23 & 24 Vict., c. 63 (Jewish Relief Act Amendment Act, 1860) . 301
25 & 26 Vict., c. 43 (The Poor Law (Certified Schools) Act, 1862) 219
26 & 27 Vict., c. 125 (The Statute Law Revision Act, 1873) . 67 *n.*
29 & 30 Vict., c. 19 (The Parliamentary Oaths Act, 1866) . . 301
29 & 30 Vict., c. 22 (The Qualification for Offices Abolition Act, 1866) 256
29 & 30 Vict., c. 117 (The Reformatory Schools Act, 1866). 219, 220
29 & 30 Vict., c. 118 (The Industrial Schools Act, 1866) . . 220
30 & 31 Vict., c. 59 (The Statute Law Revision Act, 1867) . . 246
30 & 31 Vict., c. 75 (The Office and Oath Act, 1867) 304, 228 *n.*, 256 *n.*, 258 *n.*, 261
30 & 31 Vict., c. 88 (The Indemnity Act, 1867) . . . 252 *n.*
31 & 32 Vict., c. 72 (The Promissory Oaths Act, 1868) 304–5, 228 *n.*, 252 *n.*
31 & 32 Vict., c. 118 (The Public Schools Act, 1868) . . . 212

PAGE
32 & 33 Vict., c. 56 (The Endowed Schools Act, 1869) . 213, 214
32 & 33 Vict., c. 58 (The Public Schools Act, 1869) . . . 212
32 & 33 Vict., c. 110 (The Charitable Trusts Act, 1869) . . 174
33 & 34 Vict., c. 14 (The Naturalization Act, 1870) 111 *n.*, 170 *n.*, 245
33 & 34 Vict., c. 52 (The Extradition Act, 1870) . . . 233 *n.*
33 & 34 Vict., c. 75 (The Elementary Education Act, 1870) 215–17
33 & 34 Vict., c. 77 (The Juries Act, 1870) . . Addenda, 175 *n.*
34 & 35 Vict., c. 26 (The Universities Tests Act, 1871) 208, 210–11
34 & 35 Vict., c. 48 (The Promissory Oaths Act, 1871)
305, 129 *n.*, 228 *n.*, 256 *n.*, 262, 294
34 & 35 Vict., c. 60 (The Public Schools Act, 1871) . . . 212
34 & 35 Vict., c. 116 (The Statute Law Revision Act, 1871) 258 *n.*
35 & 36 Vict., c. 33 (The Ballot Act, 1872) 247
36 & 37 Vict., c. 41 (The Public Schools (Harrow) Act, 1873) . 212
36 & 37 Vict., c. 62 (The Public Schools (Eton) Act, 1873) . 212
36 & 37 Vict., c. 87 (The Endowed Schools Act, 1873) 213, 215 *n.*
37 & 38 Vict., c. 87 (The Endowed Schools Act, 1874) 213, 215 *n.*
45 & 46 Vict., c. 61 (The Bills of Exchange Act, 1882) . 185 *n.*
2 Edw. VII, c. 42 (The Education Act, 1902) . . . 217, 218
5 Edw. VII, c. 13 (The Aliens Act, 1905) 232

THE

JEWS AND THE ENGLISH LAW

I.

When in 1655 Menasseh Ben Israel presented his famous memorial to Cromwell praying that the Jews might be received in England and permitted to exercise their religion, the Lord Protector summoned an assembly to declare their opinions on the matter. Two judges, the Lord Chief Justice Glyn and the Lord Chief Baron Steel, were members of that assembly, and they delivered their joint opinion that "There was no law which forbids the Jews' return into England." The assembly was ultimately dissolved without coming to any definite decision respecting the memorial, but shortly afterwards Jews in ever-increasing numbers settled in this country, and as we know, for a long period laboured under many disabilities; it may be not uninteresting to show by the evidence of the statute book and the law reports—in truth the only authentic means of proof—that the opinion of the judges was well founded, even if taken in its broadest meaning, namely, that the law of England imposed no burden or disability upon Jews as such. In an age of intolerance no doubt Jews felt the effects of intolerance, but these effects were also felt by all who did not conform to the religion as by law established; and if some of these effects pressed more heavily upon Jews than upon others, this was in all cases a mere accident, though it in fact made it more difficult for Jews than others to obtain absolute equality before the law. The courts of law, though they have, as in duty bound, enforced the provisions of the statute book, have always shown great tolerance and impartiality towards the Jew, and have, so far as is consistent with the faithful administration of the enactments ordained by Parliament, resisted the not infrequent attempts to make use of their machinery for the purpose of persecution; and there are even instances on record of the executive government having stepped in and prevented an abuse of the process of the Court when there were no other means of preventing injustice being done.

Let us first turn to the account the law reports have to give us of attacks made upon the exercise of the Jewish religion. In the appendix to Haggard's *Consistory Court Cases* we find that in the year 1673 certain Jews trading in and about the City of London were indicted of a riot at the Guildhall for meeting together for the exercise of their religion in Duke's Place, and the bill was found against them by the Grand Jury. A petition was thereupon presented to the King in Council at Whitehall by Abraham Delivera, Jacob Franco Mendez, Abraham de Porto, and Domingo Francia, on behalf of themselves and others, praying to be permitted to exercise their religion freely or to be given a convenient time to withdraw their persons and estates into parts beyond the seas; and on Feb. 11 it was ordered by the King in Council "that Mr. Attorney General do stop all proceedings at law against the Petitioners, who have been indicted as aforesaid and do provide they may receive no further trouble in this behalf[1]."

Yet in a few years' time they were destined to receive further trouble, for in 1685 one Thomas Beaumont caused several writs to be issued out of the King's Bench under the statute made in the twenty-third year of Queen Elizabeth against forty-eight of the Jewish nation, and thirty-seven of them were arrested "as they were following their occasions on the Royal Exchange to the great prejudice of their reputation both here and abroad." By the Statute of Elizabeth, an Act expressly directed against the Papists, and passed at a time when there were no recognized Jews in England, all persons above the age of sixteen years

[1] 1 Hag., *Con.*, Appendix, p. 2.

"which shall not repair to some church, chapel, or usual place of common prayer" were to forfeit a penalty of £20 a month, and in addition be bound with two sureties until they should conform themselves and come to church. As an indictment for riot could no longer be laid, the upholders of intolerance availed themselves of this old statute, even in those days obsolete, which was not formally repealed till 1844 (7 & 8 Vict. c. 102). However, a petition was presented by Joseph Henriques, Abraham Delivera (one of the petitioners in 1673), and Aaron Pacheco, overseers of the Jewish synagogue, on behalf of the Jewish nation, praying His Majesty to permit and suffer them as heretofore to have the benefit of the free exercise of their religion during their good behaviour towards His Majesty's Government. It was accordingly on Nov. 13 ordered by the King in Council "that His Majesty's Attorney General do stop all the proceedings at law against the Petitioners: His Majesty's intention being that they should not be troubled upon this account, but quietly enjoy the free exercise of their religion, whilst they behave themselves dutifully and obediently to his government[1]."

From this time forth there is no record in the law reports of any attempt to interfere with the free exercise of the Jewish religion. This is not a little surprising in an intolerant age, when the many statutes directed against Papists and Protestant Nonconformists were equally applicable to Jews and might have been rigidly enforced against them. It must not, however, be supposed that there were no Anti-Semites in those days; indeed in the year 1702 they succeeded in passing through Parliament an Act—entitled An Act to oblige Jews to maintain and provide for their Protestant children—the avowed purpose of which was to assist the conversion of the Jews to the religion of the land. The Act (1 Anne, st. 1, c. 30) provides that "to the end that sufficient maintenance be provided and allowed for the children of Jewish parents who shall turn

[1] 1 Hag., *Con.*, Appendix, p. 3.

Protestants be it enacted . . . that 'if any Jewish parent, in order to the compelling of his or her Protestant child to change his or her religion shall refuse to allow such child a fitting maintenance suitable to the degree and ability of such parent and to the age and education of such child, then . . . it shall be lawful for the Lord Chancellor, Lord Keeper or Commissioners (for the great seal for the time being) to make such order therein for the maintenance of such Protestant child, as he or they shall think fit.'" It may be mentioned that there were similar and even more stringent provisions in favour of the Protestant children of "Popish Parents" inserted in the Act to prevent the further growth of Popery (2 Anne, c. 1) passed in the following year.

Although not repealed until quite recent times, the statute had become quite obsolete; yet in the early days of its existence vigorous attempts had been made to enforce it, and there had even been a disposition on the part of zealous Chancellors to give the words of the enactment the most extensive interpretation. An example of this tendency is the case of *Vincent* v. *Fernandez,* which was decided in 1718 by Lord Chancellor Parker, afterwards created Earl of Macclesfield. In that case a Jew had a daughter who turned Protestant. The Jew had a very considerable personal estate, and dying in May, 1717, after having by his will left several charities and given his personal estate from his daughter to his executor, the daughter, who was married and forty-four years old, petitioned the Lord Chancellor for a maintenance under this statute. It was objected that this case was not within the Act, for that, first, the child is above forty years old, and so the care of her education over; secondly, she is married and not now to be called a child, but to be provided for by her husband; thirdly, that the parent being dead could not be said to have refused to allow her fitting maintenance, &c., and so the power given by the Act is at an end. In answer to these objections, the

Lord Chancellor said: "I strongly incline to think this case within the Act upon the following reasons; the petitioner is a Protestant child of a Jewish parent, though the parent be dead. Suppose the child of a Jew turns Protestant, and the Jew, the parent, by will gives his estate to trustees, upon a secret trust, that if the child turn Jew the child shall have the estate, and not otherwise. As this would be clearly within the mischief, so every one must wish it to be within the meaning of the Act. It is not said the complaint shall be against the father; that would indeed take this case out of the Act; neither is it said that the order should be made upon or against the father, so that this case fits every word made use of by the legislature. Suppose a suit or petition had been exhibited, and the Jew, the parent, had died pending the petition, and had given all away from his Protestant child because the child had turned Protestant, doubtless the complaint might be against the executor, and the order likewise against the executor; every one will allow this to be a hard case, and if the words be large enough (as they are), why should they not be construed to extend to it?

"Then as to the refusal of the parent, it is not to be intended that the parent, the Jew, must make an actual refusal in words, for by that construction the statute might easily be evaded and rendered useless. If the Jewish father do by will dispose of all his estate from his child, this is in law a refusal; and unless some other reason be made appear, it shall be intended, because the child was a Protestant. The obligations of nature plead so strongly on behalf of a child, that when such a case happens, some great provocation must be supposed to have occasioned it; and if no other reason be made appear, this difference in religion shall be intended the reason.

"Possibly these charities given by the Jew's will may be under some secret trust for the child if she should turn Jew, wherefore let all this be inquired into by the Master [1]."

[1] 1 Peere Williams, pp. 524, 525.

The learned reporter, however, adds a note to the effect that the Court did not appear to have made any order on the petition, and that probably the parties came to some agreement.

The effect of the statute and the method of enforcing it in the earlier part of the eighteenth century may best be gathered from the report of the proceedings in the case of one Marcus Moses given in Sanders' *Orders in Chancery*, of which I append an abridgment:—On the 22nd of January, 1723, Moses Marcus preferred a petition setting forth that he is the eldest son of Marcus Moses of London, merchant, who is by profession of religion a Jew, and as such educated his son in the best manner that he could in the mystery of that religion, and in all other respects as a gentleman and a scholar, both at home and in travels in foreign parts, for improvement suitable to the degree and ability of the petitioner's father, who has a plentiful estate, and lives in great repute and esteem in the City of London. That the said petitioner is now of the age of twenty-two years and upwards, and being by such education become capable of judging of the true religion, and having diligently searched the Scriptures and inquired into the Christian religion as well as the Jewish, and being fully convinced of the truth of the one and of the errors of the other, hath from a full conviction and from a lively faith in God's mercies through Jesus Christ our Saviour, without any worldly views, but on the contrary well knowing that he should thereby become the hatred and scorn of his parents and relations who are all Jews and with whom he was before in great esteem, and be cast off from his parents notwithstanding all those discouragements, embraced the Christian religion, the only true one, and hath been baptized therein, and is become a Protestant of the Church of England as by law established. That by means of the petitioner's conversion to the Christian faith and becoming a Protestant (as he before well knew he should), he finds himself hated and scorned by his parents and cast off by his said father; and in order to compel him to exchange his religion is by his father refused to be allowed a fitting maintenance suitable to the degree and ability of his said father and to the petitioner's age and education, whereby the petitioner, who was educated as a gentleman and a scholar, and with the dependence of a plentiful fortune from his said father, is now become destitute and without any subsistence, and not being educated in the way of business otherwise than as a gentleman and a scholar, &c., is not at present capable of getting his living, &c., &c., wherefore it was prayed that directions should be given touching an allowance for the petitioner's maintenance. Whereupon an inquiry was ordered into the circumstances of Marcus Moses, the number of his family and the amount of his estate and the education of the petitioner, and the father Marcus Moses was ordered to give £5,000 security to pay such allowance to the petitioner from time to time as the Lord Chancellor should think fit. "And it being alleged that the said petitioner hath had only five guineas from his father since his baptism, so that he hath occasion for money for his present subsistence, and that part of his clothes and wearing apparel are detained from the petitioner by his father, it is thereupon further ordered that the said Marcus Moses the petitioner's father do pay him £50 on Tuesday next and deliver him his clothes at the same time."

The inquiries appear to have been duly held, and as a result of them the father, Marcus Moses, was ordered to pay his son £60 per annum by quarterly payments, yet in the year 1726 the son presented another petition alleging that the maintenance had not been paid in pursuance of the Order of the Court; the father preferred a counter-petition setting forth that even before the making of the said Order his son Marcus Moses returned to the Jewish worship and professed himself to be a Jew, and kept the Passover with Jews, and as soon as the same was over voluntarily went over to Holland and there renounced the

Christian religion, and went publicly to the Synagogue and did penance for his having turned Christian in England, and continued in Holland a year and five months and behaved as a Jew all that time, during which time he by several letters applied to his said father to maintain and provide for him as a Jew, which he did, and paid several large sums for him more than his maintenance came to. And the said Marcus Moses being come over again to England has professed himself a Jew and behaved as such according to their ceremonies, and still continued so to do, whereby he hath forfeited the maintenance allowed him as aforesaid, and therefore praying that the said Order might be discharged. Upon these petitions all the parties were ordered to attend the Lord Chancellor (Lord King), who after hearing the evidence, including a declaration by the son in Court that he was a Christian, ordered that the sum formerly allowed for maintenance be continued until the 10th of February instant, and as to any demand of the money since the 10th of February the Bishop of London was to examine whether the said Marcus Moses be a Christian [1].

It may be seen from the record of this case that the allowances given by the Chancellors were not excessive, and that maintenance was only given in case the child claiming it was unable to maintain itself, and would not be continued unless the conversion was genuine, the question, if there were any doubt about it, being referred to the bishop of the diocese. In any case the statute was not instrumental in procuring numerous conversions; and though well known to the judges, and acted upon on occasion, there was a growing tendency on the part of the Chancellors to restrict its operation, as may be seen from Lord Hardwicke's judgment in the well-known case of *Villareul* v. *Mellish*, decided in 1737 [2]. It gradually became obsolete, and was

[1] Sanders, *Orders in Chancery*, vol. I, pp. 457 seq., 524 seq.

[2] 2 Swanston, pp. 533, 539; and 2 Atk., p. 14, under name of *Mellish* v. *Da Costa*.

finally repealed in the year 1846 by the Act to relieve Her Majesty's Subjects from certain penalties and disabilities in regard to Religious Opinions (9 & 10 Vict. c. 59).

Since the petition already referred to, which was presented in 1685, there is no trace in the law reports of the statutes directed against Nonconformists, some of the most stringent of which, e.g. the Act of Uniformity (1662, 14 Car. II. c. 4) and the Conventicle Act (1670, 22 Car. II. c. 1), were only passed after the restoration of the Stuart dynasty, being enforced against the Jews. In the case of Protestant Dissenters the severity of these statutes was in a great measure mitigated by the Toleration Act (1688, 1 Will. & Mary, c. 18), which is expressed to be enacted "Forasmuch as some ease to scrupulous consciences in the exercise of religion may be an effectual means to unite their Majesties' *Protestant* subjects in interest and affection." The Jews, though in no way protected by this Act, remained undisturbed in the exercise of their religion; and those who were hostile to them had therefore to resort to tactics which have frequently been used as instruments of persecution, and which were immediately suppressed by the courts of law, to the great credit of English justice. In the year 1732 a paper was published by one Osborne containing an account of a murder committed the latter end of February on a Jewish woman and her child by certain Jews lately arrived from Portugal and living near Broad Street, because the child was begotten by a Christian, and showing that the like cruelty had often been committed by the Jews. In consequence of this publication, several Jews recently arrived from Portugal and living in Broad Street were attacked by multitudes in several parts of the city, barbarously treated, and threatened with death in case they were found abroad any more. Accordingly in Easter term the Court of King's Bench was moved for a rule calling upon the said Osborne to show cause why a criminal information for libel should not issue against him for publishing the paper above referred to. Upon the motion, Lord Raymond the Lord Chief Justice, said that he believed the Court could do nothing in this matter by reason that no particular Jews could be able to show to the Court that they were pointed at more than any others, and thought that Lord Chief Justice Holt was of this opinion in the case of Orme and Nut. In that case (which is reported in 1 Lord Raymond, p. 486) an indictment was exhibited for a libel called "The list of adventurers in the Ladies invention, being a lottery," &c., and alleged to be to the scandal of divers good subjects of the King to the jurors unknown. The jury found the accused guilty, but upon motion judgment was arrested on the ground that the persons libelled were unknown, and that it could not be said that any definite person was defamed. The Court, however, made a rule against Osborne to show cause. In Trinity term cause was shown, and the Court made the rule absolute. They distinguished the case from Orme's case, saying, "that in the present case it is related in the paper that the fact there told is a fact which the Jews have frequently done; and therefore the whole community of the Jews are struck at," and further adding that "admitting an information for a libel may be improper, yet the publication of this paper is deservedly punishable in an information for a misdemeanour (apparently inciting to a breach of the peace), and that of the highest kind; such sorts of advertisements necessarily tending to raise tumults and disorders among the people and inflame them with an universal spirit of barbarity against a whole body of men, as if guilty of crimes scarce practicable and totally incredible [1]." This is undoubtedly a strong case, and one which, it is to be hoped, will be acted upon in case any similar attack should be made upon the Jews; but it is only right to point out that a libel on the Jewish religion would not be so dealt with unless it was such as to tend to stir up the hatred of the Queen's subjects against persons professing that

[1] See 2 Barnardiston, pp. 138, 166; Wm. Kelynge, p. 231; 2 Swanston, p. 503 (note), and Sess. Cas., p. 260.

religion, and so conduce to a breach of the peace. For later cases tend to show that, assuming that the decencies of controversy are observed, the fundamental doctrines of any religion, not excluding that of the Established Church, may be attacked with impunity. There are no doubt competent authorities who hold, on the strength of certain old cases, that any attack upon Christianity, being part of the law of the land, is punishable. But there will always be great difficulty in inducing a jury to convict. Indeed, in the year 1883, when Mr. Bradlaugh was tried for publishing a periodical called the *Freethinker*, which was advertised as being an Anti-Christian organ and as waging relentless warfare against superstition in general and against the superstition of Christianity in particular, it was laid down by the Chief Justice, Lord Coleridge, in addressing the jury, that publications discussing with gravity and decency, and in an argumentative way, questions as to Christian doctrine or statements in the Hebrew Scriptures, and even questioning their truth, are not to be deemed blasphemous so as to be fit subjects for criminal prosecution; but that publications which in an indecent and malicious spirit assail and asperse the truth of Christianity or of the Scriptures, in language calculated and intended to shock the feelings and outrage the belief of mankind, are properly to be regarded as blasphemous libels. In the subsequent case of the *Queen* v. *Ramsey* and *Foote*, arising out of the publication of the same periodical, Lord Coleridge, in dealing with this point, said: "Now according to the old law, or the dicta of the judges in old times, these would undoubtedly be blasphemous libels, because they asperse the truth of Christianity. But, as I said in the former trial, and now repeat, I think that these old cases can no longer be taken to be a statement of the law at the present day. It is no longer true in the sense in which it was true when these dicta were uttered—that 'Christianity is part of the law of the land.' Nonconformists and Jews were then under penal laws, and were hardly allowed civil rights. But now, so far as I know the law, a Jew might be Lord Chancellor [1]. Certainly he might be Master of the Rolls; and the great Judge whose loss we have all had to deplore [2] might have had to try such a case; and if the view of the law supposed be correct, he would have had to tell the jury, perhaps partly composed of Jews, that it was blasphemy to deny that Jesus Christ was the Messiah, which he himself did deny, and which Parliament had allowed him to deny, and which it was part of 'the law of the land' that he might deny. Therefore to asperse the truth of Christianity cannot *per se* be sufficient to sustain a criminal prosecution for blasphemy. . . . Therefore to maintain that merely because the truth of Christianity is denied without more, that therefore a person may be indicted for blasphemous libel, is, I venture to think, absolutely untrue [3]."

[1] A question which will be considered later.

[2] Sir George Jessel, who died on March 21, 1883.

[3] 15 Cox, C. C., p. 235.

II.

We have seen that since the year 1685[1] the Jews have been allowed the free exercise of their religion in this country and have been protected by the courts of law against a gross libel upon it—such as the oft-repeated blood-accusation—when published in such a way as to stir up hatred against the Jews and thereby ultimately lead to a breach of the peace; but it must not be supposed that the law of England ever encouraged the propagation of doctrines subversive of the Christian religion, which has always been and is still considered part of the common law of the land. In the year 1698 an Act of Parliament was passed entitled "An Act for the more effectual suppressing of Blasphemy and Profaneness[2]." The preamble runs: "Whereas many persons have of late years openly avowed and published many blasphemous and impious opinions contrary to the doctrines and principles of the Christian religion, greatly tending to the dishonour of Almighty God and may prove destructive to the peace and welfare of this kingdom, wherefore for the more effectual suppressing of the said detestable crimes" it is enacted that "if any person or persons, having been educated in or at any time having made profession of the Christian religion within this realm, shall by writing, printing, teaching, or advised speaking, deny any of the Persons in the Holy Trinity to be God, or shall assert or maintain there are more gods

[1] The Order in Council in answer to the Petition of Joseph Henriques and others having been made on November 13 of that year.

[2] 9 Will. III. c. 35, more commonly cited as 9 & 10 Will. III. c. 32.

than one, or shall deny the Christian religion to be true, or the Holy Scriptures of the Old and New Testament to be of divine authority," he or they shall upon being convicted for the first time be rendered incapable to hold any office ecclesiastical, civil, or military, and if convicted a second time of all or any the aforesaid crimes, then he or they shall from thenceforth be disabled to sue in any court of law or equity, or to be guardian of any child, or executor or administrator of any person, or capable of any legacy or deed or gift, and shall also suffer imprisonment for the space of three years without bail or mainprize from the time of such conviction. This Act still remains in the statute-book, and may at any time be enforced. In the year 1819 the full Court of King's Bench held that the offences aimed at were in many cases misdemeanours at common law, and that the Act enabled the judges to inflict cumulative punishments in addition to the ordinary common law punishment of fine and imprisonment[1]. It was, however, recognized that there might be cases in which persons could be dealt with under this Act, though guilty of no offence under the common law. Mr. Justice Best in his judgment says: "The Legislature, in passing this Act, had not the punishment of blasphemy so much in view as the protecting the government of the country, by preventing infidels from getting into places of trust. In the age of toleration in which that statute passed, neither churchmen nor sectarians wished to protect in their infidelity those who disbelieved the Holy Scriptures. On the contrary, all agreed, that as the system of morals which regulated their conduct was built on these Scriptures, none were to be trusted with offices who showed they were under no religious responsibility. This Act is not confined to those who libel religion, but extended to those who in the most private intercourse, by advised conversation, admit that they disbelieve the Scriptures. Both the common law and this

[1] See *Rex* v. *Richard Carlile*, 3 B. & Ald. 161 (1819). See also Lord Eldon's remarks, 3 Mer. p. 406 seq. (1817).

statute are necessary; the first to guard the morals of the people; the second for the immediate protection of the government[1]." In the year 1813, in favour of Unitarians, the Act, so far as it relates to persons denying any one of the Persons in the Holy Trinity to be God, was repealed[2], and this concession was at the time regarded as a signal proof of the liberality and religious toleration of the age; but the remainder of the Act is still nominally in force. It might be made use of to prevent conversions from Christianity to Judaism, if these should ever take place upon a large scale, or any active missionary organization were established among the Jews for this purpose. For though the offence struck at by the statute can only be committed by persons who have been educated in or made profession of the Christian religion, still by the law of England all persons who instigate or aid and abet or are accessory to a misdemeanour committed by others are themselves guilty of a misdemeanour and punishable in the same way as those guilty of the principal crime; the law not recognizing any distinction in the punishment of crimes lower than felony. Hitherto there has been no occasion to attempt to use the statute in this way; should, however, one arise, the bitterness of religious controversy would probably prompt such an attempt, there being no other mode of repressing proselytism by the criminal law not foredoomed to failure.

The statute has a curious history for the Jews, though it may safely be affirmed that no Jew was ever prosecuted under it. It originated in a humble address presented by the Commons to His Majesty asking for the suppression of "profaneness and immorality in all books which endeavour to undermine the fundamentals of the Christian religion and to punish the authors[3]," and that His Majesty should issue a Royal Proclamation to that effect. The address was drawn up by a committee of the House of Commons

[1] 3 B. & Ald. p. 166. [2] 53 Geo. III. c. 160, s. 2.
[3] Cobbett's *Parl. History*, vol. V, p. 1172.

appointed on February 9, and was presented to the King on the 17th. The King expressed his satisfaction at the receipt of this address, and immediately gave directions for the publication of the Proclamation asked for, and at the same time expressed a wish that more effectual provision should be made by the Legislature for suppressing the evils complained of. This Royal Proclamation or its successor, framed in a great measure upon the words of the parliamentary address presented to the King, is still publicly read in every county town throughout the country at the opening of every commission of assize and quarter sessions. The Bill for more effectual suppressing of blasphemy and profaneness, the substance of which has been already set forth, was also introduced in deference to the expression of the royal wishes contained in the King's answer. When the Bill reached the Lords, an amendment to omit the words "having been educated in or at any time having made profession of the Christian religion" was proposed and carried. The effect of this amendment would obviously be to render every Jew resident in the kingdom liable to the same pains and penalties provided by the enactment, including three years' imprisonment in the case of a second conviction. The House of Commons rejected the amendment, and appointed a committee to draw up reasons to be offered at a conference of the Lords for disagreeing with it[1]. Reasons were accordingly drawn up, read to the House, and agreed to; they are of sufficient interest to be given verbatim, and are as follows:—

"The Commons do conceive, That the First Amendment in the First Skin, Line 14, 15, made by your Lordships, will subject the Jews who live amongst us to all the Pains and Penalties contained in the Bill; which must therefore of necessity ruin them, and drive them out of the Kingdom; and cannot be thought was the intention of your Lordships, since here they have the means and opportunities to be informed of and rightly instructed in the principles of the

[1] Commons' Journals, May 18, 1698.

true Christian Religion; for which Reasons the Commons disagree with your Lordships in the said Amendment[1]." The Lords showed that the ruin and expulsion of the Jews was not intended, by allowing the Bill to pass without the obnoxious amendment.

The conduct of Parliament in preventing an injustice being done to the Jews then but recently settled in the kingdom should not pass unnoticed, especially as it could not in any way have been influenced, as Parliament is nowadays so often, by a desire to conciliate Jewish votes, for at the time there was probably no Jew entitled to exercise the Parliamentary franchise. The alleged motive of the Commons in protecting the Jews, strange as it may seem to us, is probably the true one. The gentlemen of the House of Commons perhaps really thought that the Jews, if they only had an opportunity of being instructed in the principles of the true Christian religion as enunciated by the Church of England, would be ultimately converted to Christianity, a result which would not ensue if they were driven by unjust laws to lands belonging to Christendom no doubt, but shrouded by the darkness of false Papal or Lutheran doctrine. At any rate, we can see that there was in those days, as in these, an intense desire to bring the Jews into the Christian fold. As no exception in their case was made, and the matter had been discussed, it was evidently intended that Jewish proselytes to Christianity, if they relapsed into Judaism, should be dealt with under the Act. Though such cases are constantly arising, there is no trace of any prosecution under the Act having ever taken place. It may be that the knowledge of the revelation of the methods employed by the conversionists which in such a case would inevitably be made has effectually deterred those imbued with the missionary spirit from undertaking such a prosecution; or it may be that it has never been thought worth while to exact the penalty which in the case of a first conviction is merely incapacity

[1] Commons' Journals, May 21, 1698.

to hold any office, ecclesiastical, civil, or military, a punishment which would be of little effect in almost every case of double apostasy, for the persons who publicly indulge in numerous changes of their religious profession have rarely any reasonable expectation of attaining any of the offices from holding which the Act debars them. In any cases the Act, though it still appears in the statute-book, has been allowed to become a dead letter.

The freedom accorded to the practice of the Jewish religion in this country has now been dealt with in outline. It has been shown how the Acts compelling outward conformity with the religion of the Established Church were not enforced against the Jews, and how, when a gross and malignant libel upon the rites of the Jewish religion likely and intended to lead to violence against its votaries was published, the courts of law were ready to inflict punishment upon its author. On the other hand, two Acts were placed upon the statute-book, one compelling Jews whose children might become converted to Protestantism to provide them with suitable maintenance; the other enabling a criminal prosecution to be brought against Jews who should obtain proselytes from Christianity. Of these statutes the first was repealed in 1846; the second has never been acted upon, though it still remains a part of the law of England. I will now turn to the legal position of endowments created for the purpose of furthering the Jewish religion. Such endowments are constituted by vesting the property which is the subject of them in a trustee or trustees in trust for or to the use of the institution intended to be benefited. But any trust which has for its object the propagation of religious views not tolerated by the law in force at the time will be held void by a court of justice as being contrary to the policy of the law. If a charitable purpose can be discovered in the document creating the trust, the court will apply the property to some other charitable purpose; and if no charitable intention appears, will vest it in the person who would have been entitled if the trust had never been created. Thus before the year 1688, when the Toleration Act was passed, gifts in favour of the places of worship, ministers, and schools of Protestant Dissenters were invalid [1]. As to the effect of the Toleration Act, Lord Mansfield is reported to have said that Nonconformity is rendered by it "not only innocent but lawful," and that the protecting clauses of the statute "have put it not merely under the connivance but under the protection of the law—have established it. For nothing can be plainer than that the law protects nothing in that very respect in which it is at the same time in the eye of the law a crime. Dissenters by the Act of Toleration therefore are restored to a legal consideration and capacity [2]."

It has already been shown that the provisions of the Toleration Act were confined to Protestant Nonconformists, and that the Jews received no benefit under it, and it was not until 1846 that Jewish religious endowments were made valid. Several cases came before the courts; for instance, in the year 1744 the case of *Da Costa* v. *De Paz* was tried. It is reported in Ambler at p. 228, and in 1 Dickens at p. 258; but as Lord Eldon, in giving his decision in *Moggridge* v. *Thackwell*, complained that these reports are not very accurate [3], the subjoined account is taken from a note extracted from Mr. Coxe's MSS. in Lincoln's Inn Library by Mr. Swanston [4]. Elias de Paz, by his will dated November 4, 1839, directed his executors to invest a sum of £1200 in some government or other security, and directed that the revenue arising therefrom should be applied for ever in the maintenance of a Yesiba or assembly for daily reading the Jewish law, and for advancing and propagating their holy religion, and directed that his executors during their respective lives should have

[1] *Att.-Gen.* v. *Baxter*, 1 Vern. 248, decided in Trinity Term, 1684, revised in 1689 after the Revolution, 2 Vern. 105.

[2] 3 Mer. p. 376 (note).

[3] See 7 Ves. p. 76.

[4] 2 Swanston, p. 487 seq.

the management of the assembly. The bill was to have this £1200 laid out according to the will. Lord Hardwicke, the Chancellor, in delivering his judgment, said: "This case requires two considerations: first, whether the legacy in question is good and such as this court can or ought to establish? and secondly, if not, whether it is void absolutely, or only to the particular intent, so as to leave it a general legacy, and such as the crown may dispose of? As to the first, I am of opinion that it is not a good legacy, and ought not to be established, no such instance being found. Nobody is more against laying penalties or hardships upon persons for the exercise of their particular religion than I am; but there is a great difference between doing this and establishing them by acts of the court. The cases of dissenting ministers before the Toleration Act were different; particularly Baxter's case, was not of an illegal bequest, but was a bequest for poor ejected ministers; and even as to this case of the Jewish religion, it would be for a different consideration were it for the support of poor persons of that religion. Orders are made by me and the Master of the Rolls every year upon petitions made for their support as poor people. But this is a bequest for the propagation of the Jewish religion; and though it is said that this is a part of our religion" (it having been argued that this bequest was only for propagating and reading that law which is allowed in the Church, and which is the foundation of the Christian religion), "yet the intent of this bequest must be taken to be in contradiction of the Christian religion, which is a part of the law of the land, which is so laid down by Lord Hale and Lord Raymond; and it undoubtedly is so; for the constitution and policy of this nation is founded thereon. As to the Act of Toleration, no new right is given by that, but only an exemption from the penal laws. The Toleration Act recites the penal laws, and then not only exempts from those penal laws, but puts the religion of the Dissenters under certain regulations and tests. This renders those religions legal, which is not the case of the Jewish religion, that is not taken notice of by any law, but is barely connived at by the Legislature." The Lord Chancellor accordingly came to the conclusion that the legacy was not good in law, and ought not to be decreed or established by the court. The second question, namely what ought to be done with the sum of £1200, the amount of the legacy, was considered more doubtful, and the further consideration of it reserved. Upon the further consideration of the matter, the court decreed that the money ought not to accrue to the residue of the personal estate of the testator, but ought to be applied to some other charitable uses, and that the appointment thereof belonged to the Crown; and ultimately the King by his sign manual was graciously pleased, upon the humble petition of the Governor of the Foundling Hospital, to give £1000, part of the sum of £1200, towards supporting a preacher and to instruct the children under his care in the Christian religion and for incidental expenses, &c. It is not known what became of the remaining £200, but if it was not absorbed in costs, it was probably devoted to a similar purpose. And so the money went to a charitable purpose, upon the principle that where the court cannot carry out the intention of the testator, as being against the policy of the law, it may substitute a different charitable object for his bounty. As regards the particular substitution in this instance, I cannot refrain from quoting the words of Lord Eldon: "It would have caused some surprise to the testator if he had known how his devise would have been construed [1]." The same judge says in another case: "It is very difficult, I think, seeing that intention to build a Jewish Synagogue, to discover an intention to build [2]

[1] In *Att.-Gen.* v. *Mayor of Bristol*, 2 J. & W. 308 (1820).

[2] But the money was not employed in building, but in supporting a preacher and instructing children in the Foundling Hospital in the Christian religion. This was probably unknown to the Chancellor, who could not consult the second and more correct edition of Ambler, which was not published till 1828.

a Foundling Hospital, rather than that the money should not be applied: but the court has said so always[1]."

Da Costa v. *De Paz* was not an isolated case; the principle laid down by Lord Hardwicke, that bequests for advancing the Jewish religion were invalid, though bequests for the support of poor persons of that religion were good, was regularly acted upon when similar dispositions came before the court. An example is the case of *Isaac* v. *Gompertz*, which came before the Master of the Rolls in 1783, but was not finally decided till 1786. Benjamin Isaac by his will left several annuities: first, an annuity of £20 for teaching and instructing ten poor Jews' children at Bromsall; £40[2] for the support and maintenance of the Jews' Synagogue in Magpie Alley; and £30 for teaching and instructing ten poor Jews' children in London; £20 to be given away every New Year's Day among poor Jews; and £30 to be laid out and expended every year in the purchase of coals to be given away and distributed among poor Jews and their families, &c. All the legacies were allowed except that given to the synagogue; as to which the order of the court was: "And as to the annuity of £40 given for the support and maintenance of the Jews' said synagogue in Magpie Alley, it was declared that the same ought not to fall and accrue to the personal estate of the said testator, but ought to be applied to some other charitable use, and that the appointing and directing that charitable use was in the Crown; and this court doth recommend it to His Majesty's Attorney-General to apply to the King for a sign manual to appoint and direct to what charitable use or uses the said annuity of £40 and the arrears shall be applied[3]." The legacy was ultimately divided into

[1] *Moggridge* v. *Thackwell*, 2 Ves. p. 81 (1802).

[2] Ambler's note gives £10; but this must be a misprint. See the end of the note.

[3] See Ambler, p. 228 (note), and 7 Ves. p. 61.

moieties; one moiety being given to the Magdalen Hospital, the other to the London Infirmary [1].

It would not be right while dealing with this subject to omit the case of *Straus* v. *Goldsmid*, heard by Sir L. Shadwell, Vice-Chancellor of England in 1837. There the testator bequeathed one-third of his residuary personal estate in the following words: "The remaining third of the above residue to be given to the Rulers and Wardens of the Great Synagogue in this City of London in the manner hereinafter mentioned: that is to say, the interest or dividends arising from this third to be, every year on the Eve of the Passover, distributed at least among ten worthy men who have wives and children, among whom there ought to be some learned men, to purchase meat and wine fit for the service of the two nights of Passover." The reporter states that the Vice-Chancellor held that the bequest, being intended to enable persons professing the Jewish religion to observe its rites, was good [2]. I cannot help thinking that this decision is misreported; for otherwise it is contrary to the accepted authorities already quoted. It might have been based on an intention to support poor persons of the Jewish faith by providing them with suitable viands on stated occasions, but could not, conformably with the generally received theory of the law, have been founded on intention to maintain Jewish rites and observances, for the Jewish religion had not yet received the benefit of the Toleration Acts. This benefit had already been conferred on Roman Catholics by the Roman Catholic Charities Act of 1832 [3], but it was not extended to Jews till 1846. On August 18 of that year the Act "to relieve Her Majesty's subjects from certain penalties and disabilities in regard to religious opinions [4]" became law. It expressly repealed many Acts imposing religious disabilities, and in section 2 provides: "That

[1] See note to *Att.-Gen.* v. *Burgman*, 1 Dickens, p. 169.

[2] 8 Simon, pp. 614–5.

[3] 2 & 3 Will. IV, c. 15.

[4] 9 & 10 Vict. c. 59.

from and after the commencement of this Act Her Majesty's subjects professing the Jewish Religion in respect to their Schools, Places for Religious Worship, Education and Charitable Purposes and the Property held therewith, shall be subject to the same Laws as Her Majesty's Protestant Subjects dissenting from the Church of England are subject to, and not further or otherwise."

The legal status of the religious endowments of Protestant Dissenters is well summarized by Lord Eldon in the following words: "I take it that, if land or money were given (in such a way as would be legal notwithstanding the statutes concerning dispositions to charitable uses) for the purpose of building a church or a house, or otherwise for maintaining or propagating the worship of God, and if there were nothing more precise in the case, this court would execute such a trust, by making it a provision for maintaining and propagating the Established Religion of the country. It is also clearly settled that, if a fund, real or personal, be given in such a way that the purpose be clearly expressed to be that of maintaining a society of Protestant Dissenters—promoting no doctrines contrary to law, although such as may be at variance with the doctrines of the Established Religion—it is then the duty of the court to carry such a trust as that into execution and to administer it according to the intent of the founders [1]."

At the present time therefore Jews are practically in the same position as Protestant Dissenters in respect of their religious endowments, and can as a general rule with reason anticipate that any endowments they found will be carried into effect. But it must be remembered that the operation of the Act is expressly confined to schools, places for religious worship, education, and charitable purposes, and that any endowment which cannot be brought under one of these four heads will still be subject to the old law, and might therefore be declared void on the principle of the old cases. However, the courts of law, which have

[1] *Att.-Gen.* v. *Pearson* (1817), 3 Mer. 353, at p. 409.

always given a wide interpretation to the Acts of Toleration and even made them retrospective in their operation[1], would in all probability be favourably inclined to include a Jewish endowment under one of the four heads mentioned in the statute, if that were possible. If it were impossible, it might be argued—whether successfully or not cannot be predicted, as no such case has yet arisen—that the law, having now recognized the Jewish religion and in some ways protected it, has made it legal not merely for some but for all purposes, and therefore that the reasoning on which the old cases are based no longer holds good, and the principle evolved from them is no longer law.

It should also be stated that Jewish are in no better position than other endowments. They are subject to be defeated by reason of non-compliance with the statutes relating to mortmain, or on account of infringing the rules against perpetuity (unless they can be brought within the category of trusts recognized by the law as charitable) or as being contrary to public policy. There are no reported cases relating to the failure of endowments under the first two heads of special interest to Jews, but it will not be out of place to mention here two cases arising under the third. The first is *Habershon* v. *Vardon*, which came before Vice-Chancellor Sir P. L. Knight-Bruce in 1851. Nadir Baxter had by his will, dated in 1842, directed as follows: "That other £1000, out of such part of my personal estate as may by law be devoted to charitable purposes, be paid towards the contributions that I do confidently believe and earnestly pray will speedily be begun to be raised under the sanction of our hitherto so highly favoured church and nation, in evidence of Christian faith towards the political restoration of the Jews to

[1] See *Bradshaw* v. *Tasker*, 221 (1834, before Lord Brougham). The correctness of the decision in this case was doubted by Sir Ed. Sugden (L.C.) in *Att.-Gen.* v. *Drummond*, 1 Dr. & War. p. 380 (1842), but was followed by Sir John Romilly (M.R.) *in re Michel's Trusts*, 28 Beav. 39 (1860).

Jerusalem, and to their own land." The Vice-Chancellor held that the gift of £1000 was void. "If," said he, "it could be understood to mean anything, it was to create a revolution in a friendly country. Jews might at present reside in Jerusalem; and, if the acquisition of political power by them was intended, the promotion of such an object would not be consistent with our amicable relations with the Sublime Porte[1]." This case was decided five years after the legal recognition of the Jewish religion in 1846, and is therefore still binding on the courts of first instance. Trusts in favour of the present Zionist propaganda, unless very carefully framed, might on the same principle be declared void.

The other case is in the matter of Michel's Trust. It occurred in 1860, and was a special case seeking the opinion of the court under the following circumstances. The testator, Abraham Michel, a Jew, by his will made the following bequest, which was to take effect on the death of his widow. "I give and bequeath unto my executors so much money as will produce in government securities the sum of £10 sterling per annum, upon this special trust and confidence (that is to say), upon trust to invest the same in government securities, as they shall think best, and to pay the interest thereof or dividends, yearly or half-yearly, so as they my executors shall think proper, unto the parnosim or wardens of the congregation of Ostrovesy, near Opateir, in Little Poland, for the time being; but my will and mind is, that the said parnosim or wardens do pay the said sum of £10 to three qualified persons, chosen by them from and out of my family, to learn, in their Beth Hammadrass or college, two hours daily for ever, and on every anniversary of my death, to say the prayer called in Hebrew Candish[2]; and in case there should be no one of my family qualified thereto, then or in such case my will and mind is, that the said parnosim or wardens pay the same to three persons qualified."

[1] 4 De G. & Sm. 467.

[2] Thus spelt in the report; properly *Kaddish*.

The testator died in 1821, and his widow in 1822. The executors appropriated the sum of £300, £3 per cent. consolidated annuities, to answer the above trust, and for some years after such investment had taken place the dividends were remitted to the parnosim or wardens of the congregation at Ostrovesy, but, many years since, the remittance was discontinued, in consequence of its being considered that the bequest was invalid.

The stock not having been dealt with, the surviving executor presented a petition seeking the opinion of the court on the following points: first, whether the legacy in question was a valid charitable legacy, and secondly, if valid, how the stock and cash representing the legacy, and in particular how the sums representing arrears of dividend and the accumulations thereof, ought to be paid and applied.

It was stated that the term to "learn in the Beth Hammadrass or college for two hours daily" signified to study either the Bible or the Talmud, and that the "Candish" was a short Hebrew prayer in the praise of God, and expressive of resignation to his will. That both were acts of piety, and that the prayer was generally said by the sons of the deceased, during the year of mourning and on the anniversary of the death, but if there were none, it was either said by the relatives or by some other person.

The Master of the Rolls, Sir John Romilly, had no doubt of the validity of the bequest, and held, on the analogy of the cases decided with regard to Roman Catholic charities, that the Act of Parliament (9 & 10 Vict. c. 59) was retrospective in its operation. Referring to the argument advanced on behalf of the residuary legatees that the gift was void as a superstitious use, as an anniversary or obit, and similar to praying for the testator's soul, the learned judge said, "I see nothing in the bequest which is superstitious. It was attempted to show that it was so, by importing into it the assumption that the prayer offered up on the anniversary of the death of the testator must be intended to be for the benefit of the soul of the testator.... There are many cases of superstitious uses unconnected with prayers for the soul; but in regard to *West* v. *Shuttleworth*[1] and *Heath* and *Chapman*[2] I have always felt this difficulty:—so far as relates to their places for religious worship and the property held therewith, Roman Catholics and Jews are now placed in the same position as Protestant Dissenters; and if it be part of the forms of their religion that prayers should be said for the benefit of the souls of deceased persons, it would be difficult to say that, as a religious ceremony practised by a dissenting class of religionists, it could be deemed superstitious in the legal sense in which these words were used prior to the passing of the statutes in question, which practically have authorized them. In the time of Edward the Sixth and Elizabeth the ceremony of the mass was considered superstitious, and I do not know that the law made any distinction between masses generally and masses for souls, or any distinction between those said for the general purpose and object of their religion in the worship of God and those which are for more limited objects, which were formerly considered superstitious, and which the court now, considering them in a Protestant point of view, still regards as superstitious. I express no opinion on this point, however, as no such case arises here.

"Here nothing is said as to praying for the soul of any one. Three persons are to learn in their Beth Hammadrass or college, and to say a prayer called Candish, and from the information given to the court, it appears that this means that they are to study either the Bible or the Talmud, and with respect to the Candish, that it is nothing but a short Hebrew prayer in the praise of Almighty God. This has no reference to praying for souls of the founders, and I do not know that there would be anything superstitious in a bequest by members of the Church of England to wardens to select a scholar to learn the Greek Testament

[1] 2 Myl. & K. 684. [2] 2 Drew. 417.

two hours daily, and on a certain day to repeat the Lord's Prayer, although the day selected may be the anniversary or birthday of the founder. There is nothing here to show that this was to be done under the notion that the soul of the testator would derive any benefit from it. I think that this is a valid gift for the benefit of a Jewish charity, and that the executor must pay over the dividends to the parnosim or wardens, who are to select the three qualified persons as directed by the will[1]."

In re Michel's Trusts the bequest was upheld, but the case shows that a religious trust may still be set aside as being a superstitious use, and therefore contrary to public policy. It would be extremely difficult to define precisely what is a superstitious use; but the term undoubtedly includes, and is perhaps confined to, any trust which has for its object the performance of any acts for the supposed benefit of the soul of any person whatsoever. This doctrine that all such trusts are void has never come before the House of Lords, but has been repeatedly acted upon by the other courts, and must be considered part of the law of England. The doctrine is somewhat anomalous, inasmuch as prayers for the dead are not prohibited by the Church of England, as was judicially held in the Court of Arches by Sir H. Jenner so long ago as 1838[2]. Before the Reformation trusts of this nature were considered valid and enforced by the courts, but in the reign of Henry VIII and Edward VI two statutes[3] were passed annulling them in certain cases, and though such trusts do not as a rule come within the letter of these statutes, for there is no statute making superstitious uses void generally, they are nevertheless held to be void by the general policy of the law. We have already seen that Lord Romilly *in re Michel's Trusts* was inclined to doubt the validity of this doctrine

[1] *In re Michel's Trusts*, 28 Beav. pp. 39–43.

[2] *Breecks* v. *Woolfrey*, 1 Curt. Eccl. Rep. 880; and see *Egerton* v. *All of Odd Rode*, L. R. [1894] P. 15, and *Pearson* v. *Stead*, id. [1903] P. 66.

[3] 23 Hen. VIII. c. 10, repealed by the Mortmain and Charitable Uses Act, 1888, and 1 Edw. VI. c. 14.

after the legalization of the Roman Catholic religion, but in the following year he was constrained to acquiesce in it. Speaking of his remarks *in re Michel's Trusts*, he said, "I expressed my difficulty in the case referred to, as to whether gifts for religious ceremonies practised by a dissenting class of religionists might not be permitted, if not opposed to public morality; but I think the decided cases too strong, and that the House of Lords alone can alter the settled law. It is clear that I must act on *West* v. *Shuttleworth*, which I cannot overrule[1]." And in a recent case Vice-Chancellor Hall held as a matter of course that a bequest of £10, to be expended in saying masses for the testator's soul, was void[2].

I have dealt with this subject at some length because it is a practice in certain synagogues on the second day of the festivals, and on the day of Atonement in some congregations which have adopted a reformed ritual (though happily it has not been recognized by the West London congregation of British Jews, the principal body of reformers in this country), to hold prayers for the benefit of the souls of deceased members, who are mentioned by name—a certain sum as a rule being paid on account of each name which is read out. It seems to me upon the decided cases that any legacy left for this purpose is invalid, nor would the case be different, provided that the testator was a domiciled Englishman, if the money so bequeathed is to be paid for a religious service of this kind to be performed in a country where it is not considered superstitious[3].

Gifts given for this purpose are simply void, but there is no power in the court or in the Crown to apply them

[1] *In re Blundell's Trusts* (1861), 30 Beav. p. 360.

[2] *In re Fleetwood, Sidgreaves* v. *Burder* (1880), 15 Ch. D. 594, at p. 609.

[3] See *in re Elliott* (1891), W. N. p. 9, where Mr. Justice North held that a bequest of £2000 to the Priests of the Society of Jesus at Richmond, Victoria, to be spent in masses for the souls of the testator (a domiciled Englishman) and his wife, was bad, although by the law of Victoria the gift was good.

to some other religious or charitable purpose different from that indicated by the donor, as was done in the cases, already cited, relating to endowments for the purpose of promoting the Jewish religion before the benefit of the Toleration Acts had been extended to the Jews. The reason for this is that charity is not the object of such gifts. The intention is not to benefit the place of worship, or priest officiating in it, but to secure some supposed benefit to the donor's soul. This principle is well laid down in the judgment of the Privy Council delivered by Sir Montague Smith in the case of *Zap Chea Neo* v. *Ong Cheng Neo*, in which a devise of a house for performing religious ceremonies to the testatrix and her late husband was declared void. "The remaining devise to be considered is the dedication by the testatrix of the Soro Chong House for the performance of religious ceremonies to her late husband and to herself." It appears to be the usage in China to erect a monumental tablet to the dead in a house of this kind, and for the family at certain periods to place, with certain ceremonies, food before the tablet, the savour of which is supposed to gratify the spirits of their deceased relatives. This usage, with the accompanying ceremonies, is minutely described by Sir P. Benson Maxwell, in his judgment in the case of *Choah Chron Nish* v. *Spottiswood*[1]:—

"Although it certainly appears that the performance of these ceremonies is considered by the Chinese to be a pious duty, it is one which does not seem to fall within any definition of a charitable duty or use. The observance of it can lead to no public advantage, and can benefit or solace only the family itself. The dedication of this Soro Chong House bears a close analogy to gifts to priests for masses to the dead. Such a gift by a Roman Catholic widow of property for masses for the repose of her deceased husband's soul and her own was held, in *West* v. *Shuttleworth*[2], not to be a charitable use, and, although not

[1] Wood's *Oriental Cases*.

[2] 2 Myl. & K. 684.

coming within the statute relating to superstitious uses, to be void[1]."

It would seem to follow that before the year 1846 Judaism was not a religion recognized by law, and that a Jewish synagogue was an illegal establishment. There is, however, a reported case which seems to point in the opposite direction. On May 6, 1818, the case of Israel and others against Simmons was heard by Mr. Justice Abbott, at that time a puisne judge in the Court of King's Bench. The plaintiffs were the surviving lessees of certain premises in Denmark Court, Strand, which were used as a synagogue. The defendant had become a member of the synagogue twenty years before, and had paid his seat-rent up to the year 1810; he then seceded and attended another synagogue, but he retained the key, by which possession of the seat had been given to him, till the year 1813. The action was brought to recover the amount of the rent for that space of time, and also for certain offerings and sums alleged to be due from the defendant in respect of certain rites and ceremonies peculiar to the Jewish religion. The latter part of the claim was at the suggestion of the judge abandoned by the plaintiffs. It was contended by counsel on behalf of the defendants that the action was not maintainable in point of law, because the law of England did not tolerate Jewish synagogues. Great pains had been taken to investigate the subject, and it did not appear that there was any law which legalized the establishment of Jewish synagogues. The principal synagogue in this kingdom had been established under a royal grant, in the reign of Charles the Second; but it was not open to all people of that persuasion, without any grant or licence, to erect places of worship, according to their own pleasure, and to employ preachers at their own discretion. The Toleration Act did not embrace Jewish synagogues of any description; and since the doctrines preached there were in direct hostility to the Christian religion, such establish-

[1] L. R. 6 P. C. p. 396 (1875).

ments were to be considered as illegal. In answer to a question from the court, it was admitted that there was no written law which prohibited such establishments. In reference to this argument Mr. Justice Abbott said that since no authority could be produced to the contrary, he should certainly hold that such establishments were lawful, and consequently that the plaintiffs were entitled to recover[1]. The objection was accordingly overruled; however, a highly technical point referring to a misjoinder of plaintiffs was raised, and this being decided in the defendant's favour, judgment was entered for him. The case being decided upon a different point, Mr. Justice Abbott's ruling is of no great authority upon the matter now under discussion, and though it correctly represents the law as it exists at present, it is at least doubtful whether it could have been upheld at the time when it was given. The point was raised in the midst of a trial at Nisi Prius, and apparently decided at once without due consideration and without reference to the existing authorities, and under the impression that no authority to the contrary could be produced. The cases of *Da Costa* v. *De Paz* and *Isaac* v. *Gompertz* were, however, valid authorities to the contrary, and there can be little doubt that, if these had been cited to the learned judge, his ruling on this point would have been greatly modified. He might of course have attempted to distinguish the case before him from the earlier ones on the ground that it was a matter of contract and not the case of a trust; but such a distinction it would be difficult to uphold. The case is, however, of interest as showing the tolerant spirit which animated the court at the time; it being assumed that the Jewish religion was legal, unless an authority to the contrary was produced.

[1] 2 Starkie, pp. 356–9.

III.

THE history of the way in which the courts treat endowments for Jewish religious and communal purposes has been sketched in outline, and it has been shown how, though at one time trusts for the maintenance or propagation of the Jewish religion or religious doctrines, as distinguished from trusts for the benefit of poor adherents of that religion, would not be enforced, such trusts, with very unimportant exceptions, have since the year 1846 been carried out by the courts: it remains to deal with the view the courts have taken of claims by Jews to participate in general endowments and charities not specifically confined to any religious creed or denomination. The right of Jews to establish charities in favour of their co-religionists exclusively has been always asserted, and has been firmly established by the judicial decisions previously enumerated; on the other hand, the right of non-Jews to create endowments from which Jews or the members of any other especially designated class or religion are prohibited from deriving any advantage has never been doubted. It may be laid down that Jews are entitled to the benefit of all institutions and foundations which are not by the instrument creating them restricted either expressly or by necessary implication to members of a particular denomination. If duly authorized regulations are laid down for the distribution of a charity, with which it is impossible for a Jew to comply, it is plain that he cannot participate in the benefits of it, but he will not be excluded by the mere fact that the endowment he wishes to take advantage of was founded at a time anterior to the readmission of Jews into this country.

The principles upon which the courts will act were laid down in the year 1818 by Lord Eldon, sitting as Lord Chancellor, in the matter of the Masters, Governors, and Trustees of the Bedford Charity. Of this case there is an excellent report by Mr. Swanston[1], which contains a whole mine of learning upon the subject in hand, but as it covers seventy pages, it is impossible to set it out in full here. It must therefore suffice to give an abstract of the facts, together with the most important portions of the judgment. The Bedford Charity had been originally established in the reign of King Edward the Sixth by Sir William Harper, Knight, and alderman of the city of London, and Dame Alice, his wife; and two Acts of Parliament had been passed, the last in 1793, for its regulation. The charity consisted of (1) a free school in the town of Bedford for the education, institution, and instruction of children and youth in grammar and good manners, and the Wardens and Fellows of New College, Oxford, were constituted Visitors of the grammar school: (2) a provision of £800 per annum for the marriage portions of forty poor maids of the town of Bedford, of good fame and reputation, in equal shares; all poor maidens resident in the town of Bedford, and being of the age of sixteen years or upwards, and under the age of fifty years, whose fathers had been occupiers of a house in the town for the space of ten years or had been born in the town and had occupied a house therein for three years, were to be at liberty to send to the Mayor an account in writing of their Christian and surnames, their ages, the places of their birth, and the names of their parents; and, if not of bad fame and reputation, were to be permitted to draw lots for sums of £20 each; and each of those who drew the beneficial lots was to be entitled to receive on the day of her marriage £20 for her portion, provided that she

[1] 2 Swanston, pp. 470-539.

should marry within two calendar months from the time of claiming such beneficial lot, and that she should not marry a vagrant or other person of bad fame or reputation: (3) a house or hospital for the habitation of poor boys and girls, born and resident within the town of Bedford, who were proper objects of charity, where they were to be suitably maintained until they were of a proper age to be put out to trade, agriculture, or other business: (4) a provision of a yearly sum of £700, to be applied, by two half-yearly sums of £350, in placing out twenty poor children apprentices every half-year, viz. fifteen boys, not being under the age of thirteen nor above the age of fifteen years, and five girls, not being under the age of twelve nor above the age of fifteen years, whose respective fathers had been occupiers of a house in the town for the space of ten years or had been born in the town and occupied a house therein for the space of three years. All such poor boys and girls, whose names had been sent in at the proper time, were to be permitted to draw lots; and the sum of £20 was to be paid as the apprentice fee with each of the fifteen boys and £10 as the apprentice fee with each of the five girls who should draw the beneficial lots upon their being respectively placed out apprentices to masters and mistresses of good character and respectability. The boys were to be bound for the space of seven years, and the girls for the space of five years; and every boy and girl so put out to apprentice, who should actually serve the full term of apprenticeship, and in all respects comply with the tenor of the indentures of apprenticeship, should, on producing to the trustees of the charity a certificate signed by their respective masters or mistresses and by the minister and churchwardens of the parish where they should have respectively served their apprenticeship, testifying such actual service and compliance with the tenor of their indentures as well as their good morals and behaviour respectively, be entitled to receive such sum of money, not exceeding £20 nor less than £10 each, as the trustees should judge proper and expedient.

(5) The surplusage of the funds, remaining after the before-mentioned objects had been carried out, was to be distributed in alms to the poor of the town for the time being.

In the year 1816 Sheba Lyon, whose father, Joseph Lyon, had been an occupier of a house in the town of Bedford for more than ten years, being then between twelve and fifteen years of age and duly qualified by the Act of Parliament, and her name having been given in in the usual form one calendar month before the time of drawing lots as directed by the Act, presented herself to the masters, governors, and trustees of the Bedford Charity as a candidate to draw a lot for the apprentice fee to be paid to girls. Permission to draw a lot was refused upon the ground that her father, Joseph Lyon, was of the Jewish persuasion, and afterwards any persons of the Jewish persuasion, whatever in other respects might be their qualifications under the terms of the Act of Parliament, or the children of such persons, to partake of any benefit under the Bedford Charity. In answer to an application by Mr. Isaac Lyon Goldsmid, who interceded on behalf of Sheba Lyon, the Mayor of Bedford wrote to him that the trustees, finding the number of Jews increasing in Bedford, entertained considerable doubts whether such persons were objects of the charity, and that they had been advised to refuse and had refused to admit Jews to participate in the benefit of the charity, leaving it to the persons so refused, if they should think proper, to bring the matter before the Lord Chancellor.

Accordingly a petition was presented praying that it might be declared that the poor inhabitants of the town of Bedford in other respects duly qualified were entitled to the benefit of the Bedford Charity for themselves and their children, whether they were Jews or Christians, and that Sheba Lyon should be permitted to draw lots for the apprentice fee to be paid to girls.

The evidence showed that Michael Joseph had twice voted in the annual election of trustees of the charity, that he settled at Bedford and became a housekeeper there about thirty-one years before, and at that time there was no other person professing the Jewish religion there nor had been in the memory of man; that he had had two sons and seven daughters, all of whom were born in Bedford, and that both his sons were admitted into the free school of the charity and were educated there in the usual manner, his eldest son being in the lower or writing school, and his youngest both in the grammar and writing school; and both of them drew for and received apprentice fees from the charity, and the eldest, on being out of his apprenticeship, received the benefaction of £10; that his four eldest daughters drew for apprentice fees given to girls; the three eldest of them did not draw beneficial lots, but the youngest having drawn a beneficial lot, the apprentice fee was paid with her; that all his daughters had since claimed and received the marriage portions given to poor maidens; that no Jew had ever been proposed or elected a trustee of the charity, but that such trustees had always been elected from among the most opulent and considerable inhabitants of the town; and no Jew, during the time of Michael Joseph's first residence there, had been by his circumstances and mode of living entitled to the distinction of being elected a trustee; that no Jew boy or girl had ever been admitted into the hospital, nor any Jew into the almshouses belonging to the charity, and that no Jew girl ever received the donation given to maidservants, and no Jew ever received any part of the moneys distributed annually under the provisions of the Act among the poor inhabitants of Bedford; but that no one professing the Jewish religion since Michael Joseph's residence in the town had ever applied for or been a fitting object to partake in any of those benefactions (inasmuch as no Jew had been incapacitated by age or infirmity, so as to fall within the description of persons for whose benefit the almshouses were erected) or to receive the surplus of the charity funds annually distributed; and no Jew girl, the daughter of an inhabitant of Bedford, had ever gone out to service; that there were then three Jew housekeepers in the town and no more, and that since Michael Joseph first came to reside in the town there had been four other Jew families resident as housekeepers there, all of whom had either left the town or ceased to be housekeepers there. The other two Jewish housekeepers resident in the town, Godfrey Levi and Joseph Lyon, also swore affidavits stating that their daughters had been admitted into the preparatory free school.

Evidence was filed on the part of the trustees setting out the regulations laid down for the government of the schools, from which it appeared that there were three schools attached to the charity, namely, the grammar school, the writing school, and the preparatory school; and affidavits were sworn by the gentlemen who were or had been masters of the schools. The education in the grammar school was similar to that in other public schools, and consisted of instruction in the Latin and Greek languages. Every boy was also instructed in the principles of the Christian religion, and required to read the Bible and New Testament. Nathan Joseph, the son of Michael Joseph, had been one of the scholars in the grammar school; he had never made further progress than learning the Latin grammar, and remained altogether not more than twelve months in the school when his father took him away; Michael Joseph had requested Dr. Brereton, the master, to dispense with his son's attendance in school at the time of morning and evening prayer, on account of its being inconsistent with his faith as a Jew, and for the same reason to dispense with his attendance on the Saturday, being the Jewish Sabbath, and also on the Jewish holidays; Nathan Joseph never attended the grammar school on a Saturday nor on certain other days which were Jewish holidays; he was very irregular in his attendance in school, of which Dr. Brereton frequently complained to his father, who uniformly described his absence to be of necessity, on account of his being of the Jewish persuasion. No other boy of the Jewish persuasion had at any time applied for admission or been admitted into the grammar school.

All the boys in the writing school, without exception, were educated in the principles of Christianity, and taught to read and actually read the Bible and New Testament and learn and repeat the Church Catechism. The only boys of the Jewish persuasion who were admitted into the school were Joseph Joseph, eldest son of Michael Joseph, and Lemuel Lyon, son of Joseph Lyon. Michael Joseph, on the occasion of his son's admission, requested that Joseph Joseph might not be desired to attend the morning and evening prayers, on account of his religion; the master, however, did not dispense with Joseph Joseph's attendance, but permitted him to sit instead of kneel during the prayers. At his father's request Joseph Joseph was permitted to be absent from school every Saturday and also on such days as were Jewish holidays; Lemuel Lyon was also absent (though apparently his father made no request on his behalf) every Saturday and on the Jewish holidays; and neither Joseph Joseph nor Lemuel Lyon, on account of their religion, ever read the New Testament or learned the Church Catechism, as all the other boys did.

In 1815 a school had been founded for instructing the poor boys of the town upon Dr. Bell's system of education, by the name of the preparatory school; but no Jew boy had ever been educated in the preparatory school. On the afternoons of Tuesday and Thursday in each week, being the half-holidays of the boys, the school was opened for the education of girls residing in the town, in reading, writing, and arithmetic. Two daughters of Michael Joseph, three daughters of Joseph Lyon, and two daughters of Godfrey Levi, came to the preparatory school for education for about six months. The daughters of Michael Joseph informed the master that, being Jewesses, they were not allowed to read the New Testament, and he permitted them to read the Commandments and the Bible only. The children of Joseph Lyon and Godfrey Levi, being little children, were on the above afternoons put with children of the same class to read the parables and miracles of the New Testament. All the Jew children stayed away from the school on certain days which were Jewish holidays.

The petition was presented by the before-mentioned Joseph Lyon, his daughter Sheba Lyon, and Michael Joseph, all of the town of Bedford, by five of the elders of the congregation of the Dutch and German Jews assembling at the Great Synagogue in Duke's Place, and by a similar number of the elders of the congregation of the Dutch and German Jews assembling at the New Synagogue in Leadenhall Street[1]. A considerable part of the arguments and judgment was directed to the right of the elders of the synagogues to be petitioners, and it is upon this point that the case is usually quoted in the law books. This, however, was a purely technical question, a discourse on which would be out of place here, though it may be stated that Lord Eldon decided against the claim of the elders to be petitioners, as they had no direct interest in the administration of the charity. The arguments were put forward with great ability by Sir Samuel Romilly on behalf of the petitioners, and the Solicitor-General, Sir Robert Gifford, on behalf of the trustees. Want of space necessitates their omission here, except in so far as the Lord Chancellor commented upon them in his judgment. Among the remarks he made before giving final judgment, he said: "A doubt has also occurred to me, whether

[1] Mr. Picciotto in his *Sketches of Anglo-Jewish History*, at p. 289, mentions this case, and informs us that the matter was originally laid before the authorities of the Great Synagogue, who at once appointed a committee to investigate the subject, and sought the co-operation of the other Synagogues in London; but that the Hambro' Synagogue and the Sephardi Synagogue declined to entertain the matter, referring it to the Board of Deputies. He says that the court decided that a Jew was not a "parishioner." It is remarkable that this word is not to be found throughout the seventy pages of the very learned and accurate report.

admissibility into the school is within my exclusive jurisdiction; whether it does not belong to the Visitors, the Warden and Fellows of New College. They have introduced a variety of regulations for the conduct of the boys' school, with which no Jew boy could comply. Without now giving final judgment, I have no doubt that a Jew boy cannot have the benefit of that school, because he cannot comply with these regulations[1]."

At length, on May 11, 1819, in finally disposing of the petition, Lord Eldon suggested that a new petition should be presented by the trustees, stating that doubts had arisen as to the construction of the Act in regard to Jews, and submitting to the court what they take to be the true exposition, as far as those persons are concerned. He added: "On the letter stated in the petition, as on a great deal urged to me in argument, those liberal ideas about worshipping God in church, chapel, or synagogue, I purpose to make no observations; it is not necessary. The decision in *Da Costa* v. *De Paz* has established that no one can found by charitable donation an institution for the purpose of teaching the Jewish religion; but it is quite a different question whether property can be given to perform charitable acts to persons who happen to be Jews; and it appears to me that the present is a mere question whether these individuals are or not, within the four corners of this Act of Parliament, objects of the charity thereby given. I have no concern with general principles: I am only to construe the Act[2]."

A new petition was accordingly presented by the trustees, praying a declaration whether the poor inhabitants of the town of Bedford who were of the Jewish persuasion were entitled with Christians to the benefit of the Bedford Charity for themselves or their children. And it was not until Aug. 23 that Lord Eldon pronounced his decision on the whole case. In the course of his judgment he said: "This charity had its foundation in letters patent of

[1] 2 Swanston, p. 520. [2] Ibid., p. 522.

Edward the Sixth, who founded a grammar school at Bedford as in many other parts of the kingdom, and this is the foundation of a school, pro institutione et instructione puerorum et juvenum in grammatica literatura et bonis moribus." He then, having gone through the provisions of the Acts of Parliament and summarized the evidence, proceeded as follows:—

"Many arguments were addressed from the bar on the practice and principle of toleration. I apprehend that the present question is perfectly simple in its nature, and neither more nor less than this, whether the letters patent of Edward the Sixth and these Acts of Parliament have or have not comprehended within the true construction of their provisions persons of the Jewish persuasion? Whatever my sentiments may be of the opinions expressed in some clauses of the letter written on that occasion, I apprehend that it is the duty of every judge presiding in an English court of justice, when he is told that there is no difference between worshipping the Supreme Being in chapel, church, or synagogue, to recollect that Christianity is part of the law of England; that in giving construction to the charter and Acts of Parliament he is not to proceed on that principle farther than just construction requires; but to the extent of just construction of that charter and those Acts, he is not at liberty to forget the law of the land.

"With respect to usage, as far as usage is to be looked to for an exposition of the charter, it may be convenient first to consider it with reference to the question whether Jew boys can be admitted to the school, and next to the admission of Jewish maidens. I am not sure that the first question does not belong to the Visitors; but I have no difficulty in giving my opinion on it.

"An observation not without weight is, that this school was founded as a grammar school by Edward the Sixth, who founded many throughout the kingdom, and the words 'grammar school' have generally been construed to mean a school for instruction in the learned languages; but I believe that it has been the practice from the beginning and I hope that it still continues and will long continue, that in these schools great care is taken to educate youth in the doctrines of Christianity; to teach them their duty to God and their neighbour in the terms in which those duties are taught in the Catechism; and I remember the time when boys so educated were attended to church every Sunday by their master, thereby giving to them the opportunity of learning the principles of that establishment which the law certainly favours.

"The result of the affidavits is, that it does not appear that any Jew ever partook of the benefits of the charity till within the last thirty years; that a Jew has voted in the choice of trustees, being canvassed for his vote by one of the aldermen of Bedford, and that two or three Jewish children have been admitted into this school (in what manner conducted will be seen presently), that they have not received the benefits of other parts of the charity, the affidavits accounting for that, because, from their circumstances of age or otherwise, they were not in a situation to solicit charitable assistance, or to be appointed trustees. Here are the regulations of the school approved by the Warden and Fellows of New College; and I can find nothing to raise an argument that would authorize me to say that they have not authority to make regulations for the conduct of the school. Even though the charter and the Acts had not excluded Jews, the charter and the Acts giving to the Warden and Fellows the power of making regulations, if these regulations in a Christian country operate to exclude Jew boys, it will remain to be considered whether that is not a due exercise of visitatorial authority and such as must be submitted to.

"There is another way of considering it, whether the Visitors have not, in excluding Jews, rightly construed the charter and the Acts. I have no doubt that Edward the Sixth had not any intention for the education of Jews.

Whatever may be our sentiments, it does not appear to me that they were within the scope of the charter, nor do I think that they are within the scope of the Acts; the Acts could not mean to comprehend persons who were not comprehended by the charter. How is it possible that the education of boys professing Christianity and of boys professing Judaism can proceed together? It is in evidence that Jew boys were absent on Jewish holidays and while the New Testament was read. They cannot comply with the regulations for education at this school in what must, according to the construction of the charter, be held to be 'boni mores.' The master always chooses the Latin and Greek books, and I know none of the grammar schools in which the New Testament is not taught, either in Latin or in Greek. In prescribing the school hours, directions are given for the attendance of the boys on every day in the week except Sunday; it is impossible that Jew boys can give that attendance consistently with the observance of Jewish holidays. Prayers are to be read every morning. What kind of prayers? They are prayers in a grammar school, where the master is a clergyman, and where the scholars are to have exhibitions to the universities, to which it is impossible that any Jew boy can be sent. It is not necessary to go through all these particulars, because it seems to me that Jews resident in Bedford, acting conscientiously, could not permit their sons to attend this school. I am therefore clearly of opinion that there is no pretence to say that they are entitled to attend.

"With respect to the other objects of the charity, the only question before me relates to Jewish maidens. First, can it be that, at the time of the letters patent, Jew girls were within their scope and meaning? Next, if it is clear that boys must be educated in the principles of Christianity, is there anything in the charter to authorize me to say that, it being the intention to found an institution a great object of which was the education of boys in the Christian religion, other objects of the charity were to be persons not professing Christianity? Various articles interspersed all tend to show that the design of the charity was to benefit persons professing the Christian religion. I shall mention only one, that girls are required to send in their Christian names. It is said that Christian name means only first name, and that on the other construction an Anabaptist could not be admitted. Be it so; but I apprehend that Christian name does not necessarily mean baptismal name. Though Anabaptists do not baptize till later in life than other Christians, I think that the name which they give to their children is, in a sense, a Christian name. Another circumstance is, that the children are to attend public worship every Sunday. It is stated, and I doubt not truly, that Jewish children do attend worship every Sunday[1]; but can any one contend that the words of the letters patent, 'attending worship every Sunday,' mean more than attending on a day on which, under the Christian religion, attendance at worship is more imperative than on any other day?"

Mr. Swanston gives the order as drawn up: "His Lordship doth declare that the poor inhabitants of the town of Bedford who are of the Jewish persuasion are not entitled to any benefit of the Bedford Charity in the said petition mentioned, for themselves or their children."

It may be mentioned that the Bedford Charity was fundamentally reorganized in 1874, when the Endowed Schools Commission enacted a scheme by which the whole amount of the funds is expended upon the schools except a comparatively small sum which is allotted to the endowment of forty-five almshouses. Under the new scheme there is no provision which excludes Jews from participating in the charity.

The judgment of Lord Eldon is now no longer of practical importance in regard to the particular charity in respect of which it was pronounced; but the reasoning upon which

[1] Sir S. Romilly had argued that the synagogue was open every day, and a Jew might attend worship there on a Sunday.

this decision (delivered by one of our ablest and most careful judges after mature deliberation) was based, and the principles underlying it, are still of great moment in discussing the question which is now being dealt with. A few comments upon it will therefore not be out of place. On the admission of Jewish boys to the school the Chancellor felt no doubt, and upon this point his judgment is conclusive, founded, as it really is, if carefully examined, upon the impossibility of Jewish boys complying with the regulations properly laid down for the government of the school by the duly constituted Visitors of it. He, however, as his custom was, supports this reason by others which, though cogent, are not so convincing. For instance, the fact that there were no Jews living in England at the time no doubt leads to the inference that Edward the Sixth had no intention to provide for the education of Jewish children, but it by no means compels the conclusion that it was his purpose, in the event of Jews being in the future allowed to settle in the country and openly practise their religion, to exclude their children from the advantages of the institution he was founding by the charters; and though of some weight in estimating the power of the Visitors to make the rules they had drawn up, this fact, taken by itself, could not operate to deprive any class of persons of the benefits to which they would be otherwise entitled. The impossibility of educating Christian and Jewish boys together is not now so apparent as it was at the beginning of the nineteenth century, and the mere fact of calling a school a grammar school would not at the present time be taken to necessarily imply that instruction in the doctrines of Christianity should form part of the curriculum. But men's notions upon these matters have changed; indeed, even in Lord Eldon's time they had been relaxed, for he mentions with regret that it was no longer customary for the scholars of a grammar school to attend the church service every Sunday accompanied by their master.

With regard to the portions for poor maidens and the

apprenticeship fees, Lord Eldon felt some doubt; but his decision is justified by the regulation requiring attendance at public worship on Sunday. The ingenious argument upon this point, that, inasmuch as the Jewish synagogue was open every day, Jews could comply with this requirement, was rightly overruled. On the other hand, the reasoning founded on the meaning of Christian names is far from conclusive. It will be remembered that the surplus of the funds of the charity was to be distributed in alms to the poor of the town. The effect of the order as drawn up was to exclude poor Jews from such distribution. Upon this point no argument was addressed to the court, nor is there anything in the judgment to indicate that this result was deliberately contemplated. In any case it is submitted that this particular result was not in accordance with law, and that the true principle is, as stated at the outset and borne out by the judgment delivered in the case, that charitable endowments may be confined to members of a particular faith only if words imposing such restriction are used in their creation, and that all persons, to whatever race or faith they may belong, who can and do comply with the conditions properly laid down for the distribution of an endowment are entitled to participate in it.

IV.

HAVING already passed in review the law in its bearing on the Jewish religion and endowments founded for the purpose of propagating that religion, as well as the conditions under which Jews are entitled to a share of general endowments and charities, the laws concerning the civil and political status of the Jews next claim attention. For a period of more than three and a half centuries Jews were not permitted to live in England, nor is the date when they were first allowed to settle here by any means certain. However, in considering the course of legislation, so far as it concerns the Jews, the time of the legal recognition of their resettlement is of great importance, and was much discussed in the recent case of *Dr. Wilton* v. *Montefiore*, where Mr. Justice, now Lord Justice Stirling, decided it to be November 13, 1685. The words of the learned judge are: "The history of the Jews in this country, so far as it is material to the present question, is given in a note to the report of *Lindo* v. *Belisario* [1]. After stating that the Jews appeared to have been brought here in considerable numbers by William I from Rouen in 1070, and that they lived as bondsmen of the kings, and under special protection, regulations, and exemptions, till they were banished in 1290, the note proceeds as follows: 'They did not appear

[1] 1 Hag. Cons. 216.

again in this kingdom as a distinct body[1] till the time of Charles II. They had petitioned in 1648 to be allowed to return and enjoy their religion, and the question was much agitated but nothing was done. On the Restoration, Charles II promised them protection and the use of their religion, and an order of Council issued to that effect.' The order is given in the Appendix, p. 3. It is dated November 13, 1685, and it provides as follows: 'Upon reading this day at the board the petition of Joseph Henriques, Abraham Delivera, and Aaron Pacheco, overseers of the Jewish synagogue, and the rest of the Jewish nation, setting forth that his late Majesty, of blessed memory, having found the petitioners and their nation ever faithful to the government, and ready to serve him on all occasions, was pleased in February, 1673, to signify his royal pleasure, that whilst they continued quiet, true, and faithful to the government, they should enjoy the liberty and profession of their religion, which they accordingly peaceably exercised till Michaelmas Term last; that several writs out of the King's Bench, on the statute made in the twenty-third year of Queen Elizabeth, had been taken out against forty-eight of the Jewish nation by one Thomas Beaumont, and thirty-seven of them arrested thereupon, as they were following their occasions on the Royal Exchange, to the great prejudice of their reputation both here and abroad; and therefore praying his Majesty to permit and suffer them, as heretofore, to have the benefit and free exercise of their religion during their good behaviour towards his Majesty's government. His Majesty having taken this matter into his royal consideration, was pleased to order, and it is hereby accordingly ordered, that his Majesty's Attorney-General do stop all the said proceedings at law against the petitioners; his Majesty's intention being that they should not be troubled upon

[1] By these words Dr. Haggard probably means having a synagogue and communal organization and openly practising their religion.

this account, but quietly enjoy the free exercise of their religion, whilst they behave themselves dutifully and obediently to his government.' From that time forward the Jews appear to have been permitted to reside in England and to practise the rites of their religion[1]."

This date, November 13, 1685, in the reign of James II, is inconsistent with the popular theory that the Jews came over during the Protectorate of Oliver Cromwell in the wake of their great Rabbi, Menasseh Ben Israel, in the year 1655, and have been legally settled here ever since, nor is it much less at variance with the view of the historians, that the Jews obtained a legal settlement in England sometime during the reign of Charles II, though the precise date is not given. The true date is of some importance when the course of subsequent legislation as it affects the Jews is placed under review; and as much may be said on behalf of either theory, and as the legal theory is not necessarily correct, it will not be out of place to summarize the evidence upon which the rival theories are based, so that the reader may be enabled to form an impartial judgment on the subject under discussion. Here it will be necessary to travel outside the contents of the statute book and the law reports, and to extract, though it is to be hoped not at undue length, certain entries in the public records. It must not of course be forgotten that an actual settlement is one thing, and the legal recognition of it another. The former must necessarily precede the latter. The date adopted in Mr. Justice Stirling's judgment is therefore a late one, and in reality marks the last occasion on which a serious attempt was made in due form of law to prevent the Jews who had already an organized community from continuing their residence in the country.

In order to understand the conditions for the solution of this problem, it is necessary to glance at the previous

[1] Law Reports [1900], 2 Ch. 489.

history of the Jews in this country. There can be little doubt that from the earliest times, that is, ever since England may be said to have come within the pale of civilization, Jews, prompted by that commercial instinct which has always been their characteristic, came here for the purposes of trade, and reaped the profits to be derived from it, and even settled here, though probably not in such considerable numbers as to establish distinct communities of their own until the connexion between England and the continent of Europe became closer by reason of the Norman Conquest and the events immediately preceding it. Therefore though there are at the present day few or no traces remaining of any Jewish settlements in England prior to the time of the Norman kings, it is a mistake, founded upon a passage in Prynne's *Demurrer*, to assert that the residence of Jews in England was illegal before that time. Prynne's words [1] are: "I have deduced their introduction into England only from William surnamed the Conqueror, because I finde not the least mention of them in any of our British or Saxon Histories, Councils, Synods, Canons, which doubtlesse would have mentioned them, and made some strict Laws or Canons, against their Jewish as well as against Pagan Superstitions, had they exercised them here, as they would have done as well as in Spain, and other places, had they resided here." But apart from Edward the Confessor's law, the authenticity of which Prynne disputes, there are contained in the *Liber Poenitentialis* of Theodore, who was Archbishop of Canterbury from 668 to 690 A. D., and the *Excerptiones* of Ecbert, who was Archbishop of York from 735 to 766 A. D., a not inconsiderable number of canons and regulations relating to the Jews: e. g. it was provided that a Christian woman committing fornication with a Jew should undergo severer penalties than if guilty of the same offence with a Christian [2];

[1] Prynne's *Demurrer*, part I, p. 5.

[2] Theod. *Lib. P.*, XVI, § 35.

and that if any celebrated the feast of Passover with the Jews, he should be expelled from every church[1]; and that if any Christian received unleavened bread or any food or drink from the Jews, he should do penance on bread and water for forty days[2]; and that if a Christian were to sell another Christian, although his own slave, to Jews, he was to suffer severe penalties until he redeemed him[3]. Again, mass was not to be celebrated in any place where the bodies of Jews or infidels were buried[4], and no Christian was to turn Jew or take part in Jewish feasts[5].

However this may be, there can be no doubt that after the Norman Conquest separate Jewish communities were to be found in many of the more important towns. The Jews, or "Iudaei," as they were called, living in these communities, possessed a separate and distinct legal status. This status was very similar to that of the villein, with this distinction, that the Jew was not *ascriptus glebae*, and was in every case subject to the king, and not to the lord of the manor, as the villein was. It is well described in the twenty-fifth law of Edward the Confessor, which may be translated as follows: "All Jews, in whatever part of the kingdom they may be, are under the liege protection and guardianship of the king; nor can any of them attach himself to any rich man without the king's licence, because the Jews themselves and all their chattels are the king's. But if any one detains them or their chattels, the king may claim them as his own[6]." Such a status was consistent

[1] Theod. *Lib. P.*, XXX, § 4.

[2] Ibid., XLII, § 1.

[3] Ibid., § 4; Ecb. *Ex.* 150.

[4] Theod. *Lib. P.*, XLVII, § 1.

[5] Ecb. *Ex.* 147.

[6] As to this law Prynne says: "I cannot but reject it as counterfeit, and esteem it rather a Declaration of the Jews' condition in England in Hoveden's time (inserted by him, as well as some other things of punier date, amongst these Laws) rather than any Law of, or in the Confessor's days, wherein I can find no evidence of any Jews' residence here, but only this interpolation and forged Law, which Mr. Selden wholly omits in his Collection of his Laws." Hoveden lived in the reign of Henry II, and probably died in 1201 A.D.; and though Prynne thinks the law

with a large amount of freedom: as against all the king's subjects they were free and possessed of all the rights of freemen, but their persons and property were under the absolute control and disposition of the king, whose exactions were only restricted by that prudence which warns the owner not to slay the goose that lays the golden eggs. So important a source of revenue did the Jews become that a special court, the Exchequer of the Jews, was established in the reign of Richard I; this court had jurisdiction in all causes whether civil or criminal in which Jews were implicated; though purely civil cases in which both parties were Jews were frequently, if not generally, remitted to a purely Jewish tribunal, to be decided by Jewish and not by English law. The Jews were not popular; they were the licensed money-lenders of the land—in this trade they had an absolute monopoly[1]—and the creditor is rarely beloved by his debtor. The barons looked with jealous eyes on the Jews' wide privileges in relation to their fellow men; but it was not till towards the close of Henry III's long reign that their civil rights were materially abridged by statute, though they were always subject to such restrictions as the king in his discretion might think fit to impose. In the year 1271 a statute[2] was enacted prohibiting Jews from holding lands in fee (the houses they then possessed being expressly excepted), and also from having Christian servants, while about the year 1275 the famous statute *de la Jeuerie* or *de Iudaismo* was passed, which forbade usury to the Jews, and enjoined that every Jew should wear a yellow badge on his outer garment and pay a yearly tax of threepence to

spurious, he admits that it correctly represents the legal status of the Jews in the latter part of the twelfth century. See Bracton, f. 386 b. The law is now accepted as genuine, and is included in the Ancient Laws and Institutes of England printed under the direction of the Commissioners on the Public Records of the Kingdom in 1840.

[1] Usury was most strictly forbidden to Christians as being contrary to the law of God and of the land. See Co. 3 Inst., p. 251.

[2] Rymer's *Foedera*, I, 489.

the king; on the other hand, the Jews were to be under the king's protection, and might gain their living by lawful merchandise and labour, and might buy houses in the cities where they lived and hold them in chief of the king, and might take farms or land for the term of ten years or less. But the licence to take lands to farm was to endure for only fifteen years[1]. Such was the position of the Jews before their final departure from the country in 1290[2]. This event is accurately described in Stubbs's *Constitutional History*: "At the same time (as the July Parliament) by an act done by himself in his private council" ("per regem et secretum concilium," Hemingb. II, 20) "he banished the Jews from England: the safe-conduct granted them on their departure is dated on the 27th of July[3]." These safe-conducts are the most important documents still in existence relating to this event. The one referred to by Bishop Stubbs is addressed to all the bailiffs, barons, and shipowners of the Cinque Ports, commanding them that, inasmuch as a certain time has been fixed for all the Jews to quit the realm, to give them a safe passage for themselves, their wives, children, and chattels, and to charge them no more than the ordinary and accustomed freight, and enjoining them under pain of severe forfeiture from injuring or, so far as in them lay, allowing others to injure or molest any of the Jews in property or person[4].

[1] Statutes of the Realm, I, 221.

[2] For further detail the reader is referred to Pollock and Maitland's *History of English Law before the time of Edward I*, vol. I, pp. 451–459, and Gneist's *Constitutional History*, p. 228 note, and also *The Expulsion of the Jews from England in* 1290, by B. L. Abrahams, and the Introduction to the Jewish Historical and Selden Societies' edition of *Select Pleas*, Starrs, &c., by J. M. Rigg, which has appeared while these pages were in the press.

[3] Stubbs, *Const. Hist.*, II, 126.

[4] Rymer, *Foed.*, vol. I, part 2, p. 736. Coke gives from the Close Rolls a similar writ addressed to the sheriff of G. and dated July 18, 1290. Inst., II, p. 507, and see Tovey's *Ang. Iudaica*, p. 241, and at p. 232 the entry in the Red Book of the Exchequer is given.

The decree of banishment itself is no longer extant, but Dr. C. Gross has discovered a document which throws much light upon it. This document is in the form of a writ issued from King's Clipstone on November 5, 1290, and addressed to the Treasurer and Barons of the Exchequer. It recites that though by the statute passed at Westminster (the statute *de Iudaismo*) the Jews had been forbidden to take usury of any Christian, nevertheless they still exacted interest under the name of "courtesy[1]," and thereby oppressed the people; wherefore on account of their crimes and in honour of Christ, the king had compelled them to quit the realm as being perjured, and proceeds to order that no penalty or interest should be exacted in respect of debts due to the Jews, and that the debtors should pay only the principal moneys they had actually received from the Jews[2]. The exile of the Jews did not annul debts due to them, but such debts became payable to the king, whose bondmen the Jews had been. They had been ordered to leave the kingdom before a fixed time, which is not stated in any of the documents, but is generally believed to be the first of November[3]; the writ in question was therefore issued immediately after their final departure.

In consideration of having issued this decree of banishment, the Parliament which was then sitting, composed as it was in a great measure of landowners to whom Jewish usury had been a heavy burden, granted the king a fifteenth "pro expulsione Iudaeorum." But the transaction was not a very profitable one to the crown, for by it a plenteous

[1] The original word is *curialitas*, which is quite distinct from the "curialitas Angliae" or interest which the husband has in his wife's freehold land. It probably does not occur elsewhere in this sense in mediaeval jurisprudence, and is not to be found among the terms explained in "Termes de la ley." It is used in the *Corpus iuris*, but with a very different meaning. *Novell. Valentinian.* tit. 3, § 3.

[2] Add. MSS., Mus. Brit. 32,085, fol. 122, *Publications of the Anglo-Jewish Historical Exhibition*, I, 229; Rigg, *Select Pleas*, pp. xl–xlii.

[3] Mathew of Westminster, a contemporary chronicler, says the king had allowed them to stay till the Feast of All Saints (Tovey, p. 233).

source of the revenue was for ever cut off, and that at a time when the king was expected to defray the ordinary expenses of the state out of his hereditary revenues, and subsidies were only voted by the Parliament on special and extraordinary occasions. Yet in the year 1290 this source could not be expected to yield as rich a harvest as it had done in former days. The prohibition of usury in the third year of Edward I, even if occasionally evaded, had greatly diminished the resources of the Jews, and the licence to take lands to farm, which was to endure for only fifteen years, was now about to expire, and thus another road to the acquisition of wealth was closed to them. Had they been allowed to remain, the Jews hampered by these restrictions imposed by Act of Parliament, and therefore removable only by Act of Parliament, would no longer have been as profitable to the king as they had been in former times, when, in the words of Lord Coke, "a great revenue by reason of the usury of the Jews came to the crown; for between the fiftieth year of Henry III and the second year of Edward I, which was not above seven years complete, there was paid into the king's coffers four hundred and twenty thousand pounds of and for the usury of the Jews[1]." This is a truly enormous sum, having regard to the value of money and the total wealth of the country in the thirteenth century. But after the statute *de Iudaismo* such rich harvests were no longer to be reaped, and in all probability this knowledge had considerable influence on the king's mind, in addition to the proffered gift of a fifteenth by the Parliament and the knowledge that a great part of the property still remaining to the Jews would come to him by way of escheats[2].

[1] 3 Inst., 151.

[2] Madox, *History of the Exchequer*, p. 261. See note r. "MCCLXXXX eiecti sunt Iudaei ab Anglia cum facultatibus suis; salvis cartis Christianorum penes Dominum Regem residentibus," ex Cod. Vet. MS. (*Annals of the Church of St. Augustine at Canterbury*), 4. 7, p. 102. At p. 221 Mr. Madox says: "The King of England was wont to draw a considerable Revenue from the Jews residing in this Realm: namely, by Tallages, by Fines

Looking back over the gulf of centuries, this event can be descried with sufficient clearness, but the loss of the proclamation of banishment has left it wrapped in some obscurity that has given rise to several erroneous theories that should here be mentioned. Lord Coke says that there was no banishment of the Jews, but only a voluntary exodus in consequence of the suppression of usury. "Our noble King Edward I and his father Henry III before him sought by divers Acts and Ordinances to use some mean and moderation herein, but in the end it was found that there was no mean in mischief, and as Seneca saith, 'Res profecto stulta est nequitiae modus.' And therefore King Edward I, as this Act" (the statute *de Iudaismo*) "saith, in the honour of God, and for the common profit of his people, without all respect (in respect of these) of the filling of his own coffers, did ordain, that no Jew from henceforth should make any bargain or contract for usury, nor upon any former contract should take any usury, from the Feast of Saint Edward then last past; so in effect all Jewish usury was forbidden."

"This Law struck at the root of this pestilent weed, for hereby usury itself was forbidden; and thereupon the cruel Jews thirsting after wicked gain, to the number of

relating to Law-proceedings, by Amerciaments imposed on them for Misdemeanour, and by the Fines, Ransoms and Compositions, which they were forced to pay, for having the King's Benevolence, for Protection, for Licence to trade and negotiate, for Discharges from Imprisonment, and the like. He would tallage the whole Community or Body of them at Pleasure; and make them answer the Tallages for one another. If they made Default at the Atterminations or Days of Payment prefixed to them, they were charged with great Fines or Compositions for it. In Sum, the King seemed to be absolute Lord of their Estates and Effects, and of the Persons of them, their Wives and Children. 'Tis true, he let them enjoy their Trade and bequests; but they seemed to trade and acquire for his Profit as well as their own: for at one Time or other, their Fortunes or great part of them came into his Coffers. They were a numerous Body (being settled in many, especially the great Towns of the Realm): and by Traffic and taking of usuries and mortgages of the King's subjects, they became very wealthy both in Money and Land. But as they fleeced the subjects of the Realm, so the King fleeced them."

15,060 departed out of this Realm into foreign parts, where they might use their Jewish trade of usury, and from that time that Nation never returned again into this Realm. Some are of opinion (and so it is said in some of our Histories) that it was decreed by authority of Parliament, That the usurious Jews should be banished out of the Realm; but the truth is, that their Usury was banished by this Act of Parliament, and that was the cause that they banished themselves into forein Countries, where they might live by their Usury; and for that they were odious both to God and man, that they might passe out of the Realm in safety, they made Petition to the King, that a certain day might be prefixed to them to depart the Realm, to the end that they might have the King's Writ to his Sherifes for their safe conduct, and that no injury, molestation, damage or grievance be offered to them in the mean time[1]."

Coke's error is due to his post-dating the statute *de Iudaismo*, and attributing it to the Parliament of 1290. It is still placed among the statutes of uncertain date by the commissioners responsible for the statutes of the realm. In the Harleian MS. it immediately succeeds the Statute of Westminster I, passed in the third year of Edward I, and in the document discovered by Dr. Gross at the British Museum it is stated to have been enacted "in quindena Sancti Michaelis anno regni nostri tertio"; so that the date is now placed beyond all doubt[2]. The basis of Coke's theory is thus destroyed.

Prynne, on the other hand, is very positive that the banishment was effected by Act of Parliament; his words are: "This their banishment was by the unanimous desire, Judgment, Edict, and Decree both of the King and his Parliament; and not by the King alone: and this Banishment, total, of them all, and likewise final, never to return

[1] 2 Inst., 507.

[2] Add. MSS., Mus. Brit., 32,085, fol. 122. Prynne in his *Demurrer*, at p. 34, places the statute in the year 1287, but in his *Records*, vol. III, p. 153, he attributes it to 4 Edw. I.

into England. Which Edict and Decree not now extant in our Parliament Rolls (many of which are lost) nor printed Statutes; yet it is mentioned by all these Authorities[1]." Prynne here alludes to different chroniclers, extracts from whose works he had already given; but these extracts when carefully examined do not bear out his assertion.

This view held by Prynne was undoubtedly very widely spread, and at one time held by both the supporters and opponents of the Jews' readmission; for the first petition presented on behalf of the Jews to the Council of War on Jan. 5, $164\frac{8}{9}$, some seven years before Prynne wrote his *Demurrer*, is entitled, "The petition of the Jews for the repealing of the Act of Parliament for their Banishment out of England," and speaks of the instrument of expulsion as "the inhumane, cruel statute of banishment." But those responsible for this petition seem to have been but ill acquainted with English history and jurisprudence, for the banishment is said to have taken place in the reign of Richard II[2]. Prynne has the candour and honesty to admit that the alleged statute was no longer in existence, but "B. B.," the anonymous author of *A Historical and Law Treatise against the Jews and Judaism*, a virulent diatribe against the Jews, published in 1703, which was so popular with the anti-Semites here that it was reprinted in 1721 and again in 1753 as the second edition—perceiving the weakness of this theory on account of the total disappearance of the alleged statute, unblushingly asserts that it is to be seen on the Roll of Parliament in the Tower. From internal evidence it is clear that this writer had carefully studied Prynne's *Demurrer*, and it is impossible to escape the conclusion that his statement is a wilful falsehood, made in reliance on the improbability of any of his readers taking the pains to verify it. Prynne was above such a statement as this, but feeling that the authorities he had cited were not conclusive, and fearing

[1] *Demurrer*, p. 49.

[2] Hag., *Cons. Cas.*, I, Ap. No. 1.

that the term "groundless conceit," which he had applied to Sir Edward Coke's theory, might with equal justice be applied to his own, he concludes his argument with the statement that by the fundamental laws of England, "No Freemen and Natives of England can be justly banished or exiled out of it but by special judgment of Parliament, or by Act of Parliament," as authority for which he cites Magna Charta, c. 29, and a large number of Acts of Parliament banishing individuals at various times. Therefore, he says, the Jews being banished by Act of Parliament "(never since repealed or reversed) neither may nor can by Law be readmitted, reduced into England again, but by common consent and Act of Parliament: which I conceive they will never be able to obtain[1]." It can hardly be denied that Prynne was carried away with excessive zeal to make good the proposition, to prove which he had sat down to write his *Demurrer*. He had, as he says in his "Preface to the Christian Reader," been asked by Mr. Nye, the minister, "whether there were any law of England against bringing in the Jews amongst us? for the Lawyers had newly delivered their opinions, there was no law against it." To which he had answered "That the Jews were in the year 1290 all banished out of England, by Judgment and Edict of the King and Parliament, as a great Grievance, never to return again: for which the Commons gave the King the fifteenth part of their Moveables: and therefore being thus banished by Parliament, they could not now by the Laws of England, be brought in again, without a special Act of Parliament, which I would make good for Law." The conference to consider the demands of Menasseh ben Israel was still sitting at Whitehall, and party feeling ran high; otherwise so sound a lawyer as Prynne would not have overlooked the fact that the famous clause of Magna Charta applies only to freemen, and that in the year 1290 no Jew could claim to be a *liber homo*. As has been already shown, the Jews

[1] *Demurrer*, p. 50.

were serfs or villeins, and by the statute *de Iudaismo* passed only fifteen years before, the privilege had been granted to them of not being challenged or troubled in any court, except in the court of the King, "whose Bondmen they are" ("ky serfs yl sunt"). The Jews consequently had no right to the benefit of Magna Charta or any other fundamental law of the land that applied to freemen only, and could accordingly be banished, as in fact they were, by decree of the King alone. There is yet a third theory of the expulsion which need be but briefly mentioned here. It is that sentence of exile was passed upon the Jews by a synod held in London. This does not rest on very strong authority, and it is certain that the clergy, whatever their wishes might have been, had no legal power to effect the expulsion of the Jews[1].

It has been lately suggested that in spite of the decree of banishment and the severe penalties which disobedience to that decree would undoubtedly have entailed, some Jews still remained in this country. The suggestion is based upon little trustworthy evidence, and does not call for any comment here; for if any did remain they were very soon amalgamated with and became indistinguishable from the general mass of the population. Then, again, as the centuries rolled on individual Jews from time to time can be proved to have landed on our shores, but they never attempted to establish a Jewish community here or to celebrate their worship publicly in this country; they were treated as other foreigners and subject to the laws which governed aliens[2]. It is therefore true to say that for a period of more than three centuries English history is a blank so far as the Jews are concerned; but in that long interval occurred two events of great importance in relation to the return of the Jews here. Those events

[1] See Wilkins's *Concilia*, II, p. 180; Pike, *History of Crime*, vol. I, p. 465.

[2] See "The Middle Age of Anglo-Jewish History," by L. Wolf, in *Publications of the Anglo-Jewish Historical Exhibition*, vol. I, and other works there cited.

were the extinction of villenage and the reformation of the English Church.

The disappearance of villenage is one of those great changes which has been brought about without the intervention of the legislature. To a great extent this result was effected by the attitude of the courts of common law, which admitted every presumption in favour of liberty, and in practice made it difficult and finally impossible to sustain a claim to a villein, if it was seriously contested. The last reported case in which villenage was pleaded was tried in Hilary Term, 1617 (15 Ja. I), and, as in numerous other instances, the claim was not upheld[1]. From the 15th of James I, says Mr. Hargrave in his learned argument in Sommersett's case, "the claim of villenage has not been heard of in our courts of justice; and nothing can be more notorious, than that the race of persons, who were once the objects of it, was about that time completely worn out by the continual and united operation of deaths and manumissions[2]." Had the case of the Jews occurred to him, he might have added banishment also. Villenage had thus become obsolete, but the laws and rules relating to villenage had never been repealed, and by these laws the sovereign as much as the private citizen was bound; therefore if Queen Elizabeth had laid claim to Rodrigo Lopez as her villein, it would have been necessary for her to prove either that Lopez had made confession that he was her villein in a court of record, or that he and his ancestors had been villeins to herself and her predecessors time out of memory—that is to say, for a period of sixty years, as limited by 32 Hen. VIII, cap. 2. Such proof would obviously not have been forthcoming, and no such claim was ever made by any of our sovereigns against those Jews who from time to time landed on our shores. But if they were not villeins then the disabling statutes enacted before

[1] Pigg v. Caley, Noy 27.

[2] J. O. Howell's *State Trials*, p. 41.

the expulsion did not apply to those Jews who might return and reside here. The disabling acts no doubt applied to "Iudaei" or Jews, nor were any exceptions made in the statutes, but the Jews who came back to England in the seventeenth century were free men; they were no longer villeins or quasi-villeins, and were not "Iudaei" within the meaning of the Acts. This principle of interpretation is well known to English law, and after much discussion and considerable disagreement among our greatest judges as to its application, was acted on in a recent case in which it was held that the enclosure at Kempton Park was not a place within the meaning of the Betting Act[1]. In that case reliance had to be placed on the preamble of the Act, and also upon extrinsic evidence of the circumstances existing at the time when the Act was passed, and it was the necessity of going outside the words of the statute itself which occasioned the difference of opinion among the judges; but in the very body of the statute *de Iudaismo*, the Jews, as has been already pointed out, are repeatedly called the King's bondmen, and therefore this difficulty would not arise. Certain it is that many generations of Jews lived in this country in open and flagrant violation of these obsolete statutes. They did not wear yellow badges on their outer garments; they employed Christian servants, and in some cases they did put out money to usury and held lands and houses; and yet no attempt was ever made to enforce the laws prohibiting such things, and that though, as contemporary pamphlets prove, there were undoubtedly many persons willing, nay eager, to annoy and injure the Jews had it been in their power. And yet in the year 1846 it was thought advisable to solemnly repeal by Act of Parliament "the Statute or Ordinance of the fifty-fourth and fifty-fifth years of the reign of King Henry the Third, and the Statute or Ordinance commonly called *Statutum*

[1] Powell *v.* The Kempton Park Racecourse Company, Limited, [1897] 2 Q. B., 242, and [1899] A. C., 143.

de Iudaismo[1]." If the view here stated is correct this was a work of supererogation, but in any case if there ever existed any doubt after the resettlement as to the absolute freedom and equality of the Jews with their fellow citizens before the law, it has now been removed.

Much as the decay of villenage might have facilitated the return of the Jews by rendering the former disabling enactments no longer applicable to them, the various laws passed in consequence of the Reformation of the English Church and the events which immediately preceded and led up to it were no less effective in retarding a resettlement. These laws may be classified under two heads: (1) those constituting the proclamation, teaching, or propagation of doctrines at variance or inconsistent with the tenets held for the time being by the Church as by law established, a criminal offence—the law of heresy; (2) those making criminal, failure to attend the service of the Church as by law established, and also the attendance at services other than those of the Established Church—the law of uniformity, to a great extent embodied in the statutes known as the laws against recusants.

At the time of the expulsion of the Jews, and indeed until the days of Wycliffe and the rise of the Lollards nearly a century afterwards, heresy was almost unknown in England; and if there was any legal machinery other than excommunication and ecclesiastical censure, by which such a crime could be punished, there were but few occasions when it was brought into operation, and the fact that Wycliffe and his earlier disciples escaped all temporal penalties goes far to show that though heresy even in those times was regarded as a heinous crime, there was no regular procedure by which those tainted with it could be brought to justice and punished. In any case the Jews, who had lived here as the King's villeins and under the special protection of the King, had not been liable to be charged with heresy; but if they converted a Christian

[1] 9 & 10 Vict. cap. 59.

to their religion, the apostate would have been treated with extreme rigour. Perhaps the best-authenticated case of capital punishment for heresy before the year 1400 A.D. is that of a deacon who in the year 1222, because he had become a Jew for the love of a Jewess ("pro quadam Iudaea"), was degraded by Stephen Langton, Archbishop of Canterbury, at a provincial council held at Oxford, and then delivered over to the sheriff as representing the civil power and forthwith burned[1]. There is grave doubt as to the legality of the latter part of this punishment; there seems to have been no sort of judicial proceeding of any kind when once the unfortunate cleric was handed over to the civil power; nor can it be determined under what precise enactment the capital punishment was ordered, and the sheriff who carried it out was Fawkes of Breauté, a man notorious for high-handed and lawless acts of violence. The infliction of the death penalty for heresy was, however, common on the continent, and this particular case (the offence being a flagrant one), though viewed with surprise by contemporaries, seems to have met with general approval. It cannot, however, be taken as an authority that heresy would in ordinary cases be visited with severe temporal punishment. The impotence of the law is made manifest by the complete failure of the measures taken against Wycliffe and his followers, and in May of the year 1382, when the Wycliffite controversy was at its height, the clergy actually managed to fraudulently introduce into the statute book an ordinance enabling the arrest and imprisonment of heretics; but in October of the same year the Commons represented to the King that the pretended statute had never received their assent and it was accordingly repealed[2]. Wycliffe, the arch-heretic,

[1] Bracton, f. 124, vol. II, p. 300. Ann. Wykes, p. 63. Matthew Paris, vol. III, p. 71, says he was hanged. See Maitland, *Canon Law in the Church of England*, pp. 158–179.

[2] The statute is 5 Rich. II, stat. 2, cap. 5. See *Statutes of the Realm*, II, p. 25; *Rot. Parl.* III, 125 and 141; "The case of Heresy," 12 *Rep.* 56.

was allowed to die a natural death, and it was not until the beginning of the reign of Henry IV that a thoroughly reliable weapon for the suppression of heresy was placed in the hands of the Church. In the year 1401 the famous statute *de Haeretico* was passed; it enacted that no one should preach or write contrary to the Catholic faith or determination of holy church, or hold any conventicles or schools for teaching such doctrines, or favour or maintain any such teacher, and it empowered the diocesan to cause any one "defamed or evidently suspected" of being guilty of any of the offences enumerated in the statute to be arrested and detained in prison until he should canonically purge himself and abjure his heretical and erroneous opinions. The diocesan was to openly and judicially proceed against him according to the canonical decrees within three months of the arrest, and if he were convicted he was to be imprisoned and fined after the "manner and quality of the offence" at the discretion of the diocesan, but if he should refuse to abjure or after abjuration should relapse, so that according to the holy canons he ought to be left to the secular court, then he is to be handed over to the sheriff or other proper officer who shall receive him and "before the People in a high place do to be burnt[1]." Before the statute was promulgated, and while the Parliament which passed it was still sitting, William Sawtre was pronounced by Arundel, Archbishop of Canterbury, in the provincial council, a relapsed heretic, degraded and committed to the secular court. A writ was accordingly issued by the King in Parliament ordering the heretic to be burned[2], and the sentence was

The Act declaring 5 Rich. II, stat. 2, cap. 5 void was omitted (it is said through the craft of the clergy) from the published editions of the statutes; therefore in the days of the Reformation 5 Rich. II, stat. 2, cap. 5 was treated as still subsisting, but it could hardly have been acted upon until the action of the House of Commons had been forgotten. It was finally repealed by the Statute Law Revision Act, 1863.

[1] 2 Henry IV, c. 15. *Statutes of the Realm*, II, p. 125.

[2] A copy of the writ is to be found in *Rot. Parl.* III, 459.

carried out. The writ is dated February 26, though the Parliament which passed the statute *de Haeretico* did not break up until March 10, and this fact is the main basis of the argument that after the statute *de Haeretico* had been formally repealed, heretics might still be committed to the flames because the writ *de Haeretico comburendo* could issue at common law independently of the statute. Fourteen years later it was thought right to still further increase the severity of the law. 2 Hen. V, stat. 1, cap. 7 provides that the chancellor, justices, and magistrates shall make an oath to use all diligence in destroying all manner of heresies and errors, commonly called Lollardries, and that all persons convict of heresy and left to the secular power according to the laws of holy church shall forfeit their lands and tenements as in the case of attainder for felony, and that their goods and chattels shall also be forfeited to the King. These acts remained in full force till the year 1533, and were frequently resorted to. They placed almost unlimited power in the hands of the Church. There was no definition of heresy, and the bishops were thus empowered to punish any views which were at variance with their own. The procedure was also most drastic; a person once pronounced to be an obstinate or relapsed heretic was handed over to the civil power, which had no alternative but to execute the utmost rigour of the law. We can thus explain the total absence of any effort to establish a Jewish colony in England after the banishment from Spain in 1492. The knowledge of the severity of the English law combined with the memory of the cruelties that accompanied the expulsion two hundred years before would effectually discountenance any such attempt.

Under Henry VIII and Edward VI the law as to heresy was considerably altered, but it was not varied in such a way as to give any sort of toleration to those who held principles in conflict with the doctrines proclaimed by the sovereign as supreme head of the Church as binding on all its members. Many heretics were put to death in the reign of Henry VIII, and in the short reign of Edward VI at least two persons were burned for heresy[1]. Mary, shortly after her accession, procured the passing of an "Acte for the renueing of three Estatutes made for the punishment of Heresies," providing that the three statutes enacted in the reigns of Richard II, Henry IV, and Henry V, already mentioned, should "from the xxth day of Januarye next coming be revived and be in full force strengthe and effecte to all Intentes construcions and purposes for ever[2]." The fierce and merciless persecution that ensued has caused a horrible but not undeserved epithet to be added to the name of the first Queen regnant of England, and though the number of the victims may have been exaggerated in after years, hundreds were brought to the stake within the short period of less than four years that elapsed before the Queen's death[3]. When Elizabeth came to the throne, the law was again recast. The first Act of Parliament passed in her reign, commonly called the Act of Supremacy (1 Eliz. cap. 1, sect. 15) expressly repealed the Act of Philip and Mary under which the persecutions had taken place, as also the former statutes for the punishment of heresies revived by that Act; but it was by no means intended to allow heresy and error to go unpunished, and therefore by sect. 17 jurisdiction for the visitation "of all manner of errors, heresies, schisms, abuses, offences, contempts, and enormities" was annexed to the crown, and by the following section the Queen was empowered to appoint commissioners to exercise her ecclesiastical jurisdiction, and to visit, reform, and correct

[1] The principal statutes are 25 Hen. VIII, cap. 14, and 31 Hen. VIII, cap. 14 (the Act of the Six Articles), 1 Edw. VI, cap. 12, 1 Edw. VI, cap. 1, and 2 & 3 Edw. VI, cap. 1 (see sect. 3). The last two, though obsolete, are still technically in force. For the whole subject see Stephen's *History of Criminal Law*, vol. II, pp. 453–460.

[2] 1 & 2 Phil. and Mary, cap. 6.

[3] The exact number is given as 277. For the persecution see Dodd's *Church History*, vol. II, pp. 101–109; Pike's *History of Crime*, vol. II, pp. 57–60, and 613.

all errors, heresies, &c., "to the pleasure of Almighty God, the increase of virtue, and the conservation of the peace and unity of this realm"; but a later section (sect. 36) limited the power of the commissioners so appointed, by declaring that nothing should be adjudged heresy unless determined to be heresy by the authority of the canonical scriptures, or by certain general councils, or by the high court of Parliament, with the assent of the clergy in their convocation. This restriction was no doubt intended, and did in fact operate, to exempt Roman Catholics from prosecution for heresy—Papists obnoxious to the government were proceeded against for other crimes—but it could not in any way relieve or exempt Jews, or any one who impugned the sacred doctrine of the Trinity. Although the procedure established by the statutes passed under the Lancastrian kings was abolished, it seems to have been assumed that a culprit in the case of contumacy could be burned, and that the writ *de Haeretico comburendo* would issue at common law. There are several instances of this having taken place. Two Anabaptists were burned in the year 1575, and two Arians as late as 1612. One of these last, Bartholomew Legatt, was charged with holding thirteen damnable tenets, most or all of which are held by every believing Jew; the last two are short and are here inserted from the collection of state trials: "12. That Christ by his Godhead wrought no miracle. 13. That Christ is not to be prayed unto[1]." There has been considerable discussion among lawyers as to the legality of the punishment in these latter cases; into this discussion it is not our purpose to enter; it is enough to state the fact that the convictions took place and that the extreme penalty was enforced, to show what might have been the position of professing Jews openly living and practising their religion in this country.

Since the year 1612 no execution for heresy has taken place in England, nor were offenders, if it was intended to

[1] 2 *State Trials*, p. 729.

deal severely with them, brought before the ecclesiastical courts. They were, however, dealt with by the Court of High Commission, which had been constituted in its ultimate form in the year 1583 under the powers supposed to be conferred on the crown by the eighteenth section of the Act of Supremacy, the substance of which has already been given. The commissioners had no power to order capital punishment, but they were authorized to award "such punishment by fine, imprisonment, censure of the church or otherwise, or by all or any of the said ways, and to take such order for the redress of the same, as by their wisdom and discretions should be thought meet and convenient"; and these penalties were unsparingly inflicted. Their mode of procedure was most arbitrary, and by contemporaries not inaptly compared to that of the Inquisition. There was as a rule no jury, though the court could if it wished summon a jury; arrests were made without any legal warrant; the accused were punished, though there was no evidence against them, except such as was wrung out of their own mouths by means of the *ex officio* oath. "In two points alone it was distinguished from the Inquisition of Southern Europe. It was incompetent to inflict the punishment of death, and it was not permitted to extract confessions by means of physical torture." Such a court could be made a terrible engine of oppression by a zealous persecutor, for it assumed authority not merely to try but to seek out offenders; for example, on April 1, 1634, when Laud had held the primacy but a few months, a circular letter was sent by the commissioners to all officers of the peace in the kingdom, of the following tenor: "There remain in divers parts of the kingdom sundry sort of separatists, moralists, and sectaries, as namely—Brownists, Anabaptists, Arians, Traskites, Familists, and some other sorts, who, upon Sundays and other festival days, under pretence of repetition of sermons, ordinarily use to meet together in great numbers in private houses and other obscure places, and there keep private conventicles and exercises of religion by law prohibited, to the corrupting of sundry his Majesty's good subjects, manifest contempt of his Highness's laws and disturbance of the Church. For reformation whereof the persons addressed are to enter any house where they shall have intelligence that such conventicles are held, and in every room thereof search for persons assembled and for all unlicensed books, and bring all such persons and books found before the Ecclesiastical Commission as shall be thought meet[1]." The circular makes no mention of Jews; had Laud and his associates known that they were at this very time beginning to creep secretly into the kingdom, this omission would hardly have been made.

The court had always been unpopular, and the oppressive use made of it by Laud caused its abolition by the Long Parliament in 1640 by a statute (16 Car. I, cap. 11). After reciting, "Whereas by colour of some words . . . in the Act (of Supremacy) . . . commissioners have to the great and insufferable wrong and oppression of the King's subjects, used to fine and imprison them, and to exercise other authority not belonging to ecclesiastical jurisdiction . . . and divers other great mischiefs and inconveniences have also ensued to the King's subjects," section 18 of the Act of Supremacy, under which the letters patent constituting the High Commission were issued, was repealed. A further section dealt with the other ecclesiastical courts, depriving them of all power to inflict "any pain, penalty, fine, amercement, imprisonment, or other corporal punishment upon any of the King's subjects," or to administer the *ex officio* oath. Thus after 1640, though heresy was not removed from the list of crimes, there was no court which could inflict any higher punishment than a purely ecclesiastical penalty. After the Restoration all the provisions of this statute, excepting those abolishing the Court of High Commission and the *ex officio* oath, were repealed (13 Car. II, stat. 1, cap. 12), and the power of inflicting physical punishment

[1] *Cal. S. P. Domestic*, 1633–4, p. 538.

was thus restored to the ecclesiastical courts, but some years afterwards, in 1679, it was further abridged by 29 Car. II, cap. 9, which abolished the writ *de Haeretico comburendo*, and all punishment by death in pursuance of ecclesiastical censures," reserving to the ecclesiastical courts only the power to punish atheism, blasphemy, heresy, &c., "by excommunication, deprivation, degradation, and other ecclesiastical censures not extending to death." This is still the law, but there is no record of any prosecution for heresy ever having taken place since the ecclesiastical courts were shorn of their power of inflicting corporal punishment by the Long Parliament in 1640.

Such was in outline the law of heresy; it remains now to consider the second impediment to a Jewish resettlement, the Law of Uniformity. The expression Church and State is a common, almost a hackneyed one, and we are apt to forget that there was once a time when no one, who was not an adherent of the Church, could be a citizen of the State; and when severe pains and penalties were incurred by non-attendance at church or by attendance at any religious meeting not sanctioned by the ecclesiastical authorities. Prior to the Reformation the Church had been content with punishing under the name of heretics those who ventured to proclaim doctrines inconsistent with her creed; the zeal engendered by the movement for reform prompted the punishment, though with somewhat milder penalties, of those who neglected or refused to take part in public worship as by law established. The first statutory provision was a very mild one. The Act of Uniformity (1 Eliz. cap. 2) after enacting that the Book of Common Prayer should be used in all churches and ordaining penalties for those who depraved it, provides (sect. 14) that "all and every person inhabiting within this realm, or any other the Queen's Majesty's dominions, shall diligently and faithfully, having no lawful or reasonable excuse to be absent, endeavour themselves to resort to their parish church or chapel accustomed, or upon reasonable let thereof, to some usual place where common prayer and such service of God shall be used in such time of let, upon every Sunday, and other days ordained and used to be kept as holy days, and then and there to abide orderly and soberly during the time of the common prayer, preaching, or other service of God there to be used and ministered," upon pain of punishment by the censures of the Church and of forfeiting for every offence twelve pence to the use of the poor of the parish. The penalty was only small, but sufficient to cause all except the very wealthy to conform, especially as the law was strictly interpreted. Serjeant Hawkins[1] says of it: "he who misbehaves himself in the church, or misses either morning or evening prayer, or goes away before the whole service is over, is as much within the statute as he who is wholly absent; and he who is absent from his own parish church shall be put to prove where he went to church[2]." It was, however, thought too lenient and was supplemented by an Act to retain the Queen's Majesty's subjects in their due obedience (23 Eliz. cap. 1), sect. 5 of which ordains that every person above the age of sixteen years who does not attend church shall forfeit to the Queen's Majesty twenty pounds for every month's absence. This penalty was in addition to the forfeiture of twelve pence imposed by the Act of Uniformity, and a month was interpreted as a lunar month, so that thirteen penalties might be imposed every year. If the penalty was not paid, the offender was liable under a later statute (29 Eliz. cap. 6, sect. 4) to have all his goods and two-thirds of his lands seized to the use of the crown; one-third of his lands (if he was fortunate enough to be a landowner or a leaseholder) being left him for the maintenance and relief of his family. But even this was not enough.

[1] *Pleas of the Crown*, Bk. I, cap. 10, sect. 4.

[2] It was not till 1704 that Chief Justice Holt decided "that if a man repaired to any other chapel, it would be good excuse for his not coming to his parish church, but then he must plead it." See *Britton* v. *Standish*, Cases Temp. Holt 141 & 3 Salk. 88.

Twelve years later a still more stringent Act (35 Eliz. cap. 1) bearing the same title was passed. Any one who obstinately refused to come to church without any lawful cause, and in addition (1) persuaded any other person to abstain from going to church or receiving the communion administered according to the rites of the Church, or to be present at any unlawful assemblies, conventicles, or meetings, or (2) "either of himself or by the persuasion of any other" willingly joined in or was present at any such assemblies, conventicles, or meetings under colour or pretence of any exercise of religion contrary to that prescribed by the Act of Uniformity, was to be committed to prison until he should conform and make open submission and declaration of his conformity. If he did not conform within three months he was to abjure the realm of England and all the Queen's dominions for ever. If he refused to abjure or after abjuration did not depart out of the realm, he was to be adjudged a felon and suffer as in the case of felony (i. e. death and forfeiture of lands, goods, and chattels), without benefit of clergy.

Persons neglecting to come to church were called Recusants; and if they absented themselves because they were Papists, Popish Recusants[1]. This latter class was subject to still further disabilities. In Elizabeth's reign they were not allowed to remove more than five miles from home without licence (35 Eliz. cap. 2). The alarm which succeeded the discovery of Gunpowder Plot—an event making so great an impression on the popular mind that its anniversary is still celebrated with more public enthusiasm than any other event in our history, not excepting the destruction of the Spanish Armada or the battle of Waterloo—caused the enactment of still more stringent measures. These were the Act for the better discovering and repressing of popish recusants (3 Jac. I, cap. 4) and the Act to prevent and avoid dangers which grow by popish recu-

[1] The term Popish Recusants was afterwards defined by statute, so as to include many persons who were not Roman Catholics.

sants (3 Jac. I, cap. 5). As many of the provisions of these Acts might not have applied to Jews, it is unnecessary to enter into them here. One provision, however, which was undoubtedly not confined to Papists, cannot be passed over. By sect. 13 of the former Act "for the better trial how his Majesty's subjects stand affected in point of their loyalty and due obedience," all persons over the age of eighteen who had been convicted or even merely indicted of any recusancy for not attending divine service, or who had not received the sacrament twice within the year might be compelled to take an oath, afterwards known as the oath of allegiance, the terms of which are set out in sect. 15. They are framed with the intention of being obnoxious to Papists, and expressly renounce and deny any authority to the Pope, so that many Roman Catholics who were ready to take the oath prescribed by the Act of Supremacy (1 Eliz. cap. 1, sect. 19) found themselves unable to take the new oath, the last clause of which must have been unacceptable to a religious Jew. It reads as follows: "And all these things I do plainly and sincerely acknowledge and swear, according to these express words by me spoken, and according to the plain and common sense and understanding of the same words without any equivocation or mental evasion, or secret reservation whatsoever: and I do make this recognition and acknowledgment heartily, willingly, and truly, *upon the true faith of a Christian*, So help me God." The oath itself was abolished in 1688 by the Bill of Rights (1 W. & M., sess. 2, cap. 1, sect. 3); but the final words, now for the first time introduced, were retained in other forms of oaths and declarations and, as will be hereafter shown, for a long time proved an insurmountable obstacle to the Jews in their struggle for the acquisition of political rights[1]. The Acts contain other sections also which were not confined to Popish recusants;

[1] Four years afterwards provision was made for more effectually administering this oath to persons neither indicted nor convicted of recusancy. See 7 Jac. I, cap. 6.

e.g., sects. 8 and 11 of the former enable the crown to refuse the penalty of twenty pounds a month for not attending church imposed by the statute of Elizabeth, and to seize and retain two-thirds of all the lands belonging to the offender, even although no default had been made in the payment of the penalty or the amount had been actually tendered. And by sects. 3 to 5 of the latter all persons with certain exceptions, who had not repaired to church for the space of three months, were ordered to depart from the city of London and ten miles compass of the same; and by sect. 8 of the same Act convicted recusants were disabled from holding legal, military, or naval offices, and from practising the professions of the law and medicine. Moreover, to prevent evasion of these penalties and disabilities by merely formal attendance at church, it was enacted that a recusant who conformed and repaired to church should also be required to take the sacrament of the Lord's Supper once at least every year.

Such was the legislation against recusants, which was not finally repealed until the middle of the last century [1]. We are now able to sum up the legal position in which Jews, in the early years of Charles I's reign, when they undoubtedly began to settle here, would find themselves. There was no law to prevent their coming here. If the banishment in 1290 had been effected by royal proclamation, the force of that proclamation had long been spent; if on the other hand it had been by Act of Parliament, as many persons at that time believed, the Act itself had long been lost, and any Jew for whose expulsion legal process might be brought could challenge his adversary to produce the Act. If this initial difficulty had been got over and the court had been induced by reasoning similar to Prynne's that there must have been such an Act of Parliament and that it was lost, then it would remain to

[1] 7 & 8 Vict. cap. 102 repealed most of the penal enactments so far as Roman Catholics were concerned; 9 & 10 Vict. cap. 59 repealed the remaining penal enactments, including those against Jews.

consider what effect that would have upon Jews coming to England in the reign of King Charles. The first precedent cited by Prynne is the Act banishing the Despensers, and it would have been necessary to assume, as Prynne does, that the Act banishing the Jews was in similar terms. The enacting words of that statute are as follows: "Wherefore we Peers of the Land . . . do award that Sir Hugh le Despenser the Son and Sir Hugh le Despenser the Father, be disherited for ever . . . and that they be utterly exiled out of the land of England, without returning at any time, unless it be by the Assent of our Lord the King and by the Assent of the Prelates, Earls and Barons, and that in Parliament duly summoned . . . and if they do return, then be it done unto them, as enemies of the King and of the Kingdom[1]." Substitute the words "Jews in England" for the words "Sir Hugh le Despenser the Son and Sir Hugh le Despenser the Father" and it is seen at once that the Act would apply only to the persons actually banished, for there are no words to include heirs, issue, or children; but even if such words were embodied in the Act, it would have been quite impossible to prove that a Spanish Jew living in the seventeenth century was an heir, descendant, or in any wise connected with the English Jews, all of them of German origin, of the thirteenth century. The residence of Jews in England was therefore lawful, but they would of course be subject to all the laws which bound aliens living here; though they would not be liable to the disabilities imposed on the Judaei by the legislation of Henry III and Edward I, because the special status of serfdom or villenage to which those disabilities had been attached, though not legally abolished, had practically become obsolete. On the other hand, if they attempted to practise their religion they were liable to be charged with heresy in the ecclesiastical courts or to be summoned and persecuted by the Court of High Commission; in any case the common law would compel them to

[1] *Statutes of the Realm*, vol. I, p. 184.

regularly take part in the services of a church, which they believed to be idolatrous. If they neglected to attend they were subject to severe penalties, and if in addition they took part in a Jewish service they could be made to abjure the realm, and should they still remain here they were guilty of felony and denied all benefit of clergy. Thus the real impediments to a Jewish settlement were the impossibility of setting up a Jewish synagogue and the necessity of taking part in the religion of the established church. The first of these obstacles was not removed until the reign of Charles II; we will now explain how the second was obviated in the time of that king's father.

Before the commencement of the seventeenth century, it had become customary for the monarchs of Europe to maintain legations in each other's capitals, and these legations were, by the principles of international law, which were even at this time beginning to be recognized, regarded as exterritorial—i.e. as not subject to the ordinary law of the land. Accordingly the law of heresy and the statutes against recusants would not apply to persons attached to any foreign embassy, but they would apply to all other foreigners coming to this country. Therefore on the marriage of Charles I with Henrietta Maria elaborate provision was made by treaty for the religion of the queen and her suite. However, in the treaty made with Spain in the year 1630 a clause was inserted which was interpreted as entitling all Spanish subjects, though not belonging to the embassy, to exemption from the penal laws against recusants. In express words the King of Spain undertook that subjects of the King of England who might be in his dominions for the purposes of commerce should not suffer any molestation or disturbance on account of their religion, provided that they gave no occasion for scandal. No similar promise was made by the King of England in respect of Spanish merchants, but the reason for this was that there were very few likely to remain here for more than one month and so render themselves liable to the laws against recusants, and it was well understood that the promise was reciprocal and that it would not be fulfilled unless a like measure of toleration was extended to Spanish subjects in England[1]. It was shortly after the signature of this treaty that a few Jews ventured to permanently settle in England, but they came not as Jews but as Spaniards, and sheltering themselves under the protection of the treaty were able to avoid taking part in the services of the English church. They were crypto-Jews and thought by all their neighbours to be Catholics, and no doubt occasionally attended mass at the ambassador's chapel, in order to ingratiate themselves with the embassy. Some had fled from Spain through fear of the Inquisition, but there is no evidence of any kind that they ever attempted to practise the Jewish religion here, and as it was necessary to keep on friendly terms with the representative of the Catholic king they were not likely to do anything to forfeit his protection. Among the earliest of these new comers was Antonio Fernandez Carvajal; he must have arrived here in or before the year 1635, long before the Great Rebellion commenced, for in the letters of denization which were granted to him by Cromwell on Aug. 17, 1655, he is described as having "for the space of twentie yeares and upwards

[1] The treaty is printed in Rymer's *Foedera*. The words of clause 19 are: "Et quia iura commercii quae ex pace consequuntur infructuosa reddi non debent, prout redderentur si subditis Serenissimi Regis Angliae dum eunt et redeunt ad Regna et Dominia dicti Serenissimi Regis Hispaniarum, et ibi ex causa commercii, vel negotii moram trahunt, eis molestia inferatur ex causa conscientiae, Ideo ut commercium sit tutum et securum tam in terra quam in mari, dictus Serenissimus Rex Hispaniarum curabit et providebit, ne ex praedicta causa conscientiae contra iura commercii molestentur et inquietentur, ubi scandalum alii non dederint." *Foedera*, vol. VIII, pt. 3, p. 143 (edition of 1742). In the treaty of 1667, which was renewed by the treaty of Versailles in 1783, the same clause occurs, but the reciprocal clause is expressed, "and the said King of Great Britain shall likewise provide, for the same reasons, that the subjects of the King of Spain shall not be molested or disturbed for their conscience against the laws of commerce, so long as they give no public scandal or offence." Hertslet's *Collection of Treaties*, vol. II, p. 152.

been an Inhabitant in this nation." When he had been here for some years he with other merchant strangers was prosecuted as a recusant, but the English merchants who had factors in Spain petitioned the House of Lords to stay the proceedings on the ground that the result of a conviction would be that their own factors would be similarly treated in Spain and thereby be compelled either to forsake their religion or abandon the country, which would be a matter of great concernment, as there were above one hundred English subjects resident in Spain for every Spaniard resident here. The petition appears to have been granted and the proceedings stayed [1]. Whether the other merchants attacked at the same time as Carvajal were also Jews we do not know, but we do know from the depositions in the Robles case that there were at this time several other Jews in London who were or professed to be Spaniards and therefore obtained immunity from the penalties imposed upon recusants. It is important not to exaggerate this indulgence; it did not extend to the toleration of any sort of Jewish worship and it was itself withdrawn by the outbreak of the war with Spain in 1656.

This position could not have been satisfactory to the Jewish communities abroad. If they knew of the existence of and held communication with the crypto-Jews here, they must have seen that the situation of their brethren in England was little if at all better than that of the Marranos in Spain; they were bound to take part week by week in the idolatrous worship of the Protestant church or else to obtain the protection of the Spanish embassy, as the price of which they would have to be occasionally present at the no less objectionable Catholic mass, and furthermore to completely disguise their Jewish faith even to the extent of refraining from entering into the covenant of Abraham.

[1] For the petition see *Lords' Journals*, vol. VII, p. 141. It was presented Jan. 16, 164$\frac{4}{5}$. For Carvajal see "The First English Jew," by Lucien Wolf, *Trans. Jewish Hist. Soc.*, vol. II, pp. 14–46.

In neither case could they meet for worship according to Jewish rites. The establishment of a synagogue or the organization of a community was impossible, and even private prayers could only be indulged in under the cover of the strictest secrecy.

At length a brighter prospect seemed to open out; the Great Rebellion had broken out and proved successful, and the Protestant Dissenters who had formerly inveighed against the persecution of the church and advocated universal toleration were invested with the powers of government. And yet in the moment of their triumph they forgot or repudiated the precepts and maxims which had been so dear to them in the hour of persecution. True it is that the law against heresy was practically repealed by the abolition of the Court of High Commission and the power of temporal punishment formerly exercised by the ecclesiastical courts, but the Parliament claimed the right to itself take cognizance of offences against religion, and in the assertion of this claim, which was not abandoned until the Restoration, inflicted penalties even more severe than those formerly imposed by the Court of High Commission[1]. It was only with exceptional cases that it could itself deal, and accordingly in May, 1648, it made an Ordinance for punishing Blasphemies and Heresies. The ordinance enumerates eight distinct heresies or errors (including, for example, maintaining that Jesus Christ is not the Son of God and that the New Testament is not the word of God), and provides that persons found guilty of any of them, unless they recant and abjure their errors, shall suffer the pains of death as in case of felony, without benefit of clergy; if they recant they are to be imprisoned until they find sureties against a repetition of the offence, but if they repeat the offence after having recanted they are to suffer death as in case of felony without benefit of

[1] See the case of Paul Best, who had asserted that Christ was merely and properly a man (Goodwin, II, pp. 252 seq.), and James Nayler (5 *State Trials*, 801).

clergy. The ordinance also enumerates other errors, which are to be visited with less severe penalties [1]. The laws against recusants were not interfered with, but the church services at which attendance was compulsory were to be conducted in accordance with the new Service-book, called the Directory, which had recently been framed by the Westminster Divines; and two ordinances were passed, one in March, 1645, providing that "the Book of Common Prayer shall not be henceforth used, but the Directory for Publique Worship," and the other on the 23rd of August of the same year ordering "the Directorie to be put in execution with penalties for using the book of Common Prayer [2]." The penalties were five pounds for the first offence, ten pounds for the second offence, and for the third offence "one whole year's imprisonment without bail or mainprize." These ordinances gave great satisfaction to the Presbyterians who possessed a majority in the Long Parliament, and who, having destroyed the power of the church were eager to establish their own form of worship and invest themselves with all the powers of the church they had supplanted, including the right to persecute all who held religious opinions different from their own. But this the Independents, who besides having a strong minority in the House, had the preponderating voice in the council of the army, which in those troublous times really governed the land, were bound to dispute. After a prolonged struggle the Independents gained the upper hand, and on December 6, 1648, succeeded with the help of the army in excluding their Presbyterian opponents from all share in the deliberations of the Parliament and the government of the nation. Again the party which had stood for toleration was successful, and the Jews who had long cast anxious eyes upon the growing commerce of England and desired to share it, were not slow to take advantage of so favourable an opportunity. The Council of Mechanics at

[1] Scobell, part 1, p. 149.
[2] Scobell, part 2, pp. 75 and 97.

Whitehall had at the end of December voted a toleration of all religions whatsoever, "not excepting Turkes nor Papists nor Jews[1]." A petition on their behalf was prepared by the Jews of Amsterdam; it was in the name of Johanna Cartwright a widow, and Ebenezer her son, freeborn of England, and resident in the city of Amsterdam, and prayed that the Statute of Banishment made against the Jews might be repealed and that they under the Christian banner of charity and brotherly love, might "be again received and permitted to trade and dwell in this Land as now they do in the Netherlands." The petition was presented to the General Council of the Officers of the Army, under the command of Lord Fairfax, at Whitehall on January 5, $164\frac{8}{9}$, and favourably received with a promise to take it into speedy consideration "when the present more public affairs" were dispatched[2]. The present more public affairs were the trial and execution of the king and the settlement of the government, and proved to be of such momentous concern that the petition of the Jews was completely overlooked; at least nothing was done upon it nor was the law altered or relaxed in their favour. And yet a belief was spread abroad that the petition had been granted. A circular was published by the disappointed and defeated Presbyterians entitled "the last damnable Designe of Cromwell and Ireton and their Junto or Caball," in which it is stated that "their real designe is to plunder and disarme the City of London and all the country round about . . . and so sell it (the plunder) in bulk to the Jews,

[1] Pragmaticus, Dec. 19–26. The Council of War had also on Christmas Day voted "a Toleration of all religions." *History of the Independency*, part 2, p. 50.

[2] The petition was printed and there is a copy of it in the British Museum, King's Pamphlets, E 557, Art. 17, and is reprinted in Hag., *Cons. Cases*, vol. I, Ap. No. 1. For the whole transaction see the *Clarke Papers*, vol. II, p. 172; *History of the Independency*, part 2, pp. 60 and 83; and "A Perfect Diurnall of some passages in Parliament and the daily proceedings of the Army under His Excellency the Lord Fairfax, from Munday the 1 of Janu. till Munday the 8 of Janu. 1648."

whom they have lately admitted to set up their banks and magazines of Trade amongst us contrary to an Act of Parliament for their banishment[1]." Nor was this belief confined to the political opponents of the dominant faction here, for in the collection of original letters found among the Duke of Ormonde's papers is to be found the following:—

"Rouen, March $\frac{17}{27}$, 164$\frac{8}{9}$.

"This morning I happened to have some discourse with a Jew that spake English, and asking him how he liked the Parliament and Army of England, now they had revoked the Laws that were made against the Jews; he told me, that nevertheless he thought that there were no such villains in the world as they are, and believed that none of his Religion would ever adventure themselves among such bloody traitors as had murdered their own King[2]."

But yet no one at the present time would seriously argue that the readmission of the Jews into England dates from January, 1649, nor should we give more weight to similar expressions which seem to indicate a successful issue to the negotiations conducted by Menasseh Ben Israel some six or seven years later, which in the end proved equally abortive. The ascendency of the Independents lasted till the death of Cromwell in 1658, but during the whole of it, the law was in no way altered to the advantage of the Jews. True, a milder ordinance was passed for the punishment of atheistical, blasphemous and execrable opinions; as for instance maintaining that there is neither heaven nor hell, neither salvation nor damnation, the penalty being six months imprisonment for the first offence and banishment for the second, and if any one returned after being banished he was to suffer as in case of felony without benefit of clergy[3]. This ordinance, cruel as it is, is milder than the one passed by the Presbyterians in May, 1684,

[1] *History of the Independency* [4to, 1649], at p. 61.

[2] Ormonde's *Letters*, vol. I, p. 233.

[3] See the ordinance of Aug., 1650, cap. 22, given in Scobell, II, p. 124.

for the extreme penalty could only be inflicted in the case of a second offence, but the earlier ordinance was not repealed, and as the offences enumerated by the two enactments were different, both were technically in force at the same time. The advocates of toleration throughout the period of their power showed no disposition to abandon the weapons of persecution :

Et qui nolunt occidere quenquam
Posse volunt.

It may be said on their behalf that the earlier and more cruel ordinance was never put into execution by them, but on the other hand there is no record of its having been enforced by the Presbyterians either, and the later ordinance was undoubtedly acted upon; the proceedings against George Fox, the Quaker, being a well-known instance [1].

Though the Independents did not repeal the law relating to blasphemy, they found it necessary to materially amend the laws against recusants. In spite of having obtained the supreme power, they formed, if numbers only were counted, a small if not insignificant minority of the general population. They had as strong objections to the new Directory as to the old Book of Common Prayer, nor could they hope to establish any form of worship which should be both consonant to their own religious ideas and acquiesced in by the other rival sects. Accordingly, shortly after the victory of Dunbar the Parliament passed an Act for the repeal of several clauses in Statutes imposing penalties for not coming to church. It recites that "divers religious and peaceable people, well-affected to the prosperity of the Commonwealth, have not only been molested and imprisoned, but also brought into danger of abjuring their country, or in case of return to suffer death as felons, to the great disquiet and utter ruin of such good and godly people, and to the detriment of the Commonwealth," and repeals all clauses of the Act of Uniformity (1 Eliz. cap. 2),

[1] Goodwin, vol. IV, p. 309.

and the Acts for retaining the Queen's subjects in their due obedience (35 Eliz. cap. 1, and 23 Eliz. cap. 1), and all clauses in any other Act whereby any penalty is imposed on any person whatsoever, for not repairing to their respective parish churches. But the exemption from penalties was subject to this proviso, that "to the end that no profane or licentious persons may take occasion . . . to neglect the performance of religious duties . . . all and every person and persons within this Commonwealth . . . shall (having no reasonable excuse for their absence) upon every Lord's day . . . diligently resort to some public place where the service and worship of God is exercised, or shall be present at some other place in the practice of some religious duty, either of prayer, preaching, reading, or expounding the scriptures or conferring upon the same [1]." Every person not so attending was to be deemed to be an offender against the law and proceeded against accordingly. This proviso would prevent any real measure of relief to the Jews, for attendance at a synagogue, if there had been one in existence, would assuredly not have been held to be a compliance with the Act. Should there be any doubt upon this point, it is cleared away by the religious clauses of the Instrument of Government; the document under which Oliver claimed to exercise his power as Lord Protector. The terms of the Instrument were finally settled before December 16, 1653, on which date it came into force. The clauses relating to religion are Articles 35, 36, and 37, and provide that the Christian religion shall be publicly professed, but that to this public profession none shall be compelled by penalties or otherwise, and all who professed faith in God by Jesus Christ (though differing from the doctrine publicly held forth) should be protected in the profession and exercise of their religion "so as they abuse not this liberty to the civil injury of others and to the actual disturbance of the public peace on their parts, provided this liberty be not extended to Popery or Prelacy,

[1] Ordinance of Sept. 27, 1650; Scobell, II, p. 131.

nor to such as under the profession of Christ, hold forth and practise licentiousness[1]."

If one thing is certain among the doubts occasioned by the hasty and manifold changes of law which took place during this revolutionary period, it is that freedom of worship was not extended even to all Christian sects; indeed, the majority, as events afterwards proved, were expressly excluded from protection by the last recited article, and no form of worship not in accordance with Christian dogma was at any time legal or authorized throughout the whole period.

Nevertheless, the Jews, encouraged by the reception their overtures had met with in the early part of 1649, had not given up their hopes. The Navigation Act which became law on October 9, 1651[2], caused such friction between England and the Dutch against whose carrying trade it was principally directed, that war between the two nations became almost inevitable, and actually broke out. While the war lasted the negotiations which had been carried on from Amsterdam were naturally suspended. In the month of April, 1654, peace was again proclaimed, and the negotiations were almost immediately resumed. Manuel Martinez Dormido, a member of the well-known family of the Abarbanels, arrived in London early in September, and presented to the Protector two petitions for the readmission of the Jews. These were in due course recommended to the speedy consideration of the Council, but they met with the reception which throughout the interregnum was accorded to all attempts to relax the law in favour of the Jews; the Council did not see its way to make any order in the matter[3]. But the cause was not yet hopeless; in the October of the year following, Menasseh ben Israel, brother-

[1] Gardiner's *Constitutional Documents*, p. 324.

[2] Scobell, II, p. 176.

[3] See *Cal. State Papers*, 1654, pp. 393 and 407; Goodwin, IV, p. 47, note; *Trans. Jewish Hist. Soc.*, vol. III, where the text of the petitions is given at pp. 88–93.

in-law to Dormido, and a learned Rabbi, came from Amsterdam to London, and was hospitably received by the Protector; who was willing to admit the Jews and even tolerate their worship, if conducted privately and without scandal, but who was at the same time determined not to risk a popular tumult which might not improbably break out if protection was extended to a strange religion without the previous sanction and approbation of the leaders of the people. It was with this view that a conference was summoned to meet at Whitehall to discuss the question. So much has recently been written about the conference and the events which led to it, that it will be sufficient here to extract from the old Parliamentary History the Narrative published by order of Cromwell and his Council [1].

"Whitehall, December 4.

"Divers eminent Ministers of the Nation, having been called hither by Letter from the Lord Protector, were present with his Highness and the Council in the Council-Chamber; when the following Proposals, made by certain Jews, of whom Rabbi Menasseh Ben Israel, of Amsterdam, was the Chief, were read to them.

"'These are the Graces and Favours which, in the Name of my Hebrew Nation, I Menasseh Ben Israel do request of your Most Serene Highness, whom God make prosperous, and give happy Success to, in all your Enterprises, as your humble Servant doth wish and desire.

"'I. The first Thing I desire of your Highness is, That our Hebrew Nation may be received and admitted into this puissant Commonwealth, under the Protection and Safeguard of your Highness even as the Natives themselves. And, for greater Security in Time to come, I do supplicate your Highness to cause an Oath to be given (if you shall think it fit) to all the Heads and Generals of Arms to defend us upon all Occasions.

[1] Printed by Henry Hills, printer to His Highness the Lord Protector. *Parl. Hist.*, vol. XX, p. 474.

"'2. That it will please your Highness to allow us public Synagogues, not only in England, but also in all other Places under the Power of your Highness; and to observe in all Things our Religion, as we ought.

"'3. That we may have a Place or Coemitery, out of the Town, to bury our Dead, without being troubled by any.

"'4. That we may be permitted to traffic freely in all Sorts of Merchandise, as others.

"'5. That (to the end those who shall come may be for the utility of the People of this Nation, and may live without bringing Prejudice to any, and not give Offence) your Most Serene Highness will make Choice of a Person of Quality, to inform himself of and receive the Passports of those who shall come in; who, upon their Arrival, shall certify him thereof, and oblige themselves, by Oath, to maintain Fealty to your Highness in this Land.

"'6. And (to the Intent they may not be troublesome to the Judges of the Land, touching the Contests and Differences that may arise betwixt those of our Nation) that your Most Serene Highness will give License to the Head of the Synagogue, to take with him two Almoners of his Nation to accord and determine all the Differences and Process, conformable to the Mosaic Law; with Liberty, nevertheless, to appeal from their Sentence to the Civil Judges; the Sum wherein the Parties shall be condemned being first deposited.

"'7. That in case there have been any Laws against our Jewish Nation, they may, in the first Place and before all Things, be revoked; to the end that, by this Means, we may remain with the greater Security under the Safeguard and Protection of your Most Serene Highness.

"'Which things your Most Serene Highness granting to us, we shall always remain most affectionately obliged to pray to God for the Prosperity of your Highness, and of your illustrious and sage Council, that it will please him to give happy Success to all the undertakings of your Most Serene Highness. Amen.'

"The Ministers having heard these Proposals read, desired Time to consider of them, and the next Day was spent in Prayer and Fasting.

"*Dec.* 7. This Day, in the Afternoon, a Conference was held with the Ministers about these Proposals, in the Presence of his Highness the Lord Protector, the Lord President Lawrence, Lord Lambert, Lord Fiennes, and divers more of the Council, with the Lord Chief Justice Glynn, and the Lord Chief Baron Steel. Of the Ministers there were Dr. Thomas Goodwin, Dr. Wilkinson, Dr. Tuckney, Mr. Manton, Mr. Nye, Mr. Bridge, and many others; but nothing being concluded on, another Conference was appointed to be held on the next Wednesday. Accordingly,

"*Dec.* 12. The Conference was renewed in a Withdrawing Room in the Presence of the Lord Protector, where a Committee of the Council were met by the greatest Part of the Ministers and other Persons, approved by his Highness to take the said Proposals into Consideration; but nothing then resolved upon.

"*Dec.* 14. There was another Conference on the same Subject. And,

"*Dec.* 18. The Committee broke up without coming to any Resolution or even a further Adjournment.'

"The Narrative concludes with this Remark, 'That his Highness, at these several Meetings, fully heard the Opinions of the Ministers touching the said Proposals; expressing himself thereupon with Indifference and Moderation, as one that desired only to obtain Satisfaction in a Matter of so high and religious a Concernment; there being many glorious Promises recorded in Holy Scripture, concerning the Calling and Convention of the Jews to the Faith of Christ. But the Reason why nothing was concluded upon was, because his Highness proceeded in this, as in all other Affairs, with good Advice and mature Deliberation.'"

Thus the famous Conference resulted, like all the attempts made during the interregnum, in nothing being done and no alteration in the law being made; Cromwell's good-will was not proof against the prejudice which was displayed at the Conference and which was rampant among the mob outside. Nor did the Lord Protector, actuated as he was at this time by the motives of the astute politician rather than by the feelings of the religious enthusiast, care to press the cause of religious toleration in the teeth of popular opposition; and yet he did not give the petitioners a formal dismissal. And so Rabbi Menasseh remained in London, but with far different hopes to those he cherished on his first arrival. On March 24 of the following year he again took part with six other Jews in presenting a petition to the Protector. The boons prayed for by the petitioners were now very small; they were two only, (1) protection in writing for meeting privately in their own houses for purposes of devotion; (2) a license to bury their dead in a convenient place without the city. But even this petition was not granted. It was referred to the consideration of the Council and no answer was ever returned to it. A few days later, on April 10, Menasseh published his *Vindiciae Iudaeorum*, his last effort to gain the cause he had come to plead. Speaking of the Conference he says: "Mens judgements and sentences were different. Insomuch, that as yet, we have had no finall determination from his Serene Highnesse. Wherefore those few Jewes that were here, despairing of our expected successe, departed hence. And others who desired to come hither, have quitted their hopes, and betaken themselves some to Italy, some to Geneva, where that Commonwealth hath at this time most freely granted them many and great priviledges [1]." But Menasseh, though his *Vindiciae* effected nothing, though no response came to his second petition with its very humble prayer, still

[1] *Vindiciae Iudaeorum*, the seventh section.

stayed behind at his post, hoping against hope. In September, 1657, his son Samuel died in his house, and the pious father having solemnly promised to take his mortal remains to Holland and lay them to rest in consecrated soil there, "at length with his heart ever broken with griefe on losing heer his only sonne and his presious time with all his hopes in this iland he got away with so much breath as lasted, till he came to Midleburg and then he dyed[1]." His mission had proved an utter failure.

[1] Petition of John Sadler to Richard Cromwell (S. P. Dom. Inter., cc. 8), and Petition from Menasseh to Oliver, Sept. 17, 1657 (S. P. Dom. Inter., clvi. 89), both printed in Wolf's *Menasseh Ben Israel's Mission to Oliver Cromwell*, p. lxxxvii.

V.

MENASSEH BEN ISRAEL'S mission had failed. The Conference summoned to consider his proposals had broken up without coming to any resolution; the petition presented in the following spring had received no answer, and at length, after waiting two years, the great Rabbi had returned to his home and friends, giving up the cause for lost. But the publicity given to the mission and the hopes founded upon it were such that many undoubtedly believed that it had met with some measure of success. There are accordingly some few references in contemporary literature to favours conferred upon the Jews by Cromwell. It is probable that all of these refer to the Conference at Whitehall in December, 1655, and there is little doubt that, owing to the attitude that Cromwell had adopted towards Menasseh both before and at the Conference, the impression had got abroad that special privileges had been formally accorded to the Jews. It was to officially contradict this widespread impression that the narrative set out at full length in the last article was published by order of Cromwell and his Council. It would serve no useful purpose to enumerate or comment on all the statements made by the writers of the period, but it will be sufficient to mention the most explicit of them all. John Evelyn writes in his *Memoirs*, December 14, 1655, "Now were the Jews admitted[1]." This must allude to the Conference, for if we turn to the official narrative we find that this was

[1] Evelyn's *Memoirs*, vol. I, p. 288 (1st edition).

the day of the penultimate meeting of the Conference, but we also find that the diarist's statement is untrue, and that no resolution on this or any other point raised at the Conference was ever reached. Nor can there be any reason for casting doubt upon the statement in the official narrative, for it is amply corroborated by Menasseh himself in his *Vindiciae Iudaeorum*[1]. In fact the negotiations of 1655 to 1656 had resulted in precisely the same way as those of seven years earlier, and the statements made in regard to them are entitled to no more weight than those which have already been referred to in dealing with the earlier period. It is, moreover, somewhat remarkable that the learned Dr. Haggard[2] omits all mention of Menasseh and the Conference in his concise but accurate account of this subject. He does, however, allude to the petition of 1648, and it may well be that he regarded Menasseh's mission and the earlier petition as really being only one continuous effort spread over a lengthy period; if such was his view it seems to have been shared by Menasseh himself, who, writing on April 10, 1656, says: "For seven yeares on this behalf, I have endeavoured, and solicited it" (namely an entrance into this Island for the Jews), "by letters, and other means, without any intervall[3]." In any case it would at the present time be almost universally admitted that Dr. Haggard's words, "The question was much agitated, but nothing was done," apply with equal truth to the earlier petition and the great Rabbi's mission seven years later.

During our own and our fathers' times a great change has taken place in the opinions men have formed of Cromwell's character and his place in the history of his country. It was at one time the fashion to write him down a self-seeking hypocrite; but thanks to the powerful advocacy of Thomas Carlyle and other writers contemporary with and subsequent to Carlyle, he has become a great

[1] See the seventh section.
[2] *Cons. Cas.*, vol. I, p. 216.
[3] *Vindiciae Iudaeorum*, sec. 7.

statesman, nay, a hero. In 1841, when this change of view was still in the process of birth, Carlyle wrote of Cromwell: "His dead body was hung in chains; his 'place in History'—place in History, forsooth—has been a place of ignominy, accusation, blackness and disgrace; and here this day who knows if it is not rash in me to be among the first that ever ventured to pronounce him not a knave and liar, but a genuinely honest man[1]?" And so in the course of the apotheosis of the great Oliver, his virtue as an upholder of Religious Toleration has been much dilated upon; and his conduct towards the Jews has been selected as one instance of it. But it should not be forgotten that by the men of his own time Toleration, in those who held the reins of government, was regarded as a vice rather than a virtue; and accordingly it was not his supporters, but his political opponents, such as Walker, Evelyn, and Burnet, who laid most stress on the favours he was alleged to have shown to the Jews. Before he had risen to supreme power, he had been a staunch upholder of liberty of conscience, but once he had become head of the state he was too wise to attempt to carry out measures which he knew would create violent opposition among those on whose support his influence depended. As he himself said: "This hath been one of the vanities of our contest. Every sect saith, 'Oh give me liberty!' but give it him, and to his power he will not yield it to anybody else[2]." Accordingly, when the time for its actual application came, Cromwell was constrained to allow liberty of conscience only within the very narrowest limits; for instance, in dealing with the Irish Catholics he did not force them to attend Protestant churches, but he refused to allow them to hold public worship according to their own rites. "I meddle not with any man's conscience," he wrote to the Governor of Ross; "but if by liberty of conscience you mean a liberty to exercise the mass, I judge it best to exercise plain dealing

[1] Carlyle, on Heroes, p. 335.

[2] *Oliver Cromwell*, by Charles Firth, p. 306.

and to let you know, where the Parliament of England have power that will not be allowed of [1]." As head of the executive he might forbear to rigidly enforce the laws making attendance at church compulsory, but there is no reliable evidence that he at any time allowed forms of worship contrary to the Protestant religion, and therefore, in breach of the law of the land, to be publicly celebrated.

Our English historians have taken Cromwell's hospitable treatment of Menasseh and his summoning of the Whitehall Conference as examples of his Toleration, but all admit that in this instance no practical effect was given to it. Some few writers assert that, though the Conference was a failure, the Protector subsequently formally gave the Jews a legal right of settlement in the country, and permitted them to establish a synagogue here. A statement to this effect was made by Godwin [2], and of recent years much has been written by Jewish writers, and especially by Mr. Lucien Wolf, attempting to prove this statement. Some of the last-mentioned writer's theories are so widely known and have been so skilfully put forward as to call for some comment here. The first of these theories is to the effect that a "tolerance" in the shape of a "public assurance of protection" was granted to the Jews by Cromwell on February 4, 1658. The authority for this is a passage in Burton's *Diary*, under the above-mentioned date, which reads as follows: "The Jews, those able and general intelligencers, whose intercourse with the Continent Cromwell had before turned to a profitable account, he now conciliated by a seasonable benefaction to their principal agent resident in England [3]." The authorship of Burton's *Diary* is very doubtful, nor is the work, especially those parts of it which are not reports of speeches supposed to have been taken down in the House

[1] *Oliver Cromwell*, by Charles Firth, p. 267.
[2] *History of the Commonwealth*, vol. IV, c. xvii, p. 250.
[3] Burton's *Diary*, vol. II, p. 471.

of Commons, of any great authority. Moreover, to the ordinary reader it seems hardly possible that the words used can be brought to bear the interpretation which is thus sought to be placed upon them. They point only to some personal favour, such as a trade licence or money grant, conferred on an individual; not to a public declaration in favour of a religious body—a matter which would have been considered of great political and constitutional importance, and which would not have been described in language of this kind. Mr. Wolf, however, says of it: "The precise terms of this grant, which was doubtless oral, have not been preserved. But as it was preceded by the endenization of Carvajal, in defiance of the recommendation of the Council that the Jews should only be permitted the standing of ordinary aliens, and as it was succeeded by the public celebration of the Feast of Tabernacles, we may assume that it was a kind of informal *fays ce que voudras*, the Protector relying on the tried discretion of the Jews [1]." This passage contains two mistakes; in the first place, if the Council even did make a recommendation, about which more will be said hereafter, Carvajal's endenization was not in defiance of it, because the letters patent were granted to Carvajal on August 17, 1655 [2]: whereas the petition of Menasseh Ben Israel, in answer to which the alleged recommendation of the Council is supposed to have been made, was not presented until October in that year. In the second place, this event, whatever its nature, was not succeeded by the public celebration of the Feast of Tabernacles. The authority for this statement is a passage in a letter by Mr. Jo. Greenhalgh, dated April 22, 1662, in which he says, after describing a visit to the Jewish Synagogue, that he had been told that "one year in Oliver's time they did build booths on the other side of Thames, and kept the Feast of Tabernacles in them." Even if such evidence is accepted implicitly, the celebration

[1] *The Resettlement of the Jews in England*, by Lucien Wolf, p. 12.

[2] *Transactions of the Jewish Historical Society*, vol. II, p. 46.

mentioned could not have taken place after February 4, 1658, for Cromwell died on September 3 following—a considerable time before the date for celebrating the Feast of Tabernacles had come round [1]. Mr. Wolf further supports his theory by a reference to Thomas Violet's Petition against the Jews presented to the King and Houses of Parliament in December, 1660. On turning to the document cited we find that the writer is speaking of Menasseh's Petition and the Whitehall Conference; his words are: "Upon several days hearing, Cromwel and his Council did give a Toleration and Dispensation to a great number of Jewes to come and live here in London," &c.[2] The statement, whether we regard it as true or untrue, is seen at once on perusing the context beyond all question to refer to the events of December, 1655, and can have no bearing whatsoever upon an alleged grant of Toleration in February, 1658, more than two years afterwards.

The theory itself rests upon no sufficient evidence, and the statements which are put forward as corroborating it are either wholly irrelevant or absolutely inconsistent with it; the excuse for dealing with it at such length must be that for a number of years a learned society claiming an important place in the Jewish community has held a public dinner in the early days of February to celebrate what it has been pleased to call "Resettlement Day." The dinner was announced in 1900, but not held, owing to the death of Queen Victoria; it was not revived during the present year, possibly because the organizers have discovered the futility of attempting to create an anniversary for which there is no historical justification.

The next theory is, that though the Conference effected

[1] If this celebration ever took place, it would probably be in the autumn of 1655, when the question of readmission had not yet been discussed by the Whitehall Conference and was therefore still *sub judice*. If it was before Menasseh had completed his journey to London, the building of the booths on the other side of Thames would be explained.

[2] Violet's Petition against the Jews, p. 2.

H 2

nothing, the Committee of the Council of State which had been appointed to consider Menasseh's Petition, subsequently reported in favour of admitting the Jews, subject to certain limitations and restrictions. There is no sufficient evidence that such a report was ever made. It is certain that there was no formal report, for there is no notice of one in the Council Order Book. There is, however, an unsigned paper in the state archives, which Dr. Gardiner regards as a resolution agreed on by the Committee but never presented to the Council, but which Mr. Neal calls a report of the answers *pro* and *con*, given in the Council when the question was debated. From a careful perusal of the document, the latter seems to me the better view, and it is here subjoined as read in that light, the words in brackets not being in the original. [Proposal] "That the Jews deservinge it may be admitted into this nation to trade and trafficke and dwel amongst us as providence shall give occasion."

[The answer of those that were against it, was, that they could not think it lawful, for the reasons marked with Arabic numerals. Those who were of a contrary opinion said] "That as to poynt of conscience we judge lawfull for the magistrate to admit in case such materiall and weighty considerations as hereafter follow be provided for, about which till we are satisfyed we cannot but in conscience suspend our resolution in this case.

"1. That the motives and grounds upon which Menasseh Ben Israel in behalfe of the rest of his Nation in his booke lately printed in this English tongue desireth their admission in this commonwealth are such as we conceive to be very sinfull for this or any Christian state to receave them upon.

"2. That the danger of seducinge the people of this nation by their admission in matters of religion is very great.

"3. That their havinge of synagogues or any publicke meetings for the exercise of their worship or religion is not only evill in itselfe, but likewise very scandalous to other Christian churches.

"4. That their customes and practises concerning marriage and divorce are unlawfull and will be of very evill example amongst us.

"5. That principles of not makinge concience of oathes made and injuryes done to Christians in life, chastity, goods or good name have bin very notoriously charged upon them by valuable testimony.

"6. That great prejudice is like to arise to the natives of this commonwealth in matter of trade, which besides other dangers here mentioned we find very commonly suggested by the inhabitants of the city of London.

"7. We humbly represent [that they should not be admitted for the above reasons: others represented that they might be admitted subject to the following limitations]

"I. That they be not admitted to have any publicke Judicatoryes, whether civill or ecclesiasticall, which were to grant them terms beyond the condition of strangers.

"II. That they be not admitted eyther to speake or doe anythinge to the defamation or dishonour of the name of our Lord Jesus Christ or of the Christian religion.

"III. That they be not permitted to doe any worke or anythinge to the prophanation of the Lord's Day or Christian Sabbath.

"IV. That they be not admitted to have Christians to dwell with them as their servants.

"V. That they bear no publicke office nor trust in this commonwealth.

"VI. That they be not allowed to print anything which in the least opposeth the Christian religion in our language.

"VII. That so farre as may be they be not suffered to discourage any of their owne from usinge or applyinge themselves to any which may tend to convince them of their error and turn them to Christianity. And that some severe penalty be imposed upon them who shall apostatize from Christianity to Iudaisme [1]."

Except as showing the ideas current at the time, the document is of little importance; this cannot be doubted if it is a mere report of the arguments used in the Council or Committee, and even if it is a report, intended to be presented to the Council but never in fact placed before that body, it would not be entitled to any great weight as a constitutional document. Nor would its weight be materially increased if, as there is no reason to believe, it had actually been adopted by the Council of State because the recommendation in favour of the Jews was conditional upon certain matters being first provided for and no such provision was ever during the whole existence of the Commonwealth Government made or attempted to be made either by the legislature or the executive [2]."

Let us now turn to a third theory. It is that, though it cannot be proved that any formal concession was publicly made to the Jews, yet the circumstances accompanying the proceedings taken against one Antonio Robles show that the demands made by the Jews had by some secret arrangement been practically granted. To test this theory the proceedings known as the Robles case must be briefly examined. In the spring of 1656 England was at war with Spain, and in accordance with the custom of those times a proclamation had been issued for the seizure of the property of all subjects of the king of Spain that could be found either on the high seas or in the territory of the Commonwealth. In virtue of this proclamation

[1] *State Papers*, Interregnum, ci, No. 118; *Calendar*, do.; *Domestic*, p. 15; Neal's *History of the Puritans*, vol. IV, pp. 141, 142 (ed. of 1738). Gardiner's *History of the Commonwealth*, vol. III, p. 219 n.; Wolf's *Resettlement*, p. 16; and *Menasseh Ben Israel*, pp. xlv, liv, lv.

[2] If the document itself is looked at, its precise date is of little importance. Mrs. Everett Green, in the *Calendar of State Papers*, places it about November 13, 1655, and Mr. Wolf's note on p. lv of his *Menasseh Ben Israel* seems not to be justified, especially as he himself gives its date as November 13 in his *Resettlement of the Jews*, p. 11.

an information was laid on March 14, $165\frac{5}{6}$, against Don Antonio Rodrigues Robles, a Spaniard, living in Duke's Place, on the ground that he had lately received a large cargo of wine from the Canaries, and had laden a second ship with woollen goods which he was about to dispatch thither. An order was accordingly made for the arrest and seizure of the said ships and a search of Robles's house, goods and papers. The order was at once executed, and thereupon Robles addressed a petition to the Protector. He stated that he was a Portuguese born and of the Hebrew nation, and hoped that he might partake of the laws and privileges granted to all merchant strangers the rather that he had resided here many years and paid many thousand pounds for customs, and in all things submitted to the laws of this nation. If any accusation were brought against him he asked to be permitted to answer it legally, and prayed that his goods and papers might be restored to him upon sufficient bail being given to answer the charges made against him. The petition was referred to the consideration of the Council, at whose orders a formal inquiry was held and evidence taken by the Commissioners for the Admiralty and Navy.

According to Robles's own account, which was corroborated by the evidence of several of the principal foreign merchants living in London, he was born in the kingdom of Portugal in a town called Fundao, and his family by reason of being Jews had been forced to fly from Portugal to Spain, where they were persecuted by the Inquisition, and some were tortured to death, some burnt, and others sent to the galleys, but Robles himself by God's great mercy fled to the Canary Islands, and by the help of a kinsman, who was treasurer under the king of Spain, acquired some estate, which he could not long enjoy; for, having been advised that orders had been sent by the Inquisition to apprehend him as a Jew, he came to England, where he remained some years; but he afterwards went back to the Canaries, where he recovered a portion of his property and returned with it to England, where he had lived for the last four years. He confessed that he had attended mass at the Spanish Ambassador's house in London, and that he was not circumcised. Not only was this evidence supported by Robles's friends, but it was hardly impugned by those who had given information against him—namely, John Baptista de Dunnington, a merchant and factor, and Francis Knevett, a clerk and notary of Doctors Commons. The former at his examination said that he had served Robles for eight years, having left his family six months before. That Robles was reputed by some a Portugal, by some a Spaniard; that his wife came out of Portugal, and spoke a little Spanish. That he heard he was lately turned a Jew, having formerly professed himself a Catholic. When he first came to live with Robles he took him to be a Spaniard. That Robles changed his name when he went to the Canaries (from Fererino to Robles), where the deponent had lived with him about a year. That the treasurer there was cousin to Robles, called Duarto an Rigij (Henriques), who rented the office under the king of Spain, and was then in England, being with his family turned Jews. On further examination, being asked specifically whether Robles was a Spaniard, he said: "I answer that I cannot positively say whether he be or not, for I have heard several reports of him; some saying he was a Spaniard and others saying he was a Portugal; but which to believe, I cannot tell. But I did always take him to be a Spaniard."

Knevett, who had apparently been very bitter against Robles as being a Jew dog, and had desired Dunnington to swear against him, did not, when himself examined, give very damaging evidence. He said that he believed Robles "to be a Jew, not a Spaniard; though living in the Canaries he lived as a subject of the king of Spain. That he is a kinsman to one Duarto en Rigis (Henriques) who was treasurer in the Canaries, but is now in England, and lately told the deponent that the king of Spain had seized his estate in his Dominions on the account of his being a Jew."

In this state of the evidence the Commissioners reported to the Council on May 14, that they did not find any convincing evidence to clear up either the nation or religion of the petitioner. Some affirming him to be a Jew born at "ffundam" in Portugal, which they tender to testify upon oath; others who have known him long, that they always esteemed him a Spaniard, though their testimony seem not so positive as the other; but all agree that "both in the Canaries, where he was employed under one of the farmers of the king's revenue, and in England he hath professed himself a Romanist, having frequented the mass till about six months since, which with the consideration that he is yet uncircumcised induceth us to conceive he is either no Jew or one that walks under loose principles very different from others of that profession." However, upon the whole they were unable to return any satisfying opinion upon the business, but humbly submitted the same to the Council's determination.

After hearing the report read, the Council, as might have been foreseen, on May 16 ordered that the seizures should be forthwith discharged, and that Robles should be at liberty to dispose of his goods and papers notwithstanding the warrants issued against them [1].

The case is undoubtedly of great interest as showing the position of the Jews here at the time of the failure of Menasseh's mission, but it in no way points to any legal recognition having been accorded to them. Robles's property was only liable to seizure and confiscation if he was a subject of the king of Spain. As soon as the informa-

[1] *State Papers, Domestic,* Interregnum, vol. CXXV, 38. i. 76, p. 604. i. 112, p. 289. Do. CXXVI, Council, Day's Proceedings, No. 18. Do. i. 77, p. 38. Do. CXXVI, 66, Nos. 11, 12, 13, 67, 67 i, 67 ii. Do. 105, 105 i–xi. i. 77, pp. 44, 78. Do. CXXVII, 21. Do. Council, Day's Proceedings, Nos. 19, 40. The most important of these documents are printed at length in Mr. Wolf's valuable Appendix to his *Crypto-Jews under the Commonwealth, Transactions Jewish Historical Society*, vol. I, p. 77 seq.

tion was laid against him he was ready with his answer, "I am no Spaniard, but was born in Portugal, and am of Jewish parentage." The main difficulty was to explain how it was that he traded with and had property in the Canaries, and had lived there for some time. This question was put to the witnesses examined by the Commissioners, and answered in the words of one of them, that "the Portugals who took part with the king of Spain were free to live in his territories." The plea of Judaism seems to have been set up to show why the defendant had left Portugal and afterwards the Canaries. Whether successful or not, it could entail no injury here; for, as has been already shown, the mere fact of being of Jewish birth or religion was no crime provided that the laws against Recusants were complied with, and no part was taken in a religious service which contradicted or impugned the accepted doctrines of Christianity. In any case this plea the Commissioners, who were the judges of the fact, found not proven, conceiving the defendant either to be no Jew, or very different from others of that profession: so that if he had relied on that plea alone he must have failed. He was successful because it had not been satisfactorily proved that he was a Spaniard, and the Council rightly acted upon the ancient maxim of the English law, that the burden of proof is upon those who desire to exact a forfeiture. We thus see that, months after the holding of the Whitehall Conference, the position of the Jews remained exactly the same as it had been in the time of Charles I. We see from the evidence that Robles had been settled here before the Commonwealth had been established, and some of the Crypto-Jews had been settled here even longer. Moreover no change took place in the condition of the Jews until after the Restoration. Robles, it was proved by Dunnington, "always kept his moneys at a goldsmith's, whose name is Mr. Backwell, who received it and paid it out according to his order"; and the Jews of the Restoration still kept their banking accounts at Mr. Alderman Backwell's[1]. He is also found residing in the same house in Duke's Place in the year of King Charles's return[2]. He could not continue to attend mass at the Spanish Ambassador's, for such services would not be held after the outbreak of the Spanish War; but he and his friends if they did not belong to the six Jewish families to which Cromwell is said to have[3] given special privileges, would probably occasionally attend at some Protestant place of worship in order to make sure of escaping the pains and penalties of the Acts against Recusants[4].

Yet another theory claims attention; it is that Cromwell as Protector gave to John Sadler "a special authorization" to build a synagogue[5]. The authority for this statement is a passage in the account of John Sadler in the Birch Manuscripts. The account is an ordinary biographical notice, with the facts apparently stated in chronological order, which was furnished to the writer as late as the year 1738 by Sadler's grandson, Thomas Sadler, who was not alive at the time, and could have no knowledge of the facts except by hearsay. The words are "By his interest it was that the Jews obtained the Privilege to build for themselves a Synagogue in London." The words immediately preceding are "He was in high favour with Oliver Cromwell, who by his letter from Cork invited him to take upon him the office of Chief Justice of Mounster, in Ireland, with a salary of one thousand pounds per annum, which he excused himself from accepting." The letter from Cork,

[1] Wolf's *Jewry of the Restoration*, p. 11.

[2] See the Mendez da Costa lists now printed in Wolf's *Jewry of the Restoration*, p. 4. Mr. Wolf is evidently right in fixing the date of these as 1660, but his theory that they were the work of reformers attempting to procure the re-expulsion of the Jews does not seem very probable. The traditional view that they are lists of persons made out preparatory to the regular organization of a community seems better.

[3] The Question whether a Jew, &c., p. 36; and see the Petition of the Jews to the House of Commons against the special tax proposed to be laid upon them in 1689.

[4] See the Ordinance of September 27, 1650, already quoted.

[5] Wolf's *Jewry of the Restoration*, p. 6; and his *Menasseh*, p. lviii.

which appears on another folio, was dated December 1, 1649. The words immediately following are "August 31, 1650, he was constituted Master of Magdalen College in Cambridge [1]." The writer is ostensibly alluding to a grant made at the end of 1649 or at the beginning of 1650, but we know from the facts, which are now so well established as to be incontrovertible, that no such grant could then have been made. But, it may be said, there is no need to take the words in connexion with their context, and we may assume that they indicate a privilege granted not in 1650, but in 1656. This is a somewhat large assumption to make upon the authority of a writer who had been supplied with information more than eighty years after the event by one who could not have been personally cognizant of the facts; nor is it much less at variance with the known sequence of events and possibilities of the case. It is admitted that the privilege was never made use of by the Jews; no document conferring it has ever been discovered; by the constitution then existing, which Cromwell was not in the habit of disregarding except for the purpose of securing some great political advantage, the Protector had no power to make such a grant, and finally, if it had ever been made, it is unaccountable that John Sadler himself in his petition on behalf of Menasseh Ben Israel's widow, addressed to Richard Cromwell, who had succeeded his father as Lord Protector, though he speaks of his own efforts on behalf of the Jews, omits altogether to mention it [2]. It seems impos-

[1] Birch MSS. 4,223, fo. 165, 166.

[2] "To his Highness the Lord Protector the humble Petition of John Sadler Sheweth that although your petitioner being often pressed to present petitions in behalf of the Jewes, did rather dissuade their coming hither, yet by some letters of your late royall father and others of note in this nation some of their synagogs were encouraged to send hither one of their chief rabbines, Menasseh Ben Israel, for admittance & some freedome of trade in some of these ilands. And when he had stayed here so long that he was allmost ashamed to return to those that sent him or to exact their maintenance here where they found so little success after so many hopes, it pleased his Highness & the Council to settle on the said Menasseh a pension of £100 a year," &c. (*S. P. Dom. Interregnum*,

sible to come to any other conclusion than that the alleged grant was never made.

The last of these theories with which it is necessary to deal is that a favourable answer was given to the petition mentioned at the end of the last article, which was presented on March 24, 1656, praying for protection in writing for meeting privately for purposes of worship, and for leave to establish a cemetery for the burial of the dead. It is certain that no document purporting to confer these rights has ever been discovered, but it is suggested that such a document may have been given to the petitioners and subsequently lost or destroyed by them. The motive for destroying it is not very apparent, but it is said that the Jews, after the Restoration, were afraid to acknowledge the receipt of any benefit from the late Usurper; if this were so, they showed a great lack of that far-sighted shrewdness which has usually characterized their actions. To have possession of a grant from Oliver was no crime after his régime had come to an end, and it is remarkable that after the Revolution, when their rights and privileges were under discussion, no such grant was ever referred to, although at that time there would be no more prejudice against those who had received benefits from Cromwell than against those whose religious privileges depended upon the favour of the kings of the exiled house [1]. Moreover the fact of wilful destruction or voluntary loss would not explain the total disappearance of all traces of the document, if it had ever existed; for, besides the formal answer given to the petitioners, a copy of a document of this kind would have been taken and kept among the public records along with the petition which is still preserved there. No copy is to be found there, and there is no reason to differ from Dr. Gardiner's statement of the result of the reference of this petition to the Council—" As

ch. viii). The whole petition is printed in Wolf's *Menasseh Ben Israel*, p. lxxxvii.

[1] See the case of the Jews stated, 1689.

might have been expected, it met with no response. Even if that body had been more favourably disposed towards the Jews than was the case, it was hardly likely to commit itself by a formal order to the effect that the existing law should not be carried into effect [1]." There is, however, strong evidence, amounting almost to positive proof, that a Jewish cemetery was established about this time at Mile End. There is still in the possession of the congregation of Spanish and Portuguese Jews in London the counterpart of a lease dated April 13, 1670, of land at Mile End, which has undoubtedly been used as a cemetery since that time. It recites the surrender of a lease "for fourteen years of the same land granted in February, 165$\frac{6}{7}$, by John Tuffenell and another to Anthony Fernandez Carvayall and Simon de Caceres." As the lease was surrendered it would in the ordinary course be given up to the grantors and cancelled or destroyed by them, so that there is little hope of finding it now [2]. The lease of 1670 certainly does not, and that of 1656 probably did not mention the purpose for which the land was granted; nor is it likely that any separate deed of trust was drawn up, for such a deed would have been valueless, inasmuch as a trust of this nature would not have been enforceable at this time or for long afterwards. Of the joint lessees Carvajal had received letters of denization; De Caceres was still an alien, and consequently incapable of holding any estate in land other than a lease of premises for the residence of himself or his servants, or the purpose of any business, trade, or manufacture carried on by him [3]. On the death of Carvajal, in

[1] Gardiner's *History of the Commonwealth*, vol. III, p. 222.

[2] Mr. Godwin, writing in the year 1828, says: "I applied to the Rulers of the Spanish and Portuguese Synagogue in Bevis Marks, and by their permission Mr. Almosnino, their secretary, obligingly went over with me some of their oldest records. Among them I found an account of a lease of a piece of ground in the parish of Stepney, granted them in February 165$\frac{6}{7}$, for a burying-ground." It is probable that he is referring to the lease of 1670, which mentions an older lease granted in 1656 (*History of the Commonwealth*, vol. IV, p. 250).

[3] "But as to a lease for yeares, there is a diversitie between a lease for

November, 1659, the lease would vest by right of survivorship in De Caceres alone, so that if the land had been openly used as a cemetery, or for any other purpose than that of trade or habitation, it could, and it may be safely asserted would, have been claimed by the Commonwealth or, after the Restoration, by the Crown, nor could the claim have been successfully resisted.

The old book of records of interments in the possession of the Spanish and Portuguese Congregation in Bevis Marks shows that four burials took place between the years 1657 and 1660, but these interments must have been conducted with great privacy and, if they were accompanied by any religious ceremony, with the strictest secrecy. At this period, except in the case of Recusants, there was no law prohibiting the burial of the dead in a private garden [1]; but such an interment, if attended by ceremonies unknown to and inconsistent with the doctrines of Christianity, would have immediately provoked a criminal prosecution. There being no record of any such prosecution, it may safely be affirmed

yeares of a house for the habitation of a merchant stranger being an alien, whose king is in league with ours, and a lease for yeares of lands, meadows, pastures, woods and the like. For if he take a lease for yeares of lands, meadows, &c., upon office found, the king shall have it. But of a house for habitation he may take a lease for years as incident to commerce; for without habitation he cannot merchandize or trade. But if he depart, or relinquish the realme, the king shall have the lease. So it is if he die possessed thereof, neither his executors nor administrators shall have it, but the king; for he had it only for habitation as necessary to his trade or traffique, and not for the benefit of his executor or administrator" (*Co. Litt.* 26). No amendment of the law was made until 1844, when the right of holding lands was extended to all aliens, whether merchants or not, but it was still limited to lands held for the purpose of residence or occupation by the alien or his servants, or for the purpose of any business, trade, or manufacture, and to terms not exceeding twenty-one years (6 & 7 Vict., cap. 66, sec. 5). It was not until 1870 that the unrestricted right of holding lands was conferred upon aliens (see 33 Vict., cap. 14, sec. 2). As to the old law, see the case of Fish *v.* Klein (1817), 2 Mer. 431.

[1] For the law relating to the disposition of dead bodies, see the judgments of Lord Stowell in Gilbert *v.* Buzzard and Boyer (1821), 2 Hag. *Cons.* 333; and Stephen (J.) in The Queen *v.* Price (1884), 12 Q. B. D. 247.

that if the Jewish burial service was performed at all its performance was successfully concealed. It is also manifest that this mode of interment did not satisfy the religious scruples of the more observant Jews. In September, 1657, Menasseh Ben Israel's son died in his house in London, and the pious father determined, notwithstanding the greatness of the expense and the narrowness of his means, to transport the body to Holland. To enable him to do this he petitioned the Protector to commute the pension of £100 which had recently been granted him for an immediate payment of £300: the petition was not granted in full, for it was finally arranged that the pension should be resigned and a new grant of £200 be made. Menasseh was ultimately enabled to make the journey without receiving the grant[1], but the transaction shows that the right of burial with Jewish religious ceremonies had not

[1] *S. P. Dom.* Intro. cxlvi. 89, and cc. 8, printed in Wolf's *Menasseh Ben Israel* at p. lxxxvii. Mr. Wolf does not do Cromwell justice in regard to the payment of this pension. He says: "Unfortunately this pension was never paid, and Menasseh became overwhelmed with cares" (*Menasseh Ben Israel*, p. lxix). The pension was granted on March 23, $165\frac{6}{7}$, and enrolled on May 21, 1657: "Manasseth Ben Israel, a penc̃on of 100^{ll} per annum, payable quarterly and commencing from the 20th day of February, 1656[-7]" (see the Fifth Report of the Deputy Keeper of Public Records, App. II, p. 263). Before Menasseh's departure, in the autumn of 1657, only two quarterly payments of £25 each would be due, and there is ample evidence that two such payments were made, one before September 29, 1657, and one after that date. It was probably this last payment which enabled Menasseh to make his way to Middelburg. It was not suggested by Menasseh's friends that the pension was not paid; what Sadler says in his petition to Richard Cromwell is "that at length he submitted to resign his former pension for a new grant of £200 to be presently paid as the councill ordered. But notwithstanding his stay & expense in procuring several seales, he never gott one penny of the said £200." It may be that Sadler was misinformed about the seals being actually procured, at any rate they are not extant now; and if they were ever granted the financial advisers of the Protector may have thought that as Menasseh died almost directly after the commutation of the pension, and before another quarter's allowance had fallen due, there was no moral obligation to pay his widow the promised grant of £200. For the two payments of £25 each, see the Eighth Report of the Hist. MSS. Comm., Part I, App. pp. 94b and 95a.

been granted, and that the establishment of a Jewish cemetery was unknown to the authorities. Otherwise the answer to Menasseh's petition would have been, You can bury your son here, and there is, therefore, no occasion to commute your pension: this would seem to dispose of the theory that a favourable answer was given to Menasseh's petition of March, 1656. As we have already stated, the petition was a very modest one; it did not ask for the right of public worship or the formation of a synagogue, but merely permission to meet privately for the purposes of devotion at the petitioners' own houses; nor, on the other hand, did it ask for the establishment or consecration of a cemetery, but merely for a licence to bury the dead in a convenient place outside the city "with the Proprietor's leave." The Jews in England were at this time classed with Popish Recusants, and therefore such a licence was necessary, for the Act to prevent and avoid dangers which may grow by Popish Recusants (3 Jas. I, c. 5, s. 15) imposed a penalty of twenty pounds upon persons causing a Popish Recusant to be buried in any place other than in the church or churchyard, according to the ecclesiastical laws of the realm. The request was merely to exercise a right which, had it not been for the statute, could not have been denied. However, since the outbreak of the war with Spain and the decision of the Robles case, the Jews here no longer lived as Spanish subjects in close touch with the Embassy and regularly attending the mass held there; accordingly they may have been no longer considered as Popish Recusants, and so liable to the penalties of the statute. As stated above, they probably at this time attended some Protestant place of worship. And so if they buried their dead in private ground without any religious ceremony they did nothing illegal, and if Jewish religious rites were performed, the strictest secrecy was observed. When all the circumstances are taken into consideration, it can hardly be maintained that the fact that a few Jews were buried in a garden at Mile End without any publicity, and probably without any previous consecration of the ground, is any proof that any legal protection had been accorded to those professing the Jewish religion [1].

[1] For the facts concerning the first Jewish cemetery at Mile End, see an article by Mr. Israel Davis in the *Jewish Chronicle* of November 26, 1880. Some interesting letters on the subject appeared in the same periodical during the month of October, 1901.

VI.

Cromwell's attitude to the Jews.

We must now turn from the pursuit of theories which, however interesting, are either insufficiently supported by evidence or demonstrably false, and attempt to sum up what Cromwell actually did. It is clear that at one time he had been inclined to concede some legal protection to the Jews, and had accorded Menasseh both sympathy and encouragement; but the popular storm which the public discussion of the proposals had raised convinced him of the folly of trying to carry into actual operation any plan that he may have formed. Accordingly, after the Conference he never made any such attempt, and actually expressed himself as opposed to the resettlement of the Jews. "I had almost forgot," writes Colonel Whitley from Calais to Sir Edward Nicholas on Jan. $\frac{14}{24}$, $165\frac{5}{6}$, the month after the Conference had broken up, "that Cromwell says it is an ungodly thing to introduce the Jews; but, if he refuse them, it is because they refuse to purchase it at the sum desired unless they may have the authority of a parliament for their being there with safety[1]." The finances of the Commonwealth were at this time at a low ebb, and the Royalist newswriter, in repeating the statement made by Cromwell, cannot help, having regard to his previous conduct, reflecting that it was not sincere, and that privileges might yet be granted if the Jews were willing to pay a sufficiently heavy price for them. But such privileges could only have been validly granted by legislation,

[1] *The Nicholas Papers*, vol. III, p. 255.

and the Jews, with that prudent caution which they are credited with generally displaying in money matters, very wisely refused to pay for a boon which could only be securely granted under the guarantee of an Act of Parliament, when the Protector had not the courage to introduce a bill which, even if backed by his great influence, would have stood little chance of ever becoming law. At any rate, Cromwell did nothing, and the position of the Jews remained throughout his régime the same as it had been in the time of Charles I. They were liable to severe penalties if they did not attend an authorized, that is, a Christian, place of worship, and they were precluded from holding any Jewish religious service. Jewish rites may, indeed, have been privately practised, but it is evident that the strictest secrecy was observed. It is true that there were still Jews in England, as there had been in the time of the late king, but they outwardly conformed to the laws of the land, or at any rate they were careful to commit no open or flagrant breach of them. Some few of them had rendered the Protector services, especially in his expeditions to the Indies and his war with Spain, so that their presence here was well known to him. As the law then stood he might have ordered their withdrawal, but so long as they created no trouble or disturbance he was willing that they should remain. As Mr. Carteret Webb, writing it is true nearly a century after the events, but at the same time entrusted by the oldest Jewish community in London with the advocacy of their cause, and having knowledge of the traditions of the English Jews and access to all their documents, says, "Nothing more was done by Cromwell than the conniving at Alvaro da Costa and five other Jew families living in England[1]." This statement of comparatively late date is amply corroborated by *The case of the Jews stated*, which was drawn up in opposition to the very serious attempt to levy a special tax upon the Jews, shortly after the deposition of James II, the

The legal position of the Jews under Cromwell the same as under Charles I.

[1] The question whether, &c., p. 36.

opening words of which it will not be out of place to cite here:—"That about the Year 1654 there came Six Jew Families into this Kingdom, which have (since King Charles the Second's Restauration) been increased to the Number of between Three and Fourscore Families."

Cromwell did not grant and had no power to grant special privileges to the Jews in respect of their religion.

To this then all the statements about Cromwell's protection of the Jews amount, that he knowingly allowed some half-dozen families to remain in the country, even utilizing their services for the purpose of carrying out his political aims. The only favour granted was that he did not, as head of the executive, put in force the power at that time claimed by the executive of expelling foreigners[1] who might choose to come and reside here. If this can be called a resettlement he may be said to have connived at it, but if a resettlement implies, as it is in common parlance supposed to imply, the creation of some communal organization, the foundation of a synagogue, and the open worship of God according to Jewish rites, there is no reliable evidence that Cromwell ever encouraged, or even connived at, or permitted it. If he had, as is sometimes suggested, granted the Jews a charter or other document conferring special privileges upon them in respect of their religion; the charter would have been absolutely void even during the Protector's lifetime, and certainly could have been of no avail after his death. For Cromwell was a constitutional monarch; his powers, especially in religious matters, were strictly defined and circumscribed by written constitutions, the Instrument of Government from December 16, 1653, to May 25, 1657, the Humble Petition and Advice from the latter date till the day of his death. Neither of these permitted any sort of toleration or religious liberty to be

[1] Subject no doubt to the provisions of clause 30 of Magna Charta. It is said that the last time when the right was exercised on a large scale was by Elizabeth in 1575, but it was claimed by the Crown till the Revolution (see the argument of Sir Robert Sawyer, Attorney-General, in the East India Company *v.* Sandys, and Howell's *State Trials*, 457 sqq.), and there is some doubt whether it is even now abolished (see Musgrove *v.* Chun Teeong Toy, L. R. [1891], A. C. 272).

extended to any persons professing doctrines contrary to Christianity, and the Protector had no power under either to alter or interfere with the religious settlement thereby established. Therefore even assuming—and the assumption must be made not only without any evidence, but in contradiction to all the known facts—that a charter of some kind was given, but has been accidentally lost or purposely destroyed, from a legal and historical point of view the Jews could not be said to owe their re-establishment to Cromwell, not merely because he was a usurper, and in consequence all his acts, unless confirmed by a subsequent sovereign, were void, but because he had never at any time arrogated to himself the right of introducing any strange religion, or mitigating the law in favour of its adherents.

Position at the time of Cromwell's death. Previous intrigues of the Jews in Holland with the Royalists.

This was the situation of the Jews in the early days of September, 1658; it was almost precisely the same as it had been ten years before, save that the hopes which were then formed had been disappointed, and succour was no longer expected from the statesman whose tolerant words, however sincerely spoken, had not been followed by any measure of relief. And thus it was that the news that "the powerful devil is dead," brought hope and comfort to the Jews, both here and abroad, as well as to the exiled monarch. Even before Menasseh's mission the assistance of the important congregation of Amsterdam had been sought by the Royalists, as is made manifest by the following extract from a letter of Sir Marmaduke Langdale to Sir Edward Nicholas, the Secretary of State of the fugitive king, written at Brussels on September 20, 1655: "For that clause of Mr. Overton's letter which mentions the Jews, it proceeded from some discourses I had with Mr. Brokes [Saxby] about them, who seemed much to favour them as necessary to a kingdom, and I believe their tenets do not much differ. I desired Mr. Overton to sound their intentions by some of his party in Holland. I am very sorry they agree with Cromwell. The Jews are considerable all the world over, and the great masters of money. If his Majesty could either have them or divert them from Cromwell, it were a very good service. I heard of this three years agone, but hoped the Jews that understand the interest of all the princes in the world, had been too wise to adventure themselves and estates under Cromwell, where they may by his death or other alteration in that kingdom run the hazard of an absolute ruin: but they hate monarchy and are angry for the patent that was granted by King James to my Lord of Suffolk for the discovery of them, which made most of the ablest of them fly out of England [1]."

At this time the hopes of the Jews centred in Cromwell's

Menasseh's failure made the Jews of Holland incline to Charles II.

[1] *The Nicholas Papers*, vol. III, p. 51. It is evident that the Jews of the Low Countries had at this time great expectations from Cromwell's readiness to receive Menasseh's mission, preparations for which were far advanced. The letter here referred to was enclosed in the dispatch recited in the text, and was dated Delf, 13 Sept. 55, by Richard Overton to Sir Marm. Langdale. The material passage is: "I made inquiry into the condition of the Jewes, soe farr as was necessary. I find they are in conjunction with Cromwell; some of their Rabbies are learning English on purpose to live in England and must go speedily over. They have their meetings at London, and those Rabbies are to be sent thither for y[t] purpose, soe y[t] I am very glad I dealt with them by proxe; not one of them knowes anything of me or what my intentions were. Had they, Cromwell should have known it."—*The Nicholas Papers*, vol. III, p. 44. The reference to the patent granted by King James to my Lord of Suffolk is not very clear. Thomas Howard was created Earl of Suffolk on July 21, 1603, at which time he was Lord Chamberlain of the Royal Household; on July 11, 1614, he was appointed Lord High Treasurer, but in the autumn of 1618 he was accused of extortion and dismissed. I have been unable to find any patent or commission directed against the Jews alone, but on September 5, 1604, the Earl of Suffolk was appointed one of several commissioners for the execution of the laws against Jesuits, seminary priests, or other religious persons "being corrupted and brought up seditiously beyond the seas or elsewhere," and authorizing their banishment; and on June 23, 1618, he was appointed a member of a similar commission (see *Calendar of State Papers, Domestic*, 1603–10, p. 148, and id. 1611–18, p. 547. The first commission is printed at length in Rymer's *Foedera*, vol. XVI, p. 597). It is probably one of these commissions that is referred to. In any case the passage corroborates the view expressed in the preceding article that the unbroken residence of Jews in England dates from the first years of Charles I and not earlier.

professions of universal toleration, and had been raised to fever heat by the invitation extended to Menasseh and his followers. But these hopes were destined to bitter disappointment. Before the year had ended, the Conference had been held, but nothing had come of it; the humble petition presented in the following spring remained unanswered, and though Menasseh still stayed in England his companions had departed to their homes abroad, despairing of success. And so the Jews in Holland now turned to the exiled Charles, peradventure they might obtain from him, in the event of his ever being restored to his kingdom, the boon which had been refused them by the all-powerful Protector. Little more than a year after they had been found so unapproachable by Sir Marmaduke Langdale and Mr. Overton, the failure of Menasseh's mission having occurred in the interval, the negotiations between the Jews and the king were complete, as may be seen from the copy of a commission of King Charles II, dated September 24, 1656, at the Court at Bruges, addressed to Lieutenant-General Middleton, to treat with the Jews of Amsterdam: "That whereas the Lieutenant-General had represented to his Majesty their good affection, and that they had assured the Lieutenant-General, that the application which had been lately made to Cromwell on their behalf by some persons of their Nation, had been and was absolutely without their consent, the Lieutenant-General is impower'd to treat with them, that if in that conjunction they shall be ready to assist by any contribution of money, arms, or ammunition; they shall find when God shall restore his Majesty, that he would extend that protection to them, which they could reasonably expect, and abate that rigour of the Law, which was against them in his several Dominions, and repay them [1]." Charles was at this time in Flanders, contem-

Commission to Lt.-Gen. Middleton to treat with them.

[1] *Brit. Mus. Add. MSS.* 4,106, fol. 253. This paper, says Dean Tucker, was found among the original papers of Sir Edward Nicholas, Secretary of State to Kings Charles I and II, and was communicated to him by a friend. Second letter to a friend concerning Naturalization, p. 29, published in 1753.

plating an expedition against England with the assistance of Spain, and being almost penniless the financial assistance that might be obtained from the Jews was of considerable importance to him. Such assistance he received, and he afterwards, as will be seen, scrupulously carried out the pledge, on the faith of which it had been rendered. But for the time being the prospect for resettlement was not a bright one. Charles was not ready to start until early in 1658, but on March 1 of that year English frigates destroyed his ships at Ostend, and after the battle of the Dunes on June 8, all hope of help from Spain was gone, and the expedition had to be abandoned. The restoration of the king, and the fulfilment of his promise to the Jews, which depended upon it, seemed hopeless, when the news of Cromwell's death, less than three months later, made the first of these events almost certain, though a period of more than a year and a half was to elapse before the king came to his own again.

Their hopes destroyed by the battle of the Dunes.

In this interval no great change can be proved to have taken place in the condition of the Jews here, but the reins of government had become slacker, and the laws of intolerance, though unaltered, were less uniformly enforced. Moreover, as time went on, it became more and more certain that the monarchy would be restored, and the king's promise of protection, as well as his well-known tolerant views in matters of religion, filled with encouragement those who were here, and induced others to join them. Some of them, it is plain, did not think the situation sufficiently secure to bring over their wives and families with them, for the Petition to the King in Council, presented some six months after the Restoration by the Lord Mayor and Aldermen of the City of London, complains of the competition in the export trade of strangers, "both Christians and Jewes, who live here obscurely, free from family expences and charge of Public offices." The same petition also indicates their growing numbers by comparing them to a swarm of locusts "Who are *now daily* multiplied

Interval between the death of Cromwell and the Restoration. Increase in the number of the Jews here.

by the accession of whole families of them from all parts (as if your Majesty's dominions were condemned to be the sink into which the sewer of Mankind should be emptied for a plague to your subjects)[1]." The other petitions presented at the same time also testify to this increase in the numbers of the Jews.

First mention of a Jewish synagogue in England.

There is moreover some, though it must be admitted weak, evidence that a synagogue was established at this time. It was of course a secret, and in no sense a public building. The authority for this statement is a scurrilous pamphlet, entitled *The Great Trappaner of England Discovered*, written for the purpose of vilifying one Thomas Violet, a goldsmith and Alderman of the City of London, who at this time was taking a leading part in opposing a Jewish resettlement. The tract was apparently written in March, $16\frac{59}{60}$, and, in spite of its violent and exaggerated language, has been thought worthy of preservation among the public records. The anonymous writer describes an attempt by Violet to ruin all the Jews and procure their banishment and the confiscation of their property, half of which was to be distributed among the conspirators as their reward, by means of a plot, the object of which seems to have been to hand over a quantity of spurious foreign coins to the Jews, and then charge them with coining or procuring these counterfeit pieces. The writer says that when he discovered Violet's designs he melted down the coins again, and so the plot came to nothing. It is only incidentally that the synagogue is mentioned. The commencement of the plot is described as follows: "This Deponent saith that in the beginning of last Spring" (apparently the spring of 1659), "Tho. Violet Goldsmith came to this Deponent, and told him this Deponent, that the said Thomas Violet knew of a way that might make him the said Deponent for ever, and so desired the said Deponent to go along with him, the said Tho. Violet, into Duke's Place, whereupon the said Deponent went along with the said Tho. Violet into the

[1] *Remembrancia*, vol. IX, p. 44.

place before mentioned, and was by him the said Tho. Violet brought *into the Synagogue of the Jewes, in the place aforesaid,* and spake with one Mr. Moses their High-priest that year and other Jewes; and this Deponent saith further, that the said Tho. Violet told the Jewes, this deponent was a fit man to do them service in the business which he the said Tho. Violet had treated with them about [1]."

This is the first mention in contemporary literature of a visit to a Jewish synagogue in England, and, notwithstanding the mention of the High-priest, it is not quite certain that the writer means a place of public worship; for on this occasion at least it was made use of as a place for transacting business, in which the High-priest, who is spoken of as an annually elected officer, is mentioned as having taken a prominent part, the word may be used in its etymological sense as a meeting-place, or, as is more probable, the whole story may be a fabrication on the part of the anonymous pamphleteer. In any case, it is to be observed that the building, which was so far unknown that Violet had to personally conduct his intended accomplice thither, is said to have been situated in Duke's Place, and not in King Street or Creechurch Lane, the traditional sites of the first synagogues. If used as a place of worship as well as business such user was wholly illegal and strictly secret, so that in the only one of the petitions presented against the Jews in the autumn of 1660, which has been thought worthy of preservation among the State Archives, and which contains the most sweeping and, in many cases, unfounded accusations against the Jews, the establishment of a synagogue is only hinted at, but not directly asserted, in the following words: "And moreover such of late hath been the presumption of the Jewes that as the Report hath gone and so doubtless upon inquiry it will be discovered that they have circumcised children, set up and frequented Synagogues and have had and still may have their Schools, Priests, Presbiters, and the like." Violet,

[1] *The Great Trappaner of England Discovered*, p. 3.

in his petition, dated December 18, 1660, says that at the time of the Conference with Menasseh the Jews prayed "to have liberty to erect new Synagogues or Temples amongst us for the free public exercise of their Jewish worship, Customs, and Religion; and they did *then* erect a Jewish Synagogue and it is at this day, every day they celebrate twice in the day their superstition, their fire never goes out all the year[1]." We know however that this last statement is untrue, for otherwise there would have been no object in the Jews petitioning in the spring of 1656 for protection for meeting at their private devotions in their own houses. Nor did Violet himself, an avowed and bitter enemy of the Jews, take any step in the matter until about Christmas, 1659, when he made an application to Mr. Justice Tyril, with the intention of obtaining criminal process against them, a fact which indicates that he could not earlier obtain any evidence of their having set up a synagogue, and so rendered themselves amenable to the criminal law.

No change in the legal status

There is evidence then that in the year and a half which

[1] Violet's Petition, December 18, 1660, p. 1. The previous quotation is from the Remonstrance concerning the Jews, November, 1660, *S. P. Dom.* Car. II, vol. XXI, p. 140. Mr. Wolf, in his *Jewry of the Reformation*, p. 8, note 26, intimates that this latter document is the petition actually presented by Violet to the King in Council. This is not probable; it is more likely to be the petition of Sir William Courtney and others, or one of the other petitions mentioned as being before the Privy Council on November 30, 1660 (see *Privy Council Register*, Car. II, vol. II, p. 57). If it is Violet's original petition, he does not go so far as to say that a synagogue has been actually set up, as he does in his second petition, dated December 18, 1660, and published in pamphlet form in January, 1661. Inasmuch as the debate in the Commons was ordered to take place on December 18, it is probable that this petition was never actually presented, so that it is only a political pamphlet, issued shortly after the proceedings referred to had been dropped, and accordingly little reliance can be placed on the statements of fact it contains.

Mr. Moses, the High-priest, is no doubt correctly identified by Mr. Wolf as Moses Athias, described in the Da Costa lists as "Sin. Moses Atees, Creechurch Laine, a Jewish Ribay, and Sin. Moses the Prest wer the Sinagoge is." Dr. Gaster, in his *History of the Spanish and Portuguese Synagogue* (p. 18), says that he must have acted as the temporary Hazan, and also as a kind of spiritual adviser.

succeeded Cromwell's death the numbers of the Jews increased, and their position and prospects improved so far that they ventured to hold divine service, probably in a private house, but certainly unknown to the general public or the authorities, and conducted with the strictest precautions and concealment. They may have done this also in the old days when Charles I was king, or in the more recent times of Oliver's Protectorate; but if they did they managed to leave no trace to attract the attention either of contemporary informers or subsequent historians. It is, moreover, certain that whatever hopes may have been aroused and whatever laxity there may have been in administering the law in this interval, no change was effected in the legal status of the Jews.

of the Jews till the Restoration.

On Royal Oak Day, May 29, 1660, Charles II made his triumphal entry into London, amidst the plaudits and acclamations of the citizens. Thenceforward all the acts of the late Government, unless expressly confirmed by Parliament, and all the statutes or ordinances enacted during the time of the Interregnum, were absolutely void. Thus the religious settlement effected by Cromwell was at an end, and the situation as it existed at the period before the great rebellion was revived. When Charles was firmly seated on his throne, the previous legislation against sectarianism and nonconformity, intolerant as it was, did not satisfy the bigotry of the triumphant Cavaliers, who, having themselves experienced the evils of persecution, were determined to take vengeance on their former oppressors. The history of the reign accordingly reveals a series of measures directed against all who dissented from the tenets of the established church, and it is somewhat remarkable that at the very time when these measures were being enacted and enforced the Jews obtained a permanent and legal settlement in the country. If they had a settlement before this time, it was so successfully hidden as to escape the attention of the authorities, and to baffle the keen eyes of the informers, always ready to

The Restoration of the king and Resettlement of the Jews.

swoop down upon their prey. Now, for the first time, Jews openly defied the acts against recusants by habitually neglecting to attend any Christian places of worship; now, for the first time, they organized a community, and established a synagogue where Jewish services were publicly held, notwithstanding the severe penalties to which those who took part in them were by the laws exposed. To explain this strange phenomenon it will be necessary to review briefly the general religious history of the reign, and then examine the occasions on which the still small Jewish community was brought into contact with the governing powers. The king himself was of a tolerant disposition, and again and again combatted the zeal for persecution of his Parliament, though in these contests he was often worsted, thanks to his prevailing vices of self-indulgence and indolence. At this time, as has already been pointed out, toleration did not rank high in the scale of virtues, but there can be little doubt that this was one of the few virtues (if we adopt the popular view of his character) which Charles possessed. In his early days he had had experience of the bigotry of the Presbyterians, when he was nominally a king, though really a prisoner, in Scotland, a situation from which his defeat at Worcester, despite the poverty and exile it brought in its train, came as a relief. His mother was a Roman Catholic, and he married a Roman Catholic wife. His own religious convictions were not very strong; during his exile he remained a staunch adherent to the Church of England, and even quarrelled with his mother on account of her attempt to convert his brother the young Duke of Gloucester to Catholicism; but his conduct at this time may have been actuated by policy rather than by conviction. His leanings in later life were certainly towards the ceremonies of the Roman Church, though he put off his formal conversion to it till his death-bed. To him religion was of such little importance that it was absurd to punish any one on its account. He accordingly showed himself a real advocate

Charles II an advocate of toleration in an intolerant age.

of toleration; but when the cry for persecution became too pressing, the desire for ease which prompted all his actions made him yield to it, even as Cromwell, for all his firmness of will, had ultimately given way. This tolerant disposition has already been seen in the grant of the commission to General Middleton in September, 1656, previously mentioned. The promise of protection to the Jews contained in it was only an extension of the terms of the Treaty made with Spain in the spring of the same year, as the price of her assistance for his restoration, by which he agreed to suspend and, if possible, secure the parliamentary revocation of all penal laws. In the same spirit in the Declaration of Breda, issued at the time of his restoration, he says: "And because the passion and uncharitableness of the times have produced several opinions in Religion, by which men are engaged in parties and animosities against each other (which when they shall hereafter unite in a freedom of convocation, will be composed, or better understood), we do declare a Liberty to tender consciences, and that no man shall be disquieted or called in question for differences of opinion in matter of Religion, which do not disturb the peace of the kingdom; and we shall be ready to consent to such an Act of Parliament, as, upon mature deliberation, shall be offered to us, for the full granting that indulgence."

The Convention Parliament and toleration.

The Convention Parliament, by which Charles had been re-called, did not pass any legislation on the subject of religion. The House of Commons contained many supporters of the old régime, who preferred the Presbyterian Church government established under the Commonwealth to the Church of England as formerly established, and when the question came up for discussion in the House, the king was requested to convene a select number of divines to treat concerning the affair. As a result of the conference a Declaration concerning ecclesiastical affairs was issued. It provided modifications in Church government which were a compromise between the views of the

Episcopalians and the Puritans, and further renewed the promise of toleration contained in the Declaration of Breda, in the self same terms[1]. The Declaration was presented to Parliament. The House of Commons thanked the king for it, and a bill embodying it and turning it into law was presented and read a first time; but the toleration was thought too wide, and the bill rejected on the second reading by 183 to 157 votes[2].

The new Parliament, 1661.

At the end of the year the Parliament was dissolved, and in the spring of the following year the elections for the new House of Commons were held. A wave of loyalty, such as has been seldom experienced, swept over the country. The Cavaliers were everywhere successful; the Puritans everywhere defeated, and when Charles met his Parliament in May, he was confronted by a House of Commons which might truly be called "plus royalist que le roi." "The divine right of kings," "Church and State," were the mottoes and watchwords of the newly-elected representatives of the people. The Church was to be purged of all dissenting elements, and life in the State to be made endurable only to those who owned allegiance to the doctrines of the national Church. Accordingly, the first thing done by the House of Commons, after the election of Sir Edward Turner as their Speaker, was to order all the members to take the Sacrament according to the old Liturgy, on pain of expulsion, and then, in conjunction with the Lords, to order that "The solemn League and Covenant" should be burned by the common hangman at Westminster and in the City, and that all copies thereof be taken down out of all churches, chapels, and all other public places in the kingdom. Moreover, the first law that it added to the statute-

Members ordered to take the Sacrament.

[1] Baxter, the leading Puritan divine, desired to exclude from the general toleration those who denied the Trinity and Papists, as had been done in Cromwell's time by both the Instrument of Government and the humble Petition and Advice, but the king, mindful of his promises, published the Declaration without this restrictive clause.

[2] See Cobbett's *Parliamentary History*, vol. IV, pp. 79, 82, 131–42, 152–4.

book, was "an Act for the well-governing and regulating of Corporations," commonly called the Corporation Act, by which no one was eligible to hold any corporate office or be a member of any municipal corporation who should not, in addition to taking certain oaths and making certain declarations set out in the Act, "have within one year next before his election taken the Sacrament of the Lord's Supper according to the rites of the Church of England[1]." Thus all Nonconformists, of whatsoever creed or sect, were placed under a political disability, which was not removed till the year 1828. This was immediately followed by an Act restoring the bishops to their seats in the Upper House.

The Corporation Act.

The next measure passed this session to which attention must be directed was the Quakers' Act, the passage of which was delayed in the Lords, who "had not stomachs strong enough to digest quite so fast as the Commons furnished them with this sort of food." The objection of the Lords had been that the penalties of the bill extended to others besides Quakers, but after a conference between the Houses the bill was passed. It made penal a refusal to take an oath when lawfully tendered, or maintaining that the taking of oaths was unlawful, and also "if the said persons commonly called Quakers shall at any time depart from the places of their several habitations and assemble themselves to the number of five or more of the age of sixteen years or upwards at any one time in any place under pretence of joining in a religious worship not authorized by the laws of this realm." The penalties were five pounds for the first and ten pounds for the second offence, and any one found guilty after two previous convictions, was to abjure the realm, or otherwise be transported to any of the plantations beyond the seas. This Act was not repealed until 1812, after having been on the statute-book more than a century and a half. It may

The Quakers' Act.

[1] 13 Car. II, stat. 2, cap. 1, in force till 1828, when it was virtually repealed by 9 Geo. IV, cap. 17, and finally repealed by 34 & 35 Vict., cap. 48 (the Promissory Oaths Act, 1871).

be remarked that it was fortunate for the Jews that their name was not coupled with the Quakers, as it has been in several subsequent Acts of the legislature[1].

The Act of Uniformity, 1662.

The other Act of this session that it is necessary to mention is the Act of Uniformity (13 & 14 Car. II, cap. 4), which ordained the exclusive use of the newly-revised Prayer-book in all places of public worship, and rendered incapable of holding any benefice all who had not been episcopally ordained. Moreover, all professors, tutors of colleges, and schoolmasters keeping any public or private school, were required to subscribe a declaration, which included a promise to "conform to the Liturgy of the Church of England, as it is now by law established," and schoolmasters or tutors in private houses, though not compelled to sign this declaration, had to obtain a licence from the bishop of the diocese before exercising their calling, under pain of suffering three months imprisonment, "without bail or mainprize," for each offence. It is to be noted that these last provisions, though allowed to become obsolete, were not repealed till the year 1846.

First Declaration of Indulgence, 1662.

The Act of Uniformity came into force on St. Bartholomew's Day (Aug. 24), 1662. Its effect was not only to drive more than 3,000 ministers from their livings, but also, as the earlier legislation punishing non-attendance at church was now revived, to expose Dissenters of every description to severe pains and penalties. In order to prevent the execution of these cruel laws, the king, on December 20, issued "a declaration to all his loving subjects," in which, among other things, he repels the charge of not performing the promises of toleration made at Breda, as to which he says: "We remember well the confirmations of them since upon several occasions in parliament; and as all these things are still fresh in our memory, so are we still firm in the resolution of performing them to the full. But it must not be wondered at,

[1] The Act is 13 & 14 Car. II, cap. 1, the repealing Act 52 Geo. III, cap. 155. See Cobbett's *Parl. Hist.*, vol. IV, p. 233.

since that parliament to which those promises were made in relation to an Act, never thought fit to offer us any to that purpose, and being so zealous as we are (and by the grace of God shall ever be) for the maintenance of the true Protestant religion, finding it so shaken (not to say overthrown) as we did, we should give its establishment the precedency before matters of indulgence to dissenters from it. But that once done (as we hope it is sufficiently by the Bill of Uniformity) we are glad to lay hold on this occasion to renew unto all our subjects concerned in those promises of indulgence by a true tenderness of conscience, this assurance:—

"That as in the first place we have been zealous to settle the uniformity of the Church of England, in discipline, ceremony, and government, and shall constantly maintain it;

"So as for what concerns the penalties upon those who (living peaceable) do not conform thereunto through scruple and tenderness of misguided conscience; but modestly and without scandal perform their devotions in their own way, we shall make it our special care so far forth as in us lies, without invading the freedom of parliament, to incline their wisdom at this next approaching sessions, to concur with us in the making some such act for that purpose, as may enable us to exercise with a more universal satisfaction, that power of dispensing which we conceive to be inherent in us[1]."

In the face of this declaration we are not surprised to find that the penal laws were not strictly enforced, and that in particular cases, in which the declaration itself was not considered a general dispensation, the power of dispensing conceived to be inherent in the Crown was liberally exercised. Among the Cavaliers the declaration was unpopular, partly because toleration was disliked, but especially because it was thought that undue favour was shown to the Papists. The king referred to this matter in his speech

[1] The whole Declaration is printed in Cardwell's *Documentary Annals of the Church of England*, vol. II, pp. 311–20.

on opening the session of Parliament in February, 166$\frac{2}{3}$, as follows: "The truth is, I am in my nature an enemy to all severity for Religion and Conscience, how mistaken soever it be. I hope I shall not need to warn any here not to infer from thence that I mean to favour Popery. . . . I am far from meaning a toleration or qualifying them to hold any offices or places of trust in the government; nay further, I desire some laws may be made, to hinder the growth and progress of their doctrine; . . . and yet, if the Dissenters will demean themselves peaceably and modestly under the government, I could heartily wish I had such a power of indulgence, to use upon occasions, as might not needlessly force them out of the kingdom, or staying here, give them cause to conspire against the peace of it." The Commons, in their address to the king in answer, respectfully but firmly rejected all idea of indulgence to Dissenters of any kind, offering it to his Majesty's great wisdom "that it is in no sort advisable that there be any indulgence to such persons, who presume to dissent from the Act of Uniformity and Religion established." They also added that the promise of toleration made in the Declaration from Breda was no longer binding, inasmuch as it was expressly a promise of legislation which the Parliament, elected by the free choice of the nation, was unwilling to pass. During the session no further Act against Nonconformists was passed, but at the prorogation in July, the Speaker, on behalf of the House of Commons, thought fit to apologize to the king, and at the same time besought him "to issue out your Proclamation for the putting those laws which now are in force against the Popish Recusants, Sectaries, and Nonconformists in effectual execution [1]." The king made a conciliatory reply to his faithful Commons, but it does not appear that the desired proclamation was ever issued. The rancour of the Church was not to be baulked, and accordingly, at the next session (March 16—May 17, 1664), though the subject was not broached in the

[1] Cobbett's *Parl. Hist.*, vol. IV, pp. 200, 263, 286, 289.

The Conventicle Act, 1664.

king's speech, the first Conventicle Act (16 Car. II, cap. 4) was passed. It recites that the Statute 35 Eliz., cap. 1, has not recently been enforced, and declares it to be still in force, and further enacts that all persons above the age of sixteen years attending a Conventicle, i. e. any meeting "under colour or pretence of any exercise of religion in other manner than is allowed by the Liturgy or practise of the Church of England at which there shall be five persons or more assembled together over and above those of the same Household," are guilty of a crime, and liable to three months' imprisonment, or, in the alternative, a fine of five pounds for the first offence, to six months' imprisonment or a fine of ten pounds for the second, and transportation for seven years or a fine of £100 for the third or any subsequent offence, and in the last case only was it necessary that the conviction should take place before a jury. Persons transported, who escaped or returned without leave, were declared guilty of felony without benefit of clergy. The Act was only temporary, being limited to a period or rather more than three years, but, as we shall see, it was re-enacted, though with milder penalties, shortly after its expiration. In his speech at the prorogation the Speaker explains the Act and the reason for passing it, though no recommendation on the subject had been made in the king's speech at the opening of the session, in these words: "Whilst we were intent on these weighty affairs, we were often interrupted by petitions and letters and motions representing the unsettled condition of some countries by reason of Fanatics, Sectaries, and Nonconformists. They differ in their shapes and species, and accordingly are more or less dangerous; but in this they all agree, they are no friends to the established government either in Church or State; and if the old rule hold true, 'Qui Ecclesiae contradicit non est pacificus,' we have good reason to prevent their growth and punish their practise. To this purpose we have prepared a Bill against their frequenting of Conventicles, the seed-plots and nurseries of their opinions, under pretence of religious worship. The first offence we have made punishable only with a small fine of 5*l.* or three months imprisonment, and 10*l.* for a peer. The second offence with 10*l.* or six months imprisonment, and 20*l.* for a peer. But for a third offence, after a trial by a jury at the general quarter sessions or assizes, and the trial of a peer by his peers, the party convicted shall be transported to some of your majesty's foreign plantations, unless he redeem himself by laying down 100*l.*: 'Immedicabile vulnus ense recidendum, ne pars sincera trahatur [1].'"

Bill for granting Liberty of Conscience rejected.

In the following session a Bill to enable the granting of Indulgences for Liberty of Conscience was introduced into the House of Lords with the approbation of the king under the auspices of Ashley and Arlington, but without the support of the other ministers. It was opposed by Clarendon, and "In the end very few having spoken for it, though there were many who would have consented to it, besides the Catholic lords, it was agreed that there should be no question put for the commitment; which was the most civil way of rejecting it [2]."

The Five Mile Act, 1665.

The legislation of persecution was not yet complete. In the following year, 1665, by the Parliament which met at Oxford because the plague was still raging in London, the Five Mile Act (17 Car. II, c. 2) was passed which forbade under a penalty of forty pounds and six months' imprisonment any nonconforming teacher or minister of whatsoever denomination from dwelling or coming within five miles of any city or corporate town without subscribing a declaration of non-resistance, and taking the oath laid down in the Act.

No further legislation was enacted till the year 1670; the execution of the laws already passed would have satisfied the Church party; attention was, moreover, absorbed in foreign affairs and the war with Holland; but, on the other hand, the fall of Clarendon had made the cause of

[1] Cobbett's *Parl. Hist.*, vol. IV, p. 294.

[2] Ibid., pp. 311–15, taken from Clarendon's *Life*.

toleration more hopeful [1]. On March 1, $166\frac{8}{9}$, by the prorogation of Parliament the Conventicle Act according to the provisions of its last section expired. The Commons, however, made a determined effort to continue it, and a Bill for that purpose was introduced and passed by 144 to 78 votes, but it never went further than the Lower House [2]. However, during a later session, on April 11, 1670, Charles, as the price of obtaining supplies which would not be granted on any other terms, gave his consent to the second Conventicle Act (22 Car. II, c. 1, repealed in 1812 by 52 Geo. III, c. 155): by it Conventicles, defined as in the former Act, were made illegal, and all persons attending them made liable to a fine of five shillings for the first and ten shillings for the second offence. All persons preaching or teaching at such meetings were to be fined twenty pounds for the first and forty pounds for the second offence, and every person in whose house or barn such a meeting was held was to forfeit twenty pounds, and if he was unable to pay this sum, then it was to be levied on the persons present at the Conventicle. Moreover, constables and others neglecting to give information of offences committed under the Act, and magistrates omitting to enforce its execution, were made liable to penalties of five pounds and one hundred pounds respectively; half of which sums was to go to the informer. All clauses of the Act, contrary to the recognized principles of our criminal law, were to be construed "most largely and beneficially for the suppressing of Conventicles and for the Justification and Encouragement of all Persons to be employed in the Execu-

Second Conventicle Act, 1670.

[1] In his speech on opening the session on February 10, 1667, the king again recommended toleration: "And for the setting a firm Peace, as well at home as abroad, one thing more I hold myself obliged to recommend to you at this present, which is, That you would seriously think of some course to beget a better union and composure in the minds of my Protestant Subjects in matters of Religion; whereby they may be induced not only to submit quietly to the government but also cheerfully give their assistance to the support of it."—Cobbett's *Parl. Hist.*, vol. IV, p. 404.

[2] Cobbett's *Parl. Hist.*, vol. IV, pp. 421–2.

tion thereof." The Lords, however, appended a proviso, which was ultimately agreed to by the Lower House, "That neither this Act, nor anything therein contained, shall extend to invalidate or avoid his Majesty's Supremacy in Ecclesiastical Affairs; but that his Majesty and his Heirs and Successors may from Time to Time, and at all Times hereafter, exercise and enjoy all Powers and Authority in Ecclesiastical Affairs as fully and as amply as himself or any of his Predecessors have or might have done the same; any thing in this Act notwithstanding."

In the spring of the following year both Houses of Parliament petitioned the king to issue a proclamation for the banishment of priests and Jesuits, and the enforcement of the laws against Recusants. The king again complied, making, however, this reservation: "But I suppose no man will wonder if I make a difference between those who have newly changed their religion and those that were bred up in that religion, and served my father and me faithfully in the late wars[1]." For an interval of nearly two years Parliament did not meet for the effective transaction of business.

Declaration of Indulgence, 1672.

The king took this opportunity to publish his famous Declaration of Indulgence on March 15, 1672. It recites the king's desire to preserve the rights and interests of the Church, and the endeavours made to enforce uniformity by coercive measures, and proceeds, "But it being evident by the sad experience of twelve years that there is very little fruit in all these forcible courses, we think ourself obliged to make use of that supreme power in ecclesiastical matters, which is not only inherent in us, but hath been declared and recognized to be so by several statutes and acts of Parliament." The intention of maintaining the doctrine, discipline, and government of the Church of England "as now it stands established by law" is expressed, then follows this passage: "We do in the next place declare our will and pleasure to be, that the execution of all and all manner of penal laws in matters ecclesiastical,

[1] Cobbett's *Parl. Hist.*, vol. IV, p. 479.

against whatsoever sort of nonconformists or recusants, be immediately suspended." An intention of licensing places of public worship for such as do not conform to the Church of England is then announced, and "This, our indulgence, as to the allowance of the public places of worship and approbation of the teachers, shall extend to all sorts of nonconformists and recusants, except the recusants of the Roman Catholic religion, to whom we shall in no wise allow public places of worship, but only indulge them their share in the common exemption from the execution of the penal laws, and the exercise of their worship in their private houses only [1]."

According to Macaulay, of all the many unpopular steps taken by the government, the most unpopular was the publishing of this declaration; it was abhorrent to the enemies of religious freedom, and was thought by the upholders of civil liberty a violation of the constitution, and an unjustifiable exercise of the royal prerogative. The fact that it was at this very time that the Duke of York, the heir presumptive to the throne, ceased to outwardly conform to the established religion, and formally joined the Church of Rome, naturally created the impression that there was an intention to favour Papistry, and the Protestant dissenters felt no gratitude for any relief granted to them on such conditions. When at length the necessity of a supply to carry on the Dutch War forced Charles to reassemble his Parliament in February, 1673, he thus addressed them on this matter: "Some few days before I declared the war, I put forth my Declaration for Indulgence to Dissenters, and have hitherto found a good effect of it, by securing peace at home when I had war abroad. There is one part in it that has been subject to misconstructions, which is that concerning the Papists; as if more liberty were granted them than to the other Recusants, when it is plain there is less; for the others have public

[1] Cardwell's *Documentary Annals of the Church of England*, vol. II, pp. 333-7.

places allowed them, and I never intended that they should have any, but only have the freedom of religion in their own houses, without any concourse of others. And I could not grant them less than this, when I had extended so much more grace to others, most of them having been loyal, and in the service of me and of the king my father; and in the whole course of this indulgence, I do not intend that it shall in any way prejudice the Church, but I will support its rights and it in its full power. Having said thus I shall take it very ill to receive contradiction in what I have done. And I will deal plainly with you, I am resolved to stick to my Declaration[1]."

The power to issue the Declaration questioned in the Commons. The Declaration cancelled.

The question was speedily taken into consideration by the House of Commons, which, after a long and fierce debate, resolved by 168 votes to 116, "That Penal Statutes, in matters Ecclesiastical, cannot be suspended but by Act of Parliament"; and an address to that effect was ordered to be drawn up and presented to the king; a further debate took place on the proposal that the Lords should be invited to concur in the address, but it was rejected by 125 to 110 votes. The address was accordingly presented from the Lower House only. On February 24 the king returned his answer to the address, regretting "the questioning of his power in Ecclesiastics: which he finds not done in the reigns of any of his ancestors; his only design was to take off the penalties the statutes inflicted upon the Dissenters; and which, he believes, when well considered of, you yourselves would not wish executed according to the rigour and letter of the law"; he had no intention of avoiding the advice of Parliament, and if any Bill for these ends should be offered to him he would readily concur in it[2]. The answer was not satisfactory to the House because the claim to suspend penal statutes in matters ecclesiastical seemed to be still asserted, and it was resolved that a second address should be sent to the

[1] Cobbett's *Parl. Hist.*, vol. IV, p. 503.
[2] Ibid., p. 546.

king. On March 1 the king went down to the House of Lords and complained of the addresses he had received from the Commons, and requested advice thereon. The Lords in answer sent up an address to his majesty thanking him for "asserting the ancient just rights and privileges of the house of peers." On March 7 both houses joined in presenting an address against the growth of Popery, and on the following day the king came to the Parliament in person and agreed to the address; he also asked for supply to be dispatched, and added: "My Lords and Gentlemen; if there be any scruple remain with you concerning the suspension of penal laws, I here faithfully promise you, that what hath been done in that particular shall not for the future be drawn either into consequence or example." The same day the Lord Chancellor informed the House that his majesty had on the previous night caused the original Declaration under the great seal to be cancelled in his presence[1]. The thanks of both Houses were then returned to the king, and thus ended this incident which it has been thought right to relate at length on account of the light it throws on the spirit of the times as well as upon the question immediately before us.

Into the religious history of the remainder of the reign, inextricably bound up as it is with the course of politics, it is not necessary to enter at length; there was a perhaps not ill-founded suspicion that with an avowed Papist as successor to the crown attempts would be made to overthrow the established Church. In this state of feeling it was not unreasonable to take care that all places of trust and power should be filled by members of the dominant sect only. This was effected by the Test Act of 1673 (25 Car. II, c. 2), entitled "An Act for preventing dangers which may happen from Popish Recusants," by which all persons holding any office or place of Trust under the crown, whether civil or military, were compelled to publicly

The Test Act, 1673.

[1] Cobbett's *Parl. Hist.*, vol. IV, pp. 551, 556-61.

receive the Sacrament according to the rites of the Church of England, and also to take the oath of Supremacy and sign a declaration against Transubstantiation. The penalty for executing any office without complying with these requirements was incapacity to hold any office or to prosecute legal proceedings or to act as guardian or executor, or to receive any legacy, and also the forfeiture of five hundred pounds, which could be recovered by any informer for his own benefit. It will be at once seen that this Act, though expressly directed against Papists, was equally applicable to sectaries of all denominations. This was followed five years later by the Parliamentary Test Act (30 Car. II, st. 2), entitled "An Act for the more effectual Preserving the King's Person and Government, by disabling Papists from sitting in either House of Parliament," by which for the first time Roman Catholic peers were excluded from taking their seats in the House of Lords. These last enactments are often defended upon the ground that in the then existing political circumstances it was necessary to strictly exclude Roman Catholics from all share in the government of the country; on the other hand, the Anglican party took care to exclude all Dissenters, whether Roman Catholics or not; and though measures were from time to time projected for giving relief to Protestant nonconformists, these were invariably brought forward at times such as the fag end of a session, when they had little chance of ever becoming law. This excuse, however applicable it may be thought to the Test Acts, can hardly be extended to cover a great part of the earlier legislation, such as the Conventicle and Five Mile Acts, or the frequent demands for the execution of the Elizabethan and Jacobean statutes against Recusants.

The Parliamentary Test Act, 1678.

The contest over the Exclusion Bill, the proceedings against those charged with complicity in the Popish Plot, and the subsequent revenge of the court upon the leaders of the country party, did not concern the Jews, protected as they were by their insignificant numbers and exclusion from all part in the political arena. To them, and the obscure formation of their community in these times of persecution and danger to all who dared to differ in the slightest degree from the religion as by law established and worship God according to the dictates of their conscience, it is now time to turn.

VII.

Petitions against the Jews at the time of the Restoration.

At the time of the Restoration there were some thirty families of Jews in England[1], and these naturally awaited with expectation the promise of the king, given through General Middleton, "to abate that rigour of the law which was against them," and welcomed the declaration of a Liberty to tender Consciences which had been made at Breda. But they had many enemies to reckon with—religious fanatics at a time when no one was thought religious unless fanatical, and trade rivals who, thinking that every transaction of the newly-settled foreign merchants was a loss to themselves, looked with a jealous eye on the large and increasing foreign and colonial trade of the Jews, especially that with the recently-acquired colonies in the West Indies. Accordingly it creates no surprise to find that a number of petitions were presented to the king and the Privy Council praying that the laws against the Jews should be enforced, and that, if necessary, new ones should be enacted. At the meeting of the Privy Council on November 30 such a petition from Sir William Courtney and others was read, and it is plain from the Council's minutes that several other petitions had also been received. The petition of Sir William Courtney is probably the document preserved in the State Papers under the title "Remonstrance concerning the Jews," and dated November, 1660. It recites, apparently taking Prynne's *Demurrer* as a guide, the mischief said to have

[1] See the Da Costa lists published in Wolf's *Jewry of the Restoration*, p. 4.

been done by the Jews in former times and their banishment under Edward I, and how they have "by little and little and by degrees crept and stolen into England again, and together, some as Jewes aliens and others as English, are become of late exceeding numerous, and how they became so is conceived to be by the means of the late Usurper, who most apparently did protect and countenance them in their affairs and actions," and suggests the issue of a commission to inquire into their state, the imposition of heavy taxes, seizure of their property, and their banishment for residing here without a licence from the crown [1]. The Council having heard this petition read resolved that it, together with others on the same subject, should be taken into consideration again on December 7. On that day there were read at the Council a petition of the merchants and tradesmen of the City of London for the expulsion of the Jews, and also a petition of Maria Fernandez Carvajal (widow of Antonio Fernandez Carvajal already mentioned, who had died in November, 1659) and other merchants, Jews by birth, for his majesty's protection to continue and reside in his dominions. The latter petition has unfortunately been lost; the former is probably the petition of the Lord Mayor and Aldermen preserved in the Guildhall archives; it requested the king "to cause the former laws made against the Jews to be put in execution, and to recommend to the Two Houses of Parliament to enact such new ones for the expulsion of all professed Jews out of your Majesty's dominions, and to bar the door after them with such provisions and penalties as in your Majesty's wisdom shall be found most agreeable to the safety of Religion, the Honour of your Majesty, and the good and welfare of your subjects [2]." The Council, judging the business of very great importance, referred all the petitions to the consideration of Parliament, desiring advice therein, and ordered them to be delivered to a member of

[1] *S. P. Dom. Car. II*, vol. XXI, p. 140; *Calendar*, 1660, p. 366.

[2] *Remembrancia*, vol. IX, p. 44.

the House of Commons to be accordingly presented to the Parliament[1]. Though the Privy Council did not itself come to any decisive conclusion on the subject, it seems that the intention was to uphold the king's promise and not to molest the Jews, for on December 17 Mr. Hollis, no doubt under orders from the Council, presented the above-recited order to the House of Commons as specially recommended to them for their advice therein, touching *Protection* for the Jews. The House thereupon decided to take the business into consideration the next morning[2]. The next morning, however, the matter seems to have been shelved, for there is no entry in the journal of anything having been done, and a few days afterwards (Dec. 24) Parliament was dissolved without ever having given their advice on the Jewish problem as they had been requested by the Council. From the general temper of the House of Commons on religious questions during this reign it is clear that no relaxation of the law was to be effected by legislation in favour of the Jews, and the subject was not again brought forward in Parliament for a period of more than ten years. The position of the Jews, though unsatisfactory, was by no means intolerable; the laws against Recusants were not very strictly enforced against them, and their place of worship, if they had already one, was not known, and they therefore escaped all proceedings for taking part in illegal forms of public worship. On the other hand, the new Navigation Act had securely closed all the colonies and plantations against foreign merchants and factors, but this obstacle was surmounted by applying for and in many cases obtaining letters of denization from the king[3]. As early as the year 1662 they were emboldened

Position of the Jews after the Restoration.

[1] *Privy Council Register, Charles II*, vol. II, pp. 57, 67.

[2] *Com. Journal*, vol. III, p. 209.

[3] The Navigation Act is 12 Car. II, cap. 18. See sec. 2, which, being passed by the Convention Parliament, was expressly confirmed by the following Parliament. See 13 Car. II, cap. 14. Mr. Webb, in an appendix to the *Question, &c.*, gives a list of 105 Jews who received letters of denization in this and the following reign, and this list is not exhaustive.

to erect a synagogue. There is the doubtful reference to a synagogue in *The Great Trapanner of England Discovered*, published in 1660, which has already been referred to; but in a letter dated April 22, 1662, and written by Jo. Greenhalgh to his worthy friend Thomas Crompton, minister of Astley chapel, we have the description of a visit to the Jews' synagogue and the form of worship held there. It is plain that the synagogue was a separate building formed no doubt out of a private house and arranged in very much the same manner as synagogues are at the present day, the service also being very similar, lasting some three hours and conducted wholly in Hebrew. It was necessary to observe the strictest secrecy, nor was any one admitted to the building, which was in "a private corner of the city," and had three doors, one beyond another, except very privately. Mr. Greenhalgh himself had some difficulty in going to it. He had an idea that the Jewish merchants in the city must have some place of meeting together for divine worship, and was curious to see it. "Whereupon as occasion offered me to converse with any that were likely to inform me, I enquired hereof, but could not of a long time hear or learn whether or where any such thing was;" but, having taken to the study of Hebrew, he obtained as a teacher a learned rabbi named Samuel Levi, who gave him a ticket of admittance to the synagogue. We may judge the size of the congregation by the writer's statement that in the synagogue he counted "about or above a hundred right Jews and one proselite amongst them[1]." It soon became no longer necessary to maintain this strict secrecy. In

The first synagogue.

There is a curious petition for naturalization of about this date (1661) of Jacob Joshua Bueno Henriques among the *State Papers Colonial*, vol. XV, No. 74. He says he had heard of a gold mine in Jamaica, and desired permission to go there and develop it, giving the king ten per cent. He also asks for naturalization for himself and his brothers Joseph and Moses, and that they may follow their own laws and have synagogues. (See *Calendar, S. P. Colonial*, 1661–8, p. 48, and *Jews in the British West Indies*, by Dr. Friedenwald: pub. American Jewish Hist. Soc., No. 5, p. 45 seq.)

[1] Ellis's *Original Letters*, 2nd series, vol. IV, Letter cccix, pp. 3–22.

The secrecy surrounding the synagogue discarded at the end of 1662 or beginning of 1663.

the absence of any documentary evidence it is not safe to assume that a special dispensation was given by the king to the Jews by reason of that dispensing power which he conceived to be inherent in him, but it may well have been given, and if not it is most reasonable to suppose that reliance was placed on the king's declaration to all his loving subjects, which, as before stated, was published on December 26, 1662. At any rate it is quite certain that the worship of the synagogue, which had hitherto been conducted with the greatest privacy, was shortly after this time no longer concealed, but open to the public; and for a time at any rate without any evil consequences to the worshippers. On October 14, 1663, Samuel Pepys and his wife and his friend Mr. Rawlinson paid a visit to the synagogue after dinner, where they were present at what was evidently the afternoon service for the rejoicing of the law. There was no difficulty as to admission, and no attempt at concealment. The clerk of the acts of the navy remarks upon the disorder, want of attention and confusion in the service, and observes that he could not "have imagined there had been any religion in the whole world so absurdly performed as this[1]." It was in the course of this year that the hitherto isolated Jewish families formed themselves into a community. Henceforth regular records were kept; the synagogue, in addition to being made public, was renovated and improved, and in 1664 a lease was taken; in September, 1663 the *Finta*, or contributions of the individual members of the synagogue, was fixed, and in the following November the *Ascamoth*,

An organized community formed.

[1] *Diary of Samuel Pepys*, Oct. 14, 1663, Wheatley's edition, vol. III, p. 303. This description of a visit to the Synagogue gives an impression which was shared by other Christian observers; see the autobiography of Henry Newcome, M.A., A.D. 1686, "*June* 26. We went to the Jews' Synagogue. I could not have believed, but that I saw it, such a strange worship, so modish and foppish; and the people not much serious in it as it is. And I was affected to think, that many likely men of understanding should be without Christ, and live in the denial of him." Chetham Society's Publications, vol. XXVII, p. 262.

or code of laws to govern the newly-founded community, was drawn up; it was published in April, 1664, and in the same month a *Haham*, or Chief Rabbi, was appointed; the whole organization being completed by April 19, 1664[1]. It was not likely that the public exercise of a strange religion should long remain unnoticed, and the passing of the Conventicle Act, which expressly declared that the Elizabethan legislation against Recusants was still in force and ought to be put into execution, invited an attack upon the Jews. It was not long delayed. The Conventicle Act came into force on July 1, 1664. And immediately afterwards we hear of a Mr. Rycaut molesting the heads of the congregation, suggesting that they were liable to all sorts of penalties and forfeitures, and what was worse, the Earl of Berkshire, the second son of that Earl of Suffolk in fear of whom the Jews had fled the country in the reign of James I, who held a high position at court, being a gentleman of the bedchamber and privy councillor[2], intervened, saying he was verbally authorized by the king to protect them, but threatening that unless they came to a speedy agreement with him, he would himself prosecute them and procure the seizure of their estates. In these circumstances the wardens of the synagogue, the first that had been yet appointed, took the only course open to them, and petitioned the throne direct. With great wisdom they omit all mention of the religious question and the infringement of the newly-enacted law, but say they know of no law to hinder their residence in the kingdom, and ask to be allowed to remain under the protection of the law until his majesty should think fit to order them to depart, and promise to be loyal and obedient subjects of the king. The petition was referred to the Privy Council on August 22, 1664. A most generous answer was returned. The king declared that he had

1664. Threatened attack on the Jews. Petition to the king. His gracious answer.

[1] Gaster's *History of the Ancient Synagogue*, pp. 7, 9–11, 17; Wolf's *Jewry of the Restoration*, pp. 13–15.

[2] See Cockayne's *Peerage*, vol. I, p. 343.

given no orders for molesting or disquieting the petitioners, and that they might "promise themselves the effects of the same favour as formerly they had had, so long as they demeaned themselves peaceably and quietly with due obedience to his Majesty's Laws, and without scandal to his government[1]." The concession was of great importance; it was a formal recognition of a system of public worship which had been established for more than a year in open defiance of the Elizabethan statutes enforcing uniformity, and was given at the very time when Parliament had declared that those statutes should be carried out, and had even added to their severity by the enactment of the Conventicle Act. The king's claim to grant dispensations from penal laws had not yet been questioned in Parliament, and this particular dispensation granting the Jews the same favours they formerly had had, and by implication including the right of public worship which they had of late openly exercised, was never disputed in the legislature. Even assuming an express dispensation had been given to the Jews after Christmas, 1662, the new declaration was necessary to enable them to escape the severe penalties of the new Act which had just come into force.

Inquiry concerning the Jews ordered by the House of Commons.

For some years the synagogue was kept open and the services regularly held without molestation. On February 6, $167\frac{0}{1}$, the House of Commons thought fit to take this matter into their consideration. There was a scheme on foot to prevent the growth of Roman Catholicism, and in case legislation should be introduced, it was thought a good opportunity to aim a blow at Judaism also. It was accordingly ordered "that a Committee be appointed to inquire into the causes of the growth of Popery; to prepare and bring in a bill to prevent it, and also to inquire touching the number of the Jews and their Synagogues, and upon what terms they are permitted to have their residence here, and report it with their opinions to the

[1] *S. P. Dom. Car. II*, ent. Book 18, pp. 78–9; *Calendar*, 1663–4, p. 672.

House[1]." Either from want of time or knowledge, or because the subject was not thought of sufficient importance, the part of the reference relating to the Jews does not seem to have been proceeded with; the Committee's report, which was presented to the House on February 17, dealt only with the causes of the increase of Popery, and it was resolved that an address requesting a proclamation for the banishment of priests and Jesuits, and the enforcement of the laws against Recusants, should be drawn up and presented to the king; whose answer to this address excepting those who served his father and himself faithfully in the late wars has been already mentioned.

1673. Prosecution of the Jews for meeting for the exercise of their religion.

For the time being, then, the Jews were left undisturbed; nor were they concerned with the publication of the Declaration of Indulgence in the spring of 1672, for, for nearly nine years before that time they had openly exercised the right of public worship which was conferred by that instrument on all Nonconformists except Papists. But the cancelling of the declaration in the following year gave occasion for a new attack upon the synagogue; the organizers of it no doubt argued that the withdrawal of the general indulgence of itself annulled the particular dispensation granted to the Jews, which, though previously acted upon, was evidenced and confirmed by the king's answer to their petition given on August 22, 1664. Accordingly, at the winter quarter sessions of 1673 at the Guildhall, the leaders of the Jewish community were indicted of a riot for meeting together for the exercise of their religion in Duke's Place, and a true bill was found against them by the grand jury. The Jews again petitioned the king, referring to the favourable reply they had received in 1664; and, as was seen in the first of these articles[2], on February 11, 167$\frac{3}{4}$, an order was made by the King in Council "that Mr. Attorney General do stop all proceedings at law against the Petitioners who have been

The Jews petition the king and obtain an Order in Council to stay the proceedings against them.

[1] *Com. Jour.*, vol. IX, p. 198.

[2] Supra, p. 2.

indicted as aforesaid and do provide they may receive no further trouble in this behalf [1]."

Entering a *nolle prosequi* on an indictment a new way of exercising the Dispensing Power.

The method by which the Attorney General is able to stop proceedings in a criminal trial is by entering a *nolle prosequi*—a course which before these times was not unusual in the case of informations or prosecutions commenced by a representative of the crown. About this very time the system was extended to indictments or prosecutions commenced by any member of the public without the necessity of any intervention or permission from the representative of the crown as a convenient way of exercising that dispensing power which the king thought inherent in his office [2]. It is somewhat remarkable that though Parliament was sitting at the time, and the king's power of suspending penal statutes in matters ecclesiastical had recently been questioned, no protest against this particular dispensation in favour of the Jews was made in either House; this may, however, be accounted for by the fact that Parliament was prorogued within a fortnight of the issue of the Order in Council, which may not have been generally known till some time afterwards. The measure of favour now shown the Jews was a distinct advance upon the proceedings of 1664. In the earlier year a vague promise of protection had been given upon condition that the laws of the land were duly obeyed. The formal Order in Council made ten years later effectually saved the young community from the consequences of undoubted infringements of the laws then in existence. The king could not make the celebration of an unauthorized religious service legal, but he could and did, by the exercise of his dispensing

[1] Hag., *Cons. Cas.*, vol. I, Appendix, p. 2.

[2] In Goddard *v.* Smith (1764), 8 Mod. *Rep.*, p. 264, Chief Justice Holt says that it began first to be practised in the latter half of King Charles the Second's reign, but that on informations it had been frequently done, and he ordered precedents to be searched if any were in Mr. Attorney Palmer's or Nottingham's time. And on another day he declared that in all King Charles the First's time there is no precedent of a *nolle prosequi* on an indictment.

power in this formal way, render those who took part in it immune from the penalties of the law which they were habitually violating. Indeed, shortly after this event, the leaders of the community thought themselves so far secure that during this year they took the lease of a house in Creechurch Lane for a term of twenty-five years, and established there a larger and more commodious synagogue[1]. Nor was their confidence without justification, for no further attack was made upon them during the remainder of the reign.

Progress made in the Establishment of a Jewish community in the reign of Charles II.

It is well to pause here and glance at the progress made since the king's return. The resettlement, towards which, in spite of several sustained but unsuccessful attempts, no real advance had actually been made during the Commonwealth, was now actually effected, and, if the policy of Charles were confirmed by his successors, legally complete. At the time of the Restoration, Jews, though they might enter the country as freely as other aliens, were yet in no better legal position than they had been in the days of James I; they were subject to heavy fines if they did not regularly attend the Christian services of their neighbours, and were under still severer penalties debarred from setting up a synagogue of their own. It was impossible to establish a settled community or even to meet together for Jewish religious purposes except under the cover of the strictest secrecy. Those who were here are rightly called by Mr. Wolf Crypto-Jews, for they were unable to openly profess their allegiance to Judaism. The king, who in his exile had promised to abate the rigour

[1] Gaster's *History of the Ancient Synagogue*, p. 7. Creechurch Lane is in close proximity to Duke's Place, but the extreme accuracy required in an indictment shows that in 1673 the house of prayer was at Duke's Place itself. Neither Pepys nor Greenhalgh indicates the locality of the synagogue, but it was probably the same house in Duke's Place which was still used in 1673. In the old synagogue in Duke's Place, according to Greenhalgh, the women worshipped in an inner room; in the newer synagogue in Creechurch Lane there was a separate gallery and entrance for ladies.

of the law that was against them, proved as good as his word. At the very beginning of his actual reign we have the earliest reliable evidence of a meeting-place for public worship according to Jewish rites. At first these services, though open to all Jews, were carefully concealed from the general public; yet after a lapse of three years it was possible to hold them openly; and the criminal proceedings which were threatened, or actually took place in consequence, were prevented or rendered abortive by the intervention of the king, and by the year 1674 the community, already firmly established, was able to obtain a long lease of a house, and especially reconstruct it for the purposes of a synagogue. No less than seventy members of the new congregation were granted during the reign letters of denization, and thus acquired the rights of English citizenship. Questions concerning the customs and rights of Jews, as would necessarily happen as soon as an actual settlement took place, now for the first time were discussed and decided in the courts of law—for instance, it was held that a Jew should be sworn on the Old Testament in legal proceedings whether at common law or in chancery; that it was right to alter the venue in a case where a Jew would be a necessary witness so that it should not be heard on Saturday, the Jewish Sabbath, and that a Jew might maintain an action in this country unless expressly prohibited by the king from carrying on trade here[1]. Under the aegis of the king, and protected by the exercise of his dispensing power, a Jewish community had been practically established, requiring only the like recognition and protection from succeeding monarchs to make itself permanently and legally secure.

Accession of James II. His religious policy.

On February 6, 168$\frac{4}{5}$, Charles II died, and his brother James was proclaimed king. The new sovereign was from the first determined that the crushing disabilities under

[1] See the cases of Robeley *v.* Langston (1667), 2 Keble, p. 314; and Anon. (1683), 1 Vern., p. 263; Barker *v.* Warren (1675), 2 Mod., p. 271; and case in Lilly's *Practical Register*, vol. I, p. 4 (1684).

which his fellow Papists laboured should no longer press upon them, and was quite willing to give similar relief to other Dissenters. In his speech made to the Privy Council at the time of his proclamation as king he promised "to preserve the government both in Church and State as it is now by law established," and to defend and support the Church of England. On March 5, to the great grief of all Protestants, mass was publicly said at Whitehall [1], but in his speech at the opening of Parliament on May 22, the king repeated the promise he had made to preserve the government both in Church and State. This assurance, it is plain, did not give universal satisfaction, for, fashionable as it was in those early days of his reign to profess unbounded confidence in the king, there was still some misgiving and jealousy of the royal power in religious matters which was bound to find expression. On May 27, the grand committee for religion reported that they had agreed upon two resolutions, of which the second was "That the house be moved to make an humble Address to his Majesty to publish his royal Proclamation for putting the laws in execution against all Dissenters whatsoever from the Church of England." This resolution gave great offence at court, and the court party in the House managed to defeat it by moving the previous question, which was carried, and the following motion was then unanimously adopted: "That this house doth acquiesce, entirely rely, and rest wholly satisfied in his majesty's gracious word and repeated Declaration, to support and defend the Religion of the Church of England, as it is now by law established; which is dearer to us than our lives [2]." Though no proclamation was issued, an attempt was a short time afterwards made to enforce the penal laws against the Jews; for one Thomas Beaumont issued process under the statute made in the 23rd year of Queen Elizabeth, which inflicted

Jews arrested and charged with recusancy.

[1] Evelyn's *Memoirs*, vol. I, p. 551.
[2] *Commons Journals*, vol. IX, p. 721; *Parl. Hist.*, vol. IV, p. 1357.

a penalty of £20 a month for non-attendance at church, against no fewer than forty-eight Jews, of whom thirty-seven were arrested "as they were following their occasions on the Royal Exchange"; whereupon Joseph Henriques, Abraham Delivera, and Aaron Pacheco, the overseers of the Jewish synagogue, presented a petition to the King in Council praying "his Majesty to permit and suffer them as heretofore to have the free exercise of their religion, during their good behaviour towards his Majesty's Government." King James following his brother's example by a formal Order in Council, exercised his dispensing power in favour of the Jews by ordering the Attorney-General to stop all the proceedings against them; "His Majesty's intention being" (so the order runs), "that they should not be troubled upon this account, but quietly enjoy the free exercise of their religion, whilst they behave themselves dutifully and obediently to his government[1]."

On the petition of Joseph Henriques and others a formal Order in Council made staying the proceedings.

Dispute between James II and Parliament concerning the Dispensing Power.

This Order in Council was made on November 13, 1685, at the very time when Parliament, newly reassembled after the suppression of Monmouth's rebellion, was questioning the power of the king to retain in his service Roman Catholic officers who had served against the rebels by granting them dispensations from the Test Act. In his speech to both Houses, at the resumption of the session on November 9, James openly expressed his intention of continuing them in their employment, saying: "And I will deal plainly with you, that after having had the benefit of their service in such time of need and danger, I will neither expose them to disgrace, nor myself to want of them, if there should be another rebellion to make them necessary for me[2]." On November 14 the House of Commons resolved to present an address dealing with this matter which, when finally drawn up and adopted, ran as follows: "We further crave leave to acquaint your Majesty that we have with all duty and readiness taken into consideration your Majesty's

[1] Hag., *Cons. Cas.*, Appendix, p. 3.

[2] *Commons Journals*, vol. IX., p. 756; *Lords Journals*, vol. XIV, p. 73.

gracious speech to us, and as to that part of it relating to the officers in the Army not qualified for their employments according to an Act of Parliament made in the twenty-fifth year of the reign of your Majesty's Royal Brother of blessed memory, intituled an Act for preventing dangers which may happen from Popish Recusants, we do out of our bounden duty humbly represent unto your Majesty, that these officers cannot by law be capable of their employments; and that the incapacities they bring upon themselves thereby can no ways be taken off but by an Act of Parliament: Therefore out of that great deference and duty we owe unto your Majesty who has been graciously pleased to take of their services to you, we are preparing a Bill to pass both Houses for your royal assent to indemnify them for the penalties they have now incurred. And because the continuance of them in their employments may be taken to be a dispensing with that Law, without Act of Parliament (the consequence of which is of greatest concern to the rights of all your Majesty's dutiful and loyal subjects and to all the laws made for the security of their religion) we therefore, the knights, citizens, and burgesses of your Majesty's House of Commons, do most humbly beseech your Majesty, that you would be graciously pleased to give such directions therein, that no apprehensions or jealousies may remain in the hearts of your Majesty's good and faithful subjects." A motion was made that the concurrence of the Lords be desired to the said Address, but was rejected by 212 votes to 138. And so, as had happened in the year 1673, the denial of the dispensing power of the Crown was embodied in a resolution of the Lower House only. The Lords, however, did not desire to be left behind in this matter, for on Thursday, November 19, they resolved "that Monday next be appointed for reading and considering His Majesty's speech." But in the meantime the king, who had been highly incensed with the Commons Address when presented to him, and had expressed dissatisfaction and surprise at their want of confidence in him, prorogued Parliament, which never met again for the transaction of business during his short reign[1].

The struggle transferred to the Law Courts. James issues his Declaration of Indulgence.

The struggle was now transferred from the Parliament House to the Law Courts. A decision that the king had power to dispense with the penalties inflicted by the Test Act was obtained[2], and James proceeded to make the utmost use of this judgment in his favour, but not content with granting dispensations wholesale, at length in April, 1687, he published a Declaration for liberty of conscience, suspending all the penal laws, and remitting all penalties incurred under them; allowing the free exercise of every form of religion, and announcing that the oaths of supremacy and allegiance, and the recently enacted tests, should no longer be required to be taken or subscribed by any person, "and further declaring that this royal pardon and indemnity should be as good and effectual to all intents and purposes as if every individual person had been therein particularly named or had particular pardons under the great seal." A year afterwards this Declaration of Indulgence was reissued, and ordered to be read in all churches, but now the storm, which had long been brewing, at length burst, and James was driven from his throne.

[1] *Commons Journals*, vol. IX, pp. 758, 759, 761; *Lords Journals*, vol. XIV, p. 88.

[2] The case is Godden *v.* Hales, which was decided in Easter term, 1686. The action was brought against Sir Edward Hales to recover a penalty of £500 incurred by holding the office of colonel in the army without having taken the oath required by the Test Act. The defendant, in answer, pleaded a dispensation from the Crown. Sir Edward Herbert, Lord Chief Justice of the Common Pleas, after taking time to consult the other judges, declared that he and all the other judges (except Street and Powell, who doubted) were of opinion (1) that the kings of England are sovereign princes; (2) that the laws are the king's laws; (3) therefore it is an inseparable power in the kings of England to dispense with penal laws in particular cases, and upon particular necessary reasons; (4) that of those reasons and those necessities the king himself is sole judge; (5) that this is not a trust invested in or granted to the king, but the ancient remains of the sovereign power and prerogative of the kings of England, which never yet was taken from them nor can be. And therefore, such a dispensation appearing upon record, judgment ought to be given for the defendant. See 2 *Shower*, p. 475; XI St. Tr., p. 1166 seq.

Until after the decision of Godden *v.* Hales in Easter term, 1686, the king had probably not gone beyond the law, though he had undoubtedly stretched his prerogative to its furthest limits, but his proceedings after that time are rightly regarded as wholly illegal. A special dispensation to a particular person or persons is very different from a general indemnity to all who might violate and incur penalties under the penal laws. However much we may at the present time approve of the wording and the substance of the declarations of indulgence, we cannot forget that if toleration was to be established, it could be secured only by an Act of the legislature, and not by the king alone usurping the authority of Parliament. James's hopes of success had lain in uniting all the dissenting sects against the Established Church, but the great mass of Dissenters were as vehement in their opposition as churchmen, partly because they regarded the indulgence offered them as illegal and unconstitutional, and a direct infringement of the liberties of the people and their right of legislation, and partly because they feared that the real object of placing the members of the different sects on the same footing as members of the Church of England, was, after destroying the supremacy of the Established Church, to gradually transfer it to the adherents of the Church of Rome. The Jews did not avail themselves of the Declaration of Indulgence, but for different reasons from their nonconformist brethren. They were satisfied with the dispensation granted them by Charles II, and confirmed by James II in November, 1685, for it enabled them to escape the penalties of recusancy, and also to hold public worship in accordance with the rites of their religion; nor had they any desire to take any part in the political life of the country, which under the Declaration of Indulgence they might have done. For not only were they for the most part aliens and wholly absorbed in commercial enterprises, but one of the ascamoth or laws of the synagogue strictly forbade its members from

The illegality of James's proceedings.

Did not affect the Jews.

taking any part in politics[1]—a very wise provision in the then condition of the newly-organized community. The position of the Jews therefore remained throughout the reign the same as it had been under Charles II, but lapse of time and the confirmation of the dispensation given by Charles and his successor rendered their settlement more secure, and their community was rapidly increasing, and still enjoying the royal favour, as is proved by the fact that thirty-four of its members were granted letters of denization by James II during his short reign.

Views on toleration at the time of the Revolution.

The Revolution of 1688 did not affect the status of the Jews. It was indeed recognized that it was necessary to reward in some way the loyalty to the constitution of the Dissenters, who, in spite of the indulgence offered them by the deposed king, had joined entirely in the resistance to the illegal attacks on the rights and privileges of the Established Church, but it was determined that the toleration to be granted should be strictly limited. The penal laws might be divided into two classes; first those which compelled attendance at church, and punished the holding of religious services not in conformity with the ritual laid down in the book of common prayer, secondly those which disabled all who did not profess the doctrines of the Church, and join in communion with it, from sitting in Parliament, or holding any political or municipal office or any place of profit under the Crown. The gratitude felt by churchmen to their nonconformist brethren for the support rendered to the Church in her hour of need, was not strong enough to create any desire to admit them to any share of political power, and it was thought that sufficient generosity was shown in granting freedom of worship to Protestant Dissenters, and relief from the penalties incurred by absence from church. No attempt was therefore made to mitigate any of the laws falling under the second category, nor were any of those belonging to the first class amended or repealed, but, in accordance with a mode of legislation

[1] Gaster, *The Ancient Synagogue*, p. 88.

which seems peculiarly dear to the English people, the effect of disobedience was annulled by exempting Dissenters from the penalties they would have otherwise incurred. This was done by means of the statute (1 Will. & M., cap. 18) entitled "An Act for exempting their Majesties' *protestant* subjects dissenting from the Church of England from the penalties of certain laws," and generally known as the Toleration Act. In spite of its high sounding title the toleration granted was strictly limited to Protestant Nonconformists, who might take the new oaths of allegiance and supremacy, and subscribe a declaration against transubstantiation; though Dissenters, such as Quakers, "who scruple the taking of any oath," were allowed instead to subscribe a declaration of fidelity to the throne, and also a profession of their Christian belief, and it was also provided "that neither this Act nor any clause, article, or thing herein contained, shall extend or be construed to extend to give any ease, benefit, or advantage to any papist or popish recusant whatsoever, or any person that shall deny in his preaching or writing the doctrine of the Blessed Trinity, as it is declared in the aforesaid articles of religion." Dissenters entitled to the benefit of the Act were enabled to have their places of worship certified, and persons who should disturb the services held there were made liable to penalties. At the same time it was made clear that there was no intention to allow any relaxation of the strict observance of the Sunday, for by section 16 "all the laws made and provided for the frequenting of divine service on the Lord's Day, commonly called Sunday, shall be still in force, and executed against all persons that offend against the said laws, except such persons come to some congregation or assembly of religious worship, allowed or permitted by this Act." Yet, such as it is, the Toleration Act is not unjustly regarded as the charter of freedom of conscience in this country, for it in practice gave all the liberty which at the time it was intended to allow. Nonconformity was still regarded in theory as a crime, but exceptions were

The Toleration Act.

introduced, which in the course of time became so numerous as to eat up the rule. The true effect of the Toleration Act is well expressed by Lord Mansfield in his speech in giving judgment in the House of Lords in the case of the Chamberlain of London *v.* Evans in the year 1767; he says, that in former days nonconformity was "in the eye of the law a crime, every man being required by the canon law, received and confirmed by statute law, to take the sacrament in the church at least once a-year, . . . but the case is quite altered since the Act of Toleration; it is now no crime for a man, *who is within the description of that Act*, to say he is a Dissenter; nor is it any crime for him not to take the sacrament according to the rites of the Church of England; nay, the crime is, if he does it contrary to the dictates of his conscience. . . . The Toleration Act renders that which was illegal before now legal; the Dissenters' way of worship is permitted and allowed by this Act; it is not only exempted from punishment, but rendered innocent and lawful; it is established; it is put under the protection and is not merely under the connivance of the law. . . . Dissenters, *within the description of the Toleration Act*, are restored to a legal consideration and capacity; and an hundred consequences will from thence follow, which are not mentioned in the Act. For instance, previous to the Toleration Act, it was unlawful to devise any legacy for the support of dissenting congregations, or for the benefit of dissenting ministers; for the law knew no such assemblies and no such persons; and such a devise was absolutely void, being left to what the law called superstitious purposes. But will it be said in any court in England, that such a devise is not a good and valid one now?" but then he adds later, "the case of 'Atheists and Infidels'" (among whom Jews are included) "is out of the present question; they come not within the description of the Toleration Act[1]."

[1] Cobbett's *Parl. Hist.*, vol. XVI, pp. 313–27.

Extension of the benefits of the Toleration Act.

The benefit of the Toleration Act was extended to Unitarians in the year 1813, and to the Roman Catholics, who had received considerable measures of relief by statutes passed in 1778, 1791, 1829, in the year 1832, and finally to the Jews in the year 1846, but until the reign of Queen Victoria there had been no legislative enactment exempting the Jews from the penalties of the penal laws, which were finally repealed in the years 1844 and 1846[1].

[1] In 1812 three of the most intolerant Acts passed in the reign of Charles II, namely, the Act against Quakers, the Five Mile Act, and the Conventicle Act, were repealed by the Places of Religious Worship Act, 1812 (52 Geo. III, cap. 155), which also made it necessary, under a penalty of £20, to certify and register all places for religious worship of *Protestants*, at which more than twenty persons should be present.

In 1813, 53 Geo. III, cap. 160, admitted Unitarians to the benefit of the Toleration Act, by repealing the last two lines of sect. 17, which exclude any person who shall deny the doctrine of the Blessed Trinity.

The Acts relieving Roman Catholics are (1) Sir George Savile's Act (18 Geo. III, cap. 60), which exempted Roman Catholics who took the prescribed oath, expressing allegiance to King George and disclaiming the Stuarts and the deposing power of the Pope, from many of the disabilities and penalties imposed since the Revolution by 11 & 12 Will. III, cap. 4. Catholics were henceforth allowed to purchase and inherit land, and the provisions allowing a Protestant kinsman to enter and enjoy the estate of a Catholic heir, and imposing perpetual imprisonment for keeping a Roman Catholic school, were repealed. (2) The Roman Catholic Relief Act, 1791 (31 Geo. III, cap. 32), which among other things exempted all persons who should make a declaration professing the Roman Catholic religion, and take the prescribed oath of allegiance to the king and the Hanoverian succession, from all penalties for not resorting to the parish church, and from being prosecuted for being a Papist, or for hearing or saying mass, or taking part in any other ceremony of the popish religion, provided that all places of worship should be certified, and provided also "that all the laws made and provided for the frequenting of divine service on the Lord's Day, commonly called Sunday, shall be still in force, and executed against all persons who shall offend against the said laws, unless such persons shall come to some congregation or assembly of religious worship permitted by this Act or by the" Toleration Act, i.e. a Roman Catholic or Protestant Nonconformist chapel. (3) 43 Geo. III, cap. 30, substitutes the declaration and oath prescribed in the Catholic Relief Act of 1791 for the oath prescribed in Sir George Savile's Act of 1778. (4) The Roman Catholic Relief Act, 1829 (10 Geo. IV, cap. 7), admitted Roman Catholics to full political rights, with certain exceptions, by exempting them from the provisions of the Test Acts and the Corporation Act. (5) The Roman Catholic Charities Act of 1832 (2 & 3 Will. IV, cap. 115) extended to Roman

Relief from the Test and Corporation Acts.

No relief was formally given to enable Nonconformists to fill municipal, political, or military offices, from which all who did not take the Communion according to the rites of the Church of England were excluded; but after the beginning of the reign of George II such offices were practically thrown open to Protestant Dissenters by passing annual Indemnity Acts, the first of which is 1 Geo. II, st. 2, cap. 23, in favour of those who had omitted to qualify themselves under the Corporation and Test Acts. At length in the year 1828 the statute 9 Geo. IV, cap. 17, substituted a Declaration, "upon the true faith of a Christian,' not to disturb or injure the Established Church for the Sacramental test, thus sweeping away all the political disabilities of Protestant Nonconformists, and in the following year the obligation to make a Declaration against transubstantiation was repealed, and Papists also, under certain conditions, were admitted to full political rights by the Roman Catholic Relief Act of 1829.

Legislative relief from the penal laws at length given to the Jews.

It is somewhat remarkable that, until the year 1846, no *legislative* relief from the penal laws, except in so far as some of them had been repealed in the year 1812 and the year 1844, was granted to the Jews.—The repealing Acts were not intended to benefit the Jews; but were made in favour of Protestant Dissenters and Roman Catholics respectively.—Indeed the statute passed in the last-mentioned year, which is entitled "An Act to repeal certain Penal enactments made against Her Majesty's Roman Catholic Subjects," expressly restricted the repeal of many of the statutes it dealt with, to the extent to which they related to or in any manner affected Roman Catholics. The Commission for revising and consolidating the criminal law, which was appointed in February, 1845, recommended in its first report, published three months afterwards, that the

Catholics the benefit of the Toleration Act, by making them subject to the same laws as Protestant Dissenters "in respect of their schools, places for religious worship, education, and charitable purposes." (6) 7 & 8 Vict., cap. 102, expressly repealed many of the penal enactments, so far as they "relate to or in any manner affect Roman Catholics."

clauses in the Uniformity Acts by which a penalty is inflicted for repairing to other places of worship than churches, and also those inflicting penalties on Roman Catholics, Dissenters, and Jews for professing, exercising, or promoting any religion other than that of the Established Church, and also the Laws of Recusancy, be repealed, and further that the religious worship of the Jews be protected in like manner as that of Roman Catholics and Dissenters. These recommendations were carried out in the following year by the Act to relieve Her Majesty's Subjects from certain penalties and Disabilities in regard to Religious opinions (9 & 10 Vict., cap. 59). At length, therefore, after the lapse of more than a century and a half, the Jews were formally, by a solemn Act of the legislature, admitted to the benefits of the Toleration Act, and their religion was no longer merely connived at, but was placed under the protection of the law. During this long period the Jewish question was frequently brought to the notice of Parliament, and the Jews had always both friends and enemies in that assembly; but the Jewish question never became a burning question of the day [1]. The enemies of the Jewish religion, having the letter of the law in their favour, did not feel the necessity of taking any legislative action, though they may have deplored their inability to enforce the penal laws against the Jews. The friends of the Jews, on the other hand, did not care to introduce remedial measures, which would have certainly been opposed and possibly if not probably defeated, because in fact the Jewish religion, though not sanctioned by Parliament, had under the king's dispensing power, as exercised by the Orders in Council in 1674 and 1685, all the protection that was necessary. The synagogue was always open; its worshippers were not prosecuted, and a considerable and

[1] An exception should perhaps be made of the events following the ill-fated Naturalization Act of 1753, but even then the right of public worship and the practical freedom from the penalties of recusancy were never seriously brought in question.

increasing Jewish community gradually grew up both in London and the principal commercial centres. Every year the position became more secure, and premature attempts at legislation would have only endangered it.

Parliament and the Jews. Attempt to lay special taxation upon them.

It cannot, however, be disputed that the Jews were deliberately excluded from the Toleration Act, for almost immediately after its passage their status was the subject of discussion in the House of Commons. In order to provide funds for the reduction of Ireland, which still held out for the Stuart king, and the vigorous prosecution of the war against France, it was resolved in the autumn of 1689 to raise an additional supply of two million pounds. On November 7, the Committee of the whole House, which was sitting to consider the means of raising this sum, recommended that a tax of one hundred thousand pounds be laid upon the Jews, and a bill for that purpose was ordered to be brought in. On November 11 the Jews presented a petition to the House of Commons against the proposed tax. The rule of the House then was that no petition against a bill imposing a tax would be entertained, or if presented entered upon the Journals of the House. This rule, founded on the assumption that as a tax extended over all parts of the kingdom, no individual should be allowed to treat it as a special grievance to himself, was not rescinded until 1842, when standing order 82, discontinuing the former usage and enabling the House to entertain such petitions, was passed. Consequently the petition and the debate upon it are not mentioned in the Commons Journals. The petition gave a very interesting account of the condition of the Jews in England at this time: stating that about the year 1654 there came six Jew families into this kingdom, which since the Restoration of Charles II had been increased to the number of between three and four score families, who had settled in the cities of London and Westminster, under the public faith and protection of King Charles II; that many of them had been made denizens by the last two kings, and that though one half of them had moderate or indifferent estates, the other half consisted partly of persons assisting the better sort in the management of their commerce, and partly of poor people maintained by their richer brethren, and in no ways chargeable to the parish; that they paid all the taxes and fulfilled all the duties imposed upon them, and by their large commercial transactions they greatly enriched the nation, and increased the revenue from Customs: that they were wholly unable to pay the large sum proposed to be levied upon them, and could not expect any assistance from their brethren abroad; so that if the tax were proceeded with they would be utterly ruined. Though not mentioned in the petition, the rumour was spread abroad that the Jews would be forced to leave the country, and that they would remove themselves and their effects into Holland, rather than submit to the imposition [1]. On Nov. 19 the petition was delivered by Mr. Paul Foley, member for Hereford, and afterwards Speaker; and a debate as to whether it should be received ensued. It was questioned whether the Jews were subjects of the king having the right to petition Parliament, and stated that, if they were, they had no more right than their fellow subjects, and could not petition against an Aid. Sir Thomas Lee said: "Pray let not such petitions be received. You will not receive it from others, pray begin not with the Jews." And though Mr. Foley answered these arguments by declaring "I think that for the honour of the House you are to hear what they will say. When you lay a general tax on a whole kingdom, you can receive no petition against it, because all are represented here, but when there is a particular tax on men they may petition." Mr. Speaker Powle stated that he never knew a petition against a Bill before the House was seised of it, and it was decided not to receive the petition [2]. On Dec. 30 the Bill was read a first

[1] See the *Greenwich Hospital News-letter*, 3, No. 77, Nov. 12; *Cal. S. P. Dom.*, 1689, p. 318; and Luttrell's *Diary*, vol. I, p. 303.

[2] Cobbett's *Parl. Hist.*, vol. V, p. 444, and Gray's *Parl. Debates*, vol. IX, pp. 437–8.

time, and it was resolved that it should be read a second time, but it went no further, for men saw how dangerous a precedent it would be to single out for special taxation a small, defenceless, and wholly unrepresented class, which was unable to bear the burden sought to be imposed upon it. The projected tax was accordingly withdrawn[1]. Therefore the Jews did not become subject to a separate system of taxation, as in our West Indian colonies. They were, however, expected to bear the burdens of the country in the same way as their neighbours, and about this very time great disappointment was expressed that they were not ready to advance or lend, on the security of the new taxes, large sums of money for the purposes of the Government, and the Lord Mayor was actually requested by the Earl of Shrewsbury, then Secretary of State for the North, to send for their elders and principal merchants, and to impress upon them the great obligations they were under to the king for the liberty and privileges they enjoyed, and endeavour to induce them to raise the sum of £12,000, which they had offered to provide, to £30,000, or at the very least £20,000[2]. It is probable that the response to this appeal did not come up to the expectations of the Government, and that it was partly in consequence of this that the exemption from certain of the alien duties, which had been granted in the reign of James II, and continued since the Revolution, was finally withdrawn by an Order in Council made in the October of this year[3].

Mention of Jews in the Act imposing taxation on marriages.

On other occasions also the permanent settlement of the Jews here was recognized by Parliament, and they are more than once expressly mentioned in Acts of Parliament. The first of these Acts is 6 & 7 Will. and Mar. cap. 6, entitled "An act for granting to His Majesty certaine rates and duties upon Marriages, Births, and Burials, and upon

[1] See Macaulay's *History*, ch. xv; *Commons Journals*, vol. X, pp. 281, 319; *Calendar S. P. Dom.*, Dec. 31, 1689, p. 374; *Greenwich Hospital News-letter*, 3, No. 83.

[2] *S. P. Calendar*, Feb. 10, 1690. [3] See Tovey's *Anglia Iudaica*, pp. 287–95.

Batchelors and Widowers, for the terme of 5 years, for carrying on the War against France with Vigour." It imposed a duty of two shillings and sixpence upon the marriage of every person not in receipt of alms, and additional taxes in case of the marriage of persons of rank or property, and contained a proviso that Quakers, Papists, and *Jews*, and any other persons living together as man and wife, should be liable to the duties they would have been obliged to pay, if they had been married according to the law of England, but at the same time the Act was not to be construed as in any way making good or effectual any such marriage.

The Act against Blasphemy.

Again a few years later, in the spring of 1698, when "the Act for the more effectual suppressing of Blasphemy and Profaneness" was before Parliament, and an amendment was inserted after its return to the Lords, by which all persons openly professing the Jewish religion would have been made liable to the severe penalties it imposed; the House of Commons recognized the right of the Jews to remain here and continue the exercise of their religion by rejecting the amendment by a substantial majority. This incident is thus described by Narcissus Luttrell in his *Diary*, under the date March 22, $169\frac{7}{8}$: "The Commons yesterday divided about a clause in the bill against prophanesse, relating to the Jews, who deny Jesus Christ; 144 were for it, and 78 against it: so the clause was added that the Jews shal not be molested [1]."

The Act to oblige Jews to maintain their Protestant children. The de Breta case.

The next occasion on which this subject was raised in the legislature was in the year 1702, when the Act to oblige the Jews to maintain and provide for their Protestant children was passed. The way in which this statute was put in operation has already been described in the second of these articles, and calls for no further comment, but it

[1] The *Commons Journals* give the numbers as 140 and 78. In reality no clause was added, but the words which had been struck out by the Lords were restored to the Act. For the history of the Act, see supra, pp. 13–18.

may be advisable to recall the circumstances which led to its enactment. A few years earlier the Commons had rejected the Lords' amendment to the Act against Blasphemy and Profaneness, on the express ground that it would drive the Jews out of the country, and so deprive them of the means of being rightly instructed in the principles of the true Christian religion. It soon became clear that this desire of gaining proselytes would not be gratified to any great extent if the converts were exposed to financial ruin, nor, as there was not in those days a rich and highly endowed society for the promotion of Christianity among the Jews, were the conversionists prepared to support a burden which they had reasonable hopes of removing to other shoulders. In the year 1701 a case arose which gave an opportunity for introducing legislation. In May of that year Mary Mendez de Breta, a girl nearly eighteen years of age, who had been brought up as a Jewess, embraced the Christian faith, and was baptized by Mr. Thorold, a minister of the Church of England. Thereupon her father, Jacob Mendez de Breta, disowned her for his child, turned her out of doors, and refused to allow her any maintenance, and she, being afraid of her father's anger, applied to the Lord Mayor for protection, and at his order the churchwardens of St. Andrew's Undershaft, in whose parish the father lived, provided for her and maintained her at the charge of the parish. The churchwardens lodged a complaint against the father at the Quarter Sessions at the Guildhall, and an order was made under the Relief of the Poor Act of Elizabeth that the father should allow her twenty shillings a-month for her maintenance, but this order was subsequently quashed by the Court of King's Bench, on the ground that there was no jurisdiction to make it[1]. A petition was then presented

[1] See the Inhabitants of St. Andrew's Undershaft *v.* de Breta, Lord Raymond's *Reports*, vol. I, p. 699. Before the Committee of the House of Commons it was stated that the allowance for maintenance was twenty shillings a-week. *Commons Journals*, vol. XIII, p. 799.

to the House of Commons by the ministers, churchwardens, and overseers of the poor of the above-mentioned parish and the five neighbouring parishes, stating that most of the Jews in London lived in their parishes, and that, "though they enjoy the protection of the government and the free exercise of their religion and grow rich, yet they bear such a hatred to our national religion, that in case any of their children embrace the same, they utterly disown them and treat them with great cruelty; an instance whereof appears by the daughter of Jacob Mendez de Breta, a rich Jew in St. Andrew's Undershaft, who being converted to the Christian Faith, he utterly disowns her for his child and refuses to maintain her; so that she is now kept by the said parish for her encouragement, suitable to her education," and praying that a bill might be brought in to oblige Jacob Mendez de Breta in particular and the Jews in general to maintain and provide for their Protestant children. The petition was at once referred to a Committee. The Committee heard a large number of witnesses on both sides, including the father himself, who said that Mary was not his daughter, but with two or three more children had been laid at his door in Portugal, and that he had maintained them purely out of charity, and further that he had never owned her as his daughter, but had always treated her as a servant, and that if she was entered in the parish books for the poll-tax as his daughter it was without his knowledge or consent. The Committee, however, found that the allegations in the petition were fully proved, and recommended that a bill be brought in according to the prayer of the petition. When the bill was read a second time a petition from several Jews, merchants in London, was presented against it, and after certain amendments had been made in the Commons, it was passed in the Lords without any amendment and almost without debate[1].

On other occasions occurring at frequent intervals before

[1] *Commons Journals*, vol. XIII, pp. 748, 798–800, 813, 839, 848, 886, 889, 895, and *Lords Journals*, vol. XVII, pp. 125, 126, 128, 131, 148.

1846 Parliament took cognizance of the presence of the Jews, generally with the view of mitigating in their favour new enactments which would have otherwise pressed heavily upon them, but it will for our present purpose be sufficient to enumerate briefly the principal of these occasions. For instance, in the year 1722, in order to place a check upon the Jacobites, many of whom were Roman Catholics, it was enacted by 9 Geo. I, cap. 24, that all persons owning land, who refused or neglected to take the oaths appointed for the security of the king's person and government, which included the oath of abjuration as framed in the reign of James I, and ending with the words "on the true faith of a Christian," should register their names and real estates before a fixed day, or in default should forfeit their lands. But, in the following year, an amending Act, 10 Geo. I, cap. 4, was passed, which allowed persons professing the Jewish religion to take the oath without the final words, in like manner as Jews are admitted to be sworn to give evidence in Courts of Justice.

Relaxation of the Act compelling landowners to take the oath of abjuration in favour of the Jews.

Again in the year 1740 an Act was passed enabling all persons who had settled for a period of seven years in any of the British colonies in America to be naturalized, under certain conditions, without the necessity of obtaining a private Act of Parliament, by which naturalization was granted in those days, but it contained a proviso that all such persons should first receive the Sacrament of the Lord's Supper in some Protestant and reformed congregation in Great Britain or one of the colonies, except the people called Quakers, "or such who profess the Jewish religion." It was also further provided that Jews taking the necessary oaths for the purposes of this Act might omit the words "on the true faith of a Christian," in the same way as they were enabled to do under 9 Geo. I, cap. 24[1]. Thirteen years later Lord Hardwicke's Act for the better preventing of clandestine marriages (26 Geo. II,

Similar privileges given the Jews by other Acts of Parliament. The Colonial Naturalization Act, 1740.

Lord Hardwicke's Marriage Act, 1753.

[1] 13 Geo. II, cap. 7, repealed by the Naturalization Act, 1870; see especially secs. 2 and 3.

cap. 33), which made null and void all marriages solemnized without the publication of banns or licence, expressly excepted marriages amongst the people called Quakers or amongst the persons professing the Jewish religion, and most of the subsequent marriage Acts have contained similar exceptions. In the same year was passed the famous Jew bill (26 Geo. II, cap. 26), which permitted persons professing the Jewish religion to be naturalized by Act of Parliament without having previously taken the Sacrament. The Act passed through the House of Lords with great ease, but when it came down to the House of Commons met with strong opposition; indeed it would have possibly been wrecked in the Lower House, had not some of the enemies of the Government slackened their efforts against it, in the belief that it would cause widespread unpopularity throughout the country against the party in power. Nor was this belief ill-founded, for the storm of prejudice and fanaticism that arose during the recess compelled the Government to pass as their first effective measure of the next session an Act repealing the obnoxious Jew bill. For more than seventy years the Jews were not specially mentioned in any Act of Parliament, but they were again expressly excepted from the provisions of the marriage Acts of 1824, 1836, and 1840, and the Registration Act, 1836, provided for the due registration of Jewish marriages by the Secretary of a synagogue certified by the President of the London Committee of Deputies of the British Jews.

The Jewish Naturalization Act, 1753.

This brings us down to the years 1845 and 1846, when the measures of relief were granted, and the Jewish religion finally admitted to the benefit of the Toleration Act. Till then the immunity of the Jews from the consequences of the penal laws had rested on the royal dispensations granted by the king in Council in answer to the petitions of Abraham Delivera and others in 1674, and of Joseph Henriques and others in 1685, and the preceding summary of Parliamentary enactments concerning the Jews shows

The Jews admitted to the benefit of the Toleration Act, 1845 and 1846. Till then they were protected only by the Dispensing Power of the king.

that the legislature tacitly acquiesced in this particular exercise of the dispensing power formerly claimed by the Crown, nor was there any individual bold enough to challenge it by persisting in a prosecution in a court of law. This fact is not without significance, when it is remembered that the laws against recusants, though by no means uniformly enforced, had not become quite obsolete, even at the time when they were finally repealed. The Criminal Law Commissioners, in their first report published in 1845, mention a considerable number of convictions, followed by actual imprisonment of the offenders, which had recently to their knowledge taken place in different parts of the country [1]. Though never questioned in a court of law, the immunity of the Jews did in truth rest upon sufficiently sure foundations. It could not indeed be proved that any charter or formal document of exemption had been executed in their favour, but the fact of the dispensation was sufficiently evidenced by the story of the proceedings taken against them on two important occasions in two different reigns.

There can be little doubt that in the reign of Charles II, when the Jews re-established their community here, the king still retained the power of dispensing with laws, though subject to certain limits, which even in those times could not be precisely defined, but which it was generally acknowledged that James II had in the latter part of his reign undoubtedly transgressed. Accordingly it was not absolutely condemned by the Declaration of Rights, but it was thought sufficient to declare that "the pretended power of dispensing with laws or the execution of laws, by regall authoritie, *as it hath beene assumed and exercised of late*, is illegall." To prevent such abuse in the future, the Bill of Rights absolutely abolished the power, except in such cases

[1] See first report of Her Majesty's Commissioners for revising and consolidating the criminal law, note on pp. 32–3, and also Lord Brougham's remarks, *Hans. Parl. Debat.*, vol. 59, p. 815 (1841), and id., vol. 85, p. 1264 (1846).

as should be specially provided for by statute, and contained a special saving clause, providing no charter, grant, or pardon granted before October 23, 1689, should be in any way impeached or invalidated. Though the Jews had no formal charter in their possession, they could claim the final words of the Order in Council of 1685—"His Majesty's intention being that they should not be troubled upon this account, but quietly enjoy the free exercise of their religion, whilst they behave themselves dutifully and obediently to his government"—as a grant within the meaning of the proviso [1].

Resulting anomaly in the law as to the Registration of Synagogues.

When the facts are properly analysed, it is difficult to suggest any other foundation for the freedom of the Jews to establish synagogues, and to absent themselves from church, than the exercise of the dispensing power of the Crown. From this an anomalous consequence of no small practical importance resulted, namely, that there never was any necessity to certify or register a synagogue in the same way as places of religious worship belonging to other Dissenting bodies. The benefit of the Toleration Act of 1688 was confined to persons who attended divine service at some place permitted by the Act, and no place for religious worship was permitted by the Act until certified to the Bishop, Archdeacon, or Quarter Sessions, and duly registered or recorded, and the Roman Catholic Relief Act of 1791 contained similar provisions for the certification and registration of Roman Catholic places of worship. Furthermore, the second section of the Places of Religious Worship Act, 1812, which is still in force, imposed a penalty of twenty pounds upon every person permitting a congregation or assembly for religious worship of Protestants, at which more than twenty persons should be present, to meet in any place occupied by him before it had been duly certified.

[1] For the dispensing power see the cases of *non-obstante*, 12 Rep., fo. 18: Thomas *v.* Sorrel (1674), *Vaughan*, p. 330, and Godden *v.* Hales (1686), 2 *Shower*, p. 475, and XI St. Tr., p. 1,166, with the notes, especially those at pp. 1,187 and 1,251, and generally Broom's *Constitutional Law*, pp. 492–506; Anson's *Parliament*, pp. 311–17; and Burnet's *Reign of James II*, pp. 458–60.

In the year 1855 the Act for securing the liberty of religious worship (18 & 19 Vict., cap. 86) considerably modified this stringent provision, by excepting from its operation assemblies for religious worship conducted by the incumbent of the parish, or a person authorized by him, and congregations meeting in a private dwelling-house, or meeting *occasionally* in a building not usually appropriated to religious worship. The second section of the same Act, by providing that the expression in the Act of 1846, Her Majesty's subjects professing the Jewish religion, in respect of their places for religious worship, shall be subject to the same laws as Protestant Dissenters are subject to, shall mean are subject to for the time being after the passing of this Act, seems to imply that at that time it was necessary to certify a Jewish synagogue. But it is certain that there was no provision for certifying a synagogue before 1846, and it is hardly consonant with the true principles of the interpretation of statutes to extend the scope of a highly penal section of an Act of Parliament in this indirect way, especially by an enactment entitled "An Act to relieve Her Majesty's subjects from certain penalties and disabilities in regard to religious opinions," the manifest intention of which was to grant relief from former burdens, but not to impose any new obligations. However, by the Places of Religious Worship Registration Act, 1855 (18 & 19 Vict., cap. 81), a Jewish synagogue *may* be certified in writing to the Registrar-General of births, deaths, and marriages, and will then be registered in due time. Although, as has been said, this course is optional and not compulsory, it is to be recommended, because it ensures the following advantages. A building so certified is exempt from uninvited interference by the Charity Commissioners, and is also, if exclusively appropriated to public religious worship, not liable to be rated for parochial or municipal purposes [1]. In

Advantages of certifying a synagogue.

[1] See 16 & 17 Vict., cap. 137, sec. 62; 18 & 19 Vict., cap. 81, sec. 9; and 32 & 33 Vict., cap. 110, sec. 15, as to the provisions of the Charitable Trusts Act; and as to the exemption from rates, 3 & 4 Will. IV, cap. 30; 5 & 6 Will. IV, cap. 50, sec. 27; and 38 & 39 Vict., cap. 55, sec. 151.

addition, a synagogue not certified is not entitled to any of the advantages conferred by the legislature in 1846: a gift or legacy to it is void, nor can contracts to hire seats in it be enforced, or disturbers of the service be punished.

Summary of the foregoing account of the legal recognition of the Jewish religion.

With the mention of this somewhat curious anomaly, the consequence of this method in which full legal recognition has been given to the Jewish religion, it is time to bring the foregoing inquiry to a close; nor is it necessary to recapitulate at any length the conclusions already arrived at. In the year 1290 the Jews were banished from the kingdom by royal edict, but this edict, now lost, would not avail to absolutely exclude from the country centuries afterwards Jews in no way connected with the former bondsmen of the king. From time to time isolated Jews came and lived in England, but the severity of the laws enforcing uniformity of religion was sufficient to prevent the formation of a Jewish community, and as late as the reign of James I the Jews that were here fled the country through fear of the commissioners appointed to execute the laws against Jesuits. The treaty with Spain in 1630 made it somewhat easier for Jews to settle here, by allowing them to evade some of the penalties imposed on recusants, but this advantage, such as it was, was lost by the outbreak of the war with Spain in 1656, though restored after the return of Charles II. Availing themselves of this advantage a small number of Jews settled in the country in the reign of Charles I, and at the time of the execution of that king a formal request was made for the recognition of the Jewish religion, but it was not successful, and being renewed seven years later, in spite of the fair words used and the courtesy shown to Menasseh, it again proved a failure. During Cromwell's régime nothing was done; but there is evidence that the Protector allowed some half-dozen families of persons he knew to be Jews to remain in the realm, but this was a special favour which did not enable them to form a distinct body or set up a synagogue. During his exile Charles II made a formal promise to relax the law in their favour; but no legislation was introduced, nor, if introduced, would it have had a chance of success. But the promise was fulfilled. A considerable number of Jews received the rights of citizenship; a distinct Jewish community arose, and a synagogue was established. At first the services were kept strictly secret, for fear of the enforcement of the penal laws, but, under the protection of the king's dispensing power, before the end of 1663 it was possible to hold them with open doors, and the attacks made upon the Jews were successfully repelled. On the accession of King James II a further and last attempt was made to visit with the rigour of the law the still young and struggling community, which was again saved by the exercise of the dispensing power of the Crown. After the Revolution the power of dispensation was swept away, but it was expressly provided that charters or grants already made should not be held invalid, and the formal Order in Council of November 13, 1685, granting the Jews the free exercise of their religion, was thus confirmed. At length, in 1846, after an interval of more than a century and a half, the Jewish religion, the profession of which had been frequently recognized by the legislature, was formally made legal by Act of Parliament.

VIII.

THE CIVIL RIGHTS OF ENGLISH JEWS.

HAVING already surveyed the manner in which a Jewish community was allowed to grow up in England, and the Jewish religion, which was at first extra-legal and the profession of which, but for the dispensing power of the Crown, would have involved serious criminal consequences, was at length legalized by being admitted to the benefit of the Toleration Act; it remains to consider the legal rights of professed Jews.

Distinction between civil and political rights.

This subject may be conveniently divided here into two heads, civil and political rights; for though it is true that these two adjectives are really synonymous, the one being a Latin word and the other its Greek equivalent, and that, in a country with a popular form of government, no very sharp line of demarcation can be drawn between them, yet the distinction is intelligible and useful for our present purpose; civil rights including the power to protect from wrong both person and property, and political rights the power to take part in the legislation and government of the country. The obvious intention of some of the enactments of the latter half of the seventeenth century was to exclude from any share in the government all who were not members of the Anglican Church; but as to civil rights, with which we will first deal, there were no special enactments concerning the Jews, and they had to take the law as they found it, without any exceptions in their favour in cases where, owing to their own peculiar customs and laws, it would have been not unreasonable to look for them.

We have seen that before the expulsion of the Jews in

The law of the land applied to the Jews on their return; but the abolition of villenage exempted them from the operation of the ancient statutes concerning the Judaei.

1290 there had been in force several statutes exclusively relating to them, but that these statutes could not affect the Jews on their return in the seventeenth century because they were no longer in the position of bondsmen of the king; but, on the other hand, the method of applying the common law of the land to the Jews that had been in vogue before their banishment, in so far at least as it was not a necessary consequence of the status of villenage which no longer existed, could be and, when substantial justice would thereby be done, actually was revived by the courts of law. The cases in which such application was most necessary were the celebration of marriage and the administration of the oath in courts of justice. The law as to the marriage of Jews must be left to a separate chapter, and it will suffice now to deal with the capacity of a Jew to be a witness, and his right to be sworn in a manner binding upon his own conscience, namely, on the Pentateuch or the Old Testament, instead of upon the New Testament.

Right of a Jew to be a witness in a Court of law.

Lord Coke[1], writing anterior to the resettlement, lays down that an infidel cannot be a witness, and there is little room for doubt that he meant to include Jews, whom he generally calls infidel Jews. Sir Matthew Hale—in a passage of his *History of the Pleas of the Crown*, which, though the work was not published till after his death, on Christmas Day, 1676, must have been written before the point was decided by the Courts, for there is no reference to the decision—takes a very different view. "It is said," he writes, "by my Lord Coke that an infidel is not to be admitted as a witness, the consequence whereof would also be that a Jew (who only owns the Old Testament) could not be a witness. But I take it, that although the regular oath, as it is allowed by the laws of England, is 'tactis sacrosanctis Dei evangeliis,' which supposeth a man to be a Christian, yet in cases of necessity, as in foreign contracts between merchant and merchant, which are many times transacted by Jewish brokers, the testi-

[1] Co. Lit., 6 b.

mony of a Jew 'tacto libro legis Mosaicae' is not to be rejected, and is used, as I have been informed, among all nations. Yea, the oaths of idolatrous infidels have been admitted in the municipal laws of many kingdoms, especially 'si iuraverit per verum Deum creatorem,' and special laws are instituted in Spain touching the form of the oaths of infidels. And," he adds, "it were a very hard case, if a murder committed here in England in presence only of a Turk or a Jew, that owns not the Christian religion, should be dispunishable, because such an oath should not be taken, which the witness holds binding, and cannot swear otherwise, and possibly might think himself under no obligation, if sworn according to the usual style of the Courts of England. But then it must be agreed that the credit of such testimony must be left to the Jury[1]." It was not long before the point had to be decided. In the case of Robeley *v.* Langston, which was tried in the Court of King's Bench in the month of January, 1667, several Jewish witnesses were produced and the Chief Justice swore them upon the Old Testament only; whereupon an objection to their evidence was taken on the ground that if it was false, it would not render them liable to a prosecution for perjury, but the Court overruled the objection[2]. The same practice was adopted in the Court of Chancery, though it was apparently not found necessary to introduce it until Michaelmas Term, 1684, when "a Jew being to put in an answer upon a motion, it was ordered that he should be sworn upon the Pentateuch, and that the plaintiff's clerk should be present to see him sworn[3]." Nevertheless the swearing of Jews in this manner was for some time regarded as exceptional, and as such we find references to it in the reports, for instance, in the report of Francia's trial for high treason, in 1717, mention is made of the fact that the witness Gonsales was sworn on the books of Moses; and as late as the year 1729,

[1] *Hist. Placit. Coronae*, part II, p. 279.

[2] 2 Keble, p. 314.

[3] 1 Vern., p. 263.

in the case of Gomez Serra *v.* Munez, there is a note that "the bail in this case being both Jews were suffered to put on their hats while they took the oath[1]." At length, in Michaelmas Term, 1744, the whole question was discussed in the well-known case of Omychund *v.* Barker, in which Lord Chancellor Hardwicke, assisted by the heads of the three common law courts, decided that all persons who believe in a supreme being, who will punish them if they swear falsely, are competent witnesses, and should take the oath in the form binding upon them according to the tenets of their religion. In the course of his judgment Chief Justice Willes says, "It is plain both from Madox's *History of the Exchequer*, pp. 167 and 174, and from *Selden*, vol. III, p. 1469, that the Jews here in the time of King John and Henry the Third were both admitted to be witnesses and likewise to be upon juries in causes between Christians and Jews, and that they were sworn upon their own books or their own roll, which is the same thing. I will likewise oppose" [to Lord Coke's assertion] "the constant practice here almost ever since the Jews have been permitted to come back again into England; viz., from the 19 Car. II (when the cause was tried which is reported in 2 Keble 314) down to the present times, during which I believe not one instance can be cited in which a Jew was refused to be a witness and to be sworn on the Pentateuch[2]."

Witnesses not sworn on the New Testament may be guilty of perjury.

The Court further held that perjury might be assigned in cases where the special form of oath had been administered. The objection that this could not be done was taken by counsel for the defendants, who desired to exclude the evidence of persons of the Gentoo religion taken on commission in India on the ground that the words *tactis sacris evangeliis* were necessary words in an indictment for perjury. Upon this objection Lord Chief Baron Parker said, "This is not true in fact; but supposing it was, yet this is not the only case where witnesses cannot be prose-

[1] See XV St. Tr., p. 961 and 2 Strange, p. 821.

[2] Willes, p. 543.

cuted, for there is no possibility of prosecuting them where the depositions are taken out of England; but if they were here, I should be of opinion they might be indicted upon a special indictment, for I do not think *tactis sacris evangeliis* are necessary words, for several old precedents are that the party was *iuratus* generally, or *debito more iuratus*[1]." And Chief Justice Willes dealt with the point in the same way, saying, "This objection has been in a great measure already answered by the Chief Baron, and it may receive two plain answers; first that these words, *supra sacrosancta Dei Evangelia* or *tactis sacrosanctis Dei Evangeliis* are not necessary to be in an indictment for perjury. They have been omitted in many indictments against Jews, of which several precedents have been laid before us; and they are not in the precedents of such indictments which I find in an ancient and very good book, entitled *West's Simboliography*; but it is only there said *supra sacramentum suum dixit et deposuit* or *affirmavit et deposuit.* Besides, this argument if it prove anything, proves a good deal too much; for if there were anything in it, many depositions of Christians have been admitted, and many more must be admitted or else there will be a manifest failure of justice, where the witnesses are certainly not liable to be indicted; for when the depositions of witnesses are taken in another country, it frequently happens that they never come over hither, or if they do cannot be indicted for perjury because the fact was committed in another country[2]."

It is plain from the report that several prosecutions had been instituted against Jews for perjury because precedents had been searched and brought before the Court; but, on the other hand, such prosecutions must have been very rare, for when in the course of his argument the Solicitor-General was requested by the Lord Chief Justice to deal with the point, he declared, "There is no instance of a Jew's being indicted for perjury." Lord Chief Justice Lee, "I have tried a

[1] 1 Atk., p. 43.

[2] Willes, pp. 553, 554.

Jew myself upon an indictment of perjury." Mr. Solicitor-General insisted, "That the indictment would not be wrong against a Jew if it was *tacto libro legis Mosaicae*[1]."

A Jew may be sworn on the New Testament if he does not object.

Half a century later it became necessary to hold that a Jew who professed belief in the doctrines of Christianity might, although never formally admitted to Christianity, be sworn in the common form on the New Testament. In the case of the King against Gilham, one John King, a money broker, was called as a witness and sworn in the ordinary way. He said that he was born a Jew but had been of the established religion since he had been of capacity to judge for himself, and that he now professed to be of that persuasion. He admitted that he had been married according to the Jewish rites, and that his first wife had been a Jewess, and that he had never been baptized or formally renounced the Jewish religion or been admitted a member of the Established Church. Lord Kenyon ruled that as the witness considered himself bound by the precepts of Christianity, that the obligation of an oath so taken was sufficiently binding[2].

The Oaths Act, 1838.

As questions of this kind occasionally arose[3] the Act

[1] 1 Atk., p. 35. For the report of the case see 1 Atk., pp. 21–30; 1 Wilson, p. 84, and Willes, pp. 538–54.

[2] Rex *v.* Gilham (1795), 1 Esp., p. 286. See also 6 T. R., p. 265. The validity of King's second marriage to Lady Lanesborough had been before Lord Kenyon five years before this time. See Ganer *v.* Lady Lanesborough, 1 Peake, p. 25.

[3] For instance, during the trial of Queen Caroline in the House of Lords in 1820, a discussion arose as to the proper mode of swearing an Italian witness, in the course of which Lord Erskine related the following anecdote. "I remember a case to have occurred when I was at the bar. A person came into the court of King's Bench, in the time of Lord Kenyon or Lord Mansfield, I think Lord Kenyon. Lord Chief Justice Eyre was sitting in the other court—a witness came who did not describe himself to be of any particular sect, entitling him to an indulgence, but stating that from certain ideas in his own mind he could not swear according to the usual form of the oath; that he would hold up his hand and would swear, but would not kiss the book. . . . He gave a reason which appeared to me a very absurd one—'because it was written in the Revelations that the angel standing upon the sea held up his hand.' . . .

to remove doubts as to the validity of certain oaths (1 and 2 Vict., cap. 105) was introduced and passed in the year 1838. It provides "that in all cases in which an oath may lawfully be and shall have been administered to any person, either as a juryman or a witness or a deponent in any proceeding, civil or criminal, in any court of law or equity in the United Kingdom, or on appointment to any office or employment, or on any occasion whatever, such person is bound by the oath administered, provided the same shall have been administered in such form and with such ceremonies as such person may declare to be binding; and every such person in case of wilful false swearing may be convicted of the crime of perjury in the same manner as if the oath had been administered in the form and with the ceremonies most commonly adopted."

Arrangement of cause lists so that Jewish cases should not be taken on the Jewish Sabbath or holidays.

From the earliest times after the resettlement the judges of the courts of law admitted Jews as competent witnesses and allowed them to take the oath according to their own usages. They also showed, still further, a spirit of toleration by no means universal in the seventeenth century, for they in some instances actually arranged their cause lists in such a way as to allow cases in which it was known Jews would be material witnesses to be heard on days other than the Jewish Sabbath; for example, in the year 1677 the plaintiff in the case of Barker *v.* Warren had leave given by the Court to alter the venue from London to Middlesex because all the sittings in London were on a Saturday and his witness was a Jew and would not appear that day[1]. Similar indulgences when no serious inconvenience has been caused have frequently been

I said this does not apply to your case, for in the first place you are no angel, secondly, you cannot tell how the angel would have sworn if he had been on shore." Lord Kenyon, having consulted Chief Justice Eyre held that, though the witness was not of any particular sect, the form of oath which he said would be binding on his conscience (whether his reason was a good one or a bad one) ought to be administered to him. (*Hans. Parl. Deb.*, 2nd series, vol. II, p. 912).

[1] 2 Mod. Rep., p. 271.

granted, and in the year 1900 Mr. Justice Ridley postponed the sitting of the Long Vacation Court, which would have taken place on the Day of Atonement, to the following day, at the request of Mr. D. L. Alexander, Q.C., the present President of the Board of Deputies, who at that time was the leading counsel practising in the Vacation Court. This example was still more recently followed by Mr. Justice Bigham, who sat late and so arranged his list at the Liverpool Winter Assizes of 1904 that the evidence in the Jewish libel case of Fineberg *v.* the Chief Rabbi and the members of the Liverpool Schechita Board should be concluded before the commencement of the Jewish Sabbath.

Jewish religious scruples recognized by the law merchant. A Jew excused from giving notice of dishonour of a bill of exchange on a Jewish holiday.

In the same generous spirit, if we may make a short digression, the courts in enforcing the law merchant, which is incorporated in the common law, have had regard to Jewish religious scruples and have held the necessity of observing the Jewish Sabbath or other holy day set apart by the Jews for religious purposes a special circumstance excusing a Jew in the habit of observing it from performing on that day any act of business which otherwise would be incumbent upon him; for instance, in the case of a bill of exchange or promissory note notice of dishonour must be given within a reasonable time of the actual dishonour of the bill or note, and in the absence of special circumstances the notice is not given within a reasonable time unless it is sent off on the day after the dishonour of the bill; but the fact that such day is Sunday, Christmas Day, Good Friday, or a Bank Holiday is a sufficient excuse entitling the holder or indorser of the bill to give the requisite notice upon the day following, and on the same principle it has been held that a Jew is not bound to give such notice on the Day of Atonement but may wait till the next day, and the same principle would extend to the Jewish Sabbath and New Year, and the first and last days of the Festivals in the case of a person accustomed to keep his place of business closed on those days.

The point was decided as long ago as 1811, in the case of Lindo *v.* Unsworth. There the bill sued on had been dishonoured on Saturday, Oct. 6, and Messrs. Hoare, the bankers, in whose hands the bill was, sent to give notice of the dishonour to the plaintiff on Monday the 8th, but that being the Day of Atonement, and he being by religion a Jew, his counting-house was shut and there was no way to communicate the notice to him until after the post had been dispatched. On the 9th he sent off a letter by the post giving notice of the dishonour of the bill, addressed to the defendant at Lancaster. It was contended that the notice was bad, but Lord Ellenborough ruled as follows:—"I think the plaintiff was excused from giving notice on the 8th upon the score of his religion. The law required him to give notice with reasonable diligence; and I think he did so, if he sent off the letter as soon as he could after the termination of the festival, during which he was absolutely forbid to attend to secular affairs. The law merchant respects the religion of different people. For this reason we are not obliged to give notice of the dishonour of a bill on our Sunday. But it was equally impossible for the defendant to give this notice on the 8th of October. The letter sent off on the 9th is therefore sufficient," and there was a verdict for the plaintiff[1].

Capacity of Jews to bring actions.

Returning from this digression, we have seen that the capacity of a Jew to be a witness was decided soon after the resettlement in a manner contrary to the view held by Lord Coke. That great jurist had also expressly laid down that a Jew was incapable of bringing an action, and this point also had soon to be decided. The real difficulty of admitting a Jew's evidence was the mode of administering the oath, but the alleged incapacity had been based, not upon the form of the oath, but upon the argument that the testimony of infidels in whatever way they were sworn could not be accepted.

[1] Lindo *v.* Unsworth (1811), 2 Com., p. 602. See also Tassel *v.* Lewis (1695), 1 Lord Raymond, p. 743, and the Bills of Exchange Act, 1882, sec. 49 (12) and sec. 92.

The alleged incapacity to sue was also supported by similar reasoning. Christianity being part and parcel of the law of England, those who did not profess it could not have the rights of Englishmen but, whether born within the king's allegiance or not, must be aliens, nor could they be alien friends, but must be regarded as alien enemies, even though they might be here under the special permission of the king. Lord Coke, in his report of the judgment of the Exchequer Chamber in Calvin's case, thus lays down the law: "All infidels are in law *perpetui inimici*, perpetual enemies (for the law presumes not that they will be converted, that being *remota potentia*, a remote possibility), for between them, as with the devils, whose subjects they be, and the Christian there is a perpetual hostility, and can be no peace; for, as the Apostle saith, 2 Cor. vi. 15 'Quae autem conventio Christi ad Belial, aut quae pars fideli cum infideli?' and the law saith, 'Iudaeo Christianum nullum serviat mancipium, nefas enim est quem Christus redemit blasphemum Christi in servitutis vinculis detinere.' Register 287 'Infideles sunt Christi et Christianorum inimici.' And herewith agreeth the book in 12 H. 8, fol. 4, where it is holden that a Pagan cannot have or maintain any action at all[1]." In his introduction to the report Coke admits that he has exercised what he styles the right of every reporter to state the true reasons and causes of the judgment in the way that seems to him the fittest and clearest for the right understanding of them. In consequence, even at the time the report was very severely criticized. Nathaniel Bacon says of it: "In handling this case the honourable Reporter took leave to range into a general discourse of Ligeance, though not directly within the conclusion of the case[2]."

Coke's theory that infidels are perpetual enemies.

Nevertheless a statement of law made by so high an authority was generally accepted, and we find the very

[1] Rep. VII. 17 a, 17 b.

[2] *Historical Discourse on the Uniformity of the Government of England*, part II, cap. 8, edition of 1647, p. 78.

words of Lord Coke's proposition embodied in Wingate's *Maxims of Reason or the Reason of the Common Law of England*[1]. Nor was the doctrine regarded as at all unreasonable, seeing that it was undoubtedly the law that a person excommunicated by the law of holy church was at this time incapable of bringing an action[2]. It was much enlarged upon in the arguments of counsel in the great case of monopolies between the East India Company and Sandys, where the question for decision was whether the Company, which had obtained from the king letters patent conferring upon its members the exclusive privilege of trading to the East Indies, could maintain an action for damages against the defendant for trading thither without licence. It was contended that inasmuch as the inhabitants of the Indies were infidels no subjects of the king could trade with them without licence from the king for fear that they might renounce their faith; for the king has the preservation of religion by the law vested and reposed in him, and will take care to give licence to traffic to such only as he is confident will never waver from their profession. In support of this contention the passage in Coke was cited and the treatment of the Jews prior to the expulsion was referred to. Upon this topic Pollexfen in his speech for the defendant said: "My lord, pray let us consider of late times what a number of Jews have lived among us; should we declare this for law at this day, that the people ought to use them as alien enemies, strip them, plunder them, knock them on the head, kill them and slay them? What would be the consequence? What work would this make? For if this be true, what they assert that they are perpetual enemies, then we can have no peace with them; whoever owes a Jew anything may play the Jew

[1] Maxims, edition of 1658, p. 10.

[2] Co. upon Lit., 138 b. This disability continued until 1813 when it was removed by statute (53 Geo. III, cap. 127, sec. 3). For the effect of excommunication and its employment before the passing of this statute see Lecky, *Hist.*, vol. III, pp. 494–6.

with him, never pay him; whoever has a mind to anything he has, may take it away from him; if he has a mind to beat him, and knock him on the head, he may; there is no protection for him, nor peace with him. My lord, I do believe that it is true that the Jews being under the curse, and having been a vagrant people for so long a time, and having no prince to defend them, it is probable they have been made havoc of, and our kings and princes have made bold to do with them according to their own pleasures; though what is recorded of it is so long ago, that it is hard to know the whole truth. But I think they are no precedents to be followed now, unless they had been followed by a succession of practice and authority in our books of law[1]." Sir Robert Sawyer, the Attorney-General, who appeared for the plaintiffs, met this argument by saying that if infidels came into England under a safe-conduct, then until such safe-conduct was formally determined by the king, no subject could seize the person or goods of such alien enemies, and that even when the safe-conduct was determined the right of seizing the property of alien enemies did not belong to the subjects, but was expressly reserved to the king. And this he illustrates by the appropriation by the Crown of the debts due to the Jews and the property they left behind them at the time of their expulsion[2]. The court ultimately decided the case, which was pending for nearly two years, from Trinity Term, 1683, to Hilary Term, 1685, in favour of the plaintiff, but the important arguments based on the status of the Jews were not expressly dealt with in the judgments[3].

The capacity of a Jew to sue admitted in 1684.

Before, however, this judgment was given, the point was raised in a separate case in the Court of King's Bench in Michaelmas Term, 1684. The case is noted in Lilly's

[1] X St. Tr., p. 447.

[2] The fallacy of this argument is the omission of all mention of the special status of villeins of the king then attaching to the Jews.

[3] The case is reported, X St. Tr., pp. 371–554, 2 Shower, pp. 366–72, and Skinner, pp. 132–7, 165–73, 197–204, 223–6.

Practical Register as follows: "A Jew brought an action, and the defendant pleaded that the plaintiff is a Jew, and that all Jews are perpetual enemies *Regis et Religionis*." But it was held by the court that "a Jew may recover as well as a villein, and the plea is but in disability so long as the king shall prohibit them to trade; and judgment was given for the plaintiff[1]." The notorious Jeffreys, a great stickler for the prerogative, was at this time head of the King's Bench, and therefore it is not surprising that the decision given in favour of the Jews is based upon the king's right to treat them as villeins, if he pleases, in accordance with the precedents in the times of the Norman and Angevin kings.

Coke's theory over-ruled by the Courts.

A few years later, in 1697, the point was again referred to in Wells *v.* Williams in the Court of Common Pleas; in arguing which case counsel said: "A Jew may sue at this day, but heretofore he could not, for then they were looked upon as enemies. But now commerce has taught the world more humanity[2]," and Serjeant Salkeld, in his report of the case, indicates that the doctrine of Coke was expressly over-ruled by the Court. "Turks and infidels are not *perpetui inimici*, nor is there a particular enmity between them and us; but this is a common error founded on a groundless opinion of Justice Brooke; for though there be a difference between our religion and theirs, that does not oblige us to be enemies to their persons; they are the creatures of God and of the same kind as we are, and it would be a sin in us to hurt their persons. Per Littleton (afterwards Lord Keeper to Charles I), in his reading on the 27 Ed. III, 17. M.S.[3]—a statute which provides that a merchant stranger shall not be impeached for another's debt but upon good cause, and that merchants of enemies' countries shall sell their goods in convenient time and depart. Nevertheless, as late as 1744 Chief Justice Willes, in giving his opinion in the case of Omychund *v.* Barker, thought it necessary to refer to this

[1] *The Practical Register* (1719), vol. I, p. 4.

[2] 1 Lord Raymond, p. 282.

[3] 1 Salk., p. 46.

question. After citing the passage from Lord Coke, he says: "But this notion, though advanced by so great a man, is, I think, contrary not only to the scripture, but to common sense and common humanity. And I think that even the devils themselves, whose subjects he says the heathens are, cannot have worse principles; and, besides the irreligion of it, it is a most impolitic notion, and would at once destroy all that trade and commerce from which this nation reaps such great benefits. We ought to be thankful to Providence for giving us the light of Christianity, which he has denied to such great numbers of his creatures of the same species as ourselves. We are commanded by our Saviour to do good unto all men, and not only unto those who are of the household of faith [1]."

Coke's theory not altogether groundless.

This is a good illustration of the way in which the common law of England has been altered and developed so as to meet the needs of the times. When fairly considered, Sir Richard Brooke's opinion (upon which Coke's doctrine was professedly founded), as stated in the year book (12 Hen. VIII, fo. 4), cannot properly be called groundless, but it was not necessary for the decision of the case before the court, in which the question was whether an action of trespass would lie for beating the plaintiff's servant and taking away his dog ("quum servum suum verberavit et unum canem (vocat a bloodhound) cepit et asportavit"), to lay down that if a lord beat his villein, or a husband his wife, or a man beat an outlaw or a traitor or a pagan, they shall have no action because they are not able to sue an action. In the same way the statement in Calvin's case that infidels are perpetual enemies could also be treated as merely *obiter dictum*, for it also was irrelevant to the issue in the case, which was whether persons born in Scotland after the union of the crowns of England and Scotland were in England aliens or natural born subjects and so capable of inheriting lands in England. When therefore the point was raised in the courts at the end of Charles II's and in William III's reign, it was

[1] Willes, p. 542.

possible to disregard the opinions of those eminent judges, and to pronounce a decision in accordance with the views of the more enlightened portion of the country at the end of the seventeenth century [1].

Capacity of Jews to hold real property.

The capacity of Jews to hold land or other real property in England was also for a long time a question of serious doubt among lawyers. If all Jews, whether born within the realm or not, were aliens and perpetual enemies of the king, then they were incapable of holding land, for until the year 1870 no alien could hold land in England. The question could hardly be one of practical importance in the early days of the return of the Jews to England, for the newcomers were all foreigners, and it was not till their children born here had grown up that it called for serious attention. By this time Coke's doctrine that infidels are perpetual enemies had been already exploded, and accordingly, in the year 1718, Sir Robert Raymond, then Attorney-General and afterwards Lord Chief Justice of England, gave it as his opinion that a person born in England, though a Jew, could hold and enjoy an estate in fee simple in English land, and that on his death it would descend to his issue as the lands of other subjects, and not be forfeited to the Crown. Some five years later, when the oath of abjuration was modified in favour of the Jews (by 10 Geo. I, c. 4), the opinions of ten of the most prominent counsel of the day were taken upon this question. Though separately consulted, they all agreed that a subject of his Majesty born in

[1] This is of course no reason for asserting that the earlier opinions were groundless; on the other hand that they were probably well founded appears from the following passage in Lord Stowell's judgment in the Le Louis case decided in 1817. "With professed pirates there is no state of peace. They are the enemies of every country, and at all times; and therefore are universally subject to the extreme rights of war. An ancient authority, the laws of Oleron, composed at the time of the Crusades, and as supposed by an eminent leader in those expeditions, our own Richard I, represents infidels as equally subject to those rights; but this rests partly upon the ground of notions long ago exploded, that such persons could have no fellowship, no peaceful communion with the faithful," 2 Dodson, p. 244.

England or a free denizen, being a Jew, may purchase lands[1]. However, shortly afterwards, the pre-expulsion legislation against the Jews was unearthed and relied on in support of the alleged disability. There were two statutes dealing with the matter. In 1271 a statute or ordinance (55 Hen. III) had been enacted, prohibiting Jews from holding any freehold lands excepting only the houses then in their possession in which they were actually living, but four years later the statute *de Iudaismo* slightly increased their power to acquire land, for the right was granted them to "buy Houses and Curtilages in the Cities and Boroughs where they abide, so that they hold them in chief of the King; saving unto the Lords of the Fee their services due and accustomed."

Ordinance of 1271 forbidding Jews to hold land discovered by Dr. Tovey in 1738.

The first of these ordinances does not appear in any of the printed editions of the statutes, and was discovered by Tovey in an ancient MS. in the Bodleian Library, and first printed by him in his *Anglia Iudaica* in the year 1738; its authenticity is, however, firmly established, and so it was agreed that opinions given fifteen years earlier without knowledge of its existence were of little or no value. This point was much discussed during the passage and repeal of the Jewish Naturalization Act of 1753, and after the repeal of the Act Lord Temple moved in the House of Lords that some method might be taken to ascertain this question, and that for this purpose the judges might be desired to attend and give their opinions upon it, but the motion was rejected, principally upon the ground that the judges are not obliged to give their opinions to the House upon such extra-judicial questions, where no bill is depending[2]. Even as late as 1830 there were those who thought that this alleged incapacity still existed, for Mr. Blunt, in his excellent *History of the Jews in England*, published in that year, is unable to resist this conclusion[3],

[1] For copies of these opinions see Webb, "The question whether a Jew, &c." pp. 42–6.

[2] 2 Swanston, p. 508 note, from Mr. Coxe's MS. notes.

[3] See Introduction, p. v, and pp. 119–27.

and in the same year that unrivalled Master of Real Property law, Lord St. Leonards, then Solicitor-General, in presenting a petition from one Lewis Levi, asking for a declaratory law to remove all doubts as to the power of Jews to hold landed property in fee, stated in the House of Commons that he concurred entirely with the petitioner in thinking such a law was necessary. A little later in the session leave was asked to bring in a bill for this purpose by Colonel Wilson, who said that "he was aware that the opinion of the high law men at present was, that the Jews might hold landed property like other British subjects; but, though that was the present dictum of lawyers, it did not follow that it would be the opinion of their successors," and added that he had himself been dissuaded some years before from buying some landed property of a Jew by Sir Samuel Romilly who had given it as his opinion that he could not obtain a good title from a Jew. The motion was opposed by Mr. R. Grant, who had taken up the Jewish cause, on the ground that it would be prejudicial to the general question of the abolition of the Jewish disabilities to deal with them piecemeal, and negatived without a division [1]. It has already been pointed out that these ancient statutes could have no application to the Jews after their return to England centuries later, when the status of villeinage no longer existed [2]; and certain it is that the Jews long before 1846, when the Ordinance of Henry III and the Statute *de Iudaismo* were formally repealed, did with impunity openly hold and enjoy landed estates other than houses in towns or cities in which they resided; a well-known instance is given by Sir Francis Goldsmid, Q.C., in his remarks on the civil disabilities of British Jews, who says that the late Chief Justice Lord Ellenborough (who died in 1818) gave a practical proof of his concurrence in the belief that Jews might hold

[1] Hansard, 2nd series, vol. XXIV, p. 236, XXV, p. 429.

[2] See supra, pp. 63-65, the 'Return of the Jews to England,' pp. 15-17.

land, by purchasing without hesitation of Mr. Benjamin Goldsmid a valuable freehold seat at Roehampton[1].

Capacity of Jews to hold advowsons.

If a Jew born here, or otherwise having acquired the rights of a natural born subject, was capable of holding land and other real property, then there was nothing in our law to prevent his holding an advowson, a species of real property which confers upon the owner the right of presentation to a church or ecclesiastical benefice. And so a Jew, owning an advowson, might present a duly qualified person to fill any vacancy which might occur. It must, however, be evident that if this form of property had been frequently possessed by Jews, attempts, which would have almost certainly proved successful, would have been made to prevent it. Indeed, the right had been taken from Roman Catholics by various statutes, and in cases of advowsons owned by Papists the right of presenting to the benefices when they became vacant vested in the Universities of Oxford and Cambridge, according as the livings were situate in the several counties mentioned in the Acts[2]. Similarly, in the Act to permit persons professing the Jewish religion to be naturalized by Parliament, the famous Jew Bill of 1753, a clause was inserted disabling Jews from purchasing or inheriting any advowson or right of patronage, but the popular clamour raised by the passage of this Act was so great that the Houses of Parliament felt constrained to repeal it as the first measure of the ensuing session, and, as the repeal was of the whole Act, the clause imposing the disability was also annulled[3]. Henceforth, therefore, the Jews were under no such disability, unless the statutes or ordinances of the

[1] p. 4. See also Sir Samuel Romilly's argument in the Bedford Charity case, 2 Swanston at p. 511, and for the whole subject Lord Lyndhurst's remarks in introducing the Religious Opinions Relief Bill (1846) in the House of Lords. Hans., *Parl. Deb.*, 3rd series, vol. LXXXV, p. 1254.

[2] See 3 Jac. I, cap. 5, secs. 18–21; 1 W. & M., cap. 26, sec. 4; 13 Anne, cap. 13, sec. 1, and Edwards *v.* the Bishop of Exeter (1839), 7 Scott, p. 676, and 5 Bing. N. C., p. 652.

[3] 26 Geo. II, cap. 26 and 27 Geo. II, cap. 1.

pre-expulsion period, which it has already been argued were not applicable, imposed it. When in 1846 these ordinances were formally repealed, as there was no clause dealing with advowsons in the repealing Act, any doubt there may have been on this point was removed, and, however inconvenient or undesirable it may be, it is now undoubtedly the law that a Jew or any other Dissenter, except a Roman Catholic, may have the right to present to a vacant living in the Church of England[1]. In the case of Jews, though not of other Dissenters, it was thought fit in 1858 to restrict this right by enacting, in the Act which enabled the Houses of Parliament to modify the form of oath to be administered to their members in such a way that Jews could take it, that when any person professing the Jewish religion held any office in the gift of the Crown to which the right of presentation or of appointment to any ecclesiastical benefice is annexed, such right should devolve upon and be exercised by the Archbishop of Canterbury for the time being[2].

A Jew therefore, if he holds an advowson in his own right, may present to a living, but he can only present a duly qualified person, that is, a clerk in holy orders, for no one not episcopally ordained will be instituted by the bishop.

Jews and the benefit of clergy.

A Jew was, unless he had previously renounced his religion, incapable of becoming a clergyman; and therefore Jews who had committed crimes and been convicted of them could not, according to the opinion of many great legal writers, avail themselves of the benefit of clergy which other malefactors, on a first conviction for felony, were at liberty to plead in mitigation of punishment. This right, known technically as *privilegium* or *beneficium clericale*, originated in the claim which in early times, when Papal supremacy was still recognized, had been

[1] In Mirehouse *v.* Rennell, which was decided in the House of Lords in 1833 before these old ordinances had been repealed, this was stated to be the law by Lord Wynford, see 7 Bligh, N. S., 322.

[2] 21 & 22 Vict., cap. 49, sec. 4.

made by the ecclesiastics to exemption from temporal jurisdiction, and to trial, when charged with criminal offences, by the ecclesiastical courts in accordance with the provisions of the canon law. This claim had never been recognized to its fullest extent in England, but the privilege in question had been regulated by a number of statutes, the result of which was that in the time of Charles II any person convicted of felony punishable with death, as all felonies with few exceptions such as petit larceny then were, could before judgment claim his clergy. The result of the granting of this claim was that the convict, having already by conviction suffered forfeiture of all his goods and chattels, was liable to be kept in prison for a time not exceeding one year and, if a layman, to be branded in the hand, after which he could not have the benefit of clergy a second time, but was subject to no further penalty; but, if in holy orders, he was, after 18 Eliz. c. 7, discharged without any further punishment, and could again have the benefit of clergy, however often he might be convicted of a clergyable offence. Benefit of clergy did not, however, apply to cases of treason or any misdemeanour less serious than felony, and was especially ousted or abolished in the case of murder, robbery, and the more atrocious kinds of felony. It was no doubt originally allowed only to those who had been ordained priest or deacon and had "habitum et tonsuram clericalem," but had been demanded on behalf of, and gradually conceded to, all who were supposed to be capable of taking part in the service of the church, which was interpreted as meaning all who could read. But the test of reading was not a severe one, for it became reduced to repeating a scrap of Latin, in nearly all cases the same three words, "Miserere mei, Deus," which became known as the neck verse, and was probably familiar to the bulk of the criminal classes. Thus the privilege was retained long after its original cause had ceased to exist, and was defended as a relaxation of the extreme severity of the common law which punished many offences of a comparatively trivial nature with the penalty of death. But it was never extended to persons not capable of holy orders; a by no means small class, including women and, according to the books, blind persons and all who did not profess the Christian religion; as was said in Poulter's case: "The common law doth not deny *beneficium clericatus,* the benefit of his clergy, but in certain cases: as if a man be convicted of any heresy, he shall not have his clergy for any felony, &c. The same law of a Saracen, Jew, or other infidel. *Gravius est enim divinam quam temporalem laedere maiestatem*; the same law in case of high treason against the king [1]." Such persons, if they offended, were left to the extreme rigour of the common law and to the mercy of the Crown. The unfairness of this state of the law did not pass unnoticed. In 1623 women convicted of grand larceny of goods not exceeding ten shillings in value, and in 1691 women found guilty of any clergyable felony were placed on the same footing as men entitled to clergy. At length in 1706 the idle ceremony of reading, which, as the statute says, by experience had been found to be of no use, was dispensed with by 5 Anne, c. 6, s. 6, which, being liberally interpreted, according to Sir Michael Foster, "entitled those who before were supposed to be under a legal incapacity for orders, as Jews and some others were, and likewise those who in presumption of law were not qualified in point of learning, to the indulgence of the law in common with the rest of their fellow subjects [2]." It should be added that the whole system of benefit of clergy was swept away in 1827 by 7 & 8 Geo. IV, c. 28, which also abolished the death penalty for all felonies which had formerly been clergyable. Sir William Blackstone takes a view contrary to the authorities which have been quoted, and questions whether it was ever ruled for law that Jews were before 1706 incapable of the benefit of clergy. Happily for the good name of the

[1] 11 Co. Rep., p. 29 b.

[2] Foster's *Crown Cases*, p. 306. The statutes as to women are 21 Jac. I, cap. 6 and 3 & 4 W. & M., cap. 9.

Jewish community in these early days, this was a purely academic question, for the Jews in England did not commit the crimes for which this privilege in mitigation of punishment had been granted, as Tovey, speaking of the reign of Charles II, says: "But tho' so few of them were converted, in this Reign, to Christianity, yet in some measure they lived up to the precepts of it, by a regular observance of all civil duties. For I find no complaints against them of any kind, excepting such as related to the Custom-House; from which they cleared themselves by pleading the King's Patent[1]."

The practice of administering the necessary oath upon the New Testament the cause of the civil disabilities of the Jews.

The real disabilities, whether civil or political, which were imposed upon the Jews, arose almost entirely from the form of oath or the method of administering it. The political disabilities were occasioned by the tests and forms of oaths enacted by Parliament; the civil ones for the most part by the custom, almost universal at one time, of administering the necessary oath upon the New Testament, a method wholly unacceptable to a conscientious Jew. Many civil disabilities were no doubt imposed by the statutes aimed against Popish recusants, but, as has been previously stated, these statutes were not enforced against the Jews, who, though in strictness liable to the penalties enacted by them, were regarded as exempt by reason of the dispensations granted by Charles and James II. The most irksome

[1] *Anglia Iudaica*, p. 285. The passage in Blackstone is vol. IV, pp. 373, 374, but all the authorities are the other way. See Fost., p. 306; 2 Hale, p. 373; 11 Co. Rep., p. 29 b; and Hawkins, *Pleas of the Crown*, vol. IV, p. 249. Leach's edition of 1795, who says: "Not only those actually admitted into some inferior order of the clergy, but also those who were never qualified to be admitted into orders (which was tried by putting them to read a verse) have been taken to have a right to this privilege, as much as persons in holy orders, whether they were persons lawfully born or bastards, aliens or denizens, in the communion of the church or excommunicate, within the common benefit of the law or outlaws, &c., so that they were not heretics convict, nor Jews, Mahometans, nor Pagans; nor under perpetual disability of going into orders; admitting of no dispensation, as blind and maimed persons formerly were, and women still are."

of all these disabilities was the impossibility for a Jew to become a freeman of the city of London, and so no Jew could exercise any retail trade within the city boundaries, for, by the by-laws of the corporation of London, retail trade in the city was strictly confined to freemen. By the local usage of the city the oath tendered before admittance to all those entitled to the freedom was always administered upon the New Testament, and thus the Jews were excluded. In the year 1739 an attempt was made to allow Jews to take the necessary oath on the Old Testament. In Trinity term of that year a rule was obtained in the court of King's Bench against the city chamberlain, calling upon him to show cause why he should not admit Abraham Rathom, a person duly qualified, to the freedom of the city. To this rule a return was made that it was the ancient custom to administer the oath of a freeman on the New Testament, but that when the oath was tendered to Rathom on the New Testament he refused to take it, although he was not a Quaker, and therefore he was not admitted. The case was three times argued at the bar, and finally the Chief Justice Sir Robert Raymond delivered the resolution of the Court. Upon this point he said: "The last objection made is, that it is not reasonable to confine the oath to the New Testament in trading cities, where a man's religion is of no consequence, and ought not to interfere. But the question before us is not whether upon a proper application the Jews may not be allowed to swear upon the Old Testament, as they do when they give evidence; but whether this custom of taking an oath in the usual manner is unreasonable upon the face of it"; he then cites authorities as to the definition of an oath, and says that Christianity is part of the law of the land, and continues: "It was said that the law does not require the New Testament in all cases, particularly as to evidence given by Jews. But the reason of that is, because all courts desire to have the best security they can for the truth of the evidence; and therefore, as it is known they have a more solemn obligation to speak the truth when

Jews excluded from the freedom of the city of London.

sworn on the Old Testament, it is for that reason allowed. The common regular way of swearing is on the New Testament, and shall we say that a custom requiring such a regular oath is bad? The 1 Eliz., c. 1, s. 19, take notice of an oath upon the Evangelists, and the abjuration oath (till altered for the Jews by 10 Geo. I, c. 10, s. 18) runs upon the true faith of a Christian. We therefore think that this is a good return and allow it[1]."

Quakers in a better position than Jews in this respect.

In this respect Jews were in an inferior position to Quakers, in whose favour Acts of Parliament had been passed, enabling them in all cases where an oath was required (though not qualifying them to give evidence in criminal cases or to serve on juries or to bear any office or place of profit in the Government), to make an affirmation instead of the oath, and who therefore could not be excluded from civil rights upon the ground that they refused to take the oath when duly tendered in the customary form[2].

Jews and trade in the city of London. Not more than twelve allowed to be brokers.

Thus the Jews were unable to become citizens of London, and were in consequence by the by-laws of the city excluded from all retail trade within its boundaries; wholesale trade was, however, open to them, and from the first days of their return several of their number had occupied prominent positions as merchants in the city. In addition to their total exclusion from all branches of retail trades, the number of Jewish brokers permitted to carry on business in the city was strictly limited to twelve, who received licences from the court of aldermen. These licences they were allowed to transfer upon payment of a fine to the Lord Mayor, which in the course of time

[1] Rex *v.* Bosworth (1739), 2 Strange, pp. 1112–4.

[2] The statutes are 7 & 8 Will. III, cap. 34; 8 Geo. I, cap. 6 & 22 Geo. II, cap. 46, sec. 36. See Rex and Morrice *v.* the Mayor of Lincoln (1698), 12 Mod., p. 190 and 5 Mod., pp. 399–403, where the Mayor of Lincoln was compelled by mandamus to admit a Quaker to the freedom of the city; and Rex *v.* the Turkey Company (1760), 2 Burn, pp. 943 and 1,000, where a Quaker was held to be entitled to be admitted to the Turkey Company upon his affirmation without taking the oath prescribed by the Act of Parliament regulating the Company.

became a valuable perquisite[1]; but if a Jewish broker died without having transferred his licence the appointment fell to the city and might be disposed of to the highest bidder. The place of a Jewish broker was thus of considerable value and at least on one occasion became the subject of litigation in the courts. In the year 1750, upon the bankruptcy of a Jewish broker, a petition was presented to the Court of Chancery, praying that his place as broker might be sold for the benefit of his creditors, but Lord Chancellor Hardwicke held that it could not be considered as an office, and refused the petition[2].

The disability removed, Dec. 10, 1830.

It remains only to add that in the year 1829 the following motion was unanimously carried in the Court of Common Council, "That it be referred to the Committee relative to wholesale dealers to make inquiry and report as to the municipal or legal impediments by which Jews carrying on business in the City of London are debarred from taking up their freedom of the City of London." In consequence of the report subsequently sent in, an Act was passed on December 10, 1830, by the common council, for enabling persons to take the oath according to the forms of their own religion[3]. And so since the year 1831 the custom of

[1] "As much as £1,500 has been paid for a broker's medal, and a system of disgraceful jobbing has been the consequence; a Lord Mayor and four Aldermen next in succession to the chair having formerly conspired together to raise the customary fee for transferring a broker's medal from £100 to £500 in which they succeeded. Taking customary fees (however unjust) might perhaps be palliated by immemorial usage; but may it not be asked in the case just alluded to, in the offensive sense of the word, who was the greatest Jew, my Lord Mayor or the broker? It is not astonishing that cases should have occurred where a broker has retaliated upon his lordship; and it was whispered many years back, when these transactions took place, that by threats of exposure sums have been disgorged and paid back again to the broker." *Brief memoir of the Jews in relation to their civil disabilities* by Apsley Pellatt, himself a member of the Corporation, published in 1829.

[2] See ex parte Lyons (1750), Ambler, p. 89.

[3] See Welch's *Modern History of the City of London*, p. 167. *Journal*, 105, fols. 5, 6.

administering the necessary oath on the New Testament only was no longer adhered to, and Jews have without any Act of Parliament having been passed in their favour enjoyed all the privileges of the citizenship of London.

Exclusion from the legal and other professions.

In the same way the exclusion of Jews from the various professions was due to their inability or unwillingness to comply with the regulations, especially where these included the taking of an objectionable oath, laid down by those who had the right to control the admission of candidates, and not to any impediment created by the general law of the country. It is sometimes said that the profession of the law was an exception to this general rule, and some colour is lent to this theory by the existence of provisions in certain statutes, namely 1 Geo. I, st. 2, c. 13, s. 2, 2 Geo. II, c. 31, and 9 Geo. II, c. 26[1], obliging "every person who shall act as a Serjeant at Law, Counsellor at Law, Barrister, Advocate, Attorney, Solicitor, Writer in Scotland, Proctor, Clerk or Notary," under pain of incurring severe disabilities and forfeiting £500, to take the oaths mentioned in the first-named Act. Among these was the oath of abjuration (affirming the legality of the Hanoverian succession, and renouncing allegiance to the exiled House of Stuart), which ended with the words "upon the true faith of a Christian," and therefore could not be taken by a self-respecting Jew. In the year 1766 the terms of the abjuration oath were slightly altered (by 6 Geo. III, c. 53), but the obnoxious final words were still retained. But these oaths had not to be taken before admission to the legal profession, but

[1] The earlier statutes 5 Eliz., cap. 1, sec. 5, and 7 Jac. I, cap. 6, secs. 12–18, providing that persons entering the legal profession should take an oath upon the evangelists, were apparently treated as no longer in force, either because they were regarded as being superseded by the later Acts, or because the oaths specified in them had been abrogated by 1 W. & M., cap. 8, and it would seem from sec. 25 of the Act of James I that it was never intended to be more than a temporary Act. These statutes applied equally to schoolmasters, and the last one to the medical profession, and were formally repealed in 1846 by 9 & 10 Vict., cap. 59, sec. 1.

within a certain time afterwards [1]. That time was originally three months, but the second-recited Act extended it to the end of the term following admission, and the third to six months.

The annual Indemnity Acts.

In the first year of George II an indemnity Act was passed, by which all persons who had neglected to qualify themselves for any office or employment by omitting to take the necessary oaths, &c., are indemnified and recapacitated provided that they qualified themselves on or before November 28, 1728, and every year until the year 1868, when the enactment of the Promissory Oaths Act made their continuance no longer necessary, similar Acts of indemnity were passed enlarging the time for qualification till some day in the following year. Therefore, after the reign of George II, there was nothing in the Acts recited to prevent a Jew from entering the legal profession, if he was willing to take the risk, not a very serious one, of the annual indemnity Act not being re-enacted, and his accordingly becoming incapacitated to continue to follow his profession upon the expiration of the time limited by the existing Act.

Jews admitted to the Bar, 1833.

But, on the other hand, admission to the legal profession could only be obtained through the medium of certain persons or societies who, though not bound to do so by any Act of Parliament, might lay down conditions with which Jews could not comply. For instance, the right to admit to the degree of barrister-at-law, holders of which alone are entitled to plead in the superior courts and are therefore considered the higher branch of the legal profession, has from time immemorial been vested in the

[1] The position of Roman Catholics wishing to practise the law was different, for the statute 7 & 8 Will. III, cap. 24, providing under pain of incurring the penalties of praemunire that no person should practise law without first taking certain oaths (none of which were obnoxious to Jews) and making a declaration against transubstantiation, effectually excluded them, prior to the Roman Catholic Relief Act of 1791, from all participation in the legal profession except the calling of a conveyancer which was not expressly mentioned in the statute.

Inns of Court. These are voluntary societies, and no member of the public has an inherent right to be admitted to them [1]. Persons once admitted members must then become qualified for call to the bar, and one of the qualifications which, having regard to the statutes already mentioned, can hardly be considered unreasonable, was the taking of certain oaths, including the oath of abjuration. In the year 1833 Mr. Francis Goldsmid, who had been previously admitted a fellow of the society, applied to the benchers of Lincoln's Inn to be called to the bar, and to be permitted to omit the final words from the oath of abjuration. There was some discussion, at a full meeting of the benchers, during which Lord Campbell, who was then Mr. Campbell, K.C., M.P., says that he pointed out the hardship to be imposed upon the young gentleman, who had been allowed to keep his terms and whose prospects in life would thus be suddenly blasted; to which Mr. Clarke, K.C., leader of the Midland Circuit, and at that time master of the library, replied: "Hardship! no hardship at all! Let him become a Christian, and be d——d to him!" but this reply was not taken as a serious argument, for it was unanimously resolved that the application should be granted, and Mr. Goldsmid was called to the bar and afterwards became a Q.C. and a bencher of his Inn [2].

The precedent was followed by the other Inns, and so a disability, which had long been supposed to exist, was removed without the necessity of the intervention of Parliament. As this is an instance of the way in which almost all the disabilities of this kind could have been, and in many cases were, removed, it may be of interest to append the relevant entries in the records of Lincoln's Inn:—

[1] See the King *v.* the Benchers of Lincoln's Inn (1825), 4 B & C., 855; Neate *v.* Durwan (1874), L. R., 18 Eq. 127; and Manisty *v.* Kenealy (1876), 24 W. R., 918 for the legal position and government of the Inns of Court.

[2] *Lives of the Chancellors*, vol. V, p. 544 (note).

"1827. Dec. 27. Francis Henry Goldsmid (19) 1 s. Isaac Lyon G., of Dulwich Hill Ho., Surrey Esq."[1]

"Special Council held on Jan. 25, 1833.
Twenty Benchers present.

Upon the application of Francis Henry Goldsmid, gentleman, a Fellow of this Society, relative to his call to the Bar, It is ordered that the question whether a person of the Jewish persuasion is eligible to be called to the Bar, be adjourned to Wednesday next."

"Special Council held on January 30, 1833.
Nineteen Benchers present.

Upon the motion of the Rt. Hon. Thomas Erskine, Mr. Francis Henry Goldsmid was unanimously called to the Bar."[2]

Admission of Jews as solicitors, 1770.

It remains but to add that the benchers on this occasion merely followed the praiseworthy example which had been set by the leaders of the lower branch of the profession nearly sixty years before. And here again it will be well to set out extracts from the records. In the draft minutes of the Society of Gentlemen Practisers for June 25, 1770, appear the following notes, written apparently by a member of the committee:—

"No Jew to be bail for any person but a Jew.

Abraham Abrahams } Fore Street in the Artillery Ground,
Jacobs }

admitted as attorneys."

In another document, also to be found in the printed edition of the records, the exact steps by which the admission was effected, are given. It reads as follows:—

"Oath by Jewish Solicitor.

Joseph Abrahams, son of Abraham Abrahams of Mitre Court, Leadenhall Street, was on the 29th Decr., 1763,

[1] *Admission Register*, no. 19, fo. 65; *Records of Lincoln's Inn*, vol. II, p. 127.

[2] *Black Books of Lincoln's Inn*, Book XXII, pp. 233, 234; *Records of Lincoln's Inn*, Black books, vol. IV, p. 185.

articled as clerk to George Ellis the younger of Deans Street, ffetter Lane, an attorney of the Court of King's Bench.

Affidt. of due execution of the Articles sworn 25th Jan. 1764 fyled 18th ffeb. 1764.

On ye 18 July 1769 the said Joseph Abrahams was assigned over by Articles by the said George Ellis to Robt. Gill of Angel Court, Throgmorton Street, Attorney in the Common Pleas.

23rd Jan. 1770 the said Joseph Abrahams was admitted as an Attorney of the King's Bench by Mr. Justice Yates.

13th ffebry 1770 was admitted a Sollr. in Chancery. The Deputy Clerk of ye petty Bagg informed me Abrahams was sworn on the Bible.

10th Geo. 1st. cap. 4. Subjects professing ye Jewish Religion presenting themselves to take ye Oath of Abjuration (the words *Upon the true faith of a Christian* to be omitted) and deemed a sufft. taking of the abjuration Oath[1]."

The profession of schoolmasters and tutors.

The profession of a tutor or schoolmaster was also closed to the Jew in the same way as that of the law, for the statutes already enumerated ordaining the taking of obnoxious oaths embraced the followers of the teaching profession as well as the practisers of medicine and law. The disability thus imposed was, however, practically obviated in the way already described after the reign of George II by the passage of the annual indemnity Acts. Yet from this particular profession the Jew was excluded by other statutory provisions. The Act of Uniformity provided that "all masters and other heads, fellows, chaplains and tutors of or in any college, hall, house of learning or hospital, and every public professor and reader in either of the universities and in every college elsewhere . . . and every schoolmaster keeping any public or private school and every person instructing or teaching any

[1] *Records of the Society of Gentlemen Practisers*, pp. 120, 121, 288.

youth in any house or private family as a tutor or schoolmaster," shall *before* admission subscribe a declaration of which an important clause was "that I will conform to the liturgy of the Church of England, as it is now by law established," upon pain of deprivation. It is plain that this penalty was scarcely applicable to a tutor or schoolmaster in a private family, and accordingly the following section provided that such persons should obtain a license from the Bishop of the Diocese, and that if any person should instruct or teach any youth as a tutor or schoolmaster before obtaining such license and subscribing the declaration he should suffer three months' imprisonment without bail or mainprize[1].

Dissenters disabled from teaching in the public schools and colleges.

These provisions were not very rigorously enforced, at least as regards teaching in private houses, but were quite sufficient to exclude all persons not members of the Church of England from taking any part in the instruction of youth in the public schools of the country, nor can it be doubted that such was the intention of the legislature throughout the eighteenth century, for the Act of 1769, expressly passed for the relief of Protestant dissenting schoolmasters, in terms provides that nothing therein shall extend "to the enabling of any person dissenting from the Church of England to obtain or hold the mastership of any college or school of royal foundation or of any other endowed college or school for the education of youth, unless the same shall have been founded since the first year of the reign of their late Majesties King William and Queen Mary, for the immediate use and benefit of Protestant Dissenters[2]." The Roman Catholic Relief Act of 1791, which enabled Roman Catholics to be tutors or schoolmasters, has a similar proviso "that no person professing the Roman Catholic religion shall obtain or hold the mastership of any college or school of royal foundation or of any other endowed college or school for

[1] 13 & 14 Car. II, cap. 4, secs. 8–11, superseding the provisions of 23 Eliz., cap. 1, secs. 6, 7 and 1 Jac. I, cap. 4, sec. 9.

[2] 19 Geo. III, cap. 44.

the education of youth or shall keep a school in either of the Universities of Oxford and Cambridge [1]."

The Religious Disabilities Act, 1846.

No relief from this disability was ever expressly granted to the Jews, but in 1846 the Religious Disabilities Act (9 & 10 Vict. c. 59, s. 1), which, as has been already mentioned, placed the Jews as regards education on the same footing as Protestant Dissenters and thereby legalized their communal schools and any endowments attached to them, absolutely repealed the disability so far as it related to teaching in a private house or family, and a quarter of a century later the Universities Tests Act of 1871 (34 & 35 Vict. c. 26, s. 8) abolished it so far as it related to teaching in colleges or public schools.

The Universities and Dissenters.

The Universities themselves were for a long time impossible of access to the Jews, who were nevertheless in regard to the Universities in no better or worse position than all others who dissented from the Church of England. Acts of Parliament had been passed at various times (1 Eliz., c. 1, 7 Jac. I, c. 6, 1 Guil. & Mar., c. 8, 1 Geo. I, st. 2, c. 13) requiring oaths, some of which at least would have been obnoxious to Jews, to be taken by persons admitted to degrees or offices in the Universities. But by means of the annual indemnity Acts, any difficulty thus created might have been surmounted in the same way as entrance to the liberal professions had been gained by the Dissenters. The Universities and their colleges, although not originally ecclesiastical foundations [2], had always kept up a close

[1] 31 Geo. III, cap. 32, sec. 14. The Act further provided that no schoolmaster professing the Roman Catholic religion should receive into his school for education the child of any Protestant father. The rights given to Roman Catholic schoolmasters were thus, though given twenty-two years later, much more limited than those conferred on Protestant Nonconformists. The reason for this was the popular distrust of Roman Catholicism which insisted upon a declaration of the illegality of any endowment of a school or college for the instruction of persons professing that religion; see sec. 17 of the Act—a disability which was only removed by the Roman Catholic Charities Act of 1832 (2 & 3 Will. IV, cap. 115).

[2] The Universities are civil corporations and their colleges eleemosynary corporations (see Stephen's *Blackstone*, vol. III, p. 3).

connexion with the Established Church, and, so far from smoothing the way for sectarians to take degrees, actually insisted on all their members taking religious tests in addition to the statutory oaths, including in most cases subscription to the Thirty-nine Articles of the Church of England. These tests had to be taken at Oxford before matriculation or admission to membership, but at Cambridge might be deferred until candidature for a degree. In 1850 Royal Commissions were appointed to investigate and report on the constitution of the Universities of Oxford and Cambridge, and legislation was initiated in consequence of their reports. The University of Oxford was first dealt with. The Oxford University Reform Act, 1854 (17 & 18 Vict., c. 81, secs. 43, 44) provided "that it shall not be necessary for any person, upon matriculating in the University of Oxford, to make or subscribe any declaration or to take any oath, any law or statute notwithstanding," and further that no such subscription or oath should be necessary upon taking the degree of Bachelor in Arts, Law, Medicine, or Music, but a proviso was added that such degree should not constitute any qualification for holding any office which had theretofore been held by members of the United Church of England and Ireland, unless the oaths and declarations required by law had been taken and made. The opening to Dissenters of the lower degrees only was intended to prevent them from taking any share in the government of the University, and the object of the proviso was to continue the monopoly of educational appointments belonging to members of the Established Church. Two years later the Cambridge University Reform Act, 1856, carried the cause of religious liberty, so far as the younger University was concerned, one step further, by enacting that no oath, declaration, or subscription should thenceforth be required to be taken by any person either (1) upon obtaining any exhibition, scholarship, or other college emolument available for the assistance of an undergraduate student in his academical education, or (2) upon matriculating or taking any degree in Arts, Law, Medicine, or Music, provided, however, that such degree should not, until the holder subscribed a declaration stating that he is bona fide a member of the Church of England, entitle him to become a member of the Senate or qualify him to hold any office either in the University or elsewhere which had theretofore always been held by a member of the Established Church, and for which such degree was a qualification [1]. Not unnaturally, after the passage of these Acts of Parliament the University of Cambridge was more frequented by Jews and other Dissenters than the sister University; for at Cambridge all scholarships and the higher degrees (except in the faculty of theology) were thrown open to all persons irrespective of religion, but the right to hold a fellowship or take any part in the government of the Universities was still strictly confined to members of the Established Church.

The Universities Tests Act, 1871.

The position was not satisfactory, and a wider toleration was demanded. Bills to effect this end were regularly brought forward in Parliament, and at length in 1870 the government of the day took up the question, and a Universities Tests Bill was piloted through the House of Commons by Sir John Duke Coleridge, the Solicitor-General. The Lords, however, shelved it by appointing a Select Committee to consider the matter. The Bill was again introduced the following year and passed, but several amendments intended for the protection of the Church of England were inserted by the House of Lords in accordance with the recommendations of their Select Committee. The effect of the Act is that all degrees, together with all rights and privileges annexed to them, and all offices in the Universities of Oxford, Cambridge, and Durham (which was also included in the Act), or any of their colleges, subsisting at the time the Act was passed, were thrown open to all persons irrespective of their religious belief. The only exceptions are degrees in and professorships of

[1] 19 & 20 Vict., cap. 88, secs. 45, 46.

divinity, and such offices as had been previously by some ordinance or statute confined to persons in or about to enter holy orders (thereby saving the clerical fellowships and headships of houses), or confined to members of the Church of England by reason of a degree being a qualification for holding them. Moreover, no member of a university or college can henceforth be compelled to attend the public worship of any church, sect, or denomination to which he does not belong, or any lecture to which he, if of full age or, if he is under age, his parent or guardian shall object on religious grounds. On the other hand, it is expressly stated that the Act shall not interfere with the religious instruction, worship, and discipline previously established, and every college is required to provide sufficient religious instruction for all its undergraduate members belonging to the Established Church, and also to continue in its chapel as theretofore the daily use of the Morning and Evening Prayer according to the Order of the Book of Common Prayer.

The Act does not apply to new foundations [1], but refers only to colleges subsisting at the time of its passage. It is therefore open for the adherents of any legally recognized religion to establish a college or hall in any of the universities, and conduct it on purely sectarian principles. The Jews have never attempted to create such a foundation, but have liberally availed themselves of the right of becoming members of the colleges thrown open to them by the legislation of the second half of last century.

Jews and the lower branches of education.

Having now completed a summary survey of the civil disabilities of the Jews and the means by which these have been removed, before passing to the consideration of their political rights, it may be not without interest to those who have followed the story of their admission to the universities to add a short account of the religious position in the lower branches of education. The anomalies and want of system which characterize almost all our English institu-

[1] See Reg. *v.* Hertford College, Oxford (1878), L.R. 3 Q.B.D. 693.

tions are not absent from those which carry on the education of the country. In dealing with this subject it is not necessary to attempt a scientific classification of English schools, which from a legal point of view may be roughly divided into six classes:—

(1) Private schools.
(2) Public schools.
(3) Endowed schools.
(4) Public elementary schools.
(5) Public higher grade and technical schools.
(6) Poor-law, reformatory, and industrial schools.

Private schools.

In private schools, which embrace all schools not supported by endowments or money provided from public funds, there is in this country no legal restriction in matters of religion, and the master or owner of such school may at his own pleasure provide or abstain from providing religious instruction, and if he does provide it may insist on all the pupils taking part in it, or make such exceptions as he thinks fit. The instruction may be of any kind the master chooses, subject perhaps to this limitation, that it must be such that it can be brought within the tenets of one or other of the religions which have been admitted to the benefits of the Toleration Acts, and provided also that no attempt is made to make children educated in the Christian religion deny the truth of Christianity, for such an attempt might bring the master within the pains and penalties of the obsolete but still existing Act for the more effectual suppressing of Blasphemy and Profaneness (9 Will. III, c. 35), the history of which was given in the second of these articles. The only remedy of a parent who disapproves of the religious education given at a private school is to withdraw his child and place him at another school.

Public schools.

Public schools in the legal sense include only those which come under the provisions of the Public Schools Act, 1868, and its amending Acts (31 & 32 Vict., c. 118; 32 & 33 Vict., c. 58; 34 & 35 Vict., c. 60; 36 & 37 Vict., c. 41 and c. 62), namely,

Eton, Winchester, Westminster, Charterhouse, Harrow, Rugby, and Shrewsbury. The principal Act empowers the governing bodies of these schools to make, and from time to time to alter and annul, regulations with respect to various matters, amongst which those relating to religion are—(*a*) With respect to attendance at Divine service, and, where the school has a chapel of its own, with respect to the chapel services and the appointment of preachers. (*b*) With respect to giving facilities for the education of boys whose parents or guardians wish to withdraw them from the religious instruction given in the school. The head master is, however, entitled to be consulted on all such regulations, and also to submit to the governing body proposals for making new or altering or annulling old regulations. At the present time Harrow is the only one of these schools in which regulations have been made to enable Jewish boys not only to be absent from Divine service in the school chapel, but also to receive instruction in the tenets of their own religion.

It should be added that by the thirteenth section of the Act of Uniformity (14 Car. II, c. 4), which is still unrepealed as to them, the governors and heads of Westminster, Winchester, and Eton are required to conform to the Church of England and subscribe the Thirty-nine Articles.

Endowed schools.

Endowed schools are now governed by the Endowed Schools Act of 1869 and the amending Acts (32 & 33 Vict., c. 56; 36 & 37 Vict., c. 87; and 37 & 38 Vict., c. 87), and comprise all schools (other than those coming under the Public Schools Act) which are wholly or partly maintained by means of any endowment, including therefore many of the institutions popularly known as public schools. Before 1869 these schools had been divided into two classes, there being no statutory requirement as to exemption from religious education of children in schools which came under the Grammar Schools Act of 1840 (3 & 4 Vict., c. 77), but in the case of other endowed schools it was provided by the Endowed Schools Act, 1860 (23 & 24 Vict., c. 11), that it should be lawful for the trustees or governors of every endowed school to make, and that they should be bound to make, orders admitting to the benefits of the school the children of parents not in communion with the church, sect, or denomination to which the endowment belonged, unless the will, deed, or other instrument regulating the endowment expressly required all children educated under it to be instructed according to the doctrines or formularies of such church or denomination.

The Endowed Schools Act, 1869.

This provision was, however, not considered adequate, and the Endowed Schools Act of 1869 was passed on the recommendation of the commissioners appointed five years previously to consider the question. It applies both to grammar schools and other endowed schools, and as to religious teaching provides that in every scheme which the commissioners—now the Charity Commissioners—shall frame for the regulation of such schools provision shall be made that the parent or guardian of any child attending as a *day scholar* may claim by notice in writing addressed to the principal teacher the exemption of such scholar from attending prayer or religious worship, or from any lesson on a religious subject, and that such scholar shall be exempted accordingly without forfeiting any advantage or emolument to which he would otherwise be entitled, except such as may by the scheme be expressly made dependent on learning such lessons, and further that upon complaint from the parent or guardian that any teacher systematically teaches any religious doctrine to a child after such notice has been sent, the governing body shall inquire into the complaint, and if judged well founded shall take proper measures for its remedy.

This refers to day scholars only, but with regard to boarding schools it is enacted that every scheme shall provide that if the parent or guardian of any scholar about to attend such school, who otherwise could only be admitted as a boarder, desires his exemption from attending prayer or religious worship or any lesson on a religious subject, but the persons in charge of the boarding houses of the school are not willing to allow such exemption, then it shall be the duty of the governing body of the school to make proper provisions for enabling the scholar to attend the school and have such exemption as a day scholar.

Moreover, the religious opinions of any person or his attendance or non-attendance at any particular form of religious worship shall not in any way affect his qualification for being one of the governing body of such endowment. But schools which are maintained out of the endowment of any cathedral or collegiate church, or the scholars of which are required by the express terms of the instrument of foundation to be instructed according to the doctrines or formularies of any particular church, sect, or denomination, are excepted from these provisions as to religious instruction [1] or worship, other than those for the exemption of day scholars when it has been duly claimed. It is to be observed that these conscience clauses do not enable parents to claim exemption for their children from attendance upon a Saturday, or any other day to be set apart for religious observance by the tenets of their creed, nor to insist upon their admission as boarders, though they can demand that provision should be made for them to attend an endowed school, which has theretofore been confined to boarders, as day scholars, and in fact at several schools, such as Clifton, Cheltenham, and the Perse Grammar School, boarding houses for the exclusive use of Jewish boys have actually been established [2].

Public elementary schools.

In the case of public elementary schools it was necessary to make more stringent provisions upon this subject, because the Education Act of 1870 made attendance at these schools compulsory for all children whose education was not otherwise provided for by their parents. It was therefore enacted that no child should be compelled to

[1] 32 & 33 Vict., cap. 56, sec. 19, and see also 36 & 37 Vict., cap. 87, sec. 7.

[2] See *In re* the Endowed Schools Act, 1869, *in re* Christ's Hospital (1890), L.R. 15 A.C. 172, esp. pp. 181–3.

attend or abstain from attending any Sunday school or place of religious worship, and that any parent may withdraw his child from any religious observance kept or religious instruction given in the school, and also from attendance at the school upon any day exclusively set apart for religious observance by the religious body to which he belongs. In order to make the right of withdrawal from religious instruction effective it was further provided that such instruction should only be given at the beginning or the end of the school hours at times to be inserted in a time-table, which must be approved by the Board of Education [1], which last provision is sufficient to prevent the sacrifice of secular to religious education by devoting too large a proportion of the school hours to the latter.

These provisions apply to all public elementary schools, and in the case of those provided by a local authority it is further

[1] 33 & 34 Vict., cap. 75, sec. 7, the words of which are: "(1) It shall not be required, as a condition of any child being admitted into or continuing in the school, that he shall attend or abstain from attending any Sunday school or any place of religious worship, or that he shall attend any religious observance or any instruction in religious subjects in the school or elsewhere, from which observance or instruction he may be withdrawn by his parent, or that he shall, if withdrawn by his parent, attend the school on any day exclusively set apart for religious observance by the religious body to which the parent belongs.

"(2) The time or times during which any religious observance is practised or instruction in religious subjects is given at any meeting of the school shall be either at the beginning or at the end, or at the beginning and the end of such meeting, and shall be inserted in a Time-table to be approved by the Education Department, and to be kept permanently and conspicuously affixed in every school-room; and any scholar may be withdrawn by his parent from such observance or instruction without forfeiting any of the other benefits of the school. (See also sec. 74 (2).)

"(3) The school shall be open at all times to the inspection of any of Her Majesty's Inspectors, so, however, that it shall be no part of the duties of such inspector to inquire into any instruction in religious subjects given at such school, or to examine any scholar therein in religious knowledge or in any religious subject or book."

Provision for the examination of children in religious subjects is made in sec. 76, which, however, is applicable only to non-provided schools.

enacted by section 14 of the Act of 1870, commonly known as the Cowper-Temple clause, that "no religious catechism or religious formulary which is distinctive of any particular denomination shall be taught in the school." This section is not in practice any valid protection for Jewish children, because the Board of Education has held that under it, although the catechism of any particular Christian sect may not be taught, yet the Lord's Prayer and the Apostles' Creed (being common to all Christian sects) may be subjects of instruction, and that portions of the Bible, including of course the New Testament, may be read, and such explanations given as are conformable to the principles of the Christian religion. On the other hand, under the conscience and time-table clause already referred to this religious instruction can only be given at the beginning or end of the school hours, and Jewish parents have an absolute right to withdraw their children while the lessons in religion are being taught. As in most schools separate instruction in secular subjects is given to children withdrawn from the religious teaching or observances, if Jews desire that their children attending such schools shall receive instruction in their own religion, it is necessary for them to supply it at their own expense, and in hours not included in the regular school time. This is done in many of the London public elementary schools by the Jewish Religious Education Board, and there are similar Jewish bodies performing the same duty in Manchester and other towns where there is a large Jewish population.

The Cowper-Temple clause.

In non-provided or voluntary schools the religious instruction shall, as regards its character, be in accordance with the provisions (if any) of the trust deed relating thereto, and shall be under the control of the managers [1]. In order that the provisions of the trust deed may be effectually executed, it is enacted that, though the managers of such schools are bound to carry out the directions of the local education authority as to secular education, yet those

Religious instruction in non-provided schools.

[1] Education Act, 1902 (2 Edw. VII, cap. 42), sec. 7 (6).

directions shall not be such as to interfere with reasonable facilities for religious instruction during school hours. And further, the managers are given the power of dismissing a teacher without the consent of the local education authority on grounds connected with the giving of religious instruction in the school[1]. There are several such Jewish schools to be found in London and the larger provincial centres, and it should be remembered that to these schools also the conscience and time-table clauses are strictly applicable.

Higher grade and technical schools.

Public higher grade and technical schools are schools either provided by or receiving pecuniary assistance from local authorities under various recent Acts of Parliament, which provide a higher education than that given in the public elementary schools. Section 4 of the Education Act, 1902, enacts with regard to the religious instruction to be given at these schools as follows: "(1) A council shall not require that any particular form of religious instruction or worship, or any religious catechism or formulary which is distinctive of any particular denomination, shall or shall not be taught, used, or practised in any school, college, or hostel aided but not provided by the council, and no pupil shall on the ground of religious belief be excluded from or placed in an inferior position in any school, college, or hostel provided by the council, and no catechism or formulary distinctive of any particular religious denomination shall be taught in any school, college, or hostel so provided, except in cases where the council, at the request of parents of scholars, at such times and under such conditions as the council think desirable, allow any religious instruction to be given in the school, college, or hostel, otherwise than at the cost of the council: provided that in the exercise of this power no unfair preference shall be shown to any religious denomination.

"(2). (*a*) A scholar attending as a day or evening scholar shall not be required, as a condition of being admitted into or remaining in the school or college, to attend or abstain

[1] Education Act, 1902, sec. 7 (1) (*a*) and (*c*).

from attending any Sunday school, place of religious worship, religious observance, or instruction in religious subjects in the school or college or elsewhere; and

"(*b*) The times for religious worship or for any lesson on a religious subject shall be conveniently arranged for the purpose of allowing the withdrawal of any such scholar therefrom."

Poor-law schools.

The law as to poor-law schools has little interest for the Jews, who rightly pride themselves on saving their poorer brethren from resorting to the workhouse; so that there are comparatively few children in workhouse schools; where, however, Jewish children are dependent on the union, the guardians may avail themselves of the provisions of the Poor Law (Certified Schools) Act, 1862, enabling them to send a poor child to any school certified as fit for the purpose, but by the Act no child may be sent to any school which is conducted on the principles of a religious denomination to which he does not belong, and the Poor Law (now the Local Government) Board, if of opinion that any person is aggrieved by any child being so sent or kept at any school, may order its immediate removal[1].

Reformatory schools.

Reformatory schools are established for the better training of youthful offenders, i.e. of persons under the age of sixteen years convicted of an offence punishable with penal servitude or imprisonment. Such persons may by the court or justices be committed to a certified reformatory school, but in choosing the school regard must be had to their religious persuasion, which should be ascertained and specified by the committing authority in the order of committal. Moreover, they are to be allowed to receive visits from a minister of their religious persuasion at certain fixed hours of the day for the purpose of receiving religious assistance and instruction in the principles of their religion. There is also a further provision entitling the parent, guardian, or nearest adult relative to procure the removal

[1] 25 & 26 Vict., cap. 43.

of a youthful offender from one reformatory school to another conducted in accordance with his religious persuasion, by applying to the court or magistrates by whom the sentence was pronounced, provided that the application is made before the offender has been in the school thirty days, and that the managers of the school named by the applicant are willing to receive the offender[1]. The Secretary of State has also power to remove an offender from one reformatory school to another, or discharge him altogether.

Industrial schools.

Industrial schools differ from reformatory schools in that they are established not for the punishment and reform of offenders, but for the protection of children whom the benefits of the ordinary system of education fail to reach. To these schools magistrates are empowered to commit children for a variety of reasons enumerated in the Industrial Schools Act, the provisions of which in relation to the choice of a school conducted in accordance with the parents' religious persuasion, the visiting of the child by a minister of its own denomination, and the right of the parent or nearest adult relative to procure the removal of the child to another school conducted in accordance with the child's religious belief, are precisely the same as those already set out in the case of reformatory schools[2]. It has been found expedient to establish a Jewish Industrial School for boys at Hayes in Middlesex and a second Jewish Industrial School for girls has recently been organized.

[1] Reformatory Schools Act, 1866 (29 & 30 Vict., cap. 117, secs. 14, 16).

[2] See The Industrial Schools Act, 1866 (29 & 30 Vict., cap. 118, secs. 18, 25, and 20). (See Model rules, Dumsday and Mothersole, p. 715.)

IX.

THE POLITICAL RIGHTS OF ENGLISH JEWS.

The obligation to take certain oaths the cause of Jewish disabilities.

WHEN considering the acquisition of political rights by the Jews, credit is often given to our legislators for never having enacted laws with the express object of depriving Jews of all share of political power. The gratitude for this mercy need not be excessive, for, without any special legislation, the Jews were effectually excluded from such power under the law as it existed at the time of their return, nor were the governing classes at all hasty in removing disabilities which, if not intentionally imposed, were at least deliberately maintained. The disabilities in question were occasioned by the necessity for those engaged in public affairs to take certain oaths, known as the oaths of allegiance, supremacy, and abjuration, of which it becomes necessary to give a more particular account.

The oath of allegiance and supremacy.

Until the period of the Reformation the oath of allegiance appears to have been bound up with the rendering of homage and fealty, but when the Church of England repudiated all connexion with the Roman Pontiff and acknowledged the king as its supreme head, it was thought necessary to frame a new oath of allegiance, embodying also an oath of supremacy or recognition that the king to whom allegiance was sworn possessed sovereign power, and was himself subject to no foreign potentate, ecclesiastical or lay. It will be unnecessary to do more than mention the statutes on this subject passed in the reign of Henry VIII, namely, 25 Hen. VIII, c. 22; 26 Hen. VIII, c. 2; 28 Hen. VIII, c. 7; id., c. 10; and 35 Hen. VIII, c. 1, because these were repealed during the short Papist revival under Queen Mary. More attention must be paid to the Act of Supremacy (1 Eliz., c. 1), the ninth section of which creates a new oath in terms as follows: "I, A. B., doo utterly testifie and declare in my conscience, that the Quenes Highnes is thonelye supreme governour of this realme and of all other her Highnes dominions and countreis, aswell in all sp̃uall or ecclesiasticall thinges or causes as temporall, and that no forreine prince p̃son prelate state or potentate hathe or oughte to have any jurisdicc̃on power superioritie preheminence or aucthoritee ecclesiasticall or sp̃uall within this realme, and therefore I doo utterly renounce and forsake all forraine jurisdicc̃ons power sup̃iorities and aucthorities, and doo promise that from hensforthe I shall beare faith and true allegiance to the Quenes Highnes her heires and lawfull successoures, and to my power shall assist and defende all jurisdicc̃ons preheminences privileges and aucthorities granted or belonging to the Quenes Highnes her heires and successoures or united or annexed to thimperiall crowne of this realme: So helpe me God and by the contentes of this booke."

Persons on whom it was imposed.

The oath was not imposed upon all subjects, but only upon ecclesiastical persons and those who held any temporal office, such as a judge, justice, or mayor, and the penalty for refusal to take the oath was forfeiture of the office, whether ecclesiastical or lay, in respect of which it was imposed. Four years later the obligation to take this oath was extended to all persons in holy orders, holders of a degree in any university, schoolmasters, and persons engaged in practising the law; and the penalty for refusing to take the oath was increased, being made for the first offence the same as under the statutes of praemunire and for the second the same as for high treason[1].

A new oath of obedience or allegiance, 1606.

After the failure of the Gunpowder Plot in 1605 a new oath was framed for the express purpose of repressing Popish recusants. It is a long and wordy oath, called in the statute creating it the oath of obedience, and is contained in five clauses, embracing in itself oaths of allegiance, supremacy, and abjuration of the Pope's authority. It did

[1] 5 Eliz., c. 1, ss. 5–11.

not abolish or supersede the oath prescribed by the Act of Supremacy, but was concurrent with it, and was often in popular language called the oath of allegiance or abjuration, and in practice, at least after the passing of the Act for administering the oath of allegiance (7 Jac. I, c. 6), would be tendered and administered instead of the earlier and less stringent form, which became known as the oath of supremacy. The tenor of this new oath was as follows:—

"I, A. B., do truly and sincerely acknowledge, profess, testify and declare in my conscience before God and the world, that our sovereign Lord King James is lawful and rightful King of this realm, and of all other his Majesty's dominions and countries; and that the Pope neither of himself nor by any authority of the church or see of Rome, or by any other means with any other, hath any power or authority to depose the King, or to dispose any of his Majesty's kingdoms or dominions, or to authorize any foreign prince to invade or annoy him or his countries, or to discharge any of his subjects of their allegiance and obedience to his Majesty or to give license or leave to any of them to bear arms, raise tumults or to offer any violence or hurt to his Majesty's royal person, state or government, or to any of his Majesty's subjects within his Majesty's dominions.

"(2) Also I do swear from my heart, That notwithstanding any declaration or sentence of excommunication or deprivation made or granted or to be made or granted by the Pope or his successors or by any authority derived or pretended to be derived from him or his see against the said King his heirs or successors or any absolution of the said subjects from their obedience: I will bear faith and true allegiance to his Majesty his heirs and successors, and him and them will defend to the uttermost of my power against all conspiracies and attempts whatsoever which shall be made against his or their persons, their crown and dignity, by reason or colour of any such sentence or declaration or otherwise, and will do my best endeavour to disclose and make known unto his Majesty, his heirs and successors all treasons and traitorous conspiracies which I shall know or hear of to be against him or any of them.

"(3) And I do further swear That I do from my heart abhor detest and abjure as impious and heretical this damnable doctrine and position That princes which be excommunicated or deprived by the Pope may be deposed or murdered by their subjects or any other whatsoever.

"(4) And I do believe, and in my conscience am resolved That neither the Pope nor any other person whatsoever hath power to absolve me of this oath or any part thereof, which I acknowledge by good and full authority to be lawfully ministred unto me and do renounce all pardons and dispensations to the contrary.

"(5) And all these things I do plainly and sincerely acknowledge and swear according to these express words by me spoken, and according to the plain common sense and understanding of the same words without any equivocation or mental evasion or secret reservation whatsoever: and I do make this recognition and acknowledgment heartily willingly and truly, upon the true faith of a Christian.

"So help me God[1]."

The oath directed against Popish Recusants.

The concluding words of the last paragraph, though undoubtedly obnoxious to Jews, could not have been framed with any intention of imposing a disability upon them, because, as we have seen, there were at that time no Jews known to be settled in the country. The words "upon the true faith of a Christian" were apparently inserted to effectually prevent any equivocation or mental reservation, which when these words were used would in the opinion of the Jesuit doctors themselves involve the penalty of mortal sin[2]. The oath itself was a piece of

[1] 3 Jac. I, c. 4, s. 15.

[2] A small book, either written or corrected by the Jesuit Garnet, called *A Treatise on Equivocation*, was found in the chambers of Francis Tresham, one of the Gunpowder Plot conspirators. This treatise lays it down that a man when called upon, as he thinks unjustly, to make

political sharp practice, and had been cunningly framed to injure the Roman Catholics, among whom there had long been considerable controversy as to the moral right of the Pope to depose a temporal prince. Those Catholics who refused the oath incurred the penalties laid down by the statute, while those who took it were rendered contemptible by asserting to be damnable a doctrine which large numbers of their coreligionists were known to approve [1].

The oaths of allegiance and supremacy recast at the time of the Revolution.

At the time of the Revolution in 1688 the old forms of the oaths commonly called the oath of supremacy and the oath of allegiance were repealed, and the oaths were recast so as to read as follows:—

"I, A. B., do sincerely promise and swear, That I will be faithful and bear true allegiance, to their Majesties King William and Queen Mary. So help me God," &c. (the oath of allegiance).

"I, A. B., do swear That I do from my heart abhor, detest and abjure as impious and heretical that damnable doctrine and position, That princes excommunicated or deprived by the Pope, or any authority of the see of Rome may be deposed or murdered by their subjects or any other whatsoever.

"And I do declare That no foreign prince person prelate state or potentate hath or ought to have any jurisdiction power superiority preeminence or authority ecclesiastical or spiritual within this realm. So help me God," &c. (the oath of supremacy) [2].

Such were the forms of the oaths of supremacy and

a declaration or take an oath may lawfully equivocate by using ambiguous words or by reserving mentally a sense of the words used different from that actually expressed, and that even though he uses the words "without equivocation or mental reservation." But there is one exception, namely, that he cannot do this without being guilty of mortal sin if he brings his true faith towards God into doubt or dispute. (See Baron Alderson's judgment in Miller *v.* Solomons (1852), 8 St. Tr. N.S., p. 163.)

[1] Dodd's *Church History*, Part V, Art. IV.

[2] 1 Will. & Mary, c. 8, s. 12. See ibid., c. 1, ss. 6 and 7.

allegiance, nor was any change made in them, so far as our present subject is concerned [1], until the middle of the late Queen Victoria's reign, when the question of the right of Jews to sit in Parliament, which will be dealt with in greater detail later, was raised and decided. It may therefore be seen that after the accession of William and Mary the most devout Jew could conscientiously take either or both of these oaths. However, after the death of James II in 1701 and the recognition of his son, the Old Pretender, as king, not only by the Jacobite party in the United Kingdom, but also by the French monarch Louis XIV, it was thought necessary to frame a third and new oath abjuring the Pretender's title, and known as the oath of abjuration, and impose it upon various classes of persons, including all who held any public office or high position in the state. The form of this oath was closely modelled upon the old oath of obedience which had been framed in 1605 with the express purpose of penalizing the Papists for their supposed complicity in the Gunpowder Plot, and the fifth and last clause of the old oath, ending with the words "upon the true faith of a Christian," was taken bodily and incorporated into the new oath of abjuration. Changes necessitated by the death of an old sovereign and the accession of a new one were from time to time introduced into the oath of abjuration, but on the death of the Old Pretender in 1765 it assumed its final form which was retained until 1858, when by the Oaths Act of that year [2] a single oath was substituted for the three oaths of allegiance, supremacy, and abjuration. To make the record complete it will be well to give the words of the oath of abjuration in the same way as the oaths of supremacy and allegiance have already been set out; they are as follows:—

Introduction of the oath of abjuration in 1701.

"I, A. B., do truly and sincerely acknowledge, profess, testify and declare in my conscience before God and the

[1] The change made by the Catholic Emancipation Act of 1829 (10 Geo. IV, c. 7, s. 2) applied only to persons professing the Roman Catholic religion.

[2] 21 & 22 Vict., c. 48.

world That our sovereign lord, King George, is lawful and rightful King of this realm and all other his Majesty's dominions and countries thereunto belonging. And I do solemnly and sincerely declare That I do believe in my conscience That not any of the descendants of the person who pretended to be prince of Wales during the life of the late King James the Second and since his decease pretended to be and took upon himself the stile and title of King of England by the name of James the Third or of Scotland by the name of James the Eighth or the stile and title of King of Great Britain hath any right or title whatsoever to the crown of this realm or any other the dominions thereunto belonging: and I do renounce refuse and abjure any allegiance or obedience to any of them. And I do swear That I will bear faith and true allegiance to His Majesty King George and him will defend to the utmost of my power against all traitorous conspiracies and attempts whatsoever which shall be made against his person crown or dignity. And I will do my utmost endeavour to disclose and make known to his Majesty and his successors all treasons and traitorous conspiracies which I shall know to be against him or any of them. And I do faithfully promise to the utmost of my power to support maintain and defend the succession of the crown against the descendants of the said James and against all other persons whatsoever which succession, by an act intituled, 'An act for the further limitation of the crown and better securing the rights and liberties of the subject,' is and stands limited to the Princess Sophia electoress and dutchess dowager of Hanover and the heirs of her body being protestants. And all these things I do plainly and sincerely acknowledge and swear according to these express words by me spoken and according to the plain common sense and understanding of the same words without any equivocation mental evasion or secret reservation whatsoever. And I do make this recognition acknowledgment abjuration renunciation and promise heartily willingly and truly upon the true faith of a Christian. So help me God[1]."

Jews unable to take the new oath.

This new oath could not be taken by a self-respecting Jew, and though, as we have already seen, the legislature allowed Jews to omit the final words, "on the true faith of a Christian," in two particular instances, namely landowners required to take the oath, and persons seeking naturalization in the British colonies in America, this indulgence was never extended to any other cases[2]. It had, on the other hand, been expressly held by the Courts that

Later history of these promissory oaths.

[1] 6 Geo. III, c. 53, s. 2. The other statutes are 13 & 14 (13 Ruff.) Will. III, c. 6; 1 Anne, c. 16 (c. 22, Ruff.); 6 Anne, c. 11 (5 Anne, c. 8, Ruff.), art. 22; 6 Anne, c. 41 (c. 7, Ruff.), ss. 20 & 21; and 1 Geo. I, st. 2, c. 13. There is an excellent article on the oath of allegiance in Sir F. Pollock's *Essays in Jurisprudence and Ethics.* The subsequent history of these oaths is as follows: the Oaths Act of 1858 (21 & 22 Vict., c. 48) substituted a single oath for the three oaths of allegiance, supremacy, and abjuration. The new oath contained the substance of the old oaths, and was expressed to be made "upon the true faith of a Christian"; but the very next Act in the Statute Book, the Jewish Relief Act of 1858 (21 & 22 Vict., c. 49), provided that whenever any of her Majesty's subjects professing the Jewish religion shall be required to take the said oath the words "and I make this Declaration upon the true faith of a Christian" shall be omitted. The Office and Oath Act, 1867 (30 & 31 Vict., c. 75, s. 5), still further shortened and simplified the oath to be taken by office-holders. The Promissory Oaths Act of 1868 (31 & 32 Vict., c. 72) established three new forms of oaths, the oath of allegiance, the official and the judicial oath, which are still in force and none of which is objectionable to Jews. They are as follows:—

(1) The oath of allegiance. "I do swear that I will be faithful and bear true allegiance to Her Majesty Queen Victoria, Her Heirs and Successors according to Law. So help me God."

(2) The official oath. "I do swear that I will well and truly serve Her Majesty Queen Victoria in the office of . So help me God."

(3) The judicial oath. "I do swear that I will well and truly serve our Sovereign Lady Queen Victoria in the office of and I will do right to all manner of people after the laws and usages of this realm without fear or favour, affection or ill-will. So help me God."

The Promissory Oaths Act of 1871 (34 & 35 Vict., c. 48) finally repealed all the statutes establishing the old forms of oaths and declarations which had been superseded and rendered obsolete by the Promissory Oaths Act of 1868.

[2] See supra, p. 170; *The Return of the Jews to England*, p. 122.

the omission of any part of the oath as framed by the legislature would entail the same penalties as if the oath had never been taken at all[1]. Consequently after the year 1701 no conscientious Jew could hold any of the offices for which the taking of the oath of abjuration was a necessary qualification.

Mode of administering the oaths.

It is to be observed that none of the statutes lay down the mode in which the oath is to be administered; but it would not be illegal for the official tendering the oath to insist upon its being taken on the New Testament, more especially as the earlier statutes (5 Eliz., c. 1, ss. 5 and 7, and 7 Jac. I, c. 6, ss. 12–18) had directed that it should be taken on the Evangelists, and if this were insisted upon the person to be sworn would have no right to compel the official to swear him on the Old Testament[2].

Effect of promissory oaths.

It should further be added that the administration of these promissory oaths—though so dear to the law of England—has no binding effect in law, for the breach of them cannot be prosecuted or punished as perjury[3]. They have been retained only for their moral effect as bringing home to the conscience of the newly appointed official the necessity of faithfully fulfilling the duties of his office.

In dealing with political rights, the principal subjects which will come under review are (1) the right to acquire British nationality; (2) the right of exercising the franchise; (3) the right of being a member of, and holding office under a municipal corporation; (4) the right of holding office under the crown; (5) the right of being a member of and sitting in Parliament.

The acquisition of British nationality.

Most important of all was the right to acquire British nationality. Even at the present time an alien can possess no political rights, but his civil rights also were very limited at the time when the Jews first returned to England. Magna

[1] See Rex *v.* Edward Lord Vaux (1612), 1 Bulstrode, 199.

[2] See Rex *v.* Bosworth (1739), 2 Strange, pp. 1112–14.

[3] Coke, III Inst., c. 74, p. 166.

Former status and disabilities of aliens.

Charta had no doubt conferred on aliens the privilege of entering, dwelling in, and departing from the realm, but this privilege was to exist only in time of peace, and was strictly confined to merchants engaged in commerce. As has been already seen[1], an alien was incapacitated from holding land or real property of any description, with the sole exception that, if a merchant, he might lease a house for the purpose of habitation of himself and family, or the carrying on of his trade, this being an incident of commerce. The ordinary alien, not being a merchant, such as an artificer, could only occupy a house under an agreement, not amounting to a lease, such as a tenancy at will or from year to year, but any greater interest in land he might acquire was liable to forfeiture by the Crown. As he could hold no real property he could maintain no real or mixed action, but on the other hand an alien could acquire and hold any personal property, not being an interest in land, with the one exception of a British ship, or any share therein, by gift, trade, or other lawful means, and this property he could alienate during his life, or dispose of by will on his death, for in England the *droit d'aubaine*, prevalent in France, Italy, and other continental countries which vested in the Crown the possessions of a dead stranger, never existed. He was liable to pay the alien duty, even although he had obtained letters of denization from the Crown[2]. An alien friend could also

[1] See supra, p. 110; *The Return of the Jews to England*, p. 62.

The special taxation of aliens.

[2] The alien duties under the Lancastrian and Yorkist kings and earlier monarchs had taken the form of a poll-tax levied upon all foreigners resident in the country. Under Henry VI the rates were:—For (1) all merchant strangers, if not denizens—householders, 40*s.*; not householders, but resident six weeks within the realm, 20*s.*; if denizens by letters patent, 10 marks. (2) Others not merchants, householders, 1*s.* 4*d.*; not householders, 6*d.* (see Dowell's *History of Taxation in England*, vol. I, p. 154). After the accession of the Tudors the poll-tax upon aliens does not seem to have remained a permanent feature in our national finance, but in many of the acts imposing taxation upon goods whether exported or imported a double rate was frequently levied upon the goods of aliens, though the additional duty for aliens was not always so great.

maintain any personal action either for the protection of his property or the security of his person or reputation [1]. But although the alien was thus in some ways treated as a natural-born subject his rights might be greatly curtailed by statute, such as the acts against alien artificers [2] and the Navigation Act of 1660, which prohibited aliens from being factors or merchants in any of the extra-European possessions of the Crown, and he had no absolute right either to enter the country or remain in it, if the executive government ordered his departure. This right of a State to exclude or expel a foreigner from its territory is recognized in International Law, and is known under

In the Act granting a subsidy of tonnage and poundage to King Charles II (12 Car. II, c. 4) and the rules annexed to it "all merchant strangers bringing in any sorts of the said wines are to pay thirty shillings in the tonne over and above the aforesaid rates which the native pays," and for lead, tin, and woollen clothes, &c., aliens had to pay double subsidy. At length in 1784 this "petty custom" or additional tax imposed upon aliens' goods was abolished by statute (24 Geo. III, sess. 2, c. 16). Since that time aliens have been taxed in the same way as natives, but while the alien duties remained in force they could not be evaded by obtaining letters of denization (see 1 Hen. VII, c. 2; 11 Hen. VII, c. 14; 22 Hen. VIII, c. 8; and 25 Car. II, c. 6). The attempt, for some time successful, of the Jews (many of whom had been made denizens) to escape these duties has been already referred to (supra, p. 164; *The Return, &c.*, p. 116). It would seem that in pre-expulsion times the municipalities, which had a right of taxing those resident within their borders, were accustomed to make the Jews pay double the tax imposed on their Christian neighbours. My attention has been called to the following words in an address presented by the Dutch congregation of Sandwich to the mayor of that town in the year 1571: "the order for the head money was not taxed above 2 pence for a christian and but 4 pence for a jewe; which 2 pence we are hertely willing to pay . . . such as amongst our people doe goe for to passe the seas at this tyme do paye not onely 4 pence (which in tymes past was the taxe for a jewe)," &c. (Boys' *History of Sandwich*, p. 743). It has been suggested that this passage shows that a colony of Jews remained in the Cinque Ports after the expulsion in 1290 or else settled there between that date and the return of the Jews in the time of Charles II, but I see no difficulty in making the words "in tymes past" refer to a remote period before the edict of banishment had been issued.

[1] See Tirlot *v.* Morris (1611), 1 Bulst. 134, and Yelverton, 198.

[2] See the statutes 1 Ric. III, c. 9, and 14 & 15 Hen. VIII, c. 2, and 32 Hen. VIII, c. 16; and Henriques on *Aliens and Naturalization*, pp. 20–22.

the name of "droit de renvoi." It was undoubtedly in early times maintained and acted upon in this country; for until comparatively recent times no foreigner was allowed to enter without a passport, and under the Registration of Aliens Act, 1836 (6 and 7 Will. IV, c. 11), which, though by no means strictly enforced, was only repealed by the Aliens Act of 1905 (5 Edw. VII, c. 13, s. 10), an alien on his arrival in the United Kingdom had to be registered. There is, however, no instance of the general expulsion of aliens by order of the Crown alone since the year 1575, in the reign of Queen Elizabeth. The right has thus been allowed to fall into desuetude, and can no longer be regarded as one of the prerogatives of the Crown; accordingly after the outbreak of the French Revolution, in consequence of the fears occasioned by the large number of refugees and other foreigners arriving in this country, it was found advisable to pass a temporary Act of Parliament empowering the Crown by proclamation or order in Council to order the expulsion of any alien or aliens, who might be within the realm, and also to regulate or prevent the landing of foreigners. The Act known as Lord Grenville's Alien Act, 1793 (33 Geo. III, c. 4), was a temporary one, but was renewed annually during the French war and even after the declaration of peace, though with considerable modifications, until the year 1826, when it was finally abandoned and the system of the registration of aliens adopted in its stead [1].

[1] The first Registration of Aliens Act is 7 Geo. IV, c. 54. In the revolutionary year of 1848 Parliament again vested in the principal Secretaries of State, but only for the space of one year, the power of ordering any alien to depart the realm (11 & 12 Vict., c. 20). The necessity of having legislation upon this subject shows that the Crown has lost the power it once claimed of closing the realm against alien friends and of sending foreigners out of the kingdom. It should be added that even after it was recognized that the right had been lost by desuetude in ordinary cases, it was thought to be still existing in the case of an alien charged with a crime committed abroad and demanded for extradition by his sovereign; see the opinion given to the government in 1792 by Serjeant Hill, quoted in Clarke on *Extradition*, p. 25; but in such cases

Aliens, who were subject to the disabilities above described, comprise all persons born out of the King's dominions or allegiance; for the law of England has always adopted the feudal or territorial principle that all persons born in any of the dominions over which the King has at the time of their birth sovereign power, even although, as in the case of Hanover before 1837, he does not hold them in virtue of the Crown of England, owe allegiance to the King, and are consequently natural-born subjects of his realm.

Who are aliens by English law.

The contrary principle, founded on the Roman law and incorporated in the Code Napoleon and the jurisprudence of many modern nations, whereby children wherever born are always deemed to possess the nationality of their parents, has never in theory been adopted by English law. Nevertheless the class of natural-born subjects has been widened by statute by including in it persons born abroad, whose fathers, and whose grandfathers on the father's side, have been born within the realm [1].

It will thus be seen that the Jews who originally settled here must have all been aliens, and, although their children born here would be natural-born subjects, so great has been the accession to the Jewish community of new comers

the proceedings would have at the present time to be in strict accordance with the Extradition Act, 1870 (33 & 34 Vict., c. 52). (For this subject see Forsyth's *Cases and Opinions on Constitutional Law*, pp. 181 and 369 seq.; Dicey's *Law of the Constitution*, p. 220 (note); and Henriques on the *Law of Aliens and Naturalization*, pp. 13, 14.)

[1] See The Foreign Protestants' Naturalization Act, 1708 (7 Anne, c. 5), as explained by the British Nationality Act, 1730 (4 Geo. II, c. 21), and the British Nationality Act, 1772 (13 Geo. III, c. 21). It is by reason of the adoption of the system of the Code Napoleon by Roumania that the Jews of that country have been deprived of their rights of citizenship. A Jew born in that unhappy country may be told: "You are not a Roumanian, for, being a Jew, at one time or other your ancestors must have been foreigners; you have their nationality; therefore you are an alien, and require a special act of naturalization before you can become a citizen." And unfortunately the Roumanian government have never been liberal in granting naturalization to Jews, even though settled for generations in the country.

The Roumanian Law as to aliens.

from abroad, that it may be asserted that a very large proportion, if not a majority, of the Jews in England has always consisted of aliens.

How aliens can acquire British nationality.

The machinery provided by our constitution, by which aliens may acquire some or all of the rights of native born subjects, has in consequence at all times been of the greatest importance to the Jews. In the early days of the resettlement this was in practice confined to obtaining letters patent of denization from the King. The grant of such letters patent under the Great Seal is an ancient prerogative of the Crown, whereby the sovereign is enabled to confer upon the alien many but not all the rights of a native of the realm. The letters patent may be temporary or conditional, and may either specify the privileges granted or confer all the rights of a subject, save and except such as the patent expressly or the law impliedly withholds, for the King cannot alter the law otherwise than by Act of Parliament. A denizen so created "ex donatione regis" is said to be "in a kind of middle state between an alien and a natural-born subject, and partakes of both of them," for his patent can have no retrospective effect, and therefore, before the alteration of the law, until the issue of his letters patent a denizen could have no inheritable blood, and at the present time his children born abroad before his denization do not become British subjects unless they are themselves made denizens by being expressly included in the letters of denization. As has been seen he was liable to pay the alien duties, and to any other restriction upon his rights which might be imposed by Act of Parliament. In particular the Act of Settlement, passed at a time when the jealousy of foreigners, fostered, as it had been, by the dislike of the partiality of William III to his foreign favourites, was rampant in the country, expressly excluded denizens and naturalized persons also from the exercise of all important political functions by providing that "no person born out of the kingdoms of England, Scotland, or Ireland, or the dominions thereunto belonging (although he be naturalized or made a denizen) except such as are born of English parents, shall be capable to be of the Privy Council or a member of either House of Parliament, or to enjoy any office or place of trust, either civil or military, or to have any grant of lands or hereditaments from the Crown to himself or to any other or others in trust for him [1]."

The colonial trade closed to aliens by the Navigation Act of 1660.

Though the rights of denizens were thus limited they were highly prized and eagerly sought after by the first Jewish settlers in this country; more especially because the trade with the English colonies and plantations abroad, in those days the easiest avenue to the acquisition of large wealth, had been effectually closed to aliens by the Navigation Act of 1660 (12 Car. II, c. 18), which provided that "no alien or person not born within the allegiance of our sovereign lord the King, his heirs and successors, or *naturalized or made a free denizen*, shall . . . exercise the trade or occupation of a merchant or factor in any of the said places" (i. e. lands, islands, plantations, or territories belonging to the King in Asia, Africa, or America) upon pain of forfeiting all his goods and chattels. For the strict enforcement of this provision a clause was inserted in the Act of 1696 for preventing frauds and regulating abuses in the plantation trade, compelling the governor and commander-in-chief of every English colony or plantation to take a solemn oath to see that this and other provisions were punctually and bona fide observed [2].

[1] 12 & 13 Will. III, c. 2, s. 3.

[2] See 7 & 8 Will. III, c. 22, s. 4. There seems to have been a fear that this Act would have shut out from the colonial trade persons already entitled to take part in it, such as denizens, and to close it to all except persons born within the realm or the plantations. The Jews therefore petitioned against the Bill; see *Commons Journals*, vol. XI, p. 440: "A petition of Isaac Correa, Isaac Pereira and Joseph Henriques, on behalf of themselves and divers other merchants, was presented to the House and read; setting forth That the Petitioners are informed, That there is a clause in the Bill for preventing Frauds and regulating Abuses

The law was not relaxed until 1794, and then only in favour of aliens resident in places acquired by the right of conquest, and was finally repealed in 1825[1].

Jews made denizens by Charles II.

Very many Jews were made free denizens in the early days of the resettlement, and their admission to this higher status is a mark of the liberality as well as of the far-seeing wisdom of those responsible for the executive government at the time. Mr. Carteret Webb, in an appendix to his well-known pamphlet, "The Question whether a Jew can hold land, &c.," gives a list containing the names of 105 Jews who obtained letters of denization during the reigns of Charles II and James II, and this list is by no means complete[2]. The only condition as a general rule

in the Plantation Trade That no Foreigner shall use the Occupation of a Merchant or Factor, in any of his Majesty's Plantations, under a great Penalty; That such a Clause will be the Ruin of many Families, who by the Rigour of the Spanish and Portuguese Inquisitions were forced to renounce their native Countries and shelter themselves under the Protection of the English Government, to which they have ever dutifully submitted: And praying That they may be heard by their Counsel at the Bar of the House, before the Passing of the said Bill touching the Premises." This was on Feb. 12, 169$\frac{5}{6}$; on March 4 the French Protestants residing in London presented a similar petition. Both petitions were referred to the Committee of the Houses; see *Com. Journ.*, XI, p. 491.

[1] See 34 Geo. III, c. 42, s. 6; 37 Geo. III, c. 63, s. 5; 45 Geo. III, c. 32, s. 5; and 6 Geo. IV, c. 105.

[2] Supra, p. 144 (note) and p. 158; *The Return, &c.*, pp. 96 and 110. The lists of foreign Protestants and aliens resident in England published by the Camden Society in 1862 contain at p. 42 the following document: "Denization to severall persons [among them are some Jews of note]. Our will and pleasure is that you prepare a Bill for our Royall Signature to passe our Great Seale for the makinge the persons hereafter named, being Aliens borne, free Denizens of this our Kingdome, viz.": then follow the names of a great number of persons, including a number of Jews, seven of whom are included in Webb's list, but others not found in that list are Isaac Abraham, James Baruch Lonzada, Philipp Martines, Jone Mathias, Judith his wife, and Isaac their son, Judith and Frances Meres, and Samuel Sasportas. The document continues: "And that they have and enjoy all priviledges and immunityes as other free Denizens do, provided they and every of them do live and continue with their familyes in this our Kingdome of England or elsewhere within

attached to the grant of a patent of denization to a Jew was the taking of the oath of allegiance, in the form of which, as we have seen, there was nothing to which he could reasonably object [1].

Naturalization by Act of Parliament.

Though the King by his letters patent could not grant the full rights of a natural-born subject to an alien, these could be obtained from Parliament, which, in intendment of law, is assumed to be omnipotent. An alien born in Portugal, who came into England with Beatrice, Countess of Arundel, was naturalized by Parliament in the third year of Henry VI, but private Acts of Parliament by which naturalization was conferred upon an alien did not come into vogue until the reign of Queen Elizabeth [2]. Naturalization differed from denization in that it had a retrospective effect; the naturalized person being deemed

oure dominions, and this sayd Denization to be forthwith passed under our great seale, without any Fees or other charges whatsoever to be payd by the sayd persons in the passing thereof. And for so doing this shall be your warrant. Given at our Court at Whitehall the 16 of December 1687. To our Attorney or Sollicitor Generall."

[1] Though the King and his chief ministers were thus liberal in creating denizens, impediments to the carrying out the royal intentions were sometimes interposed by minor officials. Thus we find among the public records for the year 1677 a "Petition of Manuel Martinez Dormido of London Merchant and Daniel Bueno Henriques of Barbadoes, Hebrews, to the King. That His Majesty by warrant under his Sign Manual granted Petitioners letters of denization which have passed the Signet, but are denied the Privy Seal, Petitioners' religion being only objected, pray that said two bills may pass the Privy and Great Seals notwithstanding said objection, several of their nation having enjoyed lately the like privileges" (*Col. Papers*, vol. XLI, No. 146; *Cal. S. P. America and West Indies*, 1677–80, p. 201).

Both grants had been made on the same day, namely July 24, 1661, some sixteen years before. See *Cal. S. P. Dom.*, 1661–2, p. 214, and ibid., p. 42. Also ibid., America and West Indies, 1685–8, p. 633, nos. 2019 and 2020, and ibid., Colonial, 1661–8, p. 49, no. 139. Dormido, who was made a denizen with his two sons Solomon and Aaron, is another name altogether omitted in Webb's list. He had come to England in 1654; see supra, p. 188; *The Return of the Jews*, p. 40.

[2] Viner's *Abridgment*, Tit. Alien (D) Naturalization, and Henriques on *Aliens and Naturalization*, pp. 38, 39.

a subject *natura*, to all intents and purposes, as if he had been born so. So that his lands might be inherited by his son, though born before the special Act of Parliament was passed. And he was moreover free from any liability to pay the alien duties and the other restrictions to which, as we have seen, an alien made a denizen was liable. The clause in the Act of Settlement already recited however applied to him, so that his political rights were after 1714 greatly limited [1].

Naturalization confined to Protestants by a statute of 1609.

It was in early times determined that these wide rights, in those days including full political rights, should be conferred on none save those who professed the true Protestant religion; to secure which a public Act of Parliament was passed in the year 1609. It recites that "Forasmuch as the naturalizing of strangers, and restoring to blood persons attainted, have been ever reputed matters of mere grace and favour, which are not fit to be bestowed upon any others than such as are of the religion now established in this realm," and then enacts that no person "of what quality condition or place soever" shall be naturalized unless he have received the sacrament of the Lord's Supper within one month next before any bill exhibited for that purpose, and shall also take the oath of supremacy and the oath of allegiance in the Parliament house before his bill be twice read [2]. Thus a conscientious Jew, being unwilling to take the sacrament, could not obtain naturalization by means of a private Act of Parliament.

General Naturalization Acts.

In addition various Acts of Parliament, all of which are now repealed, were passed during the seventeenth and eighteenth centuries, conferring naturalization and the full

[1] This clause of the Act of Settlement did not come into force until the accession of George I in 1714. In that year 1 Geo. I, st. 2, c. 4, was passed to prevent it being dispensed with in the private Act of Parliament granting naturalization. This last Act was repealed in 1844 by Mr. Hutt's Naturalization Act (7 & 8 Vict., c. 66), but clause 3 of the Act of Settlement is still unrepealed. See Henriques on *Aliens and Naturalization*, p. 40.

[2] 7 Jac. I, c. 2.

rights and privileges of British subjects (with the exception in the case of Acts passed after 1714 of the political rights reserved by the Act of Settlement) upon foreigners in return for benefits supposed to accrue to this country by reason of their carrying on certain branches of trade here or in the colonies, or being engaged in the public service for a definite period. For example, by the Act for encouraging the manufactures of making linen cloth and tapestry, passed in 1663 (15 Car. II, c. 15), all foreigners that shall really and bona fide set up and use in England any of the manufactures mentioned for the space of three years, should upon taking the oaths of allegiance and supremacy enjoy all the privileges of a natural-born subject. This Act was not repealed till 1863, but though open to the Jews, for the oaths required did not include the oath of abjuration, does not appear to have been frequently taken advantage of by them. The Acts for the better supply of mariners and seamen gave similar privileges to foreigners who had served for two years or more upon a British ship of war or merchant or other trading ship during time of war, and no oath or other formality was required as a condition precedent to the acquisition of these rights, which were however subject to the disabling clause in the Act of Settlement already mentioned [1]. Of the provisions of these Acts also Jews could, but did not in any large numbers, avail themselves. On the other hand, the privilege of becoming British subjects, given in 1761 to foreigners who had for two years served as officers or soldiers in his Majesty's royal American regiment or as engineers in America, was strictly confined to Protestants, and those claiming it were bound to first qualify themselves by taking and subscribing the oaths, including the oath of abjuration, and also receiving the sacrament in some Protestant and reformed congregation [2]. The benefit

[1] See 6 Anne, c. 64 (37 Ruffhead), s. 20; 13 Geo. II, c. 3; and 20 Geo. III, c. 20.

[2] See the statute 2 Geo. III, c. 25.

of naturalization given to foreigners engaged in the whale fishery was similarly restricted to Protestants, who might qualify themselves in the ways above stated [1].

The Plantation Act, 1740.

A more liberal and enlightened policy animated the framers of the Acts for the encouragement of settlement in the American colonies. By the statute (13 Geo. II, c. 7) entitled an Act for naturalizing such foreign Protestants and others therein mentioned, as are settled or shall settle in any of his Majesty's colonies in America, and popularly known as the Plantation Act, foreigners who had resided in any of the American colonies for seven years or more might be naturalized upon taking the oaths of allegiance, supremacy, and abjuration, and also receiving the sacrament. But special provisions were made in favour of Quakers and Jews. Both were exempted from receiving the sacrament; the former were allowed to affirm instead of taking the oaths, and the latter to omit the obnoxious words, "on the true faith of a Christian," which formed the conclusion of the oath of abjuration. Moreover, although the persons thus naturalized had their political rights limited by the Act of Settlement, yet in their case the incapacity to hold any office or place of trust or have any grant of lands from the Crown, applied only to offices or grants in Great Britain and Ireland, and not

[1] By 22 Geo. II, c. 45, s. 8 seq., foreign Protestants serving for three years on board English ships employed in the whale fishery and qualifying themselves by taking the oaths and the sacrament were to be deemed natural-born subjects, and by 26 Geo. III, c. 50, s. 24, aliens employed in the *southern* whale fishery for five years, and by the amending Act, 28 Geo. III, c. 20, ss. 15 and 16, the foreign owners of ships so employed for a like period may be naturalized. It is to be observed that the benefit of these Acts relating to the southern whale fishery was not confined to Protestants, and the only condition precedent was the taking of the oath of allegiance; neither the sacrament nor the other oaths being necessary. But the Acts were not long in force, for they were repealed in 1795 by 35 Geo. III, c. 92. See s. 36 seq., which restrict the privilege of naturalization to forty families owning whalers and settling at Milford before Jan. 1, 1798.

to the colonies or elsewhere[1]. The Jews who had great interests in the American colonies, and more particularly in the West Indian Islands, freely availed themselves of the benefit of this Act, as can be seen from the lists of names of persons thus naturalized, which, in accordance with the provisions of the Act, the Secretary of each colony was bound annually to transmit to the office of the Commissioners for Trade and Plantations for the purpose of registration[2].

Thirteen years later was introduced the famous Jew Bill, the merit of which is ascribed both to the Lord Chancellor, Lord Hardwicke, and the Prime Minister, Mr. Pelham, by their respective biographers. No measure has perhaps been more thoroughly misrepresented. It was entitled "an Act to permit persons professing the Jewish religion to be naturalized by Parliament, and for other purposes therein mentioned." It recited first the Naturalization Act of 1609, under which no alien was to obtain a private Act of Parliament for his naturalization unless he had first received the sacrament of the Lord's Supper, and secondly the Plantation Act of 1740, under which Jews could be naturalized in the American colonies without the necessity of first receiving the sacrament, and then enacted that Jews might, in spite of the provisions of the Act of 1609, be naturalized by private Act of Parliament without receiving the sacrament. It further provided that the political rights excepted by the Act of Settlement should be excluded, and that no person should obtain such a private Act of Parliament who had not resided in Great

The Jews Naturalization Act, 1753.

[1] See 13 Geo. II, c. 7, s. 6; 20 Geo. II, c. 44, s. 5; and 13 Geo. III, c. 25.

[2] For the names of persons naturalized in His Majesty's plantations in America, 1740–61, see the *Colonial Office Records (Board of Trade), Plantations General*, vols. 59 and 66, and *Jews in the British West Indies*, by Dr. Friedenwald, Pub. American Jewish Hist. Soc., No. 5. In the debate in the House of Commons on Dec. 4, 1753, it was stated that 185 Jews had been naturalized during the thirteen years in which the Act had then been in operation, and of these no fewer than 130 resided in the island of Jamaica (see Lord Orford's *Memoires*, vol. I, p. 317).

Britain or Ireland for three years without being absent for more than three months at any one time, or who should not bring proof that he had professed the Jewish religion for the past three years. It further contained a clause disabling every person professing the Jewish religion from purchasing, inheriting, or otherwise acquiring any advowson or right of patronage or presentation or other interest whatsoever in any benefice or ecclesiastical living. The Bill passed through the House of Lords without a division, and without any serious opposition. When the Bill came down to the Commons, it was soon perceived that political capital might be made out of it by an unscrupulous opposition. The Parliament was then nearly six years old, and there was bound to be a general election in the course of the following year. It was therefore determined to make a party cry against the government in office out of the introduction of a piece of legislation which, though a measure of justice, must have been felt even by its authors to be lacking the element of popularity. A sharp debate arose on the second reading; it was urged by the opposition that Christianity itself was dishonoured, that the Established Church was menaced, that the country would be inundated by Jews, and that all landed property, public offices, and political power would be monopolized by them. It was, on the other hand, pointed out that Jews had been living in England under the protection of the law for nearly a century, that they could already be naturalized in the colonies under the Plantation Act, that at most only a limited number would be able to avail themselves of the present enactment; and that Parliament could refuse to pass any particular Naturalization Bill which might be presented to it; but the Bill would encourage persons of wealth and substance to come to the country and so increase its commerce and credit. The second reading was carried by ninety-five votes to sixteen. The agitation in the country was, however, spreading, petitions were presented to Parliament against the Bill, including one from the Mayor, Aldermen, and citizens of London. A division was again challenged when the Bill was read a third time upon a motion for adjournment, and this was only thrown out by ninety-six votes to fifty-five. The Bill accordingly received the Royal Assent and became law as the Jewish Naturalization Act, 1753 (26 Geo. II, c. 26).

The Jews Naturalization Act, Repeal Act, 1754.

The contest was not over. During the summer recess it was transferred from the Parliament House to the country. The flames of prejudice and intolerance which had been sedulously fanned during the debate in the House of Commons now burst forth with the utmost fury. Pamphlets and broadsides were issued by both parties. Sober and temperate arguments were put forward on the one side, every calumny and insult at any time levelled against the Jewish race was raked up on the other. In such an arena the issue could not be long doubtful. Reason had to yield to passion, and the cry "No Jews! No Jews! No Wooden Shoes," was heard throughout the length and breadth of the land. The Bishop of Norwich was openly insulted in several parts of his diocese when holding the annual confirmations, on account of having supported the Bill in the Lords, and members of the lower House who represented other than pocket boroughs were threatened with the loss of their seats. The Government in view of the impending general election decided to give way before the storm. On November 15, 1753, the very first day of the new session, the Duke of Newcastle, brother to the Prime Minister, and himself a Secretary of State, introduced a Bill in the House of Lords to repeal the unpopular measure, retaining, nevertheless, the clause by which Jews were disabled from purchasing or inheriting an advowson or right of patronage in the church. It was, however, objected by the enemies of the Jews that the retention of this clause in the statute book would give parliamentary sanction to the doctrine, by no means at that time universally accepted, that Jews born here are by the common law entitled to all the rights of natural-born subjects, including the right to hold real property. The clause was in consequence omitted, and the Act of the preceding session totally repealed [1].

In the Commons also no time was lost in attacking the obnoxious Act. As soon as the Address was agreed to, a motion was made and carried without opposition that the House should be called over on December 4 in order to take the Act into consideration. In the meanwhile the repealing Bill came down from the House of Lords. Both political parties being agreed upon the expediency of repeal, the debate turned upon the preamble by which Ministers thought to defend themselves from the charge of pusillanimously yielding to popular clamour. It read, "Whereas occasion has been taken from the said Act to raise discontents and to disquiet the minds of many of his Majesty's subjects"; the Ministerial contention being that the Act in reality was of no importance in the sphere of religion, and gave only a small indulgence to the Jews by relieving them from one only of the formalities the law required for naturalization as a British subject, but that it had been unjustifiably misrepresented far and wide as being of far-reaching effect upon the constitution as a whole, and the Established Church in particular, and that the uproar thus occasioned was such that to retain it on the statute book would do the cause of the Jews more harm than good. At the same time in revoking it there ought to be an expression of disapprobation at the course pursued by those who had misled the public. On the other hand it was maintained by the opponents of the Bill that the popular tumult was fully justified by so iniquitous a measure, and an amendment was moved to substitute for the words quoted, "Whereas great discontents and disquietudes had from the said Act arisen in the minds of many of his Majesty's subjects." The original preamble

[1] In consequence a Jew may at the present time have the right to present a clergyman to a benefice in the Church of England. Supra, pp. 194–5.

was ultimately adopted by 113 votes to 47, and the repealing Bill passed into law.

Notwithstanding, a few days afterwards, on December 4, the day appointed for the call of the House, Lord Henley moved for leave to bring in a Bill to repeal so much of the Plantation Act of 1740 as enabled Jews to obtain naturalization in the colonies, but the party in power feeling that they had already paid sufficient attention to mere clamour, and that it would be dangerous to still further gratify the spirit of intolerance and fanaticism that was abroad, strongly opposed the reopening of the subject, and the motion was thrown out by 208 to 88.

Unsuccessful attempt to take away the right of Jews to be naturalized in the colonies.

Such is the story of the famous Jew Bill, creditable neither to the intelligence of the mob nor the courage of the Ministry; of it let us say with Blackstone, "Peace be now to its manes [1]."

Seventy-two years afterwards Parliament passed the statute 6 Geo. IV, c. 67, which was not confined to Jews, but abolished in all cases the necessity of receiving the sacrament imposed by the Naturalization Act of James I on all applicants to Parliament for Naturalization Bills [2]. Moreover, in 1844 Mr. Hutt's Naturalization Act (7 and 8 Vict., c. 66) introduced the system of acquiring British nationality by means of a certificate from a Secretary of State. This system is as convenient and available for Jews as for other aliens. It was improved and extended by the Naturalization Act, 1870 (33 and 34 Vict., c. 14), which with the amending Acts, is still in force, and except in very exceptional cases the old systems of denization

Recent changes in the law of naturalization.

[1] The repealing Act is 27 Geo. II, c. 1. For the whole controversy see Cobbett's *Parl. Hist.*, vol. 14, pp. 1365–1431; 15, pp. 91–163; Lord Orford's *Memoires*, vol. I, pp. 310–19; Coxe's *Administration of Henry Pelham*, vol. II, pp. 245–53, 290–8; Campbell's *Lives of the Chancellors*, vol. V, pp. 123–4; and Lord Mahon's *History of England*, vol. IV, pp. 35–7.

[2] Jews could, however, obtain naturalization in Ireland after 1816 by virtue of the Irish statute 36 Geo. III, c. 48, passed in that year. See Evans' *Collection of Statutes*, vol. I, p. 4, and Gabbett's *Digest of Statute Law*, vol. I, pp. 307–9.

and naturalization by private Acts of Parliament are now obsolete [1].

The Parliamentary franchise.

Having once acquired the rights of a British subject, either by birth or naturalization, the Jew, provided he was a freeholder in a county or a freeman in a borough, or otherwise duly qualified, was at common law entitled to exercise the franchise at Parliamentary and other elections. The legislature, however, provided machinery for preventing Roman Catholic voters from exercising this right. The statute 7 and 8 Will. III, c. 27, enacted that no person should be admitted to vote in any Parliamentary election who should refuse to take the oaths of allegiance and supremacy which the sheriff or other officer taking the poll was empowered and required to administer at the request of any of the candidates. This provision would not affect Jewish voters who, as has been seen, would find nothing objectionable in either of these oaths. However, a few years later, in the Act making provision for the election of sixteen peers of Scotland, in accordance with the terms of the then recently passed Act of Union between England and Scotland, a clause was inserted disabling from voting at any Parliamentary election in Great Britain any person who refused to take in addition the oath of abjuration which the presiding officer was likewise required to administer at the request of any candidate. The oath of abjuration ended with the words, "on the true faith of a Christian," and thus Jews as well as Roman Catholics might be, and were on occasion, debarred from recording their votes [2]. This provision was not repealed until the Statute Law Revision Act of 1867 (30 and 31 Vict., c. 59), but the Roman Catholic Relief Act, 1829 (10 Geo. IV, c. 7, s. 5) allowed Roman Catholic electors to substitute an oath they were willing to take. Needless to say, in the case of Jews and other conscientious

[1] For the present law see the author's treatise on the *Law of Aliens and Naturalization*.

[2] See 6 Anne, c. 78 (Ruff. 23), s. 13.

objectors, it had been allowed to become obsolete long before 1867, or it would have been swept away when their disabilities were being removed.

Provision in the Ballot Act for voting on Saturday.

So complete a change has been effected in the attitude of the legislature towards this question, that in the Ballot Act of 1872 special provision is made to enable voters "of the Jewish persuasion" who object on religious grounds to mark the ballot paper on the Jewish Sabbath to have, "if the poll be taken on Saturday," their votes recorded by the presiding officer in the same way as votes given by persons incapacitated by blindness or other physical cause [1]. It should, however, be noted that the clause is badly drawn, for it ought to, but does not, include cases when the poll is taken on the Jewish Day of Atonement, or the first and last days of the great Jewish festivals on which observant Jews object on religious grounds to take part in the present system of voting by ballot [2].

Offices in corporations and under the Crown.

The rights of holding office in a municipal corporation, and that of holding an office or place of trust under the Crown, can up to a certain point be dealt with together. The Corporation Act of 1661 (13 Car. II, st. 2, c. 1) enacted that no person should be elected or chosen in or to any office or place in any corporation unless he had within

[1] See 35 & 36 Vict., c. 33, 1st schedule, rule 26.

[2] It is sometimes stated that Jews had greater rights than Papists as regards voting in a parish vestry. This statement is made on the authority of a note in the case of Edenborough *v.* the Archbishop of Canterbury, which was before Lord Chancellor Eldon in 1826. The note is: "His Lordship's opinion was *understood to be*; that Jews were entitled to vote in the election of a vicar, but that Roman Catholics were not so entitled: and at the next election, votes were admitted and rejected upon that principle" (2 Russ., p. 111). It is to be observed, however, that this is not a decision, but merely what the reporter understood to be the opinion of the Chancellor, and, if pronounced, it is difficult to see upon what ground it was based other than the custom which had prevailed in the parish in question, namely, St. Stephen's, Coleman Street, in the city of London. If such a custom existed, it does not appear to rest on any legal principle.

one year next before his election taken the sacrament of the Lord's Supper according to the rights of the Church of England, and the election of any person not so qualified, was declared void. The holders of such offices were likewise required to take the oaths of allegiance and supremacy. The rigour of the law was, however, to some extent modified in 1718 by the Act for quieting and establishing corporations (5 Geo. I, c. 6), by the terms of which no person, though not properly qualified under the Corporation Act, should be removed from office or incur any penalty unless proceedings were taken against him within six months after his election to the office, and were then prosecuted without wilful delay. The Test Act of 1673 (25 Car. II, c. 2) proceeded upon similar but not identical lines. By it all persons holding any office or place of trust under the Crown, whether civil or military, were required within three months after their admission to office, to receive the sacrament of the Lord's Supper according to the usage of the Church of England in some public church after divine service on Sunday. They were further required to take the oaths of allegiance and supremacy, and also to make and subscribe a declaration against transubstantiation. Non-compliance with the Act involved a penalty of £500, as well as forfeiture of the office and a number of civil disabilities. The oaths and declaration were obnoxious to Roman Catholics only, but the obligation to take the sacrament effectually excluded from office all Dissenters and Nonconformists without exception.

Motives of the Corporation and Test Acts.

Historically no doubt the motive of these two legislative enactments was different. The Corporation Act was aimed at the extreme Protestant Dissenters, the more moderate at that time being willing to take the sacrament; it was passed immediately after the Restoration of Charles II, and was intended to purge the municipalities which had become the strongholds of the Puritan and Republican party of what was then regarded as their most dangerous element. The Test Act on the other hand was aimed at the Roman Catholics, and was entitled "an Act for preventing dangers which may happen from Popish Recusants." It was passed shortly after the Duke of York, the Heir presumptive to the throne, had publicly declared his adhesion to the Roman Catholic creed and was a consequence of the popular excitement aroused by the prospect of a papist becoming king, and thereby supreme head of the Church. By insisting on the taking of the sacrament, it included in its penalties Protestant Nonconformists, who since the Act of Uniformity had become still further estranged from the Established Church. Thus as a result all Dissenters were placed under political disabilities.

Repeal of the Corporation and Test Acts.

In both cases some relief was given to Dissenters by the Indemnity Acts which were passed annually after the accession of George II, the working of which has been already referred to in the preceding chapter[1], but the law itself was not altered until the year 1828. In the meanwhile many advocates of reform had attempted to procure the repeal or amendment of the Corporation and Test Acts. At length, in the year mentioned, Lord John Russell succeeded in passing through both Houses of Parliament a measure effecting that purpose. The Act (9 Geo. IV, c. 17) in substance substituted for the taking of the sacrament a solemn Declaration "to refrain from using any power conferred by an office to the injury or detriment of the Protestant Church as by law established, or so as to disturb the Church or its Bishops and clergy in the possession of any rights or privileges to which they were by law entitled."

Declaration not to injure the Established Church substituted for the Sacramental Test.

Lord John Russell's motion had originally been for the repeal of so much of the Corporation Act and the Test Act (the Annual Indemnity Act being afterwards included) as required as a qualification for certain offices and employments the taking of the sacrament of the Lord's Supper according to the rites of the Church of England, or imposed

[1] For the precise operation of the Indemnity Acts see The King *v.* Parry (1811), 14 East 549, and in the matter of Steavenson (1823), 2 B. & C. 34.

any penalty for omission so to do, and was intended to give relief to all except Roman Catholics, who being unwilling to sign the declaration against transubstantiation would still be disabled by the Test Act. But it was intended to give them relief by a separate measure, which was in fact brought in and carried the following year, and in their case, it was argued, the disability had been originally imposed, not upon religious opinions, but upon political doctrines. Mr. Secretary Peel, who represented the Tory government in the House of Commons, did not at first support the Bill, which on account of the Annual Indemnity Act he regarded as unnecessary. In his view the Dissenters had no real grievance, for the Annual Indemnity Act enabled them to hold the offices from which they were excluded in principle, but not in fact. Nor did the Dissenters as a body look upon the existence of the excluding Act in the statute-book as an insult to themselves. But after the subject had been debated at length, and it was shown that owing to the technicalities of the Indemnity Act Dissenters might suffer more than a purely sentimental wrong, the Home Secretary gave his support to the measure, but insisted on the necessity of inserting a clause to give protection to the Established Church; which up to that time had been protected by the right which either House of Parliament possessed of refusing its sanction to the Annual Indemnity Act, if at any time the Church was thought to be in danger. The new protection proposed to be given was to take the form of a Declaration to be made and signed by all persons elected or admitted to the offices and employments now thrown open. The Declaration as framed by Mr. Peel was taken from a bill for Catholic emancipation, formerly brought forward by Mr. Grattan, and read as follows: "I, A. B., do solemnly declare, that I will never exert any power nor any influence which I may possess by virtue of my office, to injure or subvert the Protestant Church by law established in these realms, or to disturb it in the possession of those rights and privileges to which it is by law entitled." The Declaration was in reality no real protection to the Church because it did nothing to prevent the passage of an Act of Parliament disestablishing the Church, and if such an Act was passed those who subscribed the Declaration would be immediately free from any obligation it imposed. At the same time the Declaration was in this, its original form, harmless, and was acquiesced in by Lord John Russell, and became a part of the Bill as sent up to the House of Lords.

The Lords add the words 'On the true faith of a Christian' to the new Declaration.

In the Upper House the Declaration was not considered sufficiently stringent. The Duke of Wellington proposed the insertion of the words, "Sincerely in the presence of Almighty God," and the Bishop of Llandaff, that the words "on the true faith of a Christian" should be added at its commencement, and these amendments were carried without a division. The effect of this last addition upon Jews was fully recognized in the House, for Lord Holland, who had entered a protest against it, at a later stage, moved as an amendment that Jews should be permitted to omit the words, "on the true faith of a Christian"; but this was negatived "pro forma."

When the Bill was sent back to the Lower House, the Lords' amendments were all accepted, and so became law, but some discussion took place upon the amendments, and after the Bill had been read a third time, Mr. Brougham made a spirited protest against the changes effected by the Peers, explaining that he had not expressed his disapprobation before for fear of endangering a measure which in spite of its imperfections was still a step in the advancement of toleration and religious liberty[1].

Effect of the new Declaration on the political status of the Jews.

Let us now consider what was the real effect of the new statute upon the status of the Jews. The Declaration as finally settled read as follows: "I, A. B., do solemnly and

[1] See Hansard, *Parl. Deb.*, 2nd series, vol. 18, pp. 676 seq., 816-33, 1180-1208, 1329 seq., 1450-1520, 1571-1610; vol. 19, pp. 39-49, 109-37, 156-86, and 289-300.

sincerely in the presence of God profess, testify, and declare, upon the true faith of a Christian, That I will never exercise any power, authority, or influence which I may possess by virtue of the office of   to injure or weaken the Protestant Church as it is by law established in England, or to disturb the said Church or the Bishops and Clergy of the said Church in the possession of any rights or privileges to which such Church or the said Bishops and Clergy are or may be by law entitled."

This Declaration was required to be made by every person elected to any municipal office "*within one calendar month next before or upon his admission*" to any such office. It had also to be subscribed by every person admitted into any office, employment or place of trust under the Crown, but in such case it might be done "*within six calendar months after* his admission to such Office, Employment or Place of Trust." Moreover, naval and military officers below the rank of Rear-Admiral and Major-General, and persons engaged in the Customs, Revenue, or Post Office, were expressly exempted from the necessity of making the Declaration. Omission to make the Declaration rendered the election or appointment of all persons required to make it wholly void. It is obvious that a conscientious Jew would not subscribe the Declaration; indeed the status of the Jews was rendered more unfavourable by the new Act. When in future the Annual Indemnity Act was passed[1], words were added extending the time for making the Declaration in the same way as the time for taking the sacrament had been previously extended. But though the Indemnity Act might assist a Jew to hold an office under the Crown, it in no way enabled him to be elected to any post in a municipal corporation, because in that case the Declaration had to be subscribed at latest upon admission to the office[2].

[1] These Acts were still annually passed until the Promissory Oaths Act of 1868 (31 & 32 Vict., c. 72) rendered them unnecessary. The last Indemnity Act is 30 & 31 Vict., c. 88.

[2] See Blunt's *History of the Jews*, p. 113 (note).

In the following year the Roman Catholic Relief Act, 1829 (10 Geo. IV, c. 7), removed most of the political disabilities imposed upon Roman Catholics, to abolish which Lord John Russell's measure had done nothing. Quakers, Moravians, and Separatists also objected to the new Declaration, made, as it was expressed to be, in the presence of God and on the true faith of a Christian; for these expressions made the Declaration seem to partake of the nature of an oath. For their benefit the Acts for the relief of Quakers, Moravians, and Separatists elected to municipal offices (1 & 2 Vict., c. 5, and ibid., c. 15) were passed in 1837. These Acts substituted in the case of persons holding these beliefs a new Declaration which omitted the obnoxious phrases; but it was not for some time that a similar measure of relief was granted to the Jews.

Relief given to Roman Catholics and Quakers in 1829 and 1837 respectively.

In 1835 a Jew, Mr. David Salomons, was elected Sheriff of London, which is not only a city or municipality but also a county of itself. As sheriff of a city or corporation it would have been necessary for him to make the Declaration imposed by the new Act (9 Geo. IV, c. 17) before or upon admission to the office, but a sheriff of a county holding no municipal office, and therefore able to avail himself of the provisions of the Indemnity Act, was in practice under no such obligation. The new Sheriff as a Jew was unwilling to make the Declaration, and to solve the difficulty an Act of Parliament (5 & 6 Will. IV, c. 28) entitled "An Act for removing doubts as to the Declaration to be made and oaths to be taken by persons appointed to the office of Sheriff of any City or Town being a County of itself," was passed. The Act declared that no one elected to the office of sheriff of any city or town being a county of itself should by reason thereof be liable to make or subscribe the Declaration. Parliament was thus willing to remove the hardship of the particular case which had actually arisen, but was not yet prepared to grant a general measure of relief to Jews desirous of filling offices in corporations. Lord Campbell, who, as Attorney General, had been responsible

Declaration to be taken by Sheriffs Act of 1835.

for the Act, declared in the House of Lords ten years afterwards that he had desired to introduce a more comprehensive measure, but that he felt certain that if he had extended the Bill a single line further it would have been rejected[1].

Mr. Salomons refused admission to the office of Alderman.

This small concession was wholly inadequate to satisfy the legitimate aspirations of the Jews in general, or of Mr. Salomons in particular; for it was the latter's fortune to play the foremost part in fighting the battle of religious equality, both for himself and his co-religionists. In December, 1835, being already Sheriff, Mr. Salomons was elected Alderman for the ward of Aldgate, in the City of London, and presented himself to the Court of Aldermen for admission to the office. It was demanded of him whether he had signed the Declaration required by the Act of 1829 within the space of one month, to which he answered that he had not. Whereupon it was demanded whether he would then make and subscribe the said Declaration; to which he declined to say whether he would or not, but required the Court to admit him as Alderman. This the Court refused to do, and declared his election null and void. A precept for a new election was issued, and another candidate elected to fill the vacancy. Against this newly-elected Alderman proceedings in the nature of "Quo warranto" were taken. These proceedings were successful in the Court of King's Bench, the court of first instance for such matters, which held that the Aldermen were wrong in refusing to admit Mr. Salomons to the office to which he had been elected.

[1] Hansard's *Parl. Deb.*, 3rd series, vol. 78, p. 526; and Campbell's *Lives of the Chancellors*, VIII, p. 155. Lord Campbell's reluctance was justified by the state of feeling in the House. Indeed two years later when the Bill for relief of Quakers, Moravians, and Separatists, elected to municipal offices was sent into committee, Mr. Grote moved that it be an instruction to the committee to extend the relief to persons of all religious denominations, express mention being made of the Jews; the motion was rejected by 172 to 156 votes (Hansard, *Parl. Deb.*, 3rd series, vol. 39, pp. 508–20).

A writ of error was, however, brought and the judgment of the Court of King's Bench was set aside by the Court of Exchequer Chamber. The Court held that the words "upon admission" did not mean "after," but "upon the occasion of" or "at the time of admission," and accordingly that Mr. Salomons who had neither made the Declaration nor expressed his willingness to make it was not entitled to be admitted, and that the election of his successor was regular and legal[1].

The Jewish Disabilities Removal Act of 1845.

Mr. Salomons was not yet beaten; in 1844 he was again elected Alderman, this time for Portsoken Ward, and in the following year, mainly in consequence of his exertions, Lord Chancellor Lyndhurst introduced, and carried without opposition in the House of Lords, the Jewish Disabilities Removal Act of 1845. In the House of Commons its conduct was entrusted to Sir Robert Peel, and though not allowed to pass unopposed, it was carried by a substantial majority[2]. The Act permitted every person of the Jewish religion upon admission to any municipal office to substitute for the former the following new Declaration: "I, A. B., being a person professing the Jewish Religion, having conscientious scruples against subscribing the Declaration contained in an Act passed in the ninth year of the reign of King George the Fourth, intituled an Act for repealing so much of several Acts as imposes the necessity of receiving the Sacrament of the Lord's Supper as a qualification for certain offices and employments, do solemnly, sincerely, and truly declare, That I will not exercise any power or authority or influence which I may possess by virtue of

[1] See the Queen *v.* Humphery (1838), 3 N. & P. 681 and (1839), 10 A. & E. 335.

[2] 8 & 9 Vict., c. 52. See Hansard, *Parl. Deb.*, 3rd series, vol. 78, pp. 515 seq., and vol. 82, pp. 622 seq. A similar measure had been proposed by Mr. Divett (also at the instigation of Mr. Salomons in 1841) and, though it passed the House of Commons, it had been thrown out by the Lords by 98 to 64 on the third reading, having been read a second time by a majority of 1. See Hansard, *Parl. Deb.*, 3rd series, vol. 56, p. 504; ibid., vol. 57, p. 84; and ibid., vol. 58, pp. 1048 and 1449.

the office of to injure or weaken the Protestant Church as it is by law established in England, nor to disturb the said Church or the Bishops and Clergy of the said Church in the possession of any rights or privileges to which such Church or the said Bishops and Clergy may be by law entitled."

Mr. Salomons was again elected an Alderman in the year 1847, and had the satisfaction of being admitted upon making the new Declaration.

The Oaths Act and the Jewish Relief Act of 1858.

The Oaths Act of 1858 (21 & 22 Vict., c. 48) extended the benefit of the Jewish Disabilities Removal Act of 1845, granted to persons professing the Jewish religion, to all other cases in which the Declaration imposed by the Act of George IV was required to be taken, and the Jewish Relief Act of the same year (21 & 22 Vict., c. 49) enabled Jews to omit the words "upon the true faith of a Christian" when taking the newly-framed Oath of Allegiance, Supremacy, and Abjuration; so that all offices under the Crown other than those expressly excepted, as well as municipal offices, were thenceforth thrown open to the Jews. The Act also contained a proviso that any right of presentation to an ecclesiastical benefice which might be attached to any office held by a person professing the Jewish religion should be exercised by the Archbishop of Canterbury for the time being.

Subsequent legislation.

Finally, in the year 1866, the obligation to make these Declarations which had by the various statutes been imposed upon all who had been elected to any office in a corporation or appointed to any place of trust or office under the Crown, was removed by the Qualification for Offices Abolition Act of that year[1], and the statutes themselves having thus been rendered nugatory were formally repealed by the Promissory Oaths Act of 1871[2]. In consequence at the present time the only obligation incumbent

[1] 29 & 30 Vict., c. 22; see also the Office and Oath Act, 1867 (30 & 31 Vict., c. 75, s. 5).

[2] 34 & 35 Vict., c. 48.

upon persons about to enter upon any of these offices is the taking of the simplified form of the Oath of Allegiance, which has already been set out above, and the official oath, or if the office be a judicial one, the judicial oath as prescribed by the Promissory Oaths Act of 1868[1]. Neither of these oaths contains anything objectionable to Jews; the terms of the official oath are, "I do swear that I will well and truly serve His Majesty, King Edward, in the office of . So help me God." And the form of the judicial oath is, "I do swear that I will well and truly serve our Sovereign Lord, King Edward, in the office of , and I will do right to all manner of people after the laws and usages of this realm, without fear or favour, affection or ill will. So help me God."

Moreover, persons permitted by law to make a solemn affirmation or declaration instead of taking the oath may do so by substituting the words "solemnly, sincerely, and truly declare and affirm" for the word "swear," and omitting the words, "So help me God."

Taking the insignia of office to a place of religious worship.

Thus since the year 1845 a Jew has been able to be elected a member of a municipal corporation, and since 1858 to hold an office or place of trust under the Crown. But there still existed a minor disability as regards municipal officers, which was not removed for another quarter of a century. The Act which repealed the Occasional Conformity Act—a measure passed during the ascendancy of the High Church party in the latter part of Queen Anne's reign with the avowed purpose of excluding Protestant Dissenters from municipal and other offices—and the Schism Act of 1713—a still more recent and intolerant piece of legislation—in return for the relief thus afforded, created a new disability, which without giving any protection to the Established Church was calculated to foster feelings of irritation and grievance in the hearts of those against whom it was aimed. The Act

[1] 31 & 32 Vict., c. 72, and see *supra*, p. 228 (note).

contained a clause providing that if any mayor, bailiff, or other magistrate should knowingly or wilfully resort to or be present at any public meeting for religious worship, other than of the Church of England as by law established, in the gown or other peculiar habit, or attended with the insignia of his office, he should on conviction be disabled from holding any such office, and adjudged incapable of bearing any public office or employment whatsoever[1]. This enactment was directed against all Nonconformists, whether Protestants, Roman Catholics, or Jews; and such store was placed upon its efficacy that when the disabilities of Roman Catholics were finally removed in 1829, instead of being repealed it was actually re-enacted and extended, for whereas the Act of George the First applied only to England and Wales, the prohibition was extended to all parts of the United Kingdom, and a penalty of £100 was now imposed for every breach of the prohibition in addition to the forfeiture of office as provided by the earlier Act[2]. It was not till 1867 that the Office and Oath Act of that year repealed these futile and offensive enactments[3].

Device of fining Dissenters for refusing to serve the office of sheriff.

An ingenious device, which for some years was resorted to for the purpose of persecuting Protestant Dissenters in the City of London, was never employed against the Jews on account of their exclusion from the freedom of the City, to which reference has been made in the preceding chapter. By the Corporation Act of 1661 none could fill a corporate office who had not within one year next before

[1] 5 Geo. I, c. 4; the Occasional Conformity Act is 10 Anne, c. 6 (Ruff., c. 2), and the Schism Act 13 Anne, c. 7 (12 Anne, st. 2, c. 7, Ruff.).

[2] See s. 25 of the Roman Catholic Relief Act, 1829 (10 Geo. IV, c. 7).

[3] 30 & 31 Vict., c. 75, s. 4; see also 34 & 35 Vict., c. 116. The reason for their original institution is given by Sir Wm. Blackstone in a note to p. 54 of his *Commentaries*, vol. IV, as follows: "Sir Humphry Edwin, a lord mayor of London, had the imprudence soon after the Toleration Act to go to a Presbyterian meeting-house in his formalities; which is alluded to by Dean Swift in his *Tale of a Tub* under the allegory of Jack getting on a great horse and eating custard."

his election taken the sacrament of the Lord's Supper according to the rites of the Church of England. In the year 1748 the Corporation of London made a by-law imposing a fine of £400 upon every person who being nominated by the Lord Mayor for the office of Sheriff declined to be a candidate, and of £600 upon every one who being elected by the Common Hall refused to serve the office. The fines were to be used for defraying the cost of the new Mansion House. Many Dissenters were nominated and elected to the office of Sheriff, although disabled from filling it by the Corporation Act, and in all cases the fines were exacted, more than £15,000 being obtained in this way. At length a Nonconformist named Allen Evans determined to test the legality of these proceedings. In the year 1754, as many of his co-religionists had been before, he was elected Sheriff. Not having taken the sacrament within twelve months he was ineligible to serve the office, and he refused to pay the fine; whereupon an action was brought against him by the City Chamberlain in the Sheriff's Court, and he was in April, 1757, adjudged to pay the sum of £600, the amount of the fine, in addition to a sum of £174 10*s.* 7*d.* for damages and costs. Mr. Evans then appealed to the Court of Hustings, but the appeal was dismissed and the original judgment affirmed, Mr. Evans being condemned to pay a further sum of £95 3*s.* 0*d.* as the costs of the appeal. Mr. Evans then brought the case before the court of the commissioners delegates, called the Court of St. Martin's, which on this occasion consisted of five judges of the superior courts; the case was argued before them no less than three times, and at length, in 1762, they unanimously reversed the decision of the lower courts. The City Corporation then brought a writ of error in the House of Lords, which also decided in favour of Mr. Evans, upon the ground that the Toleration Act enabled persons who came within its terms to abstain from taking part in the rites of the Church of England without committing any breach of law, and consequently the plea of ineligibility for office on account of not having taken the sacrament was a good and lawful plea in answer to a claim for a penalty for refusing to serve. If the by-law was to have the effect, which the City contended it had, then it was a worse instrument of persecution than the Jesuits had ever used; for the law made Dissenters ineligible for office, and the by-law punished them for not serving. As Lord Mansfield said in his speech in moving the judgment in the House of Lords: "If it could be supposed the city have a power of making such a by-law, it would entirely subvert the Toleration Act, the design of which was to exempt the Dissenters from all penalties; for by such a by-law they have it in their power to make every Dissenter pay a fine of £600, or any sum they please, for it amounts to that. The professed design of making this by-law was to get fit and able persons to serve the office: and the plaintiff sets forth in his declaration that if the Dissenters are excluded, they shall want fit and able persons to serve the office. But were I to deliver my own suspicion, it would be, that they did not so much wish for their services, as for their fines. Dissenters have been appointed to this office, one who was blind, another who was bedridden; not, I suppose, on account of their being fit and able to serve the office. No; they were disabled both by nature and by law . . . . . In the cause before your lordships the defendant was by law incapable at the time of his pretended election: and it is my firm persuasion that he was chosen because he was incapable . . . . . They chose him that he might fall under the penalty of their by-law [1]."

[1] Sir Thomas Harrison (Chamberlain of London) *v.* Evans, 1767, 3 Bro. P. C., p. 465; *Lords' Journals*, vol. 31, pp. 457, 458–9, 461, 470, 475; Cobbett, *Parl. Hist.*, vol. 16, pp. 313–27; and 2 Burn., *Eccl. Law*, pp. 207–20. Similar by-laws had been made and acted upon to the prejudice of Dissenters in other parts of the country. Indeed as early as 1690, in the case of the Mayor of Guildford *v.* Clarke, the court decided that the defendant being a Protestant Dissenter was not liable to pay a fine of £20 imposed by a local by-law for refusing to serve the ancient office of bailiff

As has been already indicated the Jews were exempt from this particular form of persecution, not on account of any goodwill felt towards them by their Christian neighbours, but because at that time it was impossible to nominate or elect Jews to the offices in question, because the freedom of the City, and consequently the burdens as well as the privileges which it entailed, was strictly denied them. The result of one measure of intolerance was thus the means of sheltering its victims from the consequences of other intolerant enactments.

Jews not liable to these fines.

It has already been stated that in the Jewish Relief Act of 1858, which threw open to Jews the right of holding office under the Crown by enabling them to omit the final words of the qualifying oath, certain high offices, including those of Lord Chancellor and Lord Lieutenant of Ireland, were expressly excepted. The exception was based upon a similar reservation as regards Roman Catholics contained in the twelfth section of the Catholic Relief Act of 1829 (10 Geo. IV, c. 7), and is in the following words: "Nothing herein contained shall extend or be construed to extend to enable any person or persons professing the Jewish religion to hold or exercise the office of Guardians and Justices of the United Kingdom or of Regent of the United Kingdom under whatever name, style or title such office may be constituted, or of Lord High Chancellor, Lord Keeper or Lord Commissioner of the Great Seal of Great Britain or Ireland or the office of Lord Lieutenant or Deputy or other chief governor or governors of Ireland or Her Majesty's High Commissioner to the General Assembly of the Church of Scotland[1]." But after the Office and Oath Act, 1867 (30 & 31 Vict., c. 75) had opened the Chancellorship of Ireland

S. 3 of the Jewish Relief Act of 1858, disabling Jews from holding certain high offices, repealed in 1871.

in that town (2 Vent. 247), but the effect of this decision was thought to have been annulled four years later by the case of the King and Queen *v.* Larwood in which the defendant, though he pleaded the Corporation Act and that he was a Protestant Dissenter, was fined (though only five marks) for refusing to serve the office of Sheriff of Norwich to which he had been elected (1 Ld. Raymond 29 and 4 Mod. 269).

[1] 21 & 22 Vict., c. 49, s. 3.

to every subject of the Queen, this section, together with the two preceding ones, was wholly and unreservedly repealed by the Promissory Oaths Act of 1871 (34 & 35 Vict., c. 48, s. 1), so that since that date every office, the throne alone excepted, could legally be filled by a Jew, although the appointment of a Jew might be highly impolitic or improper, as, for instance, to the post of High Commissioner to the General Assembly of the Church of Scotland.

A Jew may now be Lord Lieutenant of Ireland or Lord Chancellor.

There is, however, a widespread belief that a Jew cannot legally hold the offices of Lord Lieutenant of Ireland and Lord Chancellor. This was, no doubt, the case until the year 1871, but since that time it has ceased to be so, and the view, though still very generally accepted, rests upon no sure foundation. It is argued that Roman Catholics cannot hold these offices; therefore Jews, to whom the legislature has shown no greater favour than to Roman Catholics, cannot hold them either. But section 12 of the Catholic Relief Act, 1829, has never been expressly repealed, and still remains on the statute-book, and yet nevertheless there is high authority for saying that Roman Catholics are at the present time eligible for these offices, for the statutes imposing the qualifying oaths and declarations which Roman Catholics were unable to take and by virtue of which they were formerly excluded have been abrogated without any reservation, and there is no disability directly imposed upon Roman Catholics by any Act of Parliament, nor should such disability be implied by words in Acts of Parliament which, while excepting certain offices from the relief granted in other cases, do not expressly create a new disability[1]. This at any rate is the effect of the answer given by the late Lord Coleridge, when questioned as Attorney-General in the House of Com-

[1] The sections in question are 10 Geo. IV, c. 7, s. 12, and 30 & 31 Vict., c. 62; the later Promissory Oaths Act of 1871 (34 & 35 Vict., c. 48) absolutely abolished the statutes imposing the obnoxious oaths and therefore by implication removed the disability which had been kept alive by the former Acts.

mons in 1872[1]. As to the status of Roman Catholics in this matter, there does seem to be some doubt, owing to the sections concerning them being unrepealed, but in the case of Jews there is hardly any room for doubt, and both Mr. Gladstone and Mr. Asquith in the course of the debate on the former's bill to remove the disabilities of Roman Catholics to hold the offices of Lord Chancellor of Great Britain and Lord Lieutenant of Ireland, in 1891, asserted without contradiction or correction that there was no obstacle to the holding of the Lord Chancellorship by any one other than a Roman Catholic, though he was a Jew, Mahomedan, Buddhist, or Hindoo[2]. This Bill was not accorded a second reading, so that the doubt in case of Roman Catholics has not been removed; but as to Jews it may be stated that it is the accepted view of constitutional lawyers that since 1871 they labour under no such disability[3].

Ecclesiastical patronage attached to an office held by a Jew.

It should be added that the last section of the Jewish Relief Act of 1858 is still in force, and consequently that a Jew holding office under the Crown is disabled from exercising any ecclesiastical patronage which would other-

[1] Hansard, *Parl. Deb.*, 3rd series, vol. 211, pp. 280 seq. When Lord Chief Justice he reaffirmed this view in his well-known charge to the jury in the case of the Queen *v.* Ramsay and Foote, saying: "But now, so far as I know the law, a Jew might be Lord Chancellor" (1883). 15 Cox C. C., p. 235.

[2] Hansard, *Parl. Deb.*, 3rd series, vol. 349, pp. 101, 1733–99; the passages referred to are at pp. 1749 and 1777.

[3] It would indeed be difficult to see on what foundation such a disability could now be based. Not on statute, for the section of the statute has been repealed, nor on common law on the ground that the Chancellor is the keeper of the King's conscience, and that as the King must by the Bill of Rights be a Protestant and by the Act of Settlement join in communion with the Church of England, the Lord Chancellor as keeper of his conscience must likewise be a Protestant and a member of the National Church, for if this reasoning were sound not only would Protestant Dissenters be under a similar disability, but it would have been wholly unnecessary to expressly except this particular office in the Acts for the relief of Roman Catholics and Jews, if such persons were already incapacitated by the common law.

wise devolve upon him. The words of the section are as follows:—

"Where any right of presentation to any ecclesiastical benefice shall belong to any office in the gift or appointment of Her Majesty, and such office shall be held by a person professing the Jewish religion, the right of presentation shall devolve upon and be exercised by the Archbishop of Canterbury for the time being; and it shall not be lawful for any person professing the Jewish religion, directly or indirectly, to advise Her Majesty, or any person or persons holding or exercising the office of Guardians of the United Kingdom, or of Regent of the United Kingdom, under whatever name, style or title such office may be constituted, or the Lord Lieutenant of Ireland, touching or concerning the appointment to or disposal of any office or preferment in the Church of England or in the Church of Scotland; and if such person shall offend in the premises, he shall, being thereof convicted by due course of law, be deemed guilty of a high misdemeanour, and disabled for ever from holding any office, civil or military, under the Crown[1]."

The same disability is imposed upon Roman Catholics by the seventeenth and eighteenth sections of the Catholic Relief Act, 1829, but all other Dissenters (even though atheists or heathens) are entitled to exercise the ecclesiastical patronage belonging to any office which they may hold.

[1] 21 & 22 Vict., c. 49, s. 4.

X.

THE POLITICAL RIGHTS OF ENGLISH JEWS (*continued*).

Their Admission to Parliament.

The history of the admission of the Jews to Parliament is so well known and has received so much attention from the writers on constitutional history and constitutional law that it will be sufficient to indicate here its main outlines. Immediately after the passage of the Catholic Relief Act, 1829, efforts were made in Parliament for the complete emancipation of the Jews from all civil and political disabilities. The leader of the movement was Mr. Robert Grant, who, on April 5, 1830, introduced into the House of Commons a Bill "to repeal the civil disabilities affecting British born subjects professing the Jewish religion." Leave to bring in the Bill was granted by a majority of 18, and when it came up for second reading it was thrown out by a majority of 63[1]. This was before the Reform Act of 1832. Mr. Grant reintroduced his measure in the reformed House of Commons and met with more success. Several petitions in favour of Jewish emancipation had been presented to the Houses of Parliament[2], and on April 17, 1833, Mr. Grant moved that the House of Commons should resolve itself into a committee of the whole House to consider the disabilities affecting Jewish subjects; despite a protest from Sir Robert Inglis the motion was adopted without a division. In committee Mr. Grant moved "that it is

Mr. Robert Grant's Jews' Civil Disabilities Bill, 1830-36.

[1] See Hansard, *Parl. Deb.*, 2nd series, vol. 23, pp. 1287–1336, and ibid., vol. 24, pp. 784–814; the debates are interesting, as almost all the arguments for and against the Jews were used by the supporters or opponents of the Bill.

[2] Hansard, *Parl. Deb.*, 3rd series, vol. 15, pp. 310, 559; ibid., vol. 16, pp. 10, 725, 775, 973.

expedient to remove all civil disabilities at present existing affecting His Majesty's subjects of the Jewish religion, with the like exceptions as are provided with reference to His Majesty's subjects professing the Roman Catholic religion." When after debate the question was put, the "Ayes" resounded through the House, but the "Noes" were few. The minority did not challenge a division, and the resolution was agreed to[1]. Thus the Jews' Civil Disabilities Bill was again introduced; the second reading was carried by 159 votes to 52[2], and the third reading by 189 to 52[3], but the House of Lords refused the Bill a second reading by 104 votes to 54[4]. Nothing daunted, on April 24 of the following year Mr. Grant again brought forward and carried, by 53 votes to 9, a motion to go into committee to consider the subject[5], and the revived Bill was accorded a second reading in the Lower House by 123 votes to 32, and also a third reading after a motion for adjournment had been defeated by 50 votes to 14[6]. The dwindling numbers of the advocates of the Bill in the House of Commons and the lukewarm support which it received from the Government in power encouraged the House of Lords to again reject it, and by an increased majority, only 38 voting for and 130 against the second reading[7]. Late in the session of 1836 the Bill was again revived under the auspices of Mr. Spring Rice, the Chancellor of the Exchequer; but the second reading was not moved until August 3, when the House was so thin that it was in imminent danger of being counted out. The second reading was agreed to by 39 votes to 17. Having passed through the remaining stages, the Bill was sent up to the Lords and was read a first

[1] Hansard, *Parl. Deb.*, 3rd series, vol. 17, pp. 205–44.
[2] Ibid., vol. 18, pp. 47–59.
[3] Ibid., vol. 19, pp. 1075–82. For the committee stage see vol. 18, p. 1251.
[4] Ibid., vol. 20, pp. 221–55.
[5] Ibid., vol. 22, p. 1372.
[6] For the second reading see Hansard, vol. 23, p. 1158, and ibid., p. 1349, for the committee stage, and vol. 24, p. 382, for the third reading.
[7] Ibid., vol. 24, pp. 720–31.

time on August 15, but on account both of the lateness of the session and the poor support it was likely to receive, the second reading was never moved, and the prorogation took place on the 20th of that month[1].

1836-47. Minor measures of relief from political disabilities.

A general and comprehensive measure was not again introduced, for the advocates of equal rights for the Jews recognized that their cause had not sufficient popular support to overcome the resistance of prejudiced and persistent opponents who could usually count upon a majority of votes in the Upper House. They therefore wisely confined their efforts to obtain gradually and by small instalments the end they had in view—a method so frequently adopted in the making of the English constitution and so peculiarly dear to the English people. The result was the different enactments, already enumerated, altering the oath and other methods of qualification, so as to open municipal and other offices to members of the Jewish faith, but none of these statutes had any bearing upon a Jew's right to sit in Parliament. At length the question became one of practical politics by the return of Baron Lionel de Rothschild as one of the Members for the City of London at the General Election of 1847.

1847. Baron de Rothschild elected to represent the city of London in Parliament.

At that time before a member could take his seat or vote, he was required to take three several oaths: the oath of allegiance, the oath of supremacy, and the oath of abjuration. The tenour of these oaths has been already explained, and, as has been seen, though a Jew might conscientiously take the first two, he could not with any sense of decency or propriety pronounce the words "upon the true faith of a Christian," which concluded the oath of abjuration. Moreover, it was customary to administer all these oaths upon the New Testament, which by itself would have debarred a conscientious Jew from taking any of them. This form of administration was not, however, ordained by any statute then in force and might upon occasion be waived or altered by resolu-

[1] Hansard, vol. 35, pp. 865–75, 1209, 1216, 1318.

tion of the House in favour of any particular member or class of members, though such an indulgence was a matter of favour and not of right[1]. The House, however, had no power to waive the oaths themselves or to alter their form, for the statute (1 Geo. I, st. 2, c. 13, ss. 16, 17) expressly enacted that no one should vote in the House of Commons or sit there during any debate until he had taken the oath of abjuration, and imposed a penalty of £500 as well as several important disabilities upon any one who should presume to vote without having taken the said oath[2]. These provisions being laid down by statute could not be removed or dispensed with by a single branch of the legislature, but only by an overriding or repealing Act of Parliament.

1847–48. Lord John Russell's Jewish Disabilities Bill.

Accordingly in December, 1847, the Prime Minister, Lord John Russell, who happened to be one of Baron de Rothschild's colleagues in the representation of the City of London, took precisely the same course as Mr. Grant had taken in 1833, and the House of Commons, having resolved itself into committee, moved a resolution in the same terms as that adopted fourteen years earlier. The resolution was agreed to by 257 votes to 186, the increased numbers in the division showing the increased interest aroused[3]. The Jewish Disabilities Bill, which placed Jews

[1] In 1833, Mr. Joseph Pease, the Quaker member for South Durham, had been allowed to make a solemn affirmation instead of taking the oath; this was by virtue of the Statute 22 Geo. II, c. 46, s. 36, and earlier statutes enabling Quakers to substitute an affirmation for an oath in all cases where an oath was required, thus including promissory as well as juridical oaths (see Hansard's *Parl. Deb.*, 3rd series, vol. 15, pp. 387, 476, 639. Mr. Pease had even been allowed to omit the words "on the true faith of a Christian," to which he objected as being unnecessary in the same way as if they had been "on the true faith of a gentleman" (see Hansard, vol. 113, p. 508), but then the Acts prescribed the form of the oath, but not that of the affirmation which might be substituted.

[2] But there was no provision here or elsewhere for vacating the seat of a member who omitted to take the oath of abjuration, if he did not attempt to exercise the power of voting. See May's *Parl. Practice*, p. 158.

[3] Hansard, *Parl. Deb.*, 3rd series, vol. 95, pp. 1234–1331, 1356–98.

on the same footing as Roman Catholics, was subsequently brought in and carried through the House of Commons, 277 members voting for and 204 against the second reading, but thrown out in the House of Lords by a majority of 35; 125 lords voting for and 163 against the second reading[1]. In the following session Lord John Russell brought forward another measure with a similar object, but confined its scope to an alteration of the parliamentary oath in favour of Jews. The Bill which was known as the Parliamentary Oaths Bill was successfully steered through the House of Commons, being carried on the second reading by 275 votes to 185, and on the third by 272 to 206, but it was again wrecked in the Lords, who refused it a second reading by 95 to 70[2].

1849. Lord John Russell's Parliamentary Oaths Bill.

After the failure of this measure Baron de Rothschild vacated his seat by applying for and receiving the stewardship of the Chiltern Hundreds. He offered himself for re-election and was returned by a large majority. The Government, however, brought in no Bill to enable him to take his seat, and on July 26, 1850, he came to the table of the House of Commons, and requested to be sworn upon the Old Testament, whereupon the Speaker directed him to withdraw. After a long debate, including an adjournment and three several divisions, this request was conceded. The next day the baron again came up to be sworn; the oaths of allegiance and supremacy were duly administered on the Old Testament, but when the oath of abjuration was tendered the newly elected member refused to repeat after the clerk the words "upon the true faith of a Christian," and upon

1850. Baron de Rothschild having resigned and been re-elected attempts to take his seat.

[1] Hansard, vol. 95, p. 1421; ibid., vol. 96, pp. 220–83, 460–540; ibid., vol. 97, pp. 1213–50; and ibid., vol. 98, pp. 1329–1409. Of the debate in the Lords the Earl of Malmesbury in his *Memoirs* writes: "The Jew Bill was thrown out in the Lords by a majority of 35. Mr. Lionel de Rothschild and his brother Anthony were present. I never saw the House so full. The Rothschilds stood like elder sons of Peers on the steps of the throne, and would not even retire when the division took place" (*Memoirs of an Ex-Minister*, vol. I, p. 230).

[2] Hansard, vol. 102, pp. 1188–1202; ibid., vol. 104, pp. 1395–1449; ibid., vol. 105, pp. 431–66, 670–83, 1373–1434; vol. 106, pp. 871–922.

their being read said, "I omit these words as not binding upon my conscience," and concluded with the words, "So help me God." He was then directed to withdraw. A motion was subsequently carried by 166 votes to 92 "that the Baron Lionel Nathan de Rothschild is not entitled to vote in this House or to sit in this House during any debate, until he should take the Oath of Abjuration in the form appointed by law." It was further formally resolved by 142 votes to 106 to take the form of the oath of abjuration into consideration during the next session with a view to the relief of persons professing the Jewish religion [1].

1851. Lord John Russell's Oath of Abjuration (Jew) Bill.

The following Session, in pursuance of this resolution, the Oath of Abjuration (Jew) Bill was introduced by the Government. It provided that whenever any of her Majesty's subjects professing the Jewish religion shall present himself to take the oath of abjuration the words "upon the true faith of a Christian" shall be omitted from the oath, and passed the House of Commons, though the majority on the second reading was only 25, but was rejected in the Lords by 144 votes to 108 [2].

Mr. Salomons purports to take the Oath of Abjuration without pronouncing its final words.

In the meantime Mr. David Salomons had at a bye-election been returned to the House of Commons as member for the borough of Greenwich, and on July 18, 1851, the day after the rejection of the Government's bill by the Upper House, attended at the table for the purpose of being sworn. Upon the New Testament being tendered to him by the clerk, he requested to be sworn on the Old Testament, which being reported to Mr. Speaker, Mr. Speaker asked him why he desired to be sworn upon the Old Testament; he answered because he considered it

[1] *Com. Jour.*, vol. CV, pp. 584, 590, 612; Hansard, vol. 113, pp. 298–333, 396–453, 486–533, 769–817.

[2] Hansard, vol. 115, pp. 1006–19, 1030; ibid., vol. 116, pp. 367–412; ibid., vol. 117, pp. 1096–1102; and ibid., vol. 118, pp. 142–7, 188, 859–909. "Jew Bill passed second reading House of Commons by 25; 202 to 177. This will encourage the Peers" (Lord Malmesbury's *Memoirs*, vol. I, p. 283).

binding on his conscience; Mr. Speaker then desired the clerk to swear him upon the Old Testament: there being no debate and no division such as had taken place in the case of Baron de Rothschild a year previously. The clerk then handed him the Old Testament, and tendered the oaths. The oaths of allegiance and supremacy having been duly taken, when the oath of abjuration was administered Mr. Salomons read as far as the words "upon the true faith of a Christian," which he omitted, and concluded with the words "So help me God." He then read the following declaration from a paper which he had in his hand, and then pushed over to the clerk at the table: "I have now taken the oaths in the form and with the ceremonies that I declare to be binding on my conscience, in accordance with the statute 1 & 2 Vict., c. 105. I now demand to subscribe to the oath of abjuration and to declare to my property qualification." The omission of the words of the oath being reported to Mr. Speaker, he desired Mr. Salomons to withdraw. "He thereupon retired from the table and sat down upon one of the lower benches; upon which Mr. Speaker informed him that, not having taken the oath of abjuration in the form prescribed by the Act of Parliament and the form in which the House had on a former occasion expressed its opinion that it ought to be taken, he could not be allowed to remain in the House, but must withdraw: and he withdrew accordingly." A short discussion of the subject, which was adjourned to the following Monday, July 21, ensued[1]. On the resumption of the debate on that day Mr. Salomons took his seat in the House. The Speaker rose and desired him to withdraw; but the request fell upon deaf ears, and, amidst a scene of great confusion, the Speaker appealed to the house to support the chair. The Prime Minister, Lord John Russell, then moved: "That Mr. Alderman Salomons do now withdraw." To this Mr. Bernal Osborne moved as an amendment that Mr. Salomons,

Mr. Salomons takes his seat in the House and refuses to withdraw.

[1] Hansard, vol. 118, pp. 979-86; *Com. Jour.*, vol. CVI, p. 372.

having taken the oaths required by law in the manner most binding on his conscience, is entitled to take his seat in the House. The adjournment of the debate was then moved, but was defeated, 65 voting for, and 257 against it; Mr. Salomons himself voting in the minority. After further discussion Mr. Bernal Osborne's amendment was put to the vote, and lost by a majority of 148. After the division Mr. Salomons, who had taken no part in it, as it involved a question personal to himself, re-entered the house and took his seat as before, when the debate on the original motion for his withdrawal was continued. The adjournment was again moved, and during the debate on it Mr. Salomons, being directly challenged as to the course he intended to pursue, rose amidst loud cries of "withdraw," and, having obtained a hearing, explained his position. After apologizing for his presumption in addressing the House, which he would not have done had he not been directly appealed to, he said: "But I beg to assure you, Sir, and the House, that it has been far from my intention to indulge in anything contumacious or presuming towards either. But, having been returned to this House by a large constituency, and believing that I labour under no disability whatever, and that I am in a position to fulfil all the requirements of the law, I thought I should not be doing justice to my own position as an Englishman and a gentleman did I not adopt the course which I thought right and proper of maintaining my right to appear on this floor—without thereby meaning any disrespect to you, Sir. I thought I was bound to take this course in defence of my own rights and privileges, and of the rights and privileges of the constituents who have sent me here. In saying this, Sir, I shall state to you that whatever the decision of this House may be, I shall willingly abide by it, provided that just sufficient force be used to make me feel that I am acting under coercion." In conclusion he besought the House not to come to a final decision without giving him an opportunity of addressing it on what he believed to be the rights and privileges of himself and his constituents. The motion for adjournment was again defeated, and the original motion, "that Mr. Salomons do now withdraw," was put and carried by 231 to 81 votes. "Whereupon Mr. Speaker stated that the Honourable Member for Greenwich had heard the decision of the house, and hoped that the Honourable Member was prepared to obey it.

"Mr. Alderman Salomons continuing to sit in his seat, Mr. Speaker directed the Serjeant-at-Arms to remove him below the bar.

"Whereupon the Serjeant-at-Arms having placed his hand on Mr. Alderman Salomons, he was conducted below the Bar[1]."

Subsequent proceedings in the House of Commons.

The next day the subject was resumed, the Prime Minister moving that Mr. Salomons was not entitled to vote or sit in the House during any debate, until he should have taken the oath of abjuration in the form appointed by law. To this Mr. Bethell moved as an amendment that both Baron de Rothschild and Mr. Salomons, having taken the oaths in the manner in which the House was bound by law to administer them, were entitled to take their seats as members of the house. The amendment was defeated by 118 votes to 71. After a fruitless motion for adjournment a further amendment was proposed "and that this House, having regard to the religious scruples of the Honourable Member for Greenwich, will exercise its undoubted privilege in that behalf, and proceed forthwith to cause such alterations to be made in the form and mode of administering the said oath as shall enable the Honourable Member to take and subscribe the same." After further discussion the debate was adjourned[2].

Meanwhile petitions were presented to the House on behalf of the electors of the borough of Greenwich, praying

[1] *Com. Jour.*, vol. CVI, p. 381; Hansard, *Parl. Deb.*, vol. 118, pp. 1143–1217.

[2] *Com. Jour.*, vol. CVI, pp. 386–7; Hansard, *Parl. Deb.*, vol. 118, pp. 1318–66.

to be heard by counsel at the bar in defence of their right to elect their own representatives, and also on behalf of the inhabitants of London, praying the house to forthwith adopt a resolution admitting Baron de Rothschild to his seat in the house and to hear counsel in support of the petition. These petitions were considered separately, and both were refused by substantial majorities, it being thought that the subject had been so thoroughly discussed that no further light could be thrown upon it. On the resumption of the adjourned debate the amendment pledging the House to alter the oath of abjuration was defeated by a majority of 38, and the original motion declaring Mr. Salomons not entitled to take his seat until he had taken the oath of abjuration carried by a majority of 55[1].

The case of Miller *v.* Salomons.

Such were the proceedings in the House of Commons; at the sitting last mentioned the Speaker had read to the House a letter which he had received from Mr. Salomons, in which the latter stated that actions had been commenced against him for penalties alleged to have been incurred for having sat and voted as a member of the house on the 21st of July. The action was tried in the Court of Exchequer by Baron Martin and a jury, which, under the direction of the learned judge, returned a special verdict embodying the facts already set forth. Upon this verdict a learned argument took place before the full Court of Exchequer on January 26 and 28, 1852. On behalf of Mr. Salomons four grounds were put forward for asserting that the penalties were not enforceable against him: (1) The oath of abjuration laid down by the statute contained the words "our sovereign Lord King George," and therefore it was submitted that since the reigning sovereign did not bear the name of George, the obligation to take the oath no longer existed. (2) That when the law imposes an oath upon any person, it not only permits but requires him to take it

[1] *Com. Jour.*, vol. CVI, pp. 406–7; Hansard, *Parl. Deb.*, vol. 118, pp. 1573–1629.

in such form as is most binding on his conscience. In Mr. Salomons' case this was with the omission of the words "upon the true faith of a Christian," which were not introduced as part of the substance of the oath, imposing a religious or political test, but as part of the form or manner in which the oath was to be taken, and might therefore be regarded as mere words of attestation, like the words "So help me God," which were actually omitted in the last act prescribing the form of the oath of abjuration[1]. (3) That Mr. Salomons was authorized to take the oath in the way he did by the Oaths Act of 1838 (1 & 2 Vict., c. 105). (4) That he was enabled to do this by the provisions of 10 Geo. I, c. 4, which had by implication been kept alive by the annual indemnity acts.

As the judges differed in opinion, judgment was not given until April 19, when the Court entered judgment for the Plaintiff; Baron Martin dissenting. The difference was as to the second ground put forward by the Defendant; the other three points being purely technical and manifestly untenable. Baron Martin held that as the words "upon the true faith of a Christian" were originally inserted not as a test of Christianity, but for the purpose of making the oath more effectually binding upon the consciences of Roman Catholics, it would be absurd to insist upon a Jew pronouncing them; for it was only when these words were omitted that the oath was really obligatory and binding upon him, and the advantage contemplated by the statute secured. Had it been intended that the words should be of the substance and essence of the oath, and that no one except a Christian should be permitted to take it, it was competent for the legislature so to enact, but the statutes did not manifest any such intention.

The Chief Baron (Pollock) and the other two judges, on the other hand, held that the words in question were an essential part of the oath; for a judicial and a promissory oath are different in their nature. A judicial oath may

[1] 6 Geo. III, c. 53.

be modified so as to be made binding on the taker; because such an oath is governed by the law of nations, for justice is of all countries and climes; but an oath of office or qualification is governed by the municipal laws of the State which requires it to be taken, and by those laws alone. Where the very form of the oath is prescribed by the legislature, then the directions of the legislature must be literally followed, and the oath must, and can only lawfully be taken in the prescribed form, until that form be altered by the authority which appointed it. If the prescribed form is such as to exclude the adherents of any particular religious sect, it may be unjust, but it is not absurd. In this case the express words of the oath did exclude all but Christians, and no intention to include any who were not Christians could be collected either from the Act itself or the history of the times when it was passed.

The judgment affirmed on appeal.

Judgment was accordingly entered against Mr. Salomons, who thereupon appealed to the Exchequer Chamber. In May, 1853, that Court unanimously affirmed the decision of the Court below. After pronouncing the judgment of the Court, Lord Campbell, the Chief Justice, added, "We have only to declare what the law is, not what it ought to be. I regret that the Act ever passed so as to exclude the Jews, and my wish is that it should be repealed. But it is our duty to put the best construction we can on the Act of Parliament; and, in so doing, we entertain no doubt whatever that, according to the existing law, Jews are excluded from sitting in either House of Parliament [1]."

[1] 8 Exch. p. 787. Baron Alderson had concluded his judgment in the Court below in a similar way, saying: "I do most sincerely regret, as a mere expounder of the law, to come to this conclusion—for I do not believe that the case of the Jews was at all thought of by the legislature when they framed these provisions. I think that it would be more worthy of this country to exclude the Jews from these privileges (if they are to be excluded at all, as to which I say nothing) by some direct enactment, and not merely by the casual operation of a clause intended apparently in its object and origin to apply to a very different class of the subjects of England" (7 Exch. p. 542).

A writ of error was lodged in the House of Lords, but was not proceeded with. Thus the legal validity of the proceedings which had taken place in the House of Commons was established; and Mr. Salomons was obliged to pay the fine of £500, and to retire from the House[1].

Lord John Russell's Jewish Disabilities Bill of 1853.

There is little doubt that the majority of the members of the House of Commons, though that majority was by no means overwhelming, was willing to admit Jews to the full privileges of membership, and recognized that it was only by a legal technicality that Jews were excluded. Still, while the law remained unchanged the House was resolved to administer it according to the letter. The efforts to obtain an alteration of the law were therefore renewed. In February, 1853, Lord John Russell, who was then Secretary of State for Foreign Affairs in Lord Aberdeen's coalition Ministry, again moved that the House should go into committee to take into consideration certain disabilities affecting the Jews, and, after an animated discussion, in which the old arguments were reiterated, the motion was carried by 234 votes to 205[2]. A Jewish Disabilities Bill was accordingly brought in and read for

[1] The Disabilities Repeal Act 1852 (15 & 16 Vict. c. 43), which received the Royal Assent on June 30 of that year, abolished the disabilities but not the pecuniary penalties imposed by 1 Geo. I, stat. 2, cap. 13. The Act was retrospective in its operation, and therefore relieved Mr. Salomons from all penalties except the payment of the fine. He was consequently enabled to become the first Jewish Lord Mayor of London in 1855, and, after the Jewish Relief Act had come into force, to take his seat when re-elected for Greenwich in 1859. The Disabilities Repeal Bill was introduced by Lord Lyndhurst in the House of Lords on May 4, just a fortnight after the decision of the court of first instance in Miller *v.* Salomons, and was at once accepted by Lord Derby, the head of the short-lived Conservative Government (Hansard, *Parl. Deb.*, vol. 121, pp. 190–9, and vol. 122, p. 697 and pp. 1127–30). The case of Miller *v.* Salomons is reported in 7 Exch., 475, and 8 Exch., 778. See also 21 L. J., N. S., 161; 16 Jur., 375; and 8 St. Tr., new series, 111. For the want of prosecution of the appeal in the House of Lords see the debate on Lord Campbell's question in that House on July 21, 1857 (Hansard, *Parl. Deb.*, vol. 147, pp. 108–17).

[2] Hansard, *Parl. Deb.*, vol. 124, pp. 590–625.

the first time on March 1. It was opposed at all the remaining stages, the second reading being carried by a majority of 51, and the third by a majority of 58 votes[1]. The Bill was then sent up to the House of Lords, when the Prime Minister, the Earl of Aberdeen, who had on previous occasions voted against the removal of Jewish Disabilities Bills, took charge of it. The rejection of the measure was moved by the Earl of Shaftesbury, and the Bill was refused a second reading by 164 votes to 115[2]. The history of the previous Bills had led the supporters of this one to anticipate no other fate for it in the Upper House; indeed Mr. John Bright, addressing the House of Commons on this subject for the first time during the debate on the third reading, had roundly asserted that the only way of making it law, was for the Government to stake its existence as a Government upon its acceptance by the Lords, and urged the Government in case it was not passed to cast the responsibility of forming a Government upon those who voted for its rejection. Lord John Russell in winding up the debate declined to yield to this appeal, adding that he believed there would be no great resistance on the part of the House of Lords to the Bill, when once there was an overwhelming opinion in the country in its favour. "Although," he said, "we have for a long time had a majority in this house in favour of this question, I cannot say that we have anything more to urge upon the House of Lords at present than has been urged before. We have not to say—the Hon. Gentleman has forced me to the confession—that there is an overwhelming feeling in the country in favour of the measure"; it was, however, in conformity with other acts of toleration; it would be illiberal to refuse it because its benefit was confined to a small and insignificant body, and there were already signs that the members of the other house would soon be converted to its utility[3].

[1] Hansard, vol. 125, pp. 71-118, 166-72, and 1217-90.

[2] Ibid., vol. 126, pp. 754-96.

[3] Ibid., vol. 125, p. 1286.

1854. Lord John Russell's Parliamentary Oaths Bill refused a second reading by the House of Commons.

The following year, 1854, Lord John Russell, still being leader of the House of Commons, having the same end in view, elected to pursue a different line of policy, and introduced the Parliamentary Oaths Bill, the object of which was to substitute a single oath for the oaths of allegiance, supremacy, and abjuration, and the oaths appointed to be taken by Roman Catholics under the Catholic Emancipation Act of 1829 (10 Geo. IV, c. 7). The terms of the new oath were as follows:—

"I, A. B., do swear that I will be faithful and bear true allegiance to Her Majesty Queen Victoria, and will defend her to the utmost of my power against all conspiracies and attempts whatever which shall be made against her person, crown, or dignity; and I will do my utmost endeavour to disclose and make known to Her Majesty, her heirs and successors, all treasons and traitorous conspiracies which may be found against her or them; and I do faithfully promise to maintain, support, and defend to the utmost of my power the succession of the crown, which succession, by an Act intituled, 'An Act for the further limitation of the Crown and better securing the Rights and Liberties of the Subject,' is and stands limited to the Princess Sophia, Electress of Hanover, and the heirs of her body, being Protestants, hereby utterly renouncing and abjuring any obedience or allegiance unto any other person claiming or pretending a right to the crown of this realm; and I do declare that no foreign prince, prelate, person, state or potentate hath or ought to have any temporal or civil jurisdiction, power, superiority or pre-eminence, directly or indirectly, within this realm. So help me God."

The words "on the true faith of a Christian" were not contained in the new oath, and therefore the passage of the Bill into law would have entailed the admission of the Jews to Parliament. The Bill was allowed to be read a first time without a division, but serious opposition at a later stage was threatened by Sir Frederic Thesiger.

It was obvious that the Bill did three things: (1) it altered and simplified the form of oath; (2) it abolished the Roman Catholic oath, appointing one form of oath to be taken by members of all creeds; (3) it admitted the Jews to Parliament. When the discussion on the second reading took place, the threatened opposition manifested itself, and was directed as much against the alteration of the Roman Catholic oath as against the concession to the Jews. Lord John Russell in vain declared that the only subject before the House was the admission of Jews to Parliament, and that his Bill did nothing more than embody the provisions of the different bills for that purpose, which had been sent up to the House of Lords, and been rejected. Mr. Disraeli and others replied that they had consistently advocated and voted for the removal of Jewish disabilities, and would vote for the present measure if it was confined to that, but that in view of the controversy which had recently been aroused by the Papal claims, they were unable to vote for its second reading, which was ultimately refused by 251 votes to 247[1].

The narrowness of the majority, as well as the speeches made in the debate, indicate that the Bill, had it been introduced in a different form, would have successfully passed through the House of Commons, but the result was that the cause of Jewish emancipation was again delayed, and this time by a vote of the House of Commons.

1856. Mr. Milner Gibson's Oath of Abjuration Abolition Bill.

No attempt to renew the controversy was made during the following year, which saw the downfall of the coalition Ministry and the formation of Lord Palmerston's first Cabinet; but early in the Session of 1856 Mr. Milner Gibson, the Free Trade member for Manchester, introduced a Bill to abolish the oath of abjuration. The final words of this oath constituted the only impediment to Jews occupying a seat in Parliament, and it was the avowed object of the proposer of the new Bill to remove this disability; at the same time it was admitted on all hands

[1] Hansard, vol. 130, pp. 272–88; ibid., vol. 133, pp. 870–974.

that the oath of abjuration had become obsolete, and that since there were no longer any descendants of the Pretender to claim the throne, there was no necessity to require the Queen's subjects to renounce and abjure allegiance to them. The Bill, though not a Government measure, received the support of the Prime Minister, Lord Palmerston, and his followers, subject to the insertion of a clause, which was subsequently moved by Lord John Russell, providing for a declaration as to the maintenance of the Protestant Succession to the Throne; Lord Palmerston himself answering the objection that the Bill would admit Jews to Parliament by indirect means by the statement that the obstacle which prevented them from sitting had been only indirectly and unintentionally erected. Mr. Disraeli made a remarkable speech on the second reading of the Bill, giving it his support but saying that he would prefer to retain the words on the true faith of a Christian, and give special exemption to the Jews by a separate clause. Christianity itself owed its very existence to the efforts and exertions of a Jew, and a Christian community more than any other was bound to show the Jews respect [1]. The second reading of the Bill was carried by 230 votes to 195, and though at the third reading Sir F. Thesiger proposed an amendment restoring the clause ending with "upon the true faith of a Christian," the amendment was rejected by 159 votes to 110, and the Bill was sent up to the House of Lords. In that House the second reading was bitterly opposed; and on the motion of Earl Stanhope refused by 110 to 78 votes [2].

1857. Lord Palmerston's Oaths Bill.

In the April of the following year, 1857, a general election took place, the result of which was to retain Lord Palmerston in power with a substantial majority in the House of Commons. Baron de Rothschild was again returned as one of the members of the City of London. The

[1] Hansard, vol. 141, pp. 752–5. His peculiar theory is developed in the twenty-fourth chapter of his *Life of Lord Charles Bentinck*.

[2] Ibid., vol. 140, p. 1288; ibid., vol. 141, pp. 703–59; ibid., vol. 142, pp. 595–605, 1165–97, 1772–1805.

Jewish question was not allowed to remain long dormant. As early as May 15 the Prime Minister himself presented the Oaths Bill to the House of Commons, the object of which was to substitute a single oath for the oaths of allegiance, supremacy, and abjuration. In asking leave to bring in the Bill, Lord Palmerston in the first place apologized to Lord John Russell for taking the subject out of his hands. He then explained that the Bill did not in any way interfere with the oath to be taken by Roman Catholics, which would remain the same as it had been since the Catholic Emancipation Act of 1829. The new oath embraced the old oath of allegiance, and those parts of the oaths of supremacy and abjuration which were applicable to the circumstances of the time, but omitted such parts of those oaths as had become obsolete, such as abjuring the Pretender and his descendants, and did not contain the words "on the faith of a Christian[1]." In consequence Jews would be allowed to sit and vote in Parliament. The only argument for excluding them, was that it was a Christian Assembly, but would the admission of a few Jews shake the Christian Religion? He had often heard of Jews becoming Christians but never of Christians becoming Jews; the Old Testament had prepared the way for the New Testament, but the New would never lead back to the Old Testament. Sir Frederic Thesiger gave a history of the previous measures on the subject and, though he did not resist the introduction of the Bill, announced his intention of opposing it at a later stage. The Bill was accordingly brought in and read a first time without opposition[2].

The second reading stage was also passed without opposition; for, before it was reached, Sir F. Thesiger announced

[1] The wording of the new oath was primarily the same as that of Lord John Russell's Bill of 1854 (see *supra*) except that the words "jurisdiction, &c., ecclesiastical or spiritual" were substituted for "temporal or civil jurisdiction" in the last clause of the oath, the reason for the alteration being that Roman Catholics were not to be required to take the new oath.

[2] Hansard, vol. 145, pp. 318–38.

that the new oath was in many respects an improvement upon the old oaths, and that his objection to it was that it might be taken by persons who did not declare themselves Christians. He would not therefore oppose the second reading, but would propose in committee the addition of words which would preserve the Christian character of the oath. At the committee stage he accordingly moved as an amendment that the following words be added at the end of the new oath:—

"And I do make this promise, renunciation, abjuration, and declaration, heartily, willingly, and truly, on the true faith of a Christian."

The opposition to Jewish Emancipation grows weaker.

The amendment was debated with the same keenness that had been exhibited on former occasions, but it was manifest that the ranks of the opponents of Jewish emancipation were becoming thinner. Sir John Pakington, one of the leading Tories in the House, declared that though he had on previous occasions voted for the exclusion of the Jews, he was now on further consideration ready to admit them, and should vote against the amendment, though he thought it would have been better to have retained a profession of Christianity in the oath, and to have made a special provision to enable Jews to omit that part of it. When the amendment was at length put to the House, it was rejected by the substantial majority of 140; 201 members voting for and 341 against it[1].

At the Report stage the Government consented to the insertion of clauses in the Bill disabling Jews from holding the high offices of State, from which Roman Catholics were excluded by the Catholic Emancipation Act of 1829, and from exercising any ecclesiastical patronage which might be attached to offices they might hold. Nevertheless the third reading of the Bill was opposed but finally carried by 291 to 168 votes[2].

[1] Hansard, vol. 145, pp. 1101, 1341, 1794–1857.

[2] Ibid., vol. 146, pp. 143–8, 347–65.

The Bill is rejected by the House of Lords.

Thus under the auspices of the Government, and with an overwhelming majority in its favour in the House of Commons, the Bill was sent up to the House of Lords; where its second reading was moved by Earl Granville, at that time President of the Council. The Earl of Derby, the leader of the Tory opposition, moved its rejection, and was immediately followed by the aged Lord Lyndhurst, the former Tory Chancellor, who made a powerful speech in favour of the Bill. After a long debate, in which the most telling speeches were made by Lord Bingham in favour of, and by Wilberforce, Bishop of Oxford, against the Bill, the second reading was refused by 171 votes to 139[1].

1857. Lord John Russell's Oaths Validity Amendment Bill.

The friends of Jewish emancipation were not willing to let the matter rest. A week later, in the House of Commons, Lord John Russell pressed the Government to give facilities for the passage of a new Bill to remove Jewish disabilities which he was about to introduce, but Lord Palmerston, thinking that he had done enough by the introduction of his own measure and its successful passage through the Lower House, was unable to promise a day for the discussion of the new Bill[2]. It was known as the Oaths Validity Act Amendment Bill, and its object was to extend the principle of the Oaths Act of 1838 (1 & 2 Vict., c. 108), which enables persons to take an oath according to the form and ceremony binding on their own conscience, so as to make it to apply to the oaths to be taken by Members of Parliament. On July 21 Lord John Russell moved for leave to bring in the Bill. The House, he said, had already affirmed the principle of religious liberty by a majority of 140, and ought not to be baffled by an adverse vote of the House of Lords. It was open to them to admit a Jewish member by Resolution, but that would bring them into conflict with the other House; the measure, he now proposed, if carried, would settle the question without any risk of such a contest, and if strenuously supported by the Government would have a fair chance of passing both Houses; while in any case

[1] Hansard, vol. 146, pp. 1209–78.

[2] Ibid., pp. 1699–1704.

its introduction would show that they did not partake of the apathy of resting content with what had already been done.

Not receiving facilities from the Government the Bill is abandoned.

The motion for leave to bring in the Bill was opposed by Mr. Walpole, who stated that he took this somewhat unusual course for three reasons. In the first place its introduction, after a Bill for effecting the same object had already been before the House that session, was an evasion if not a breach of the rules of the House; in the second place it was likely to lead to a conflict with the House of Lords; and thirdly there was no proper time for the discussion of the measure. In the course of the debate the Prime Minister, Lord Palmerston, expressed his cordial assent to the motion for leave to bring in the Bill, but reserved for future consideration the question whether he should give it his support in its future stages, and refused to postpone Government business for the purpose of pressing the Bill forward. The motion was carried by 246 votes to 154, and the Bill read a first time. The second reading stage was postponed by its author, and ultimately abandoned, with a notice that a similar measure would be introduced next session [1].

Baron de Rothschild again resigns and is re-elected.

In the meantime Baron Rothschild had applied for and obtained the Chiltern Hundreds, and been re-elected by the citizens of London. There was some anticipation that he would attempt to take his seat and obtain a resolution from the House allowing him to omit the obnoxious words of the oath, and threatening with the penalties of breach of privilege any one who might sue him for penalties in consequence of his sitting or voting without taking the oath. Such a course would almost inevitably have caused a collision between the House of Commons and the courts of law, and, although it may have been contemplated, was never in fact attempted.

Select Committee appointed to

On the other hand, Lord John Russell on August 3 moved in the House of Commons for the appointment

[1] Hansard, vol. 146, pp. 1772–80; ibid., vol. 147, pp. 134-95, 684, 929, 1287.

consider whether a Statutory Declaration might under the Act of 1835 be substituted for Parliamentary Oath.

of a Select Committee to consider whether the Statutory Declarations Act of 1835 (5 & 6 Will. IV, c. 62), which permits a statutory declaration, containing nothing objectionable to Jews, to be substituted for an oath in certain cases, was applicable to the oaths appointed to be taken by Members of Parliament. Though there was some discussion, no division was challenged on the motion, and the Committee was appointed. In due course the Committee, having arrived at the decision by only a narrow majority, reported that the provisions of the Act were not applicable to the oaths which members of the House were bound to take before taking their seats. The report was laid upon the table and ordered to be printed. No further step in the controversy was taken during the session[1].

The autumn session of 1857: Lord John Russell's Oaths Bill.

The acute commercial crisis in the latter part of 1857 rendered an autumn session necessary, and Parliament was hastily summoned to meet in the month of December. In an interval not taken up by Government business, Lord John Russell brought in a Bill "to substitute one oath for the Oaths of Allegiance, Supremacy, and Abjuration, and for the Relief of her Majesty's Subjects professing the Jewish Religion," which subsequently became known by the shorter title of the Oaths Bill. The oath now proposed was the same as that contained in the Government's abortive measure of 1857, but with the addition at the end of the following words, "And I make this Declaration upon the true faith of a Christian." On the other hand, clause 5 of the Bill provided that a person of the Jewish persuasion to whom the oath was administered might omit this final sentence. The Bill also contained a clause to extend the Jewish Disabilities Removal Act of 1845 (which applied only to admission to municipal offices) to all offices on admission to which the Declaration prescribed by the Act of 1828 for repealing the Corporation and Test Acts (9 Geo. IV, c. 17) had to be made and subscribed. The Bill was presented and read a first time, but the

[1] Hansard, vol. 147, pp. 811, 933–60, 1010–20, 1119, 1223, 1287.

second reading was deferred until after the Christmas recess. On February 10, 1858, the Bill was set down for second reading, and at this stage also no division was challenged, but Sir F. Thesiger announced that he would move the omission of the fifth clause when the House went into Committee on the Bill[1].

Fall of Lord Palmerston's Government, and the formation of a Conservative Ministry under Lord Derby.

In the meantime Lord Palmerston's Government fell, being defeated in the House of Commons on the second reading of the Conspiracy to Murder Bill, which had been introduced by the Cabinet in deference to the wishes of the French Government on account of the unsuccessful attempt to assassinate the Emperor Napoleon. The Earl of Derby and the Conservative party came into office, but yet the change of Ministry was not thought to militate against the successful termination of the contest for Jewish emancipation. The former Ministry, though proclaiming themselves the friends of religious liberty, had never been really united in support of any of the numerous Jew Bills, and on the last occasion one influential member of the Cabinet had sanctioned the course adopted by the House of Lords by ostentatiously walking out of the House without voting. On the other hand several members of the new Ministry, including Mr. Disraeli, the leader in the House of Commons, Sir John Pakenham, the first Lord of the Admiralty, Lord Stanley, the Prime Minister's son, and Sir Fitzroy Kelly, the Attorney-General, were keen advocates of Jewish emancipation, and the Earl of Derby himself, though he had led the opposition to the previous Bill in the House of Lords, now that he had become Prime Minister was known to be wavering and ready to accept a compromise if any could be suggested, which, without having the appearance of a complete surrender on the part of the Upper House, might bring to an end the prolonged struggle between the two Houses.

The Oaths Bill read a third time in the Commons.

In due course the House of Commons went into Committee upon the Bill. Sir F. Thesiger having become Lord Chancellor, and been transferred to the House of Lords, it

[1] Hansard, vol. 148, pp. 469–99, 1084–1118.

was left to Mr. Newdegate to move the omission of clause five, which made special provision in favour of Jews when called upon to take the new oath. The motion did not however command the assent of one third of the members taking part in the division, and was defeated by a majority of 153; 144 members voting for it and 297 against it. The Bill passed through committee intact, and in due time received its third reading [1].

The Bill in the Lords. The fifth clause, enabling Jews to omit the final words of the oath, rejected in committee.

The next day the Bill was read a first time in the House of Lords. The following week the second reading was moved by Lord Lyndhurst and agreed to without a division, but the Earl of Derby announced that though several of his colleagues were in favour of clause five, he himself could see no reason for altering the course he had followed on previous occasions, and that he would vote for the omission of the clause when the House went into committee. At that stage the new Lord Chancellor, Lord Chelmsford, formerly Sir Frederic Thesiger, moved the omission of the clause. Lord Lyndhurst led the opposition to the motion, which was carried by 119 votes to 80, but the clause extending the benefit of the Jewish Disabilities Removal Act, 1845, to the case of Jews appointed to other than municipal offices was allowed to pass, and the Bill as amended was read a third time on the last day of April without opposition [2].

Baron de Rothschild appointed a member of the Commons' Committee for drawing up reasons for disagreeing with the Lords' amendments.

When the Bill thus emasculated was returned to the House of Commons, its author, Lord John Russell, stating that the chief value of the Bill had lain in the clause regarding the admission of Jews to seats in Parliament, moved that the House should disagree with the Lords' amendments. After some discussion the motion was carried, and it was also resolved that a Committee be appointed to draw up reasons to be assigned to the Lords for disagreeing with their amendments. When the names of the Committee had been decided upon, Mr. Duncombe moved "that Baron Lionel Nathan de Rothschild be one

[1] Hansard, vol. 149, pp. 294-305, 442, 466-550, 946.

[2] Ibid., pp. 946, 1477-86, 1758-97, 2009.

other member of the said Committee." The debate on his motion was adjourned in order to enable the precedents as to the legality of such a nomination to be searched. At the adjourned debate many members thought the nomination improper and inexpedient, though all agreed that it was not illegal, and the motion was carried by 251 to 196 votes[1].

The legality of the appointment.

The appointment of Baron de Rothschild as a member of the Committee was a master-stroke in the constitutional skirmish which was being maintained between the two Houses. It was a convincing proof of the absurdity of the position which the Lords maintained. The Act of George the First (1 Geo. I, stat. 2, c. 13), under which Alderman Salomons had been mulcted and driven from the House, imposed penalties upon Members of Parliament, who had not taken the oaths, only in case they voted or sat in the House during a debate, but neither that nor any other Act punished an unsworn member for exercising any of the other privileges attaching to membership of the House. One of these was the important right of sitting upon a Committee, if appointed by the House; though in order to establish this it was necessary to search the precedents as far back as the year 1715, in which year it was resolved that Sir Joseph Jekyll being a member of the House was capable of being chosen of a Committee although he had not been sworn at the Clerk's table[2]. The exercise of such important functions by a Jew, which the Lords were powerless to prevent, clinched the argument advanced by Lord John Russell that it was only by a sort of legislative fraud that Jews were excluded from the full rights of membership of Parliament, and also demonstrated to the House of Lords the futility of their insisting on debarring from the full rights of membership of the Lower

[1] Hansard, vol. 150, pp. 336–54, 430–443.

[2] 18 *Com. Jour.*, p. 59. Sir Joseph Jekyll was Chief Justice of the County Palatine of Chester, and his absence on circuit was the reason for his not having taken the oaths. See Cobbett, *Parl. Hist.*, vol. VII, p. 57.

House one whom that House was ready and willing to admit.

The Commons' reasons.

Without delay the Committee drew up the reasons which were read in the House and agreed to: they were as follows:—

"1. Because the words 'on the true faith of a Christian,' were originally introduced into the oaths to be taken by Members of Parliament with a view to bind certain Roman Catholics, and were not intended for the purpose of excluding persons of the Jewish religion.

"2. Because the exclusion of British subjects from seats in Parliament and offices in the State on the ground of their religious opinions is contrary to the general maxims of freedom of conscience.

"3. Because no charge of disloyalty or unfitness for public employment, and a fair share of legislative power has been alleged, or can be alleged, against the Jewish community.

"4. Because the infliction of disabilities upon any class of Her Majesty's subjects, solely on the ground of their conscientious adherence to their faith, savours of persecution, and is totally inconsistent with those principles of religious liberty, which, in the case of more powerful communities, have been applied by Parliament with such happy effects.

"5. Because the Commons having already on ten previous occasions, and in five Parliaments, passed Bills for removing the civil disabilities of the Jews, and having of late years agreed to such Bills by constantly increasing majorities, are convinced that the opinion of their constituents, and of the country at large, has been irrevocably pronounced in favour of the removal of such disabilities.

"6. Because such Bills have been supported by many of the most eminent Members of both Houses of Parliament, who, while differing upon other political questions, have concurred in the justice and expediency of measures for the relief of the Jews.

"7. Because the rights of the Electors of the United Kingdom have been peculiarly affected by a law which has been construed to prevent the admission to the House of Commons of persons who have been lawfully returned as members of that House.

"8. Because the first and third clauses of the Bill are open to the construction that the new Oath, which the former of them contains, should be taken not only in all cases where the Oaths of Allegiance, Supremacy, and Abjuration, are now required, but also where the Oaths of Allegiance and Supremacy are at present required, though without the Oath of Abjuration; the result of which construction, if the Bill should pass into law without the fifth clause, would be to exclude the Jews from practising as solicitors and barristers, and from offices under the Crown, to which employments and offices they are now admitted.

"9. Because such result would be contrary to the intention of the two Houses of Parliament, appearing from the sixth clause, and from the title of the Bill under consideration[1]."

Conference between the two Houses.

The House of Commons further decided to request a conference with the Lords, which the Lords agreed to, and the Commons subsequently appointed the members of the Committee, including Baron de Rothschild, to manage the Conference on their behalf. The Conference was duly held, and the reasons delivered to the Lord Chamberlain who conducted it on behalf of the Upper House[2].

Lord Lucan's suggestion for compromise

When the report of the Conference came up for consideration in the House of Lords, the Earl of Lucan, of Crimean fame, a staunch supporter of the Tory party who had always hitherto consistently voted against the different Jew Bills, moved an amendment to the effect that it should be lawful for either House of Parliament, when the oath was administered to a Jew prior to his taking his seat

[1] *Com. Jour.*, vol. 113, p. 172.

[2] Hansard, vol. 150, pp. 529-30, 763, 859.

in the House, by resolution to determine that the form of the oath, so far as it referred to the Christian faith, should be modified in such manner as should seem best calculated to adapt it to the honest and conscientious scruples of persons professing the Jewish religion.

The suggestion favourably received.

The proposal took the House somewhat by surprise, being made by Lord Lucan *proprio motu* without consultation with any political party or group. It nevertheless met with a favourable reception. Earl Stanhope, who had led the opposition to Mr. Milner Gibson's Bill of 1856, announced that he would no longer offer an uncompromising opposition to the admission of Jews to Parliament, and if the amendment now before the House should be pronounced by Lord Lyndhurst, who had throughout led the cause of Jewish emancipation, to be a fair settlement of this long-agitated question, he also was prepared to vote for it. More significant still was the position taken up by the Prime Minister, the Earl of Derby. He expressed his desire to come to a reasonable compromise with the House of Commons. If it were a question of policy or expediency, their duty was to yield to the determined expression of the views of the House of Commons, and to waive their own opinions, unless they felt that they were supported by the country. But it must be admitted that the country was extremely apathetic on the question. Lord Lucan's suggestion might be a plausible solution of the difficulty, but it would require consideration, and would have to be put into shape. Moreover, he thought, it would best be carried out by being embodied in a separate Bill. In the meantime the proper course was for the Lords to insist upon their amendments. The Earl of Malmesbury, the Secretary of State for Foreign Affairs, concurred in the Prime Minister's views, and after some discussion Lord Lucan withdrew his amendment.

The Lords insist on their amendments.

Lord Lyndhurst then moved that the House should not insist upon its amendments; and was answered by the Lord Chancellor, who went through and severely criticized the reasons put forward by the Lower House. Earl Granville and Lord Brougham appealed to the mover not to persist in his motion, considering that the cause of Jewish emancipation had made such an advance that evening owing to the attitude of Lords Derby and Malmesbury that it might be considered to be practically won. Lord Lyndhurst adopted this suggestion, and withdrew his motion, expressing the hope that the spirit of conciliation would survive. Accordingly the Lords resolved to insist upon their amendments, and appointed a Committee to prepare reasons to be offered to the Commons therefor[1].

Carrying out the compromise.

The following week two Bills, each intended to carry out the compromise arrived at, were presented in the House of Lords, and read a first time; they were Lord Lyndhurst's Bill to substitute one oath for the Oaths of Allegiance, Supremacy, and Abjuration, and for relieving the religious scruples of certain of Her Majesty's subjects, and Lord Lucan's Jewish Relief Bill. The discussion of these rival measures was postponed from time to time owing to the indisposition and consequent absence of the Prime Minister. At length, when the Bills reached the second reading stage, the Earl of Derby expressed his preference for Lord Lucan's Bill on the ground that it was more in accordance with Parliamentary procedure. Thereupon Lord Lyndhurst desiring only to attain the end in view, and having no personal object to fulfil, postponed and ultimately withdrew his Bill, which had become known as the Oaths Substitution Bill. Lord Lucan then proceeded to move the second reading of his Bill, which as originally drafted contained two clauses only. The first empowered either House of Parliament to resolve that thenceforth any person professing the Jewish religion, when taking the oath substituted by the Oaths Bill of the present session for the Oaths of Allegiance, Supremacy, and Abjuration, might omit the words "And I make this declaration upon the true faith of a Christian," and so

Lord Lucan's Jewish Relief Bill.

[1] Hansard, vol. 150, pp. 1139-93.

long as such resolution continued in force made the taking of the oath in such modified form valid so as to enable the taker to sit and vote in Parliament; the second enabled persons professing the Jewish religion to omit the abovementioned words in the said oath in all other cases in which they might be required to take it. Despite the understanding which had been arrived at by the leaders on both sides of the House, the motion for the second reading was stubbornly opposed, but was carried by 143 votes to 97[1].

At the Committee stage two additional clauses were inserted, the first excluding Jews from holding the high offices of state from which Roman Catholics were excluded by the Catholic Emancipation Act of 1829. This clause, as we have seen, was subsequently repealed by the Promissory Oaths Act of 1871. The second, which is still in force, was also borrowed from the Catholic Emancipation Act, and conferred upon the Archbishop of Canterbury the right of presentation to any ecclesiastical benefice which belonged to any office in the gift of the crown which might be held by a person professing the Jewish religion, and disabled any person professing that religion from directly or indirectly advising the Crown as to the exercise of its ecclesiastical patronage.

The third reading was also opposed, but was carried by thirty-three votes to twelve, and even then eight peers recorded their solemn protest against the Bill[2].

The Lords' reasons for insisting on their amendments.

Meanwhile the committee had framed the report of the Lords' reasons for insisting on their amendments to the Oaths Bill. After some discussion in the House these reasons were finally settled and sent down to the House of Commons along with the Jewish Relief Bill. In their final form they were as follows:—

"1st. Because, although the words 'on the true Faith

[1] See Hansard, vol. 150, pp. 1600, 1998–2000, 2218; ibid., vol. 151, pp. 154–5, 693–730.

[2] Ibid., vol. 151, pp. 916–30, 1070–4, 1257–66.

of a Christian' were originally introduced into the Oath for the immediate purpose of binding certain Roman Catholics, it is unreasonable to assume that the Parliament which so introduced them did not intend that the profession of Christianity should be a necessary qualification for admission to the Legislature, when they enacted that a Declaration of that faith should form part of the Oath required to be taken by every member of both Houses.

"2nd. Because the constant intention of the Legislature may be further inferred from the fact that neither at the time of the introduction of these words were the Jews admissible nor have they at any subsequent period been admitted to sit and vote in either House of Parliament.

"3rd. Because exclusion from seats in Parliament and offices of the State on the ground of religious opinion and for other reasons where the general good of the State appears to require it, is a principle recognized in the settlement of the succession to the Crown and in other cases; and has, moreover, been further and recently sanctioned by the House of Commons in some of the provisions of the present Bill.

"4th. Because, without imputing any disloyalty or disaffection to Her Majesty's subjects of the Jewish persuasion, the Lords consider that the denial and rejection of that Saviour, in whose name each House of Parliament daily offers up its collective prayers for the divine blessing on its councils, constitutes a moral unfitness to take part in the legislation of a professedly Christian community.

"5th. Because, when the Commons plead in support of their views, in a matter which equally concerns the constitution of both branches of the Legislature, their repeated recognition of the expediency of removing this disability of the Jews, and admitting them to their councils, the Lords desire to refer to their equally firm adherence to the principle of retaining those privileges which they believe to be peculiarly and inseparably attached to Parliament as an exclusively Christian Assembly[1]."

The House of Commons and the compromise.

The next day the Jewish Relief Bill was read for the first time in the House of Commons, and Lord John Russell made a motion for the adjournment of the House in order to explain the course he proposed to adopt. He would move the second reading of the new Bill, and ask the Government for facilities for carrying it through its remaining steps before the end of the session. If this were done the House might concur in the Lords' amendments to the Oaths Bill without proceeding to discuss their reasons. He would, of course, have preferred that the Lords should have said that the object in view, namely, the admission of Jews to sit and vote in that House, would have been better provided for in a separate Bill, instead of giving reasons why no Bill of the kind should pass at all. He was, however, assured that the course taken was not intended as an insult to the House of Commons, and the compromise, by which the Lords merely retained the right to exclude a Jew, if created a peer, from their own House, he was willing to accept as the best practical solution of the question, hoping, as he did, that in course of time Jews would be admitted into the other House also. Mr. Disraeli, as leader of the House of Commons, at once consented to grant the facilities asked for, and the motion was by leave withdrawn[2].

The Bill was rapidly passed through the House of Commons; its rejection was moved on the second reading by Mr. Newdegate, who could only muster 65 supporters against 156 opponents of his motion. It went through committee and was reported without amendment. Yet on the motion for the third reading the opposition was again renewed. It was led by Mr. Warren, who declared that the settlement was one in which nothing was settled and that from the moment that the Bill became law would

[1] Hansard, vol. 151, pp. 156, 262, 1243-57.

[2] Ibid., pp. 1369, 1371-80.

date the decline of the moral and religious influence of the House of Commons. On the division being taken, 129 voted for, and 55 against the third reading. The same evening the House took into consideration the Lords' Amendments to the Oaths Bill and the reasons given for insisting upon them, and passed the following resolutions: (1) "That this House does not consider it necessary to examine the reasons offered by the Lords for insisting upon the exclusion of Jews from Parliament, as by a Bill of the present session intituled 'An Act to provide for the relief of Her Majesty's subjects professing the Jewish religion,' their lordships have provided means for the admission of persons professing the Jewish religion to seats in the Legislature." (2) "That this House doth not insist upon its disagreement with the Lords in their amendments to the said Bill."

Two days afterwards, on July 23, 1858, the Royal Assent was given to both the Jewish Relief Bill and the Oaths Bill[1].

Baron de Rothschild takes his seat in the House.

The following Monday Baron Lionel de Rothschild again appeared at the table of the House, and was allowed to take the new oath with the omission of the final words, a resolution to that effect having been first proposed by Lord John Russell, and carried by a majority of thirty-two. He was thus at length permitted to take his seat in the House of which he had been a member for eleven years, in the course of which he had been returned as the representative of the city of London no less than five times, at three general and two bye-elections[2].

The real character of the "compromise."

The controversy which had divided the two Houses for ten years was thus settled in a way peculiarly consonant to the trend of English constitutional history. The settlement seems to be destitute of principle and innocent of logic, but it was sufficient to meet the difficulty which had actually arisen; its form, moreover,

[1] Hansard, vol. 151, pp. 1614-36, 1754-62, 1863-5, 1879-1906, 1967.

[2] Ibid., pp. 2105-15.

was so clumsy that it was in a short time found necessary to amend it. It was said to be a compromise, but it was in fact no compromise, for the whole point at issue was conceded. It is true that the Lords retained the right to prevent a Jewish peer from taking his seat in their House, but there was no intention at that time of making a Jew a peer, and before such a creation became a question of practical politics the Lords had voluntarily surrendered this very questionable privilege. On the other hand the House of Lords may have been thought to have saved its dignity and justified itself in the position it had taken up, for it had all along been maintained that the question did not concern the Lower House alone, and the Lords, while desiring to maintain the exclusively Christian character of the legislature, disclaimed any intention to interfere with the right of the other House to decide upon the validity of the returns and the admission of members elected to it. At any rate a collision between the two Houses or between the House of Commons and the Law Courts had been avoided, and in spite of the absurdity of the result achieved, when looked at from the merely formal point of view, religious liberty had in substance emerged triumphant.

The settlement hastened by the fall of the Liberal Government.

The ultimate issue was probably hastened by the advent to office of a Conservative Ministry, although the chief opponents of Jewish emancipation had always been found in the ranks of that party. Yet the successive Tory leaders of the House of Commons, Sir Robert Peel, Lord George Bentinck, and Mr. Disraeli, had been staunch adherents of the cause of religious liberty. Had the Liberal party remained in power, there is no reason to doubt that the majority of the House of Lords would have continued to reject any Jewish Relief Bills sent up to them, so long as the ministry declined to make its acceptance a cabinet question; but when the Conservatives came into office they found it necessary to have the standing cause of difference between the two Houses removed, especially as it was only by the forbearance of their opponents that they could count on a majority in the House of Commons, and they were only carrying on the Government until it was convenient to hold a general election. It would have suited neither party to make the Jewish question a ground of appeal to the country. Both the friends and enemies of religious freedom professed their belief that the country was behind them, but neither were willing to stake their political existence upon such an issue. The fact was that, taking the country as a whole, complete apathy upon the subject reigned among the electors. Lord Palmerston was right therefore from the political point of view in not placing the matter in the forefront of his programme; and Lord John Russell himself, while he remained in the cabinet, had not succeeded in converting the whole of his followers to the cause. Indeed, the measure he brought forward in 1854 had actually been defeated in the House of Commons, and he himself was thought to have become so lukewarm that the next Bill (that of 1856) was entrusted by the Jewish partisans to Mr. Milner Gibson.

The exclusion of the subject from the arena of party conflict a benefit to the Jews.

From the selfish point of view there can be little doubt that the Liberals did right in not making Jewish emancipation one of the issues of party conflict, and, moreover, its exclusion from the arena of party politics was of no little advantage to the Jews themselves, for if they had come to be regarded as the special favourites of one of the great political parties in the State, they would assuredly have been looked upon with dislike, if not with hostility, by the other. Experience has shown that it is to the leaders of political parties, more than to the rank and file of their followers or the electors as a body, that a small community like the Jews must look when it requires special treatment or protection. On the one occasion when a policy of justice to the Jews had been made the subject of an appeal to the people, viz. the Naturalization of Jews Act, 1753, the result had proved disastrous to the cause of religious liberty. The lapse of time and the extension of education, though they may have eradicated many popular prejudices, have not so altered the character of the populace as to make it welcome a policy of altering the law in order to secure political equality to the Jews with any great amount of enthusiasm.

The praiseworthy conduct of Baron de Rothschild and Mr. Salomons.

Before returning from this digression it should further be remarked that throughout the controversy the Jews acted in an open and conscientious way. Over and over again Mr. Roebuck declared in the House that, were he a Jew, he would take the oath, including the words "on the true faith of a Christian," though he would have regarded them as a mere farce and not binding on his conscience; and no doubt it was a case in which, if ever, the maxim of Euripides might be acted upon:—

ἡ γλῶσσ' ὀμώμοχ', ἡ δὲ φρὴν ἀνώμοτος [1].

To their credit, however, Baron de Rothschild and Mr. Salomons pursued a different course with the unanimous approval of their co-religionists. Had they chosen to follow Mr. Roebuck's advice, it was admitted by the opponents of Jewish rights that they could not have been excluded, for, as Sir Frederic Thesiger put it, it was impossible to bind an unconscientious man by any oath [2].

An inconvenience arising from the form of the settlement remedied by Act of Parliament.

The inconvenience of the machinery provided for carrying out the so-called compromise soon became manifest. The doors of Parliament had been opened to the Jew, but he could not enter as of right, for every session [3] a resolution must be passed enabling such Jews as might desire to

[1] Eur., *Hip.*, 612.

[2] However, means were taken by the House of Commons to prevent Mr. Bradlaugh from taking the oath which he had previously declared was not binding on his conscience. But this was a quarter of a century later. The legality of that decision of the House of Commons was affirmed by the Law Courts. See Bradlaugh *v.* Gossett (1884), L. R., 12 Q.B.D. 271.

[3] For it was held that a resolution did not remain in force after a prorogation. Report of Committee, Session I, 1859, No. 205, *Com. Jour.*, vol. 114, p. 59, and Hansard, vol. 152, pp. 459-63.

take the oath to omit the final words, and such resolution might be opposed, and was liable to be defeated on each occasion. To remedy this defect an Act of Parliament was passed two years later enabling the House of Commons to convert a resolution arrived at under the Jewish Relief Act of 1858 into a Standing Order, which would remain valid and in force until repealed, and therefore obviate the necessity of passing a fresh resolution every session[1].

The "compromise" upset by the Parliamentary Oaths Act of 1866.

Six years later Parliament was again called upon to deal with the question. The result was the Parliamentary Oaths Act of 1866 (29 & 30 Vict., c. 19). This Act substituted a new and simplified oath, which did not contain the words "on the true faith of a Christian," as the oath to be taken by members of both Houses of Parliament, in lieu of the oaths laid down by the Oaths Act of 1858 and the Roman Catholic oath, the form of which was laid down by the Catholic Emancipation Act of 1829. The object of the new Act, like that of Lord John Russell's unsuccessful measure of 1854, was to create a simplified and uniform oath which all members of Parliament alike might take, to whatever religious denomination they might belong[2]. It incidentally upset the so-called compromise of 1858 by depriving the House of Lords of the right to exclude a Jewish peer which they then retained. It met, however, with no serious opposition in either House of Parliament, and the point to which

[1] See the statute 23 & 24 Vict., c. 63, and see Hansard, vol. 157, pp. 960–63, 1916–9; ibid., vol. 158, p. 305; ibid., vol. 159, p. 1507; ibid., pp. 1745–50.

[2] The wording of the new oath as finally settled was as follows: "I, A.B., do swear that I will be faithful and bear true allegiance to Her Majesty Queen Victoria; and I do faithfully promise to maintain and support the succession to the Crown, as the same stands limited and settled by virtue of the Act passed in the reign of King William the Third, intituled 'An Act for the further limitation of the Crown, and better securing the rights and liberties of the Subject,' and of the subsequent Acts of Union with Scotland and Ireland. So help me God." The debates on the measure are to be found in Hansard, vol. 181, pp. 453–9, 1712–37; and vol. 182, pp. 289–314, 480–3, 510–18, 1322–55, 1619–28, 1759, 2176.

substantial criticism was directed was the alteration in the Roman Catholic oath. So far as it related to the Jews, Sir George Grey, the Chancellor of the Exchequer, in introducing the Bill, fairly explained its scope to the House of Commons. He said, "The members professing the Jewish religion sat now in that House not by absolute right, but by sufferance, the result of a compromise adopted to terminate a long struggle, but it was impossible not to see that that arrangement must be temporary. Those gentlemen had sat there for some years, and it would be absurd to ask if any danger had arisen to the Crown, the Church, or the Constitution from Jews sitting in that House. They had taken part with credit to themselves in the discussions of the House, and had performed their duty with integrity and ability. He thought the time was come when the members professing the Jewish religion should be admitted to all the privileges which were enjoyed by the members of other religious denominations. By the adoption of the measure he proposed members would be relieved from the necessity, on coming to the table after a general election, of ranging themselves in three divisions on taking the oaths. Let no man be asked any question as to his religion, but let him take his seat in the House if qualified to sit there, in the opinion of those who sent him there, on taking the oath of allegiance as a loyal subject of the Crown[1]."

The power of the House of Lords to exclude Jews voluntarily abandoned by the former opponents of Jewish emancipation.

When the Bill reached the House of Lords, Lord Chelmsford, who years before had been the leading opponent of Jewish emancipation, proclaimed himself content with the new proposal. Before the second reading he said: "With regard to the omission of the words 'upon the true faith of a Christian' I have always contended against the admission of Jews to Parliament as a matter of principle. I have never thought that there was the slightest danger to the state in admitting a few Jews to the legislature; but upon principle, and upon principle alone, I have main-

[1] Hansard, vol. 181, p. 456.

tained my opposition. Now, in the year 1858 an Act was passed which involved a compromise upon this long-vexed question, and it was enacted that either House of Parliament might by a resolution dispense in the case of a Jew with those words of the oath which declare it to be taken 'upon the true faith of a Christian'. Now, my Lords, it appears to me that the principle is as much violated by admitting a Jew by the side door of a resolution as it would be if you admitted him by throwing open the principal door, and giving him a seat in Parliament by the express words of the Act itself. Therefore, in my view, there really is on this subject nothing left worth contending for, and I am not at all disposed, having certainly failed in maintaining the principle which I defended, to take any further part in resisting the complete admission of the Jew to his seat in the legislature[1]." Again, at a later stage, when it was proposed to insert the words "on the true faith of a Christian" in the new oath, the same speaker repeated his former statement, and further said: "The House of Commons had chosen to adopt a resolution by means of which a person of the Jewish faith presenting himself at the table could be admitted on taking the oath, omitting the words 'on the true faith of a Christian,' and that resolution had now become a standing order of the House; it was, therefore, clear that, so far as the House of Commons was concerned there was no impediment whatever to the admission of the Jews to Parliament. The resolution had broken down the barrier completely, and the Jew walked in without any difficulty and took his seat. With regard to their Lordships' house—suppose Her Majesty were to be advised to raise a Jew to the dignity of the peerage, would their Lordships refuse to pass a resolution dispensing with that portion of the oath which required him to say he made the declaration 'on the true faith of a Christian'? Their Lordships would hardly be disposed to adopt a course which would be an insult to the Crown;

[1] Hansard, vol. 182, p. 1349.

and, therefore, he considered that there was practically no impediment to the admission of Jews to their Lordships' house. Under these circumstances there was, as he had said, nothing left to fight for! Immediately the principle he had maintained was sacrificed all grounds for further resistance were gone; therefore he did not oppose the second reading of the Bill, and must now decline to vote for the amendment [1]." The amendment was not pressed to a division, and the one relic of intolerance which had survived the eleven years' struggle between the two Houses was swept away, practically without any effort to retain it. It was not, however, for nearly twenty years that any Jew was able to avail himself of the rights now thrown open to his community. At length, in July, 1885, Sir Nathaniel de Rothschild, the first Jew to receive a patent of peerage, under the title of Lord Rothschild, was sworn in as a member of the House of Lords, and took his seat accordingly [2].

Lord Rothschild created a peer in 1885.

The Office and Oaths Act 1867.

The simplified oath established by the Parliamentary Oaths Act of 1866 was to be administered only to persons about to take their seats in either House of Parliament, but the following year another Act, the Office and Oaths Act 1867 (30 and 31 Vict., c. 75) was passed. It enacted that the new and simplified form of oath should be taken as a qualification for the exercise of any office, franchise, or civil right, instead of the Oaths of Allegiance, Supremacy, and Abjuration, or any form of oath substituted for them (as, for instance, under the Oaths Act and Jewish Relief Act of 1858). Inasmuch as the necessity for making the declaration had, as we have seen, been previously removed by the Qualification for Offices Abolition Act 1866 (29 and 30 Vict., c. 22), henceforth Jews when qualifying themselves for holding any office or civil right would go through precisely the same ceremonies as their Christian fellow subjects.

The Promissory Oaths Act 1868.

The Promissory Oaths Act of 1868 (31 and 32 Vict.,

[1] Hansard, vol. 182, p. 1622.

[2] *Lords' Journals*, vol. 117, p. 335.

c. 72), introduced by Lord Chelmsford when again Lord Chancellor, and in consequence of the report of the Royal Commission on the subject appointed in the year 1866, and reappointed after the change of government in the same year, again modified the form of the oaths, and enacted the three very simple forms of the Oath of Allegiance, the Official Oath, and the Judicial Oath, which have already been set out, and which are still in force.

The Promissory Oaths Act, 1871, throws open to Jews the high offices from which they were excluded by the Jewish Relief Act of 1858.

Finally, the Promissory Oaths Act of 1871 (34 and 35 Vict., c. 48), in addition to repealing the section in the Jewish Relief Act of 1858, which excluded Jews from some of the highest offices of state, formally repealed all the statutes establishing the old forms of oaths and declarations which had been superseded and rendered obsolete by the Promissory Oaths Act of 1868 or earlier Acts. This Act passed through both Houses of Parliament without opposition, and almost without discussion. Since it became law Jews have been on precisely the same footing in regard to political rights as their Christian fellow subjects, with this exception only, that they cannot exercise any right of ecclesiastical patronage attaching to any office they may happen to hold.

CHRONOLOGICAL TABLE.

1070. A number of Jews brought from Rouen by William I.

1194 (?). Exchequer of the Jews established by Richard I as a separate department, and Justices of the Jews appointed.

1232. Domus Conversorum opened by Henry III.

1271. Ordinance of Henry III prohibiting Jews from holding lands in fee, and having Christian servants.

1275. Statute de la Jeverie or de Judaismo.

1290. Banishment of the Jews by Edward I.

1401. Statute de Haeretico, 2 Hen. IV, c. 15.

1558. Acts of Supremacy and Uniformity (1 Eliz., c. 1 and c. 2).

1575. General expulsion of Aliens by Queen Elizabeth.

1580–1592. Legislation against recusants (23 Eliz., c. 1, 29 Eliz., c. 6, 35 Eliz., c. 1 & 2, &c.).

1605. Gunpowder Treason and Plot.
New legislation against Popish recusants.
The new Oath of Obedience and Allegiance "on the true faith of a Christian" (3 Jac. I, c. 4).

1608. Calvin's case.

1609. Applicants for naturalization required to take the sacrament of the Lord's Supper (7 Jac. I, c. 2).

1612. Last execution for heresy in England.

1617. The last claim of villenage in an English court.

1618 (?). The Jews fly from England in consequence of the issue of a commission for the execution of the laws against Jesuits, &c.

1625. Act for punishing divers abuses committed on the Lord's Day, commonly called Sunday (1 Car. I, c. 1).

1627. Act for the further reformation of sundry abuses committed on the Lord's Day, commonly called Sunday (3 Car. I, c. 2).

1630. Treaty with Spain, by virtue of which Spanish subjects were exempted from the laws against recusants.

1635 (?). Carvajal settles in England.

1640. Court of High Commission abolished (16 Car. I, c. 11).

1648. The Independents obtain control of Parliament.

1649. Petition of the Cartwrights of Amsterdam for the re-admission of the Jews.
Execution of Charles I.

1653. The Instrument of Government. The law against recusants relaxed, but not so far as to give immunity to persons not believing in Christianity.

1655. Menasseh Ben Israel arrives in England. The Whitehall Conference.

1656. War between England and Spain. Capture of Jamaica.
Case of Antonio Robles.
Commission to treat with the Jews of Amsterdam given by Charles II to General Middleton.

1657. Departure and death of Menasseh Ben Israel.

1658. Death of Oliver Cromwell.

1660. Declaration of Breda.
Restoration of Charles II.
Navigation Act (12 Car. II, c. 18) excludes from the colonial trade aliens unless naturalized or made denizens.
Petitions against the Jews referred to Parliament by the Privy Council.

1661. Corporation Act (13 Car. II, st. 2, c. 1).
And following years. A number of Jews granted letters of denization.

1662. Act of Uniformity (13 & 14 Car. II, c. 4).
Dec. 26. First Declaration of Indulgence.

1663. Public worship openly and regularly performed in the synagogue.
Organization of the Jewish community.

1664. The Conventicle Act (16 Car. II, c. 4).
Threatened attack on the Jews by the Earl of Berkshire. Their petition to the king for protection favourably answered.

1665. The Five Mile Act (17 Car. II, c. 2).

1667. Robeley *v.* Langston. Jewish witness allowed to be sworn on the Old Testament.

1670. Second Conventicle Act (22 Car. II, c. 1).

1672. Second Declaration of Indulgence.
James, Duke of York, openly embraces Catholicism.

1673. The Declaration of Indulgence cancelled.
The Test Act (25 Car. II, c. 2).
The principal Jews indicted for meeting together for the exercise of their religion.

Petition of Abraham Delivera and others. Order in Council to stay all proceedings against the Jews.

1674. Rebuilding of the synagogue. Lease for twenty-five years taken.

1677. Act for the better observation of the Lord's Day, commonly called Sunday (29 Car. II, c. 7).

The Writ de haeretico comburendo abolished (29 Car. II, c. 9).

1678. The Parliamentary Test Act (30 Car. II, st. 2).

1684. A Jew's right to maintain an action recognized by the Court of King's Bench (Lilly's *Practical Register*, vol. I, p. 4).

1685. Death of Charles II, and accession of James II.

Forty-eight Jews charged with recusancy.

Petition of Joseph Henriques and others to the king. Formal Order in Council to stay these proceedings. "His Majesty's intention being that they" (the Jews) "should not be troubled on this account, but quietly enjoy the free exercise of their religion, whilst they behave themselves dutifully and obediently to his government."

1687. Declaration of Indulgence.

1688. The Revolution. Deposition of James II.

1689. New and simplified oaths of supremacy and allegiance.

The dispensing power of the Crown, saving previous charters and grants, abolished.

The Toleration Act (1 Will. & Mary, c. 18), the benefit of which was restricted to Protestant Trinitarians [extended to Unitarians in 1813, Roman Catholics in 1832, and Jews in 1846].

Proposal to impose special taxation on the Jews. Their petition to Parliament not received. The projected tax withdrawn.

1694. Jewish marriages expressly included in the provisions for the tax upon marriages (6 & 7 Will. & Mary, c. 6).

1698. The Act against blasphemy and profaneness (9 Will. III, c. 35).

1701. The Act of Settlement (12 & 13 Will. III, c. 2).

Death of James II. His son's title to the English throne recognized by Louis XIV.

The oath of abjuration invented (13 & 14 Will. III, c. 6).

1702. Act to oblige Jews to maintain and provide for their Protestant children (1 Anne, c. 24).

1707. Voters at Parliamentary elections may be required to take the oath of abjuration (6 Anne, c. 78).

1708. The Foreign Protestants' Naturalization Act (7 Anne, c. 5).

1714. The requirement of taking the oath of abjuration imposed in 1701 on all public officers, &c., continued. Members of Parliament not to vote or sit before taking the said oath (1 Geo. I, st. 2, c. 13).

1718. The Religious Worship Act (5 Geo. I, c. 4) forbids attendance with the insignia of office at any Nonconformist place of worship.

1723. Jewish landowners required to take the oath of abjuration allowed to omit the words "on the true faith of a Christian" (10 Geo. I, c. 4).

1728. First (Annual) Indemnity Act (1 Geo. II, st. 2, c. 23).

1730. British Nationality Act (4 Geo. II, c. 21).

1732. Attempt to arouse popular animosity against the Jews by the blood accusation frustrated (Rex *v.* Osborne).

1739. The custom of requiring the oath administered prior to receiving the citizenship of London to be taken on the New Testament held to be good (Rex *v.* Bosworth).

1740. The Plantation Act (13 Geo. II, c. 7) enables Jews to be naturalized in the colonies without taking the sacrament or pronouncing the final words of the oath of abjuration.

1743. Held in Da Costa *v.* De Paz that a legacy for instructing Jews in their religion could not be so applied.

1744. Held in Omychund *v.* Barker that all persons who believe in a Supreme Being are competent witnesses, and should be allowed to take the oath in the form binding upon them according to the tenets of their religion.

1753. Jewish marriages exempted from the provisions of Lord Hardwicke's Marriage Act (26 Geo. II, c. 33).
The Jews Naturalization Act (26 Geo. II, c. 26) passed. Consequent agitation against the Jews.

1754. The Jews Naturalization Act repealed (27 Geo. II, c. 1).

1765. Death of the Old Pretender. The form of the oath of abjuration finally settled (6 Geo. III, c. 53).

1770. First Jews admitted as solicitors; being permitted to omit the final words of the oath of abjuration.

1772. British Nationality Act (13 Geo. III, c. 21).

1781. The Sunday Observance Act (21 Geo. III, c. 49). Places of amusement (admission to which is by payment) open on a Sunday to be deemed disorderly houses.

1784. The Alien duties abolished by Pitt (24 Geo. III, sess. 2, c. 16).

1791. Roman Catholic Relief Act (31 Geo. III, c. 32).

1793. Lord Grenville's Aliens Act (33 Geo. IV, c. 4) temporary but periodically renewed till 1826.

1794. Act for the better observance of the Lord's Day by persons exercising the trade of bakers (34 Geo. III, c. 61). Provisions of this Act with some modifications embodied in the Bread Acts (3 Geo. IV, c. 6, s. 16; and 6 and 7 Will. IV, c. 37, s. 14).

1811. Held in Lindo *v.* Unsworth that a Jew is excused from giving notice of dishonour of a bill of exchange on the Day of Atonement.

1812. Charities "for the benefit of any persons of the Jewish nation" exempted from the provisions of the Act for registering and securing charitable donations (52 Geo. III, c. 102, s. 11).
The Places of Religious Worship Act (52 Geo. III, c. 155) repeals the Five Mile Act and the Conventicle Act, &c.

1813. Unitarians admitted to the benefit of the Toleration Act (53 Geo. III, c. 160).

1823. Jewish marriages exempted from the provisions of the Marriage Act (4 Geo. IV, c. 76).

1825. The necessity of taking the sacrament as a preliminary to naturalization abolished (6 Geo. IV, c. 67).
Repeal of the Navigation Act (6 Geo. IV, c. 105).

1826. The temporary Aliens' Acts discontinued, and the system of registration of aliens substituted (7 Geo. IV, c. 54).

1828. Declaration "on the true faith of a Christian" substituted for the sacramental tests imposed by the Corporation and Test Acts (9 Geo. IV, c. 17).

1829. Roman Catholic Relief Act (10 Geo. IV, c. 7).

1830. Mr. Robert Grant's Bill for repealing the civil disabilities of the Jews refused a second reading by the House of Commons.
Jews admitted to the freedom of the City of London, and allowed to take the oath on the Old Testament.

1832. The Roman Catholic Charities Act (2 & 3 Will. IV, c. 118).

1833. Mr. Francis Goldsmid called to the Bar.
The Jewish Civil Disabilities Bill passed by the House of Commons, but refused a second reading by the House of Lords.

1834. The Jewish Civil Disabilities Bill again passed by the House of Commons, but refused a second reading by the House of Lords.

1835. Mr. Salomons elected Sheriff of London. The Sheriffs' Declaration Act (5 & 6 Will. IV, c. 28).

Mr. Salomons elected Alderman and unsuccessfully attempts to be admitted.

The Parliamentary Elections Act, 1835, abolishes the power of the presiding officer to administer the abjuration oath to electors (5 & 6 Will. IV, c. 36).

1836. The Registration of Aliens Act (6 & 7 Will. IV, c. 11).

The Jewish Civil Disabilities Bill passed the House of Commons a third time but sent to the Lords too late to receive a second reading.

The Marriage Act (6 & 7 Will. IV, c. 85) and the Registration Act (ibid. c. 86) recognize the validity of Jewish marriages, make special provision as to their registration and give statutory recognition to the London Committee of Deputies of British Jews.

1837. Quakers, Moravians, and Separatists Relief Acts (1 & 2 Vict., c. 5 and c. 15).

Mr. Grote's motion to extend the relief to Jews rejected by the House of Commons.

1838. The Oaths Act (1 & 2 Vict., c. 105).

1841. Mr. Divett's bill for the admission of Jews to Corporate Offices, known as the Jews' Declaration Bill, passes the House of Commons and receives a second reading in the House of Lords but is refused a third reading.

1844. The system of naturalization by certificate from a Secretary of State introduced by Mr. Hutt's Naturalization Act (7 & 8 Vict., c. 66).

Repeal of the laws against recusants and other penal enactments so far as they affected Roman Catholics.

1845. Act for the relief of persons of the Jewish religion elected to municipal offices (8 & 9 Vict., c. 52).

1846. The Religious Disabilities Act (9 & 10 Vict., c. 59) repeals the laws against recusants and other penal statutes and extends the benefit of the Toleration Act to the Jewish religion (see also 18 & 19 Vict., c. 86, s. 2).

1847. Baron Lionel de Rothschild elected Member of Parliament for the City of London.

1848. Lord John Russell's Jewish Disabilities Bill passes the Commons but is refused a second reading by the Lords.

1849. Lord John Russell's Parliamentary Oaths Bill (altering the oath in favour of Jews) passed by the Commons but rejected by the Lords.

Baron de Rothschild obtains the Chiltern Hundreds and is re-elected.

1850. Baron de Rothschild unsuccessfully attempts to take his seat in Parliament.

1851. Lord John Russell's Oath of Abjuration (Jew) Bill passed by the Commons but rejected by the Lords.

Mr. David Salomons, having been elected member for Greenwich takes his seat in the House and is forcibly removed.

1852. The case of Miller *v.* Salomons.

The Disabilities Repeal Act 1852 abolishes the disabilities but not the pecuniary penalties imposed by 1 Geo. I, stat. 2, c. 13, upon persons who should vote in Parliament without having taken the oath.

1853. Lord John Russell's Jewish Disabilities Bill passes the Commons but is rejected by the Lords.

1854. Lord John Russell's Parliamentary Oaths Bill, creating a new oath which Jews could take, refused a second reading in the House of Commons.

Oxford University Reform Act (17 & 18 Vict., c. 81).

1855. Places of Religious Worship Registration Act (18 & 19 Vict., c. 81) makes provision for the registration of Jewish synagogues.

Act for securing the Liberty of Religious Worship (18 & 19 Vict., c. 86).

1856. The Marriage Act (19 & 20 Vict., c. 119) makes special provisions as to Jewish marriages and gives statutory recognition to the West London Synagogue of British Jews.

Cambridge University Reform Act (19 & 20 Vict., c. 88).

Mr. Milner Gibson's Oath of Abjuration Abolition Bill passed by the Commons but rejected by the Lords.

1857. Lord Palmerston's Oaths Bill having passed the Commons by a large majority is rejected by the Lords.

Lord John Russell's Oaths Validity Amendment Bill introduced in the House of Commons but abandoned before the second reading stage.

Baron de Rothschild resigns and is re-elected.

1858. Lord John Russell's Bill "to substitute an oath for the Oaths of Allegiance, Supremacy, and Abjuration, and for the relief of Her Majesty's subjects professing the Jewish religion" passes the Commons and receives a second reading in the Lords, but in committee the clause enabling Jews to omit the words "on the true faith of a Christian" is struck out. The Commons appoint a Committee to confer with the Lords. Baron de Rothschild is appointed a member of and serves on the Committee. Lord Lucan's suggestion for compromise accepted.

The Oaths Act (21 & 22 Vict., c. 48), and the Jewish Relief Act (21 & 22 Vict., c. 49), the result of the compromise.

Baron de Rothschild sworn as member of the House of Commons.

1860. Endowed Schools Act (23 & 24 Vict., c. 11).

The Act (23 & 24 Vict., c. 63), enables the House of Commons to make a Standing Order for the swearing in of Jewish members.

1866. Parliamentary Oaths Act (29 & 30 Vict., c. 19) introduces a new oath to be taken by Members of Parliament not containing the words "on the true faith of a Christian," thus enabling Jews to be sworn in as members of the House of Lords.

Qualification for Offices Abolition Act (29 & 30 Vict., c. 22) renders it unnecessary to make and subscribe the Declaration imposed by 9 Geo. IV, c. 17, in lieu of the sacramental test.

1867. Office and Oath Act (30 & 31 Vict., c. 75) (1) throws open the office of Lord Chancellor of Ireland to all subjects. (2) Enables persons holding office to attend any place of worship with the insignia of their office. (3) Substitutes the form of oath created by the Parliamentary Oaths Act of 1866 for that required to be taken by office holders and others.

The last of the Annual Indemnity Acts (30 & 31 Vict., c. 88).

1868. Promissory Oaths Act (31 & 32 Vict., c. 72) introduces new and simpler forms of (1) the oath of allegiance; (2) the official oath; (3) the judicial oath.

The Public Schools Act (31 & 32 Vict., c. 118).

1869. The Endowed Schools Act (32 & 33 Vict., c. 56).

1870. The Naturalization Act (33 & 34 Vict., c. 14).

Elementary Education Act (33 & 34 Vict., c. 75).

1871. The Workshop Regulation Act Amendment Act (34 & 35 Vict., c. 19) permits Sunday labour in the case of young persons and women professing the Jewish religion.

The Universities Tests Act (34 & 35 Vict., c. 26).

The Promissory Oaths Act (34 & 35 Vict., c. 48) repeals obsolete Acts relative to promissory oaths, and removes the disability of Jews to hold certain high offices imposed by the Jewish Relief Act of 1858.

The Sunday Observation Prosecution Act (34 & 35 Vict., c. 87) forbids prosecutions for Sunday labour under the Lord's Day Act of 1677 except with the consent of the chief officer of the police district or two magistrates, &c.

1872. The Ballot Act (35 & 36 Vict., c. 33) contains provisions enabling Jews to vote on their Sabbath.

1878. The Factory and Workshop Act (41 Vict., c. 16) continues the permission of Sunday labour by Jews.

1885. Sir Nathaniel de Rothschild created a peer.

1888. The Oaths Act (51 & 52 Vict., c. 46).

1898. Jewish marriages excluded from the provisions of the Marriage Act, 1898 (61 and 62 Vict., c. 58).

1901. The Factory and Workshop Act (1 Edw. VII, c. 22) continues the recognition of the right of Jews to work on Sundays.

1902. The Education Act (2 Edw. VII, c. 42).

1905. The Aliens Act (5 Edw. VII, c. 13).

1906. Jews marrying foreigners in the United Kingdom exempted from the necessity of obtaining a certificate under the Marriage with Foreigners Act (6 Edw. VII, c. 40).

ADDENDA AND CORRIGENDA.

Page 2, line 11. 1673] 1673–4

4, l. 9. fit.'"] fit[1].'" *Footnote*: [1] For the circumstances which led to this enactment, see post, pp. 167–9.

ll. 13–14. Popery . . . year] Popery (11 Will. III, c. 4, s. 7) passed three years earlier.

8, l. 33. *Villareul*] *Villareal*

10, l. 35. Queen's] King's

12, n. 1. later.] later (see p. 262).

14, n. 1. (1817).] (1817) and id. 379 (note).

15, l. 3. in favour of] as a favour to

19, l. 20. 1744] 1743

20, l. 1. was] sought

22, n. 1. 7 instead of 7 Vesp. 81.

23, n. 1. *Burgman*] *Berryman*

n. 2. Simeon] Simon

n. 4. c. 59.] c. 59; and see the Liberty of Religious Worship Act, 1855 (18 & 29 Vict., c. 86), s. 2.

24, l. 14. God,] God[1], *Footnote*: [1] See *Att.-Gen.* v. *Lucas*, L. R. [1905] 1 Ch. 68, where a bequest for the purpose of keeping in good order burial grounds the use of which is restricted to members of the Society of Friends, was held to be a gift for the advancement of religion and therefore a valid charitable legacy.

26, l. 13. void.] void[1]. *Footnote*: [1] *In re Sidney*, *Hingeston* v. *Sidney* [1908] 1 Ch. 126. A bequest in trust for such charitable uses or for such emigration uses as the trustees shall think fit is void for uncertainty, as emigration uses are indefinite and not necessarily charitable.

29, n. 2. *Breeks* v. *Woolfrey*, 1 Curt. Eccl. Rep. 880; and see *Egerton* v. *All of Odd Rode*, L. R. [1894] P. 15, and *Pearson* v. *Stead*, id. [1904] P. 66.

30, n. 2. *Burder*] *Brewer*

37, ll. 15–16. and afterwards any] and that it had been resolved not to allow any

l. 34. Sheba . . . draw] Sheba Lyon should be permitted to draw lots for the

47, ll. 1–2. (delivered . . . was based] delivered, after mature deliberation, by one of our ablest and most careful judges) was based

49, l. 14. Dr. Wilton] De Wilton

54, n., l. 2. 386 b.] 386 b. Iudaeus vero nihil proprium habere potest, quia quicquid acquirit non sibi acquirit sed regi, quia non vivunt sibi ipsis sed aliis, et sic aliis acquirunt et non sibi ipsis.

54, n. 2. 489.] 489. This ordinance was passed by the advice of the prelates and magnates only. No doubt the King could legislate for the Jews (his villeins) without the consent of the Commons, but this ordinance contains provisions affecting Christians also. See the Report on the Dignity of a Peer (1819), pp. 162–3.

55, n. 1. 221.] 221. See Report on the Dignity of a Peer, p. 181.

63, n. 2. J. O. Howell's] 20 Howell's

73, l. 2. 1679] 1677

83, n. 1. Scobell, part 1.

86, l. 5. volunt.] volunt[2]. *Footnote*: [2] Juv., Sat. X, 96.

97, l. 4. compulsory,] compulsory[4], *Footnote*: [4] See the Ordinance for the better Observation of the Lord's Day, 1656, cap. 15 (Scobell, vol. II, p. 441, and Burton's *Diary*, vol. II, pp. 261–8; also the Humble Petition and Advice, clauses 9, 10, 11 (Gardiner's *Constitutional Documents*, p. 340, and Scobell, II, p. 378).

98, l. 34. them."] them[3]." *Footnote*: [3] Ellis's *Original Letters illustrative of English History*, 2nd series, vol. IV, pp. 1–21, Letter cccix.

99, ll. 27–8. it . . . year,] it has not since been revived,

107, n. 1. p. 11.] p. 11. An account of Edward Backwell, who died in 1683, is to be found in the *Dictionary of National Biography*, vol. II, p. 321. He was a well-known goldsmith under the Commonwealth and Charles II, to whom he had advanced over £28,000 in the year 1660 (see 12 Car. II, c. 23, s. 37), and one of the founders of the modern banking system. He was the predecessor in business of the well-known firm of Child. Owing to the closing of the Exchequer by Charles II in 1672, he lost a sum of nearly £100,000; this money was afterwards (in 1677) repaid by a cheque on the Excise, but Backwell was ultimately made a bankrupt. See *Alderman Backwell's* case (1683) 1 Vernon, 152.

n. 2, l. 1. [2] See] [2] And apparently still in the house of his kinsman Duarto Henriques. See

111, n., l. 11. 26] 2 b

l. 16. 6 & 7] 7 & 8

l. 18. 33] 33 & 34

117, n. 1, l. 7. 272).] 272, at p. 282).

122, l. 12. Violet,] Violet[2], *Footnote*: [2] In the *Visitation of London*, 1634 (MS. Coll. Arms, c. 24) we find among other persons Thomas Vyolet of London, goldsmith; grandson of Rafell V, born in Antwerp. Arms and Ped. (p. 382 b). See Lists of Foreign Protestants and aliens resident in England, 1618–88 (Camden Soc., vol. LXXXII, p. xv).

133, l. 19. or] of

145, n., l. 3. gold] copper

l. 8. seq.)] seq.) By the Proclamation for the encouraging of Planters in His Majesty's Island of Jamaica in the West Indies, issued on Dec. 14, 1661, which is regarded as the original charter of the Island, all copper and other mines (except gold and silver) within the "respective allotments shall be enjoyed by the grantee thereof, reserving only a twentieth part of the product of the said mines to our use." See Edwards' *History of the West Indies*, vol. I, p. 168 n.

146, n. 1, l. 9. 262.] 262. John Evelyn similarly describes a visit to the Synagogue at Amsterdam: see his *Diary* for August 19, 1641.

147, l. 12. Rycaut] Rycaut[3] *Footnote*: [3] In the *Visitation of London*, 1634, we find Peter Richaut of London, merchant, grandson of Peter R. of Brabant. Arms and Ped. (198 b). See Lists of Foreign Protestants in London (Camden Society's Publications, vol. LXXXII, p. xv).

170, ll. 11–12. as . . . and] *omit*

ll. 33–4. 9 Geo. I, cap. 24] 10 Geo. I, c. 4

175, l. 4. punished.] punished[1]. *Footnote*: [1] I should also add that the minister of a Jewish synagogue is not exempt from serving on juries unless the synagogue is duly registered, the words of the exemption being, "ministers of any congregation of Protestant Dissenters and of Jews whose place of meeting is duly registered, provided they follow no secular occupation except that of a schoolmaster." See the Schedule to the Juries Act of 1870 (33 & 34 Vict., c. 77).

185, n., l. 1. 2 Com.] 2 Camp.

200, l. 4. take] takes

l. 6. c. 10] c. 4

n. 2, l. 5. Burn] Burrows

216, n. 1, l. 8. observance by] observance (cf. *Marshall* v. *Graham* and *Bell* v. *Graham* [1907] 2 K. B. 112, in which it was held that Ascension Day was such a day for members of the Church of England) by

245, n. 2, l. 1. 1816] 1796

l. 4. 307–9.] 307–9. From the benefit of the previous Irish statute, 23 & 24 Geo. III, c. 38, Jews had been expressly excepted.

246, l. 10. c. 27] c. 27, s. 19,

247, l. 2. 1867,] 1867[3], *Footnote*: [3] Indeed, the Parliamentary Elections Act of 1835, which limited the time for taking the poll at Parliamentary elections in boroughs to a single day, enacted, as was necessary if the election was to last a single day only, that no elector at any election should be required to take any oath, any law or statute to the contrary notwithstanding (5 and 6 Will. IV, c. 36, s. 6). Henceforth it must have been exceedingly difficult, if not impossible, to prove that any particular elector had "refused" to take the oath or oaths.

287, l. 24. Pakenham.] Pakington

INDEX

Abarbanels, the, 88.
Abbott, Mr. Justice, 32.
Aberdeen, Lord, 277.
Abjuration, oath of, 226-9 and 202, 206, 246, 267, 271 seq., 280.
modified in favour of Jewish landowners required to take it, 170, 191.
Abraham, Isaac, 236 n.
Abrahams, Abraham, 205.
Joseph, 206.
Action, capacity of a Jew to bring, 185-91.
Advowson, capacity of a Jew to hold, 194-5, 242-4.
Alderman, a Jew could not be before 1845, 254.
Alderson, Baron, 276 n.
Alexander, D. L., 184.
Alien duties, 230 n.
Alien enemies, were Jews to be held, 186 seq.
Aliens, 229 seq.
American colonies, 240.
Amsterdam, Jews of, 84, 88, 118, 120.
Anabaptists burned, 70, 71.
Arians burned, 70, 71.
Arlington, 134.
Arundel, Archbishop of Canterbury, 67.
Ascamoth, 146, 157.
Ashley, 134.
Asquith, Mr., 263.
Atonement, Day of, 184, 185, 247.

Backwell, Mr., 106 and 107 n., 316.
Bacon, Nathaniel, 186.
Ballot Act, 247.
Bar, first Jew called to, 203-5.
Baxter (the Puritan divine), 128 n.
Baxter, Nadir, 25.
Beaumont, Thomas, 2, 50, 153.
Bedford Charity, the, 35.
Benefit of Clergy, 195-8.
Bentinck, Lord George, 298.
Berkshire, Earl of, 147.
Best, Mr. Justice, 14; afterwards Lord Wynford, 195 n.
Bethell, Mr. (afterwards Lord Westbury), 273.
Bigham, Mr. Justice, 184.
Bingham, Lord, 284.
Blackstone, Sir William, 197, 198 n., 245, 258 n.
Blasphemy, 10-12.
act for the suppression of, 13-18, 167.
Blood accusation, 9.
Blunt's *History of the Jews in England*, 192.
Bracton, 54 n.
Bradlaugh, Mr., 11, 300.
Breda, declaration of, 127, 132.
Brereton, Dr., 39.
Breta de, Jacob Mendez and Mary Mendez, 168, 169.
Bright, Mr. John, 278.
Brokers, Jews as, in the City of London, 200.
Brooke, Justice, 189, 190.
Brougham, Mr. (afterwards Lord), 172 n., 251, 293.
Burnet, 96.
Burton's Diary, 97.

Campbell, Mr. (afterwards Lord), 204, 253, 276, 277 n.
Canary Islands, 103-6.
Carlyle, Thomas, 95.
Caroline, Queen, trial of, 182 n.
Cartwright, Johanna and Ebenezer, petition of, 84.
Carvajal, Antonio Fernandez, 80, 98, 110.
Maria Fernandez, 143.
Catechism, the Church, teaching in schools, 40, 44, 217.
Cemetery, Jewish, at Mile End, 109-14.
Chancellor, *see* Lord Chancellor.
Charitable purposes, Jewish, 18 seq.
Charles I, legal position of the Jews under, 77, 106, 125.
Charles II, 50, 51, 128-31.
his toleration, 125-41, 151, 152, 164, 172, 175.
Chelmsford, Lord, *see* Thesiger.

Christianity part of the law of the land, 11, 43, 186, 199.
Christian names, 46.
on the faith of, *see* Abjuration, Oath, Declaration.
religion, denial of, 13 seq.
Civil rights of English Jews, 177 seq.
Clarendon, Lord, 134.
Clarke, Mr., 204.
Clergy, *see* Benefit of Clergy.
Coke, Lord Chief Justice, 55 n., 57, 178, 185, 189-91.
his theory of the banishment of the Jews, 58-9.
Coleridge, Lord Chief Justice, 11, 210, 262.
Colleges, 211, *see* Universities.
Colonial trade closed to aliens, 235.
Colonies, naturalization in, 240, 245.
Committee appointed by the House of Commons in 1858 to consider the Lords' Amendments to the Oaths Bill, 288 seq.
Commons, House of, orders Inquiry concerning the Jews, 148.
"Compromise," the, on the Jewish Relief Bill, 291, 296 seq.
upset, 301.
Conventicle Act (1664), 133, 147, 148.
(1670), 135, 161 n.
Convention Parliament, 127.
Corporation Act, 129, 161 n., 247 seq.
Correa, Isaac, 235 n.
Courtney, Sir William, petition of, 124 n., 142.
Cowper-Temple clause, 217.
Crompton, Rev. Thomas, 145.
Cromwell, Oliver, 51, 80, 84, 88 seq., 94, 95, 97, 107-9, 115-21, 175.
Richard, 108.
Curialitas, 56 n.

Da Costa, Alvaro, 116.
lists, 124 n., 142 n.
De Caceres, Simon, 110.
Declaration not to injure the Established Church substituted for the Sacramental Test, 162, 250 seq.
of Rights, 172.
Delivera, Abraham, 2, 8, 50, 154, 171.
Denization, 234 seq.
Denizens, Jews made, 144, 158, 236.
De Paz, Elias, 19.
De Porto, Abraham, 2.
Derby, Earl of, 284, 287, 288, 292.
Dispensers, act banishing the, 78.
Directory for public worship substituted for Book of Common Prayer, 83.
Despensing Power, 131, 150, 154-8, 163, 171-3.
Disraeli, Mr. (afterwards Earl of Beaconsfield), 280, 281, 287, 296, 298.
Divett, Mr., 255 n.
Dormido, Aaron, 237 n.
Manuel Martinez, 88, 237 n.
Solomon, 237 n.
Droit d'aubaine, 230.
Droit de renvoi, 232.
Duncombe, Mr., 288.
Dunnington, John Baptista de, 104.

Ecbert's excerptiones, 52, 53.
Ecclesiastical Patronage, Jews and, 256, 263, 294.
see Advowson.
Education, *see* Schools, Universities.
of Christian and Jewish children together, 39-40, 47.
Edward the Confessor, law of, concerning the Jews, 53.
I and the Jews, 54 seq.
VI, 68.
Edwin, Sir Humphrey, 258 n.
Eldon, Lord, 19, 21, 24, 35, 41, 46, 247 n.
Elizabeth, Queen, 63, 69, 232, 237.
Ellenborough, Lord, 185, 193.
Ellis, George, 206.
Endowed schools, 213-15.
Endowments for furthering the Jewish religion, 18 seq.
Erskine, Lord, 182 n.
Thomas, 205.
Established Church, declaration not to injure, 250 seq.
Evans, Allen, 259.
Evelyn, John, memoirs quoted, 94, 146 n., Addenda.
Exchequer of the Jews, 54.
Excommunication, 187.
Eyre, Lord Chief Justice, 182 n.

Fawkes of Breauté, 66.
Finta, 146.
Five Mile Act (1665), 134, 161 n.

Foley, Mr. Paul, 165.
Foster, Sir Michael, 197.
Foundling Hospital, 21.
Fox, George, the Quaker, 86.
Francia, Domingo, 2.
  Francis, 179.
Fundao, 103.

Gardiner, Dr., 100, 109.
Gaster, Dr., 124 n., 147 n., 151 n., 158 n.
Gifford, Sir Robert, 41.
Gill, Robert, 206.
Gladstone, Mr. W. E., 263.
Glynn, Lord Chief Justice, 1, 91.
Godwin, Mr., 97, 110 n.
Goldsmid, Benjamin, 194.
  Isaac Lyon, 37, 205.
  Francis, 193, 204, 205.
Grant, Mr. Robert, 193, 265.
Granville, Earl, 283, 293.
Grattan, Mr., 250.
Greenhalgh, Mr. Jo., 98, 145.
Grenville, Lord, 232.
Grey, Sir George, 302.
Grote, Mr., 254 n.
Gunpowder Plot, 75, 222, 224 n.

Haggard, Dr., 95.
Haham, 147.
Hale, Lord Chief Justice, 20, 178.
Hales, Sir Edward, 156 n.
Hall, Vice-Chancellor, 30.
Hardwicke, Lord Chancellor, 20, 180, 201, 241.
Hardwicke's Marriage Act, 170.
Hargrave, Mr., on villenage, 63.
Harper, Sir William, 35.
Hawkins' *Pleas of the Crown*, quoted, 74.
Henrietta Maria, 79.
Henriques, Daniel Bueno, 237 n.
  Duarto, 104, Addenda, 107 n.
  Jacob Joshua Bueno, petition of, 145 n.
  Joseph, 3, 13 n., 50, 154, 171, 235 n.
Henry III, 54, 57.
  IV, 67, 69.
  V, 69.
  VIII, 68.
Herbert, Chief Justice, 156 n.
Heresy, law of, 65-73.
High Commission, Court of, 71-3, 82.
Higher Grade Schools, 218.
Holland, Lord, 251.
Hollis, Mr., 144.
Holt, Chief Justice, 10, 150 n.
Hoveden, 53 n.

Indemnity Acts, 203, 208, 249, 250, 252 and note.
Independents, the, 83, 86.
Indulgence, declaration of, (1662), 130.
  (1672), 136-9.
  (1687), 156.
Industrial Schools, 220.
Infidels, status of, 186-91.
Inglis, Sir Robert, 265.
Inquisition, the, 71, 103.
Instrument of Government, the, 87, 117.
Ireland, naturalization in, 245 n.
Isaac, Benjamin, 22.

Jamaica, 145 n., 241 n.
James I, 119, 147.
  II, 51, 116, 152-8, 172, 176, 226.
  See also York, Duke of.
Jeffreys, Lord Chief Justice, 189.
Jekyll, Sir Joseph, 289.
Jenner, Sir Herbert, 29.
Jerusalem, Trust for the political restoration of the Jews to, 25.
Jessel, Sir George, 12.
Jesuits, 224.
Jewish disabilities removal act, 255.
  Relief Bill (1858), 293-7.
  Relief Act Amendment Act (1860), 301.
Jewish religion, attacks on, 2.
  receives the benefit of the Toleration Act, 23, 208.
  religious education board, 217.
Jews compelled to maintain their Protestant children by Act of Parliament, 3-9; 167-9.
  their right to participate in general endowments and charities, 34 seq.
  their status after the Norman Conquest, 53.
  of Amsterdam, 84, 88, 118, 120.
  their banishment, 55 seq.
  their return, date of, 49, 175.
  crypto, 80.
  period between their banishment and return, 62.
  their legal position in Charles I's reign, 77.
  and Cromwell, 115-18.
  and Charles II, 119-22, 124-7, 142-52.
  and James II, 153, 154, 157.

freedom from crime in early days, 198.
Civil Disabilities Bill, 265 seq.
Joseph, Joseph, 40.
Michael, 37, 39, 40.
Nathan, 39.
Judaei, 64.
Judicial Oath, 228 n., 276.
Jury, exemption of Jewish minister from serving on, Addenda, 175 n.

Kaddish, 26.
Kelly, Sir Fitzroy, 287.
Kenyon, Lord, 182, 183 n.
King, John, 182.
King, Lord, 8.
Knevett, Francis, 104.
Knight-Bruce, Sir P. L., 25.

Land, capacity of Jews to hold, 191–4.
Langdale, Sir Marmaduke, 118, 119.
Langton, Stephen, 66.
Laud, Archbishop, 71, 72.
Law Merchant, 184.
Lee, Lord Chief Justice, 181.
Lee, Sir Thomas, 165.
Legacies for Jewish religious purposes, 18 seq.
Legal profession, exclusion of Jews from, 202–6.
Legatt, Bartholomew, 70.
Levi, Godfrey, 39.
Lewis, 193.
Samuel, 145.
Littleton, Lord Keeper, 189.
Llandaff, Bishop of, 251.
Lollards, 65.
Lollardries, 68.
London, petition against the Jews (1660), 121, 143.
petition against the Jew Bill (1753), 243.
freedom of the City and the Jews, 199–202.
Dissenters and the Shrievalty, 258.
elects Baron L. de Rothschild to Parliament in 1847, 267.
Long Parliament, 72, 73.
Lopez, Rodrigo, 63.
Lord Chancellor, a Jew may now be, 261–3.
Lord Lieutenant of Ireland, a Jew may now be, 261–3.
Louis XIV, 226.
Louzada, James Baruch, 236 n.
Lucan, Earl of, 291, 293.
Luttrell, Narcissus, 167.
Lyndhurst, Lord, 194 n., 255, 277 n., 284, 288, 292, 293.
Lyon, Joseph, 37, 39, 40.
Lemuel, 40.
Sheba, 37.

Macaulay, Lord, 137, 166 n.
Macclesfield, Earl of, 4.
Madox, *History of the Exchequer*, 57 n.
Magna Charta, 61, 117 n., 229, 230.
Magpie Alley, synagogue in, 22.
Malmesbury, Earl of, 269 n., 292.
Mansfield, Lord, 19, 160, 182 n., 260.
Marcus, Moses, 6.
Marriages, act imposing taxes on, mentions Jews, 166.
Martin, Baron, 275.
Martines, Philip, 236 n.
Mary I, 69.
Mathias, Jone, 236 n.
Menasseh Ben Israel, 1, 51, 61, 85, 88–93, 95 seq., 112, 115.
Petition to Richard Cromwell on behalf of his widow, 108.
his son's burial, 112.
Mendez, Jacob Franco, 2.
Meres, Frances, 236 n.
Judith, 236 n.
Michel, Abraham, 26.
Middleton, Lieut.-Gen., 120, 142.
Milner-Gibson, Mr., 280, 299.
Municipal Offices, *see* Corporation Act.
Insignia of, 257.

Natural-born subjects, 233.
Naturalization, 237 seq.
Act (1740), 170, 240.
Act (1753), 163 n., 171, 241.
Navigation Act (1651), 88.
(1660) and (1661), 144, 231, 235.
Newcastle, Duke of, 243.
Newcome, Henry, visit to the Synagogue, 146 n.
Newdegate, Mr., 287, 296.
New Testament, a Jew may be sworn on, 182.
practise of administering the oath on, 198 seq., 267, 269, 270.
Nicholas, Sir Edward, 115, 118.
Nolle prosequi, 150.
Norwich, Bishop of, 243.
Notice of dishonour of a negotiable

instrument on a Jewish holiday, 184.
Nye, Mr., 61, 91.

Oath, the *ex officio*, 71, 72.
juridical, 178–83.
promissory, 198 seq., 256–7, 304–5.
effect of, 229.
mode of administering, 229.
of adjuration, 226, also 170.
of abjuration (Jew) Bill, 270.
of allegiance and supremacy, 221–9, also 76.
Parliamentary, *see* Parliament.
Office, *see* Corporation Act, Ecclesiastical Patronage, Test Act, &c.
Official oath, 228 n.
Ormonde, Duke of, Papers quoted, 85.
Osborne, the King *v.*, 9.
Mr. Bernal, 271.

Pacheco, Aaron, 3, 50, 52, 53, 154.
Pakington, Sir John, 283, 287.
Palmerston, Viscount, 280, 281, 284, 287, 299.
Papal claims, 280.
Parker, Lord Chief Baron, 180.
Parliament, admission of Jews to, 265 seq.
attitude of, towards the Jewish settlement, 164–71.
Parliamentary Committee, members though not sworn may serve on, 289.
franchise, 246.
Party politics, advantage of keeping the Jewish question out of, 298–300.
Pease, Mr. Joseph, the Quaker, 268 n.
Peel, Sir Robert, 250, 255, 298.
Peers, Jews admitted to the House of, 302 seq.
Pelham, Mr., 241.
Pellatt, Apsley, 201 n.
Pepys, Samuel, visit to the Synagogue, 146.
Pereira, Isaac, 235 n.
Perjury, 180–3.
Petitions against the Jews at the time of the Restoration, 142 seq.
Petition by the Jews of Amsterdam, 60, 84.
Menasseh's second, 92.
of the Jews for protection, 1664, 147.
167¾, 2, 149.
1685, 2–3, 154.
of the Jews against special taxation, 1689, 164–6.
Petty custom, 231 n.
Picciotto's sketches of Anglo-Jewish History, 41 n.
Political rights, 221 seq.
Pollexfen, 187.
Pollock, Sir F. (Chief Baron), 275.
Essays in Jurisprudence, 228 n.
Poor Law Schools, 219.
Powle, Mr. Speaker, 165.
Prayers for the souls of the dead, 26–30.
Presbyterians, 83.
Pretender, the, 226.
Profaneness, statute against, 13–18.
Proselytism by Jews, 15.
Prynne, quoted and commented on, 52, 59–62.

Quakers, 129, 159, 161 n., 167, 171.
admission to Parliament of, 268 n.
obtain privileges as to taking oaths earlier than Jews, 200; as to making declaration, 253.

Rathom, Abraham, 199.
Rawlinson, Mr., visits the Synagogue with Pepys, 146.
Raymond, Lord, 9, 20, 191, 199.
Recusants, 75, 113.
conviction of, in recent times, 172.
laws against, modified, 86, 87.
laws against, repealed, 163.
Reformation, the, its consequences to the Jews, 65 seq.
Reformatory schools, 219.
Registration of synagogues, 173–5.
Religious instruction, *see* Schools.
Remonstrance concerning the Jews, 142.
Resettlement Day, 99.
Restoration, the, 125.
Revolution, the, 158, 225.
Richard II, 60.
Ridley, Mr. Justice, 184.
Robles, Antonio Rodrigues, 102–7.
Roebuck, Mr., 300.
Roman Catholic Relief Acts, 161 and id. note.
Romilly, Sir John, 27, 29.
Sir Samuel, 41, 46 n., 193, 194 n.
Rothschild, Baron Lionel de, 267 seq., and 269, 281, 285, 288, 291, 297, 300.

Rothschild, Anthony de, 269 n.
Sir Nathaniel de, made a Peer, 304.
Roumanian law as to aliens, 233 n.
Russell, Lord John, 249, 251, 268, 269, 270, 271, 277, 278, 281, 284, 286, 296, 297, 299.
Rycaut, Mr., 147.

Sabbath, the Jewish, recognized by the Courts and the Law Merchant, 183–5.
see Ballot Act.
Sacrament of the Lord's Supper, 238, 245, &c.
see Naturalization, Corporation Act, Test Act.
Sadler, John, 107–9.
Salomons, David, 253, 254–6, 277 n., 300.
attempt to take his seat in Parliament, 270–7.
Sandwich, 231 n.
Sasportas, Samuel, 236 n.
Sawtre, William, 67.
Sawyer, Sir Robert, 188.
Saxon times, Jews in England in, 51–3.
Schoolmasters, Jews and the profession of, 206.
Schools, 212–20.
Shadwell, Sir L., 23.
Shaftesbury, Earl of, 278.
Sheriff, declaration by, 253.
device of fining Dissenters for refusing to serve as, 258–61.
Shrewsbury, Earl of, 166.
Solicitors, Jews admitted as, 205.
Spain, treaty with England, 79, 175.
war with England, 102.
Spaniards, Jews settle in England as, 80–2.
Spring Rice, Mr., 266.
St. Leonards, Lord, 193.
Stanhope, Earl, 281, 292.
Statutes restricting the rights of the Jews, 54.
see Table of Statutes, p. xxi.
Steel, Lord Chief Baron, 1, 91.
Stirling, Lord Justice, on the date of the return of the Jews to England, 49–52.
Stowell, Lord, 191 n.
Suffolk, Earl of, 119, 147.
Superstitious use, 27 seq.
Swift, Dean, 258 n.
Synagogues, actions for seat rents in, 32.
theory that Cromwell authorized the building of, 107–9.
first real evidence of existence of, 122, 144–9.
registration of, 173–5.

Taxation, attempt to lay special, on the Jews, 164–6.
Technical Schools, 218.
Temple, Lord, 192.
Test Acts (1673) and (1678), 139–40, 154–8, 161 n., 248 seq.
Theodore, Liber Poenitentialis of, 52, 53.
Thesiger, Sir Frederic (afterwards Lord Chelmsford), 279, 281, 282, 287, 288, 292, 300, 301.
Time-table in public elementary schools, 216.
"Tolerance" said to have been granted by Cromwell in February, 1658, 97–9.
Toleration, 96, 127–41, 152–8.
Toleration Act, 9, 19, 20, 159, 161–3, 260.
extended to the Jews, 23, 163, 171.
Tovey, Dr. De Blossiers, 192, 198.
Transubstantiation, declaration against, 140, 248, 250.
Tresham, Francis, 224 n.
Tucker, Dean, 120 n.
Turner, Sir Edward, 128.
Tyril, Mr. Justice, 124.

Uniformity, the Law of, 73 seq., 163.
Act of (1660), 130.
Unitarians, 15, 161.
Universities, the, and Dissenters, 208–11.
Usury, 54, 56–60.

Villeins, status of, similar to that of the Jews, 53, 62, 65.
special status of Jews as, 188–9.
Villenage, disappearance of, 63–5.
Vindiciae Iudaeorum, 92–5.
Violet, Thomas, 99, 122–4.

Walker's *History of the Independency*, 84, 96.
Walpole, Mr. Spencer, 285.
Warren, Mr., 297.
Webb, Carteret, 116, 144 n., 192 n., 236.
Wellington, Duke of, 251.
West Indian Islands, 241.

Whitehall Conference, 1, 89.
Whitley, Colonel, letter to Sir Ed. Nicholas, 115.
Wilberforce (Bishop of Oxford), 284.
Willes, Chief Justice, 180, 181, 189.
William I, 49.
Wilson, Colonel, 193.
Witnesses, right of Jews to be, 178–83.

Yates, Mr. Justice, 206.
Yesiba, 19.
York, Duke of (afterwards James II), 137, 249.

Oxford: Horace Hart, Printer to the University